ENVIRONMENTAL POLITICS IN THE MIDDLE EAST

HARRY VERHOEVEN

(*Editor*)

Environmental Politics in the Middle East

Local Struggles, Global Connections

جامعة جورجتاون قطر

GEORGETOWN UNIVERSITY QATAR

Center *for* International *and* Regional Studies

HURST & COMPANY, LONDON

First published in the United Kingdom in 2018 by
C. Hurst & Co. (Publishers) Ltd.,
41 Great Russell Street, London, WC1B 3PL

Printed in India

A Cataloguing-in-Publication data record for this book is available from the British Library.

This book is printed using paper from registered sustainable and managed sources.

ISBN: 9781849049672

www.hurstpublishers.com

CONTENTS

ABOUT THE CONTRIBUTORS

Jill Crystal is the Curtis O. Liles III Professor of Political Science at Auburn University. She received her PhD from Harvard University. She specializes in comparative politics with an emphasis on Middle Eastern politics, and is the author of, among other books, *Oil and Politics in the Gulf: Rulers and Merchants in Kuwait and Qatar* (Cambridge University Press) and *Kuwait: The Transformation of an Oil State* (Routledge).

Ali El-Keblawy is a Professor of Environmental Science and Plant Ecology at the University of Sharjah. He established the Sharjah Seed Bank and Herbarium, where he was the director. In his more than twenty-five years of research, he covered the biology and management of invasive plants, rangeland management, combating desertification, and domesticating native plants for landscaping and as cash crops. He has published numerous articles in top journals.

Afyare A. Elmi is an Associate Professor of Security Studies in the Gulf Studies Program at Qatar University. His research interests include international and maritime security, state-building/peace-building, conflict, and identity. He is the author of many policy papers, and academic publications, including *Understanding the Somalia Conflagration: Political Islam, Identity and Peacebuilding* (Pluto Press).

Francis Ghilès is a Senior Research Associate at CIDOB, the Barcelona Centre for International Affairs. He served as the North Africa correspondent of the *Financial Times* for many years, and has contributed to numerous reports and studies on contemporary affairs in the Maghreb. Ghilès is trilingual and has lectured at major universities in the United Kingdom, United States, and France.

Ilya Gridneff is a Nairobi-based analyst at the Horn of Africa think tank Sahan Research. Primarily working on Somalia, his topics of research cover security-sector reform, natural resources, and debt relief. Previously, he was a foreign correspondent in Papua New Guinea, South Sudan, and the broader East Africa region with Bloomberg News, the Associated Press, and other international media outlets.

Clement M. Henry is Emeritus Professor of Government and Middle East Studies at the University of Texas at Austin. After retiring from Texas, he served as chair of the Department of Political Science at the American University in Cairo, and as Visiting Research Professor, at the Middle East Institute, National Union of Singapore. He coauthored *Globalization and the Politics of Development in the Middle* East (Cambridge University Press); and *The Arab Spring: Will It Lead to Democratic Transitions?* (Palgrave Macmillan); and coedited *The Politics of Islamic Finance* (Edinburgh University Press).

Abbas Maleki is Professor of Energy Policy in the Department of Energy Engineering at Sharif University of Technology in Tehran, and Senior Associate, International Security Program at the Belfer Center for Science and International Affairs, Harvard Kennedy School. He served as Iran's Deputy Foreign Minister from 1988 to 1997. He coedited *U.S.–Iran Misperceptions: A Dialogue* (Bloomsbury); coauthored *Iran Foreign Policy after September 11* (Book Surge); and authored *Iranian Foreign Policy: Past, Present and Future Scenarios* (Routledge).

Jeannie L. Sowers is an Associate Professor of Political Science and Program Chair of the International Affairs Program at the University of New Hampshire. Her publications focus on political economy, ecology, and state–society relations in the Middle East and North Africa. She is author of *Environmental Politics in Egypt: Experts, Activists, and the State* (Routledge); coeditor of *The Journey to Tahrir: Revolution, Protest, and Social Change in Egypt*; and coauthor of *What Everyone Needs to Know about Modern Egypt* (Oxford, forthcoming). She serves on the editorial boards of *Middle East Report* and *Global Environmental Politics*.

Harry Verhoeven teaches at the School of Foreign Service, Georgetown University in Qatar, and is the Convenor of the Oxford University China–Africa Network. He is an editor of the Cambridge University Press book series on Intelligence and National Security in Africa and the Middle East. He received his doctorate from the University of Oxford, where he later served as a Junior Research Fellow at Wolfson College, and as a Visiting Scholar at the University of Cambridge.

Wessel N. Vermeulen is Assistant Professor in Economics at Newcastle University London. He studies issues in economics related to natural resources, trade, and migration in international contexts and has published in *The Economic Journal, Journal of Commodity Markets*, and *Acta Politica*. His publications also include *Failure to Prevent Gross Human Rights Violations in Darfur: Warnings to and Responses by International Decision Makers (2003–2005)* (Brill).

Eckart Woertz is Senior Research Fellow at CIDOB, the Barcelona Centre for International Affairs, Scientific Advisor to the Kuwait Chair at Sciences Po in Paris, and teaches at the Barcelona Institute of International Studies (IBEI). Formerly, he was a Visiting Fellow at Princeton University and Director of economic studies at the Gulf Research Center in Dubai. He is author of *Oil for Food: The Global Food Crisis and the Middle East* (Oxford University Press).

ACKNOWLEDGMENTS

This edited volume is the product of research, reflection, conversation, and writing by eleven scholars that occurred over a three-year period in all continents of the world, with Doha as its epicenter. That observation not only highlights the global nature of the contemporary academic enterprise, but is also a pivotal reflection of the kind of book *Environmental Politics in the Middle East: Local Struggles, Global Connections* aspires to be. The volume underscores the ways in which environmental dynamics in the Gulf, North Africa, and the Levant cannot be understood in separation from political, economic, and social developments; but also not without understanding the multifaceted links of the Middle East with Eurasia, Africa, and territories across the Arabian Sea. I thank the contributors to this volume for their enthusiasm to think, investigate, and author across disciplinary, regional, and political boundaries.

This volume developed out of two working groups held under the auspices of the Center for International and Regional Studies (CIRS) at Georgetown University in Qatar. Mehran Kamrava and Zahra Babar formulated the initial contours of this project, and generously invited me to assume its intellectual leadership. They have shown great interest throughout and provided an excellent support environment. At CIRS, the contributors and I also acknowledge Elizabeth Wanucha, Jackie Starbird, Islam Hassan, Misba Bhatti, and Umber Latafat, who all helped out in various ways. Suzi Mirgani's diligence, creativity, and professionalism made it a real pleasure to work with her. We would also like to acknowledge the contributions of those who added at various stages to the substantive discussions: Madalla Alibeli, Martin Keulertz, Laurent Lambert, and Maria Snoussi. At Hurst, Michael Dwyer, Jon de Peyer, Daisy Leitch, and Kathleen May provided, as ever, first-class editorial input and support, including soliciting several stimulating external reviews that have helped to considerably improve the volume. Finally, grateful acknowledgment also goes also to the Qatar Foundation for its support of research and reflection in a region that sorely needs it.

Finally, as the editor I would like to also personally thank my family for its unwavering support at times of momentous changes and turbulent seas to navigate. To my mother, Miek, my wife Maimuna, and my daughter Aliya: together we cultivate our garden. I am blessed to be able to do so with you.

INTRODUCTION

THE MIDDLE EAST IN GLOBAL ENVIRONMENTAL POLITICS

Harry Verhoeven

> We sent down water, as a blessing from the sky and made grow gardens with it and grain for the harvest, and lofty date palm-trees with their spathes, piled one above the other
> As sustenance for (Our) servants
> We gave (new) life thereby to a dead land.
>
> Surah Qaf (50: 9–11), al-Quran

Images and storylines of scorching scarcity and exuberant abundance shape a great many conversations about the Middle East. For every evocation of Arabian sand dunes and the seemingly existential inhospitality associated with them, there are equally powerful tropes of rivers, oases, and oil wells miraculously greening the desert and generating immense riches. The Sahara, the Nile, the Rub' Al-Khali, and the Euphrates and Tigris loom large in the geographer's imagination, in the same way that Saudi Arabia's Ghawar oilfield, the Strait of Hormuz, and the Suez Canal are avatars of the global economy. The idea that geography is a key determinant of human behavior and of the (lack of) flourishing of civilization has long been intuitive, even self-evident, to many residents of the region and external observers.

Yet what is striking in much of the extant literature is how disconnected environmental change and continuity remain from the bulging output on the region's history, internal politics, and international relations.[1] The political economy of the environment remains a relatively marginalized field of inquiry: with the notable exception of the proliferation of scholarship on rentierism and the (oil) resource curse and tropes of scarcity-induced "water wars," discussions of environmental issues still all too often tend to be framed in isolation from wider societal dialectics and broader questions about authority, ideology, identity, legitimacy, and power that form the core of the social sciences.[2] What role does resource exploitation play in the reproduction of social relations and nation-building? Can the properties of certain strategic commodities explain the origins of political order, or is it rather that particular types of state instrumentalize the environment in highly specific ways? And do our ways of evaluating sociological processes determine our understanding of ecosystems too, or can scholars observe the natural and the human in splendid isolation, recognizing that each domain is governed by its own set of laws? This book investigates the nature and form of such interconnections. It seeks to place material practices and environmental imaginaries—the assumptions, discourses, and ideas that people hold and share about their natural surroundings and that mold their behavior vis-à-vis them and each other—firmly at the center of social scientific inquiry.

Without getting bogged down in the controversy over "scale,"[3] doing so means, among other things, thinking more ingeniously about how the local, national, regional, international, and global relate to one another. What constitutes "the Middle East" and how it links to other regions has always been indeterminate and contested.[4] A history of shifting ecological, legal, and imagined boundaries points to the importance of mapping out past and future alternative geographies when rethinking the region and its place in the wider world. This is particularly urgent given that ecological changes are rarely placed in a broader geospatial context and mostly understood as site-specific in their origins and effects, but also because environmental debates are frequently conceptually isolated owing to their presumed limited relevance to the Middle East's "high politics." The chapters in this edited volume problematize such categorizations.

To give an example of what a possible reframing entails, take the small Iranian city of Zabol, officially the most polluted town in the world by World Health Organization standards.[5] While this designation elicits embarrassment among officials in Tehran and bewildered curiosity among outsiders who have never heard of the city, discussions of Zabol usually define the extraordinary levels of fine particular matter ($PM_{2.5}$) as a question of air pollution, resulting from its unfortunate geography with nigh-daily dust storms that batter the city, unplanned urban expansion, and the drying up of nearby Hamoun Lake.[6] The obvious response, in this characterization of the issue, is to tighten regulation of pollutants, improve city management, and implement infrastructural adaptations to improve the literal weathering of storms. Yet such framing entirely overlooks the much more structural—and political—causes of why perhaps more than 500 people die every year in Zabol from tuberculosis and other pollution-related diseases. Zabol's "environmental" disaster is at least as much a question of the impact of global climatic changes, international sanctions, the agrarian crisis for millions of impoverished people in Eastern Iran, and the opium trade in war-torn Afghanistan with its halting effect on the flow of the Helmand River—on which the city and its parched wetlands depend—as it is of incessant winds and the local population's bad consumption habits.

This book rejects the separation of the Middle East's ecological trajectory from its political and socioeconomic history, both locally and globally. It argues that the environmental dynamics in the region are both reflective and co-constitutive of broader global political-economic and environmental forces, as well being integral to the power politics in and of their own locales. Put differently, studying environmental change and natural resources management in the Middle East is essential to understanding the myriad political and socioeconomic hopes, illusions, and problems of its inhabitants, both in their on-the-ground manifestations and in the ways they are imbricated in broader global systems. Conversely, analyses that leave out the ways in which ecological factors are continuously shaped and reshaped, discursively and materially, by struggles over power—who gets what, when, and how, in Harold Lasswell's classic definition of politics—fall woefully short in their diagnosis and thereby also compromise any interventions they propose.

This introduction to the book provides an overview of the history of theorizing the relationship between human society and its environment, demonstrating just how central specific understandings of and practices toward the environment have been to the history of the Middle East and how the politics of the environment in the region, in turn, have shaped the global political economy and imagination. Many categorizations of the dominant traditions and discourses of environmentalism exist,[7] but, in light of its objectives, this book proposes a framework of analysis of its own. First, I briefly discuss the origins of pre-modern environmental determinism: the notion that environmental factors are the prime explanation for societal structures and political outcomes. Subsequently, I identify three major paradigms that have been particularly consequential in the modern age in molding the ways in which their adherents think about science, economic development, and political power in their respective relationships with environmental change. Finally, I introduce the different chapters in this edited volume, underlining how they connect to these different paradigms as well as to one another.

Classical environmental determinism

For centuries, the world's foremost thinkers have reflected on how the natural and the human realm relate to one another. For most of recorded history, this relationship was understood as strongly mediated—if not entirely determined—by the divine. Yet even if many philosophers continued to acknowledge God as the ultimate actor in human and natural affairs, some endeavored to theorize a less interventionist deity and to study the relationship in relative autonomy. Of special interest, from early on, was the link between the sociopolitical characteristics of a society and its ecological context. Aristotle believed that the life and growth of all living organisms was determined by experiential interaction with their physical environment and projected his understanding of the natural world onto the course of history and societal institutions. He became an early exponent of environmental determinism, arguing for a causal link between the resource abundance of a particular topographical area and the kind of political system that existed there: if democracy and ideas of egalitarian rights flourished in fertile plains, then the acropolis was better suited to stratification in the form of monarchy and oligarchy. Aristotle's belief in climate and ecology as the structural determinants of civilization was also evident in his attribution of the relative lack of technological sophistication among Northern Europeans to their colder climes, whilst east of the Hellenic world, the inhabitants of Persia, Anatolia, and the Levant were considered to be more subservient, lazy, and lacking in courage because of the lusher environmental conditions, with slavery a natural outcome.[8] Greece's civilizational success was thus environmentally determined and should be defended, if necessary through eugenics, to ensure its continued intellectual and political superiority, or so Aristotle and his teacher Plato believed.[9]

Aristotle's philosophy, and that of the physician Hippocrates, was not just influential in Western antiquity but also garnered widespread admiration in the Arab world.[10] Hippocrates, in *Airs, Waters, Places*, propositioned that "the climate, the seasons, the winds, the topography, the drinking water, and the relative exposure to those elements determine to a great extent the physique, temperament, intelligence, and therefore even the culture of the people who live there."[11] The prolific twelfth-century Sephardic Jewish scientist Moshe ben Maimon (also known as Maimonides) read the classics of antiquity and built on Hippocrates in correlating urbanization and civilizational stagnation, because, from Cordoba to Cairo, urban air—"stagnant, turbid, thick, misty and foggy"—negatively affected the intellectual faculties of city-dwellers and thus also the quality of urban governance.[12] In his masterpiece *Muqaddimah*, Abd al-Rahman Ibn Khaldun, perhaps the greatest scholar of the fourteenth century, developed Aristotelian environmental determinism into a climate theory of his own that sought to expound the key drivers of history.[13] He divided the world into seven climatic zones, each of which corresponded with a particular level of civilization, societal temperament, and set of customs: thus it was the exogenous influence of climate that accounted for the backwardness of much of Africa and Northern Eurasia, whilst his "middle zone"—with the optimal environmental circumstances—represented the apogee of human progress. Ibn Khaldun explained the nature of institutions and degree of affluence in function of natural endowments and ecological changes; nomads living in testing steppe or desert environments were more martial and bound together by codes of honor and solidarity (*asabiyya*), whilst sedentary peoples might live more comfortable lives in cultured cities, but over time fall prey to decadence and decline.

Ibn Khaldun's rationalist historiography, situated in the Greco-Islamic tradition of Ibn Sina and Ibn Rushd, was not always popular in his own life and times among conservatives who rejected his methods and conclusions regarding the environment and economics.[14] However, his version of environmental determinism would become majorly influential in nineteenth-century Europe, when Orientalists—not least Arnold Toynbee—celebrated his propositions linking climate, national character, and the rise and fall of polities.[15] The rediscovery of the heritage of Ibn Khaldun, Aristotle, and Hippocrates coincided with the growing fascination of Europe's intelligentsia and politicians with biology and with the renewed imperialist thrust that brought Europeans to exotic shores. Already, back in the eighteenth century, Montesquieu claimed in his *De l'esprit des lois* (1748) that the harsher climate of Western and Northern Europe instilled a sense of discipline, rationality, and political organization in its peoples, while further south societies were more prone to vice and inferior intellect. This allowed him to believe in European supremacy over "Asiatics" and other "lesser peoples," a conviction shared by many other leading thinkers of the age—David Hume, Voltaire, Johann Gottfried von Herder, Thomas Jefferson, Johann Blumenbach, Georg Wilhelm Friedrich Hegel—which paved the way for the "scientific racism" that proved so expedient in justifying nineteenth-century imperialism in Africa, Asia, and South America. Thus, in one of history's painful ironies, Ibn Khaldun's translated work was invoked to justify the French colonization of Algeria from 1830 onwards and the division of the native population into Arab and Berber "races," both represented as degenerate and inferior to the rational conquerors hailing from the temperate climate of France.[16] French administrators in Algiers were obsessed with the potentially nefarious impact of climate on the psychological and physical health of the colons and undertook expensive initiatives to "correct" the climate and change the ecology of the settler colony, so that France's *mission civilisatrice* would be preserved.[17] As the hygienist Jean Noël Perier put it: "colonizing is sanitizing."[18]

Earth in the balance: liberal views on environment and development

Environmental determinism shaped much of the debate in the nineteenth and twentieth centuries and continues to be influential,[19] but does not constitute the mainstream in thinking about the interaction between human society and the environment. Instead, the combination of the Scientific Revolution, the Industrial Revolution, and the secularization of politics propelled forward a resoundingly optimistic conventional wisdom, which has increasingly acknowledged that environmental degradation could have existential consequences for humanity and our planet itself, but interjects that the right kind of human intervention can ensure the regeneration of ecosystems and societal flourishing. The mainstream paradigm is unmistakably liberal, in that it posits an unambiguously positive evaluation of human potential and the benign and rational nature of interactions between individual citizens, enterprises, and states; aberrations such as violence and fraud do occur but are considered fully preventable if the correct mix of incentives and constraints is in place. While liberal authors have emphasized different key variables in tackling environmental degradation and resource scarcity, they all share the belief that economic growth and ecological sustainability can be reconciled—and can even be mutually reinforcing—and that the recipes for doing so can be applied universally.[20] A leading exponent of such middle-of-the-road environmentalism is Al Gore's *Earth in the Balance*, which recognizes that mankind is now the dominant cause of environmental change around the world and calls for a global Marshall Plan bringing together scientists, businesses, governments, civil society, and citizens around an agenda of responsible stewardship of a fragile global environment.[21]

Three principal mainstream approaches to the relationship between environment and development can be discerned. The first is usually termed "market environmentalism," because of its strong adherence to methodological individualism and its commitment to the (moderately reformed) neo-classical tradition of economics. Market environmentalists accept that the production models of large corporations and the voracious habits of consumers are harming the environment, but believe that capitalism itself is not to blame for the environmental crisis.[22] Flipping the argument on its head, they see ecological imbalances, such as rapid climatic changes, as a grave threat to the maintenance and expansion of prosperity.[23] They advocate the full application of the logic of the market—most prominently property rights and the price mechanism—to ecosystems and natural resources, claiming that this will eliminate negative externalities and, through incentives, stimulate productive and consumptive behavior that is both economically and ecologically sustainable.[24] Putting a price on carbon through tax, demanding water recovery fees from urban consumers and farmers, regulating—rather than prohibiting—the trade in ivory, and privatizing communally held or government-owned land are all classic examples of what market environmentalists might prescribe.[25] International trade too is considered a highly efficient instrument in reducing an economy's ecological footprint and is mutually beneficial for importers and exporters; Middle Eastern states like Egypt or Saudi Arabia would long ago have run out of water and food were it not for the option of importing commodities—"virtual water"—from producer countries where such resources are abundantly in supply, and can be poured into cultivating vast quantities of produce for export markets.[26]

Underpinning the market environmentalist view is the conviction that scarcity is not so much of a constraint, but actually a source of tremendous human ingenuity and creativity, provided that market tools are available for innovators to develop and disseminate their adaptive strategies.[27] This, then, is where many green capitalists would situate the reason for the persistent—and worsening—environmental problems of the Middle East: the lack of economic freedom and the disincentives put in place by overbearing states produce not just financial stagnation but also unchecked carbon emissions, air pollution, and terrible waste and water management. Despite attempts by the International Monetary Fund and the World Bank in the neoliberal 1980s and 1990s to promote a market-friendly approach to development—e.g. by scrapping subsidies for food producers and consumers that encourage environmentally and fiscally disastrous agriculture—market environmentalism has never really taken root in the Middle East.[28]

A more widely adopted approach in the region to environment and development is "technocratic environmentalism." This prism deems the magic of prices insufficient in getting to grips with the seriousness of the ecological challenge. Instead, it prioritizes the top-down translation of rigorous, experiment-based insights into public policy.[29] This requires a strict analytical separation of the natural world and human society and an emphasis on objectivity in observation and intervention. Only by maintaining a critical distance and ignoring romanticized views of society or nature can knowledge be accumulated over time and interactions between humans and their environment be rendered less harmful. This view echoes the elitist approach to science and policy of Auguste Comte, the nineteenth-century founding father of modern positivism, who dismissed Montesquieu's climate theory by arguing that social forces trumped natural variability and coined the cognoscenti-led science of "sociology" as clearly distinct from the speculative *physique sociale*. Technocratic environmentalism over the past century has meant rule by experts, and is resolutely apolitical in that a strictly positivist methodology of problem diagnosis, intervention, and evaluation overseen by scientific authorities is seen to be the only adequate response to degradation and growing scarcity.[30] Politicians, activist groups, and citizens might mean well, but ultimately risk corrupting the scrupulous, complex, and fine-grained work of technocrats.[31] This is especially so in the Age of the "Anthropocene": mankind has now become a geological force that is fundamentally altering Earth's bio-geochemical cycles, driving a sixth wave of mass extinction of species. This urgently requires an all-encompassing collective effort to keep human civilization within planetary boundaries—a biophysical imperative that might be at odds with neoclassical economics.[32] The main instruments envisaged by technocratic environmentalists are, apart from a specialized, highly autonomous bureaucracy, the environmental impact assessment and the expert advisory commissions, alongside strong planning agencies that "coordinate" efforts and "horizontally mainstream" priorities throughout organizational structures.

An example of both the promises and pitfalls of this approach in the Middle East is the International Center for Agricultural Research in the Dry Areas

(ICARDA), which has promoted sustainable agricultural development and poverty reduction in rural regions since 1977. ICARDA employs more than 600 experts drawn from top research institutes across the globe and belongs to a worldwide "epistemic community" of scholars with a strong *esprit de corps* and commitment to both expert-generated knowledge and bringing about on-the-ground change in key complex policy areas.[33] As part of the global Consortium of International Agricultural Research Centers (CGIAR), ICARDA specializes in research and training and works alongside governments in dry land countries. Headquartered in Aleppo, the technocrats of ICARDA developed a close relationship with the Assad regimes of father Hafez (1970–2000) and son Bashar (2000–current), helping to turn Syria into a regional agricultural powerhouse through the rapid expansion of cultivated land and the doubling of water wells to irrigate the new acreage. When, however, the rains began to fail Syria in 2006, and aquifers around the country were rapidly depleted, the shaky foundations of the agrarian boom that ICARDA had helped to engineer became evident. Rural poverty and anger with belated government reforms soared in the years leading up to the outbreak of the Syrian civil war in March 2011, a combustible mix that explains some of the opposition to Baathist rule.[34] Focused almost entirely on its relationship with the Syrian government and its model of technocratic environmentalism, ICARDA remained silent when confronted with disastrous feedback from the supposed beneficiaries of the policies that it had helped to craft.[35]

The third and final current in the mainstream paradigm is that of "liberal institutionalism," which shares the assumptions of market and technocratic environmentalists about development and the universality of its (optimistic) outlook. But rather than putting all its faith in markets or experts/epistemic communities, its main thrust is to focus on the structures of global cooperation, international law, and domestic regulation. States and international organizations should take the lead in driving meaningful change in the environment–development relationship, but universities, multinational corporations, and non-governmental organizations play vital roles too.[36] Institutionalists see a world of complex interdependence in which survival is possible only through multi-level cooperative structures, and they are increasingly focused on multi-actor "governance" in rapidly evolving networks rather than traditional "government."[37] In the context of the Middle East, there is therefore a growing emphasis on studying the institutional determinants of technological innovation, diversifying the domestic energy mix, and addressing pollution by state and non-state actors.[38] Approaching sustainability from a network perspective is also evident in the growing scholarship on the nexus between water, energy, and food.[39] Liberal institutionalism as a frame to approach the environment–development debate is strongly present in international law and quantitative political science, not least when it comes to the sharing of transboundary resources like water.[40] Much work has been done on which institutional permutations might best manage the competing claims of Turkey, Syria, and Iraq over the Euphrates and Tigris Basin,[41] and what forms of regional integration around the waters of the Nile—particularly between Egypt, Sudan, and Ethiopia—might be legally and environmentally feasible.[42]

Rediscovering old—and crafting new—governance mechanisms for natural resources has also been popular among economists. The New Institutionalism School investigates how principles of collective action and other institutional arrangements function in local communities that manage common-pool resources.[43] This literature adopts a more decentralized perspective to sustainability.[44] It stresses the institutionalized livelihood strategies deployed by local actors in navigating environments with great climatic variability and legal landscapes with multiple, sometimes overlapping, systems of tenure. In pre-2011 Syria, for example, Bedouin communities were neither Arcadian traditional societies living in open-access environments, nor fully integrated citizens engaging in incipient capitalist production for urban markets. Rather, the Bedouin blended customary claims to land, tribal authority structures, and semi-sedentary production to adapt to the continuously changing demands of their badiya steppe environment.[45] New Institutionalists have documented how pastoralists in Sudan respond to conditions of high rainfall variability and risk of drought with a collective strategy that relies on constant mobility and provides their herds with access to as many different communally held grazing areas as possible. In such a context, strong, egalitarian socio-legal structures that collectively pool the risks of ecological change have proven much more effective in helping people weather adversity than private property regimes.[46]

Limits to growth: the dystopianism of Malthus and his disciples

The sanguine liberal view on the ability of markets, scientists, and governments to reconcile society's appetite for economic growth with environmental sustainability has long been the scholarly and policy mainstream, but has always had to contend with a powerful critique emanating from environmental determinists. No challenger has had a more enduring impact than the

English reverend Thomas Malthus, whose dystopian linking of demography, environmental degradation, and political economy in the late eighteenth and early nineteenth centuries continues to influence many today, not least in the Middle East.

Already in the fifth century BCE, Plato had postulated that the growing ability of Hellenic civilization to mold—and thus damage—the natural world should lead it to adopt a system of government led by philosopher kings, rather than a rancorous democracy where the unbridled pursuit of self-interest risked undercutting the resource base on which the political community depends for its survival.[47] Two thousand years later, Malthus became convinced that a scenario in which humanity's impact on the Earth's resources would reach a point of no return was no longer hypothetical. Malthus believed that food production only grew arithmetically—2, 4, 6, 8, 10...—but that population expanded geometrically—2, 4, 8, 16, 32...—and that the numbers of mouths to feed was rapidly bringing society to the brink of an environmental apocalypse, with the onset of industrial civilization only exacerbating the problem: "the race of plants and the race of animals shrink under this great restrictive law and man cannot by any efforts of reason escape from it."[48] He rejected the Enlightenment optimism of the Marquis de Condorcet and William Godwin for whom a peaceful, free, and equitable world lay within reach, thanks to intellectual and technological progress. Instead, Malthus reframed environmental factors as exogenous, blaming ecological limits to food production and the very nature of humanity—its proneness to vice and procreation—for the inevitable resetting of human population to lower but more sustainable levels.[49] Hunger, disease, and war—the pitiless "checks" on population and prosperity—were thus primarily the consequence of ignoring the laws of nature. They would disproportionately cull the numbers of poor people, whose blindness to environmental limits and lack of sexual restraint meant that they had no one but themselves to blame for their misery. Malthus stridently criticized the Poor Laws of his era for merely postponing the inevitable day of reckoning. In doing so, he helped provide an ecological rationale for the laissez-faire policies articulated by his contemporaries, Jeremy Bentham and David Ricardo. Fearing diminishing returns on ever scarcer land and the fiscal burden of an expanding population dependent on state-organized charity, the liberal paragons of the age claimed that their economics were inextricably rooted in iron laws of nature. In Polanyi's words, for them "poverty was Nature surviving in society; its direct physical sanction was hunger."[50]

The reverend's ideas thwarted neither the gradual development of workers' rights and a British welfare state, nor the extraordinary expansion of industrial civilization. Moreover, his predictions of an imminent environmental doomsday, and of the steady-state economics that he and his ideological confreres had fretted about, failed to materialize.[51] However, Malthusianism lives on and has become the master narrative for framing violence, poverty, and environmental degradation in the non-Western world.[52] Malthus saw India as the exemplar of the cruel but unmistakably efficient natural system of self-regulation through hunger, disease, and war. His ideas informed the British imperial administration of the subcontinent, and in part explained the civil service's decision barely to intervene in food markets when catastrophic famines ravaged India in the late nineteenth century and millions of people died.[53] The conviction that the poor have no one but themselves to blame if they choose to have endless numbers of children, and that the most charitable form of public policy is one of non-intervention in food markets, was also carried to the Middle East. Malthus disparagingly noted that the explanation for poverty and hunger in Egypt clearly lay in the want of industry of the procreating poor; the notion of a demographic time bomb under the Egyptian economy survived British colonialism and has been central to post-independence politics and development policy.[54]

Malthusianism lost much of its appeal in early-twentieth-century Europe and North America and could have ended up as an ideological relic. But the growing awareness in the 1960s of the environmental dark side of industrialization and urbanization, combined with the Middle Eastern oil shock of 1973, terminated the West's cornucopian era of post-1945 record growth in disposable incomes. The broadcast images of famine in Ethiopia, Bangladesh, and the Sahel (1972–4), and the simultaneous price hikes for energy products in European cities, revived the message that perhaps Malthus' prophecies were not just of relevance to a distant Third World, but augured a dismal global future. This was the context in which some discerned a "population bomb,"[55] the Club of Rome published its warnings about "Limits to Growth,"[56] and a new generation of Neo-Malthusians emerged who detected resource scarcity as the defining variable of the modern era.[57]

For Lester Brown, the re-emergence of resource scarcity and its links with political instability called for a redefinition of national security—a view echoed by others working in the same tradition.[58] That security prism has been carried over into one of the most influential environmental tropes of our times, that of "water wars" in South Asia, Africa, and, perhaps most prominently, the Middle East.[59] As the MENA region's population is projected to increase to over 400 million people in 2025—up from 100 million in 1960 and 300 million in 2005—limits to growth, and pressures on water tables especially, appear very tangible indeed: Neo-Malthusian voices predict that existential scarcity will increasingly pit nations against each other, leading to deadly clashes over dwindling supplies.[60] The conflict between Israelis and Palestinians—and Israelis and Arab states more broadly—is one over competing nationalisms and land, with increased instrumentalization of religion by different conflict actors, but also one over the Jordan River and the limited amount of groundwater in the region.[61] Neo-Malthusians argue that the geopolitical maneuvering by the Syrian, Iraqi, and Turkish governments in the context of the regionalized civil wars in Syria and Iraq must be seen in light of the earlier-mentioned hydropolitics of the Euphrates and Tigris,[62] which have been exacerbated dramatically by the conflict, inducing local impact of global climate change.[63]

As evidenced—in the eyes of the twenty-first-century heirs of Malthus—by the Syrian case, "water wars" and, increasingly, "climate wars" are no longer merely a question of inter-state conflict, but also intra-state violence.[64] According to the United Nations Development Programme:

> Spreading drought, reduced water levels in rivers, stunted agricultural production, and incursion by sea water will force large numbers of people to emigrate, turning millions of people, particularly in the Nile River Delta and coastal areas in the Arab Gulf, into "environmental refugees." ... Such severe changes may also affect political stability and increase domestic tension. Sudan has experienced internal conflicts in Darfur, for example, between pastoralists and farmers over access to water sources.[65]

Thus, Yemen's intractable water and food crises are often depicted as a key contributor to state failure, and alleged to be co-responsible for the underdevelopment that is underpinning terrorism in the country, even before the Houthi takeover of Sana'a in January–February 2015 and the subsequent Saudi–Emirati bombing campaign.[66] Similarly, some have attributed the revolts of the 2011 Arab Spring and their violent outcomes to the explosive cocktail of a youth bulge, environmental degradation, and economic stagnation.[67] Food prices are seen as an especially apt predictor of political instability.[68] No case study of a (supposed) climate change conflict has been more cited than that of the genocidal violence in Darfur, including by the UN secretary general, the United Nations Environment Programme, and one of the world's most influential development economists.[69] Despite significant analytical problems with attributing the war in western Sudan to "climate" or "environmental scarcity,"[70] Darfur continues to be framed in Malthusian terms and presented as a dark harbinger of storms gathering across the MENA region.

(Neo-)Malthusians, like other environmental determinists, struggle to design a wide range of democratically supported policy proposals because of their scapegoating of the impoverished masses and their strong conviction that mankind has already crossed a point of no return—only draconian measures might address the escalating crisis. Theoretically, this penchant for authoritarianism can be explained by the reliance of most water/climate war models on a combination of Hardin's "Tragedy of the Commons" dilemma—in a context of open access, a shared and finite resource will be destroyed by a community of rational individuals, even if it is in no one's long-term interest for this to happen—and the political philosophy of Thomas Hobbes.[71] In Hobbes' view, because man is like a wolf to other men, perennial conflict is inevitable unless a Leviathan imposes law and order. Theorists of scarcity-induced conflicts have therefore tended to warn that unless a powerful government constrains the choices of people—and the poor in particular—Malthusian checks like war and famine kick in. In Ancient Greece, Aristotle already worried about ecological limits to society, suggesting that slavery and other restrictions on the actions of many people might be a necessary precondition for civilization.[72] But perhaps the most articulate formulation of the links between resource scarcity—especially water—and the centralization of power can be found in *Oriental Despotism*.[73] Based on his interpretation of the historical trajectories of, *inter alia*, Mesopotamia and Pharaonic Egypt, Wittfogel theorized "hydraulic civilizations" as highly hierarchical, bureaucratized states where water flows were tightly controlled from the top down and huge infrastructure works and forced labor were essential to Leviathan's projection of power. Such vintage environmental determinism makes authoritarianism less a matter of greedy rulers and their eccentric personalities than of the natural structural characteristics of the lands they rule over. The upshot is that resource-scarce regions like the Middle East either have to face tragedies of the commons and water wars, or submit to enlightened despotic rule that rationalizes production and consumption patterns.

Political ecology: critiquing the naturalizing of power

Alongside the mainstream liberal approach and Malthusian dystopianism, a third paradigm seeks to understand and interpret the environment–

development dialectic. While scholars with a broad range of views could be categorized under this umbrella, what political ecologists share is the conviction that there can be no neat analytical separation between the environment and human conceptualizations of it: the positivist illusion that one can study environmental change and management devoid of any subjectivities, and faraway from discussions about the distributional implications of that which the scientist claims to observe, is challenged.[74] This paradigm highlights the political and social construction of the environment, both materially and discursively, and is primarily concerned with how power evinces itself in particular environments and how (narratives of) environmental degradation affect authority and legitimacy.[75] Environmental processes, and their observations, in this reading are endogenous: they are not independent variables but are co-determined by political, economic, and cultural dynamics. Science and values are co-produced, which is not to say that environmental problems like climatic change or species extinction are not real, but rather to underscore that framing them is always a political act. For example, by describing the loss of biodiversity or global warming without putting these processes in the context of a global political economy of the environment that clearly benefits certain constituencies at the expense of many losers, one silences the voices of some and strengthens those of others.[76]

The paradigm of political ecology is highly critical of both the liberal and the Malthusian approach, notably in how they link the environment, society, and force. Political ecologists agree with (neo-)Malthusians that mainstream environmentalists underestimate the omnipresence of violence, particularly in the developing world, and overestimate the power of rationality—whether in the form of science, markets, and "win–win" institutions—in guaranteeing a peaceful future. But political ecologists are equally critical of the simplistic understanding of politics that Malthusians hold. They underline that their anti-poor bias and their framing of the environment as an exogenous variable amounts to a blindness to political economy and the ways in which the most vulnerable are disproportionately affected by both direct physical violence and the everyday oppression of economic, social, and political exclusion.[77] Contrary to the Malthusian narrative, the empirical record shows that international water wars, in the Middle East and elsewhere, are exceedingly rare.[78] Yet, as political ecologists insist, analysis should not end by underscoring how misguided the environmental conflict trope is. The fact that Malthusian discourses not only survive but thrive is of itself politically important, as it allows powerful actors to absolve themselves of responsibility—whether the Ethiopian Derg regime denying how it exploited the great famine of the 1980s, the Sudanese government washing its hands of Darfur in the mid-2000s, or the Baathists today seeking to hide how their disastrous policies exacerbated the Syrian population's vulnerability to drought and starvation.[79]

The strategic deployment by powerful elites of what has aptly been termed in another context an "ecology of fear" was a cornerstone in the capture of Middle Eastern lands for the European imperialist project in the nineteenth and twentieth centuries.[80] French and British colonial administrators believed that the region's ecology had faced a devastating collapse after classical antiquity, during which the Middle East had been associated with civilizational flourishing and high agricultural productivity. Through science, literature, and education, they spun a narrative lamenting the demise of a romanticized past, which contrasted starkly with the dystopian present. This legitimized not only the establishment of colonial states but also the programs of political-economic reform and environmental engineering on which European *savants* embarked.[81] For instance, British colonialism in Iraq drew heavily on environmentally determinist storylines of the otherworldliness of Mesopotamia because of its vast, desolate deserts, shifting rivers, and unnavigable marshes. Not only did this "impossible" geography of impenetrability serve to excuse early military failures to conquer the land, the British imperial mission was subsequently presented as a selfless attempt at undoing the Malthusian curse and reclaiming what had once been the "cradle of civilization." Such representations enabled the roll-out of technologies of surveillance and diverting water flows, both of which served as bedrocks of control over the Iraqis and their environment.[82]

The French domination of Algeria drew on similar themes: establishing mastery over both disease and the desert was seen as a heroic demonstration of tricolore supremacy and as an instrument with which to bolster confidence in imperialism back home. Environmental interventions in the Sahara meant not just changing water flows or planting trees, but amounted to social engineering, both of colonial subjects and of the imperialists themselves.[83] The obsession with public health and ecology followed from the fact that the reach of French troops and administrators across Africa was, for decades, limited by the hygienists' inability to neutralize debilitating disease. However, groundbreaking experiments with quinine in Algeria caused death rates from malaria among French soldiers to plummet, and appeared to vindicate the "environmental" approach to state-building.[84]

The links between technology, accumulation, and the consolidation of political power through the material taming of nature and the instrumentalization of environmental imaginaries did not end with decolonization. In many Middle Eastern states, the transfer of formal sovereignty amounted to the recycling of such strategies, *mutatis mutandis*, for the purposes of the new incumbents in the post-independence era. In Sudan, imperialists and local elites built the modern state in function of the idea that the Nile represented political and economic power, and that establishing centralized control over it gave incumbents a chance to remake the political economy and establish durable hegemony over society. After 1956, successive democratic, military, socialist, and Islamist regimes have stuck to the view that "dams are development," warning that a deviation from top-down engineering of water flows risked keeping the country mired in poverty.[85] As mentioned earlier, Egypt's rulers have been similarly obsessed with their dependence on the Nile and have consistently evoked population pressures to justify costly activities of land reclamation, ostensibly to promote economic development but often in function of patronage politics and wealth accumulation in Cairo under the guise of "reform" and "greening the desert."[86] Israel has sought to build its post-1948 economy, as well as justify its claims to statehood, through successful settlement of the land for which a strong hydro-agricultural thrust was essential; water has occupied a special place in Zionist ideology from the start, because—in the words of Prime Minister Levi Eshkol (1963–9)—water was the "blood flowing through the arteries of the nation."[87] Similar ideas about the nation-building effects of hydraulic projects inspired Muammar Qaddafi, when he pushed his Great Man-Made River—a system of pipelines under the desert sand transporting groundwater across the country—in a colossally expensive, ecologically unsustainable but politically shrewd bid to make Libya self-sufficient in food and fiber.[88]

The central importance of commodities to Middle Eastern state-building, patronage systems, and the self-image of its elites is also evident in the vast literature on rentierism, energy politics, and the resource curse.[89] The overdependence of economies on fossil fuels and associated rent-seeking through control over the commodity has been discussed in terms of its implications for political stability, the volatility of economic growth, neglect of education, and delayed (or wholly absent) democratization.[90] The Gulf states, Libya, and Algeria are usually cited as examples.[91] Apart from the implications for domestic power struggles, political ecologists underline that the Middle East's most strategic resources have also determined the ways in which the region has been integrated into the global political economy and its international normative complexes and how it has come to shape them in turn. The Arabian American

Oil Company (Aramco) embodies this, not just because of its crucial role in global oil markets and as the linchpin of the post-1945 Saudi–American alliance, but also because of the ways in which it anchored the modernization paradigm at the heart of the Saudi state. US corporate executives and Saudi royals engaged in mutually beneficial myth-making about how their partnership brought the desert to life through cutting-edge science, exemplary treatment of workers, and uniquely benign stewardship of oil and water resources.[92] Decades after the introduction of US-style modernization, the baton has been so successfully relayed to the Gulf states that they have now become themselves symbols (and exporters) of high modernism, with global ideational influence.[93]

This volume

This book begins by exploring how the consolidation of state authority and political contestation intersects with natural resources management and environmental change. Post-2012 resurgent authoritarianism in the Middle East is met with strong resistance, often formulated through the language and symbols of environmental politics—a trend that most scholarship on the region has so far missed.[94] Demonstrators around Istanbul's Taksim Gezi Park in 2013 protested against the conversion of the park into a shopping mall and high-end real estate, but the unrest morphed from a contestation of the disappearance of urban green spaces into a broader questioning of the state of democracy, the links between financial capital and politics, and the rights of minorities in Recep Tayyip Erdoğan's Turkey.[95]

The opening chapter of this volume, "Environmental Activism in the Middle East and North Africa," analyzes the sociological origins of such new modes of social mobilization. By drawing on case studies from Algeria, Egypt, and Lebanon, Jeannie Sowers charts the ways in which myriad forms of protest can scale up from focusing on a local environmental hazard to challenging national and transnational threats to livelihoods and political rights. Sowers underlines how environmental issues—because of their embeddedness in the domains of public health, identity formation, and core–periphery relations—are central to the high politics of the MENA region. Environmental activists often attempt to frame grassroots issues, such as pollution and waste management, in broader critiques of corruption and legitimacy, and seek support in transnational networks and coalitions. Such innovative tactics, Sowers hopefully notes, have in several cases forced governments to negotiate, accommodate, and even make fundamental reforms.

One case of relatively successful resistance against resource exploitation and political oppression is examined in detail by Francis Ghilès and Eckart Woertz in "Tunisian Phosphates and the Politics of the Periphery." The late-nineteenth-century discovery of a lucrative commodity in a remote region that became crucial to the political economy of the (post-)colonial state is a story that has a familiar ring to it in many developing countries. Ghilès and Woertz show how the wealth generated in the phosphate mines of Metlaoui in the Gafsa Governorate accrued to a coastal elite and its international network, but resulted in the entrenched economic marginalization of Tunisia's western hinterlands and widespread health hazards due to water pollution and land degradation. The workers of the basin around Metlaoui propelled forward the struggle for independence and remobilized with a vengeance against the dictatorship of Zine el Abidine Ben Ali; local branches of the Union Générale Tunisienne du Travail revolted in 2008 and then joined the first of the Arab uprisings in 2010–11. For the workers, economic marginalization and environmental problems were intimately connected with the nature of the political system—both its authoritarian character and the centralization of money and power in Tunis, with the complicity of international financial institutions such as the IMF and the European Investment Bank. As Ghilès and Woertz emphasize, the struggle to lend genuine democracy to Tunisian politics and give communities a greater say over the wealth generated in the mines has continued after the fall of the dictator. Fearful of business-as-usual and echoing environmental justice movements elsewhere,[96] strikes still regularly paralyze Metlaoui. The region refuses to demobilize until a better, comprehensive deal is offered—one that does not just provide token compensation for past harms and meager wage increases, but genuinely reforms Tunisia's political economy of phosphate.

As evident in these first two chapters, the dominant response of state elites and security agencies in the Middle East has been to stymie bottom-up political-environmental activism and curtail transnational connections. Sowers highlights the powerful role of both state and private media in framing environmental counter-narratives that seek to criminalize activists and portray them as foreign agents—processes in evidence in Tunisia and in Erdoğan's draconian purges following the failed coup attempt in July 2016. Turkey's emboldened president has steamrollered infrastructural megaprojects, accusing any opposition to them of undermining the state and seeking to keep the country underdeveloped.[97] The language of security and brute force thus shut down discussion of alternative constructions of ecological, economic, and political governance.

The unassailability of the hegemonic developmental paradigm and strategies of repression are also the main theme of Jill Crystal's contribution, "The Securitization of Oil and its Ramifications in the Gulf Cooperation Council States." She points to the ways in which Gulf states have increasingly invoked threats to their natural resources as a pretext to crack down on dissent and further restrict space for any form of opposition over the last decade. Crystal highlights the fusion of two powerful narratives, one around the Global War on Terror and one around hydrocarbon resources as the bedrock of Gulf wealth and society. The result is the emergence of a discourse coalition—a group of actors with disparate interests assembled around a compelling set of storylines, pushing a new set of material practices[98]—which is imposing a new political framework on the region. In a poignant illustration of the power of framing, the chapter suggests that this discursive strategy at a time of historically low oil prices is helping Gulf monarchs shift the ruling bargain with their citizens from a patronage-based contract to political acquiescence in exchange for security.

Ali El-Keblawy illustrates the environmentally ruinous decisions generated by the prevailing approach of thinking about natural resources in the Gulf. His chapter documents years of efforts by Gulf states to transform their landscapes—desert space, agricultural lands, sprawling cities, and degraded natural habitats—into more economically productive and aesthetically more appealing environments. As a technocratic environmentalist, he warns in "Greening Gulf Landscapes" against the unsustainable cost and questionable scientific basis of many contemporary policies and their dependence on massive consumption of groundwater. El-Keblawy is skeptical of the modernization paradigm that for so long has dominated environment-development discussions in the region and argues for a fundamental rethink of both priorities and instruments in environmental and economic policy. He sees existing Gulf landscapes as resourceful, productive, and ecologically valuable, rather than as enemies to be vanquished at all costs. He advocates a return to widespread use of native plants in greening parts of the desert and restoring degraded landscapes. Not only does he argue that such species are naturally well adapted to the local environment—including being drought-resistant—and require little or no fertilizer, he also argues that incremental, homegrown strategies have a much greater chance of mitigating climatic changes and boosting water conservation than counterproductive mega-projects that misread the landscape.

The environmental impact of consumption patterns is not just limited to the region itself, as Ilya Gridneff reminds us, but stretches far beyond the borders of the Gulf states. "Burning Somalia's Future" is the first thorough study of the illicit charcoal trade between the Horn of Africa and the Arabian Peninsula. By exploring how the appetite of Gulf restaurants, cafés, and tea houses for Somali charcoal to heat shisha water pipes and grill meat is one of the main drivers behind deforestation in Somalia, the chapter highlights the environmental dark side of regional connectivity. Moreover, the illicit trade is not just environmentally ruinous—increasing Somalia's proneness to flooding and drought, worsening land erosion, and undermining people's livelihoods—but is also politically destabilizing for the country's fledgling central government. Both the Al-Shabaab jihadists as well as foreign armies—notably the Kenya Defence Forces—are embroiled in the trafficking, and benefit from taxing charcoal. This fuels the violence and invites further external intervention—directly by Ethiopia and the African Union and indirectly by Gulf states and Western powers—thereby strengthening the vicious cycle that keeps Somalia's political institutions weak, its agricultural population impoverished, and its ecosystems progressively more degraded. Gridneff's study again underscores how what is often perceived as a local environmental hazard is not only driven by a transnational political economy, but is integral to core political and security concerns, domestically and internationally. The enmeshing of multidimensional environmental, political, socioeconomic, and security problems at multiple scales is particularly challenging to address from a policy perspective,[99] but mapping out these links, as the chapter does, is a necessary, if not sufficient, condition to break the vicious cycle.

Very similar conclusions regarding the interconnections between resource exploitation, economic marginalization, and transnational insecurity spillovers emerge from Afyare Elmi's "Illegal Fishing and Piracy in the Horn of Africa." Maritime resources are greatly under-researched by the social sciences, despite their importance to food security, reliable employment, and healthy ecosystems.[100] Illegal fishing worldwide accounts for almost one in every four fish caught and is a multi-billion-dollar business, making it a lucrative activity that has attracted the interest of criminal syndicates whose capacities overwhelm those of any Somali law enforcement agency. Elmi emphasizes the links between illegal fishing—not least by vessels and fishermen from Egypt, Iran, and Oman—and the rise of piracy off the Somali coast. One cannot comprehend the wave of hijackings and kidnappings in the Indian Ocean without understanding the utter devastation of livelihoods in mainland Somalia and in its territorial waters following three decades of war, external intervention, and looting of its natural resources. This chapter highlights linkages between environmental degradation and violence that are anything but

Malthusian. Instead, the key drivers are changing cost–benefit ratios for organized criminals with transnational operations and perverse forms of globalization that considerably facilitate the illicit flows of commodities, money, and weapons.[101] Elmi debunks the oft-cited narrative that Somali pirates are well-meaning protectors of Somalia's maritime riches after state collapse, showing instead how both piracy and illegal fishing are relatively new phenomena, forming nodes in international criminal networks that stretch from Oman and Dubai to London.

If Gridneff and Elmi focus on the barely regulated dark underbelly of globalization, then Clement Henry surveys what institutional arrangements might help the world reduce its climatologically disastrous addiction to oil and simultaneously stabilize the international relations of the Middle East. "Learning Geopolitical Pluralism: Toward a New International Oil Regime?" situates the shifting politics of the "devil's excrement" both in its twentieth-century evolution and in the changing global order of the early twenty-first century. Henry draws on the concept of geopolitical pluralism, as developed by Zbigniew Brzezinski, to analyze how resource politics are impacted by the withering of the Pax Americana. Contrary to those who see the post-2008 reduced US willingness to micromanage Middle Eastern politics as signaling dangerous weakness—recall, in particular, the tensions between Barack Obama and Saudi King Abdullah over Washington's refusal to save the Mubarak regime in Egypt in 2011 and to punish the Assad regime in 2013—Henry alerts us to the creative potential that the new age holds. An attempted return to the old Saudi–American and OPEC modes of governing oil markets is doomed to fail, but the chapter instead suggests expanding the membership of the International Energy Agency with (re-)emerging global players like China and India. Such steps would put broad foundations under a new international oil regime that facilitates contact between suppliers and buyers and assures safe transit. Rather than seeing oil as the classic Achilles heel of global politics,[102] Henry optimistically concludes with the hope that the crafting of a rekindled energy regime might underpin a stable global order, because it would bolster the cooperative tendencies between the Great Powers and because the return to high oil prices he foresees could lead to a critical mass of investment in renewable energy sources, thereby mitigating the impact of climate change.

The conviction that a different set of institutions and incentives might facilitate reforming entrenched environmental and economic practices in the Middle East is also the focus of the next chapter. In "Scarcity Drives Economic

Development," Wessel Vermeulen examines the impact of lavish energy subsidies. The stratospheric levels of energy consumption in most Middle Eastern states undermine public finance, economic growth, and the fight against climate change and air pollution. Reform has often been portrayed as environmentally necessary, but politically impossible and economically controversial—under the assumption that many MENA-based enterprises would lose international competitiveness without the subsidies. Vermeulen makes the opposite, market environmentalist argument. Scarcity could drive innovation: subsidy reductions would force businesses in economies like Saudi Arabia's to develop highly energy-efficient products that are actually in demand in global markets, rather than being net contributors to climate change and serving only a domestic clientele. Properly pricing energy would thus enhance economic diversification and encourage pro-green technological development, or so Vermeulen contends. The ongoing fiscal consolidation in many Gulf economies at the time of writing (2017) is thus welcome, economically as well as environmentally.

The final contribution in this collection touches on several themes of the book with its study of "The Politics of Natural Resources in the Caspian." Abbas Maleki explores the changing geopolitical and environmental landscape of the Earth's biggest inland sea and the surrounding nations, chronicling the rise of Central Asia as an international backwater to a key site in the global political economy, owing to its resurgent hydrocarbon production. Maleki dissects how the inflow of petrodollars transformed domestic politics and helped entrench authoritarianism and vast patronage networks in states like Azerbaijan, Turkmenistan, and Kazakhstan. The oil and gas windfall also led to a complex new international landscape. On the one hand, the Global War on Terror has given the Caspian littoral states—adjacent to both Iraq and Afghanistan—further strategic relevance and alliances with the United States and other Western partners; on the other hand, as Maleki shows, international oil majors have been frustrated in their Caspian operations, caught between rent-seeking by powerful bureaucracies in the region and virulent criticism by global civil society over their environmental practices and collusion with autocratic regimes. While hydrocarbon production is scheduled to grow considerably in the next decade despite such contestation and uncertainty, the oil price remains the wild card on which the future of the region's natural resources hinges. The chapter concludes pessimistically that both an increase and decrease in prices are destabilizing; neither seems likely to usher in the era of deep regional cooperation that is required to modernize decaying industries, tackle pollution in the Caspian, and adapt to climate change. The anthropocentric modernization paradigm is still deeply entrenched in the minds of decision-makers, and sovereigntist tendencies that put narrow national interest before basin-wide visions remain much more potent than institutional environmentalists would hope for.

In conclusion, then, this edited volume responds to the call of several landmark publications to mainstream the ways in which the exploitation and representation of the environment have shaped global history.[103] Even if not all of the contributions in this edited volume situate themselves squarely within that paradigm, most chapters are colored by political ecology's emphasis on historicizing and politicizing the environment–development debate and emphasizing conceptual and spatial crossovers. We have deliberately sought to blur conventional boundaries between material and immaterial, between nature and culture, and between states, societies, and regions. How "the ecological" is understood, visualized, remembered, instrumentalized, and intervened upon is fundamentally about humans and their hierarchies; deconstructing these interactions and their representations is about unravelling claims of authority and legitimacy. This is of particular importance in a region that has so frequently been seen by outsiders through the prism of environmental determinism and where ruling elites have imposed authoritarian control as the supposedly unobjectionable corollary of "environmental crisis."

This volume certainly does not contest the seriousness of what the Anthropocene implies for the Middle East—from air pollution and water scarcity to marine biodiversity loss and the impacts of climate change—yet challenges mono-dimensional framings of this multitude of grave issues. With the origins and consequences of such threats deeply rooted in questions of distribution, willfully blinding oneself to them amounts to a political act of favoring the privileged in society and the convenient causal mechanisms they identify and the blame they assign. By mapping out the complex and meandering environmental politics of the Middle East, this book problematizes much of what is presented as common sense and authoritative knowledge about the region.

What emerges instead is a multi-scalar atlas that shows how flows of resources and discourses around them link various parts of the world together in unexpected ways. The construction and reproduction of political power, financial accumulation, and ecological vulnerability are neither abstract global processes without territorial anchorage, nor dynamics that can be grasped by analyzing just one geographic unit of analysis. Our approach reveals core aspects of global and local politics and environmental change that often remain in the shadows. As this book shows, some of that occlusion is deliberate and a function of hegemonic aspirations by local elites, regional states, and global capital; but in other cases, environmental storylines and long-established biophysical practices have become so self-evident that their genesis from colonial, corporate, or scientific-bureaucratic interests has been all but forgotten. Recovering and questioning the roots of the state's manifest destiny to green the desert, of an elusive Arab consensus on how to leverage hydrocarbon wealth for peace, and of presumed local vices of deforestation and soil erosion is as much a process of meticulous scholarly inquiry as it is of political imagination.

The central message emerging from this book thus echoes one of the key tenets of political ecology, namely that "all environmental-ecological arguments ... are arguments about society and, therefore, complex refractions of all sorts of struggles being waged in other realms."[104] Environmental change is about changes in—and regularly the brutal reordering of—social relations. Ultimately, the chapters in this volume are documents of past, present, and impending clashes of interests, perspectives, and ideologies that spiral across disciplinary and administrative borders: local struggles, regional imaginaries, global connections. As such, the contributing authors urge a widening and restructuring of the ongoing debate about the future of the Middle East and associated tropes of crisis. In doing so, they emphasize that unless ecological discussions are recognized and re-centered as quintessentially political, activists, policy-makers, and scholars will continue to disappoint the ordinary people at the heart of the nexus between social injustice, political exclusion, and environmental calamities.

1

ENVIRONMENTAL ACTIVISM IN THE MIDDLE EAST AND NORTH AFRICA

Jeannie Sowers

Activism around public health and environmental issues constitutes a key element in the broader landscape of mobilization across the Middle East and North Africa. From the protests in Istanbul's Gezi Park and ninety other towns in Turkey in 2013, to demonstrations against electricity shortages in the Gaza Strip in 2017, new openings for environmental activism across the region have emerged over the past few decades. The expansion of environmental contestation has been intrinsically enmeshed in broader processes of social change that have transformed the region's political economies and ecologies. The study of environmental activism thus echoes the emphasis in the introduction to this volume on a political ecology approach—the interrelated study of ecological, social, and political change on a variety of scales.[1]

The spread of environmental activism in the region has been most evident in countries with semi-competitive political systems and long histories of collective action, including labor activism. Contestation around environmental issues, however, has also emerged in political and social contexts conventionally seen as inhospitable to activism. As this chapter shows, environmental activism across the region illustrates continuities in organization, discourse, and practice, as well as features specific to particular places and social contexts. State authorities have in turn responded with a largely predictable repertoire of action, ranging from repression to accommodation.

This chapter explores predominant modes of state–society engagement around environmental issues in the Middle East and North Africa. Elsewhere I have analyzed how networks of environmental experts and activists influenced environmental policy-making and implementation in Egypt, by analyzing efforts to control industrial pollution, relocate industries, preserve marine habitats and coastal areas, decentralize water management, and improve sanitation.[2] This chapter focuses more generally on social mobilization around environmental issues and state responses to these forms of activism across the region. I define environmental activism as the purposive engagement of individuals in the public sphere to make environmental claims. Popular concern around environmental concerns in the MENA focuses on a range of issues, from the adverse impacts of hazardous industries to demands for public services such as irrigation water and adequate solid waste collection.

The 2011 uprisings in the Arab world catalyzed scholarly and popular interest in developing a more multi-layered and granular understanding of the dynamics of social protest, which has had a long history in the region. As the popular revolts gave way to complex civil and regionalized wars in Libya, Syria, Iraq, and Yemen, however, the largely nonviolent and mass forms of social mobilization and activism have been overshadowed. Yet environmental mobilization has not diminished. Indeed, the phenomenon will most likely continue to intensify in most countries of the region, reflecting changes in political opportunity structures and activist strategies, as well as structural drivers including population growth, urbanization, migration, climate change, and scarce supplies of water and agricultural land.

This chapter proceeds as follows. It first situates Middle Eastern environmental mobilization in broader comparative studies of environmental activism, and then turns to the structural economic and social changes that created new openings for environmental mobilization. In the third section I discuss the advent of official, state-sanctioned environmentalism, before turning to the dominant modes of environmental activism that engage the state. These include widespread "wildcat" protests, typically in rural and peri-urban areas; the spread of formal environmental NGOs and voluntary associations; and the popular resistance "campaign" (*hamla*). State responses to these forms of environmental mobilization are explored in the fifth section, focusing on attempts to co-opt, delegitimize, and sometimes negotiate with environmental activists. Lastly, I explore some shared features and lessons learned from popular environmental campaigns in Egypt, Lebanon, and Algeria, and look toward future challenges for environmental activists.

Environmental activism in developing countries: the Middle East in comparative perspective

Environmental mobilization in the Middle East and North Africa has often seemed to be a *terra incognita* for scholars, whether in the fields of Middle Eastern studies or in comparative environmental politics. When studies of environmental movements emerged in the 1970s in Europe and North America, scholars rarely looked outside these regions at other types of mobilization. The emergence of large, membership-driven environmental organizations in the US, the "new social movements" linking anti-Cold War activism with feminism, peace, and ecological concerns, and the rise of Green parties in Europe all helped shape the field of environmental politics in ways that did not offer much insight into evolving state–society relations or environmental issues in the Middle East.[3]

Similarly, during the 1980s and much of the 1990s, the MENA was largely excluded from the flowering of scholarly inquiry around "environmentalisms of the poor" in South Asia and Latin America. Scholars studying liberation theology, subaltern voices, and the rise of feminist, indigenous, and democratization movements in Latin America and South Asia opened new avenues for the study of environmental politics. These focused attention on understanding the "environmentalisms of the poor." These scholars argued that since the rural poor in many developing countries depended directly upon the health and integrity of forests, pastures, water, and soil, their struggles for survival and justice were distinctive "Southern" forms of environmentalism. If Northern industrialized countries grappled with environmental problems generated by affluence and consumption, "environmentalisms of the poor" included struggles for indigenous and customary rights and resistance to centralized, large-scale projects in dam-building, resource extraction, and plantation forestry.[4] Environmentalisms of the poor thus challenged widespread (if incorrect) assumptions that states and citizens would prioritize environmental protection only once a certain level of economic development was reached.

These analyses of mobilization among the rural poor paralleled the rise of environmental justice as an organizing approach to understanding the disproportionate impact of pollution and other negative environmental impacts on communities of color and poor communities in the United States and Europe. Drawing on the fields of geography, urban and critical race studies, environmental studies, and sociology, environmental justice accounts demonstrated the ways in which race, class, and region made some communities more vulnerable to environmental hazards than others. In the United States, the siting of hazardous facilities in low-income or minority neighborhoods, unequal enforcement of environmental laws, and the unequal provision of health care inspired extensive literature on the structural causes of environmental racism and discrimination.[5]

Environmental justice and environmentalisms of the poor remain important approaches to understanding the political dynamics around environmental issues in the Middle East. While the Middle East faces a number of important and complex environmental issues, only some have proven salient to popular mobilization, and these often relate directly to concerns around public health and economic livelihoods. Popular forms of mobilization in urbanizing regions focus on pollution and public health threats from air pollution, traffic, lack of green space and recreational opportunities (especially for children and youth), inadequate solid waste collection and disposal, and industrial proximity. Rural mobilization often focuses on lack of access to land and water for agriculture, inadequate sanitation and solid waste systems, and displacement and threats to livelihoods from large state-led projects such as dams.

State elites and official media outlets often view popular environmental contestation in both rural and urban areas with suspicion. Critical voices concerned about health and environment receive short shrift across the globe, but particularly so in the MENA. Regional and local conflicts, and the continued meddling of great power patrons, allow Middle Eastern regimes to cast social or environmental challenges to state-sanctioned development projects as threats to national security, territorial integrity, and national identity. As one scholar observed in analyzing Turkish environmental movements, "the modernizing state mostly takes a confrontational position, opposing not only what are deemed 'radical' environmental demands, but also rather mild calls to conserve nature."[6] Official ambivalence about environmental claims is manifested in calls by state-owned media and government officials to respect the unity and integrity of the state, often portraying local demands for environmental justice as acts of internal division fomented by outside agitators.

As in other regions, state and corporate actors increasingly deploy their own environmental discourses and interventions, often under the rubric of sustainability. While some of these activities improve specific environmental outcomes, others are more accurately characterized as greenwashing.[7] In contexts where states or large corporate interests directly own or influence media outlets, media coverage amplifies official narratives and initiatives regarding environmental protection, whether or not these efforts lead to substantive environmental improvement. In the absence of robust and accountable mechanisms to report accurately on environmental problems, state media often frame environmental activism as divisive and contrary to national interests.

The political economy of environmental activism

As the outpouring of collective action during the 2011 Arab uprisings amply demonstrates, structural socioeconomic changes in the last few decades have created new openings for activists across the Middle East and North Africa. The exhaustion of statist populism and the turn to market liberalization, ongoing urbanization, and expansion of higher education, combined with new communication technologies and ownership, opened new spaces for political interaction and the spread of new discourses around environmental issues.

Post-colonial Middle Eastern states have long embraced a simplistic template for "modernization" and development, combined with deep distrust of social and popular mobilization. State elites sought to reshape local environments through the common template of strategies associated with "development." The template for development in arid regions—whether in California or in Egypt—focused on harnessing river systems through building large dams and extensive irrigation systems, "greening" the desert, and the extraction and consumption of fossil fuels to underpin mechanization and industrialization. In the 1950s and 1960s, under state-led programs of industrialization, many MENA states taxed agriculture to provide investment in heavy and intermediate urban industries without regard to environmental impacts. The parallel cultivation of authoritarian security states stifled alternative perspectives, as universities and voluntary associations were brought under rigid state control. The focus on creating heavy and intermediate industry was followed by fiscal crises in the 1970s and 1980s that crippled investment and modernization in these state-owned enterprises and created intense hotspots of pollution. These "hotspots" have long generated chronic conflict with local urban residents, fishermen, and farmers living nearby.[8]

Fiscal pressures eventually drove many MENA states to re-engage with the private sector, seeking economic growth and job creation. Led by Tunisia, Egypt, and Turkey, neoliberal reforms opened protected domestic markets to foreign direct investment and established special economic zones designed to attract private investors without regulatory burdens or taxation. These zones and other favorable national policies helped attract some secondary industries based on proximity to cheap natural resources (oil, gas, and phosphates), particularly in industries facing significant regulation and thus limited expansion in developed countries. In Iran, these areas have included the special economic zones of Sirjan, which saw concentrations of chemical, hydraulic oil, and motor oil companies, and Anzali, a port city on the Caspian Sea.[9] In Egypt, free zones have often been located to take advantage of existing port infrastructure, resulting in large complexes of pollution-intensive or potentially hazardous industries next to well-established, growing cities, such as Damietta, Alexandria, and Suez.

The spread of urban frontiers thus played a significant role in fostering environmental concerns and activism. Driven by population growth, ongoing rural to urban migration, and displacement due to war and climate change, over 64 percent of the MENA population currently live in cities.[10] As urban frontiers expand each year, more urban inhabitants live in proximity to industrial facilities, ports, garbage dumps, incinerators, and other "noxious" facilities. Urban areas are also well-networked in terms of media coverage, cell phones, dense neighborhoods, family, and professional networks—all of which serve to facilitate opportunities for collective action.

Neoliberal policy reforms, adopted unevenly during the 1970s through the 1990s, generally enriched small numbers of *nouveau riche* business groups with close ties to incumbent regimes, while new jobs emerged primarily in the informal private sector. State contraction eroded the subsidies, urban infrastructures, and public employment that sustained many middle- and lower-class citizens, leading to increased expressions of public discontent. Deepening corruption and inequality became widespread public concerns, as did privatization of state-owned enterprises. In Egypt, labor activism, including wildcat strikes, demonstrations, and attempts to form independent unions, increased significantly by the second half of the 1990s.[11] Highly publicized instances of state concessions to striking public sector workers encouraged the diffusion of these modes of social protest, even while public sector workers represented an increasingly small proportion of the labor force.[12]

As the state's ability to deliver public services and provide adequate safety nets declined, private voluntary organizations also emerged to fill the void.

Egypt in the 1980s—and particularly the 1990s—saw a significant expansion in charitable undertaking, welfare associations, and local development associations connected to the broader turn toward Islamic and communal forms of social mobilization.[13] This expansion in Islamic and civic mobilization reflected deepening neoliberal changes in the regional political economy, as ideas, migrants, and remittances flowed to and from the Persian Gulf to the rest of the MENA.

Generational and demographic changes have also been important in diffusing various modes of activism. New jobs in partially revitalized private sectors could not keep pace with demographic change and the number of entrants into the labor market. Population growth, particularly for youth aged 15–29, exceeded job opportunities, resulting in exceptionally high unemployment rates for women, youth, and college graduates, when compared with other world regions. By the 1990s, some of these educated cohorts in their twenties and thirties created networks of activists, some of whom worked in Islamic circles and others who worked in human rights, democracy movements, and labor organizing. These activists steadily demonstrated a greater capacity to organize direct action and capitalize on spontaneous outbreaks of protest during the 1990s and early 2000s. The Arab Barometer surveys, for instance, found that 30 percent of Egyptian youth aged 18–24 had participated in protest activity in the few years prior to the 2011 uprising.[14]

Underpinning these youth-based informal networks of activism was the expansion of what Marc Lynch termed the new Arab "public sphere."[15] Privatization of the media sector brought about a proliferation of "old" media such as newspapers and TV stations, alongside the explosion of "new" media, including satellite stations and social media platforms. The rise of Qatar's Al Jazeera, alongside a number of regional satellite stations, provided expanded coverage of issues such as the Israeli–Palestinian conflict and the US invasion of Iraq that created broader senses of solidarity. Specific protest movements grew from this sense of shared grievances, such as the widespread protests in Egypt after Israeli incursions into Gaza in the winter of 2008–9. However, state-owned satellite and new corporate-owned media outlets could also quickly turn against protest movements, as when General al-Sisi took power in a military coup against the Muslim Brotherhood in Egypt in 2013, initiating a broad crackdown on all forms of dissent that was enthusiastically embraced by most Egyptian media outlets.

Despite these challenges, transnational changes in the flows of information, communication, and education have enabled social activists to access and publicize environmental issues more readily and work with activist organizations across borders. Within the MENA, a dearth of robust social science communities or diverse media outlets had long limited local scholarship and media coverage on issues such as activism around environmental problems.[16] With more decentralized and diversified forms of communication and new ways to connect to international environmental movements, local environmental activists have found new spaces for learning and engagement. Citizen journalists, bloggers, and others have increasingly shared environmental issues with a broader range of audiences at home and abroad, documenting environmental problems and local social mobilizations.

Assistance from migrants living abroad has also helped raise the profile of environmental issues in some countries. In Turkey, for instance, transnational linkages between Kurdish communities in Germany and their home towns brought new dynamism to social and environmental movements in Turkey's south-east. As the Islamist AKP party increasingly dominated the central government—winning a plurality of seats in almost every Turkish election since 2002—popular environmental claims in minority regions were increasingly tied to claims about communal identity, authenticity, and autonomy. These movements and their transnational ties are increasingly vulnerable, however, to President Erdoğan's re-militarization of the Kurdish conflict and his expansive crackdown on a wide range of Kurdish and secularist news outlets and civil society organizations in fall 2016.

State-sanctioned environmentalism

Middle Eastern states have selectively embraced environmental concern over the past few decades. All MENA governments during the 1990s and 2000s adopted some kind of national environmental law and created an environmental agency or ministry. These institutional changes often reflected the sustained efforts of technocrats, local scientists, and expatriate consultants working within various ministries and donor-funded projects.[17] As has often been the case in bureaucratic development in the region, Egypt and Turkey led the way. Local experts with donor assistance created the Egyptian Environmental Affairs Agency in 1982, which was restructured in 1994. A minister of state for environmental affairs at cabinet level was added in 1997. In Turkey, a Prime Ministry Undersecretariat for Environment was established in 1978, and restructured in 1991 into a Ministry of Environment with expanded jurisdiction.[18] In other parts of the region, new environmental agencies were attached to ministries of water (the UAE and Yemen), sustainable development (Tunisia, Mauritania), housing or municipalities (Bahrain, Djibouti), or energy, mining, and water (Morocco).[19] The organizational trend over time, however, was to emulate the Turkish and Egyptian models to create stand-alone environmental ministries. However, environmental ministries are widely viewed as "weak" compared with the money and power concentrated in the governmental ministries of the interior, industry, mining, and oil and gas.

Environmental ministries and agencies with mandates over natural resources differ significantly in their territorial reach, institutional capacities, and legal standing. Turkey established provincial environmental offices in all eighty-one of its administrative districts, drawing up local environmental funds derived from environmental service provision.[20] Egypt formally established regional environmental bureaux, but these remained unevenly funded and staffed for years. In the poorer countries of the region, environmental capacity-building at the provincial level was typically initiated by donors, and thus faced the typical sustainability challenges associated with external initiatives.

In addition to creating environmental laws and institutions, state-owned and state-supportive media outlets increasingly devoted some coverage to select environmental issues. Media coverage was encouraged, in part to pressure firms and local authorities to comply with national environmental regulations. In China, national media coverage of "pollution controversies" is a recognized mechanism to enhance inadequate state enforcement.[21] More frequently, however, MENA media coverage focused on promoting "environmental awareness" for citizens rather than compliance for firms, exhorting citizens to behave in more environmentally friendly ways.

States also sometimes supported semi-official environmental NGOs that represented official concerns and interests. For instance, in monarchical systems such as Jordan and Saudi Arabia, leading members of the royal family took up issues such as nature conservation and wildlife preservation. Hearkening to the enclosures of common pastures in England and the creation of colonial game preserves across Africa, monarchies often focused on preserving fauna (and their habitats) that they themselves had decimated through unregulated hunting. As an exhibition at Doha's Museum of Islamic Art on hunting in the Islamic world presented, royal families exalted hunting as a princely endeavor and a symbol of authority. Ruling families in Saudi Arabia, Oman, the UAE, and Jordan have all supported breeding programs and habitat protection to reintroduce the endangered Arabian (white) oryx to the Arabian Peninsula, in cooperation with international conservation organizations such as the International Union for Conservation of Nature and the World Wildlife Fund.

Strategies of environmental activism and state responses

If we focus primarily on social activism rather than elite or state support for environmental issues, three prevalent modes of engagement between environmental activists and state authorities have emerged, as indicated in Table 1. These modes include relatively uncoordinated yet widespread phenomena, such as "wildcat" protest and "quiet encroachment;" the activities of formal environmental voluntary organizations and NGOs; and the conduct of popular resistance campaigns.

Informal activism: encroachment and wildcat actions

In an influential essay written in 2002, Asef Bayat argued that many scholars had largely missed significant forms of social action by focusing almost exclusively on formal social movements, which are rare in the Middle East and North Africa given their exclusionary political systems. Instead, Bayat called attention to what he termed the "quiet encroachment of the ordinary."[22] Faced with unaccountable, overwhelmed bureaucracies; police forces intimately tied to security forces; and emergency laws that stripped citizens of basic civil rights, the urban poor sought to obtain what they needed through direct action and by using connections to obtain services and employment. These "non-collective but prolonged direct actions of dispersed individuals and families to acquire the basic necessities of their lives ... in a quiet and unassuming illegal fashion" had transformed urban landscapes across much of the region.[23] What Bayat termed "social non-movements" in turn forced states to extend services, upgrade informal areas, and recognize "illegal" squatting. Quiet encroachment thus joined urban mass protest, trade unionism, community activism, social Islamism, and non-governmental organizations (NGOs) as an important form of regional activism.[24]

Encroachment, however, is not the only type of small-scale, informal, and localized action to appropriate and demand access to natural resources and environmental services. Local media and online platforms regularly report that small groups of community members, peasants, urban residents, fishermen, and others block roads and public places, petition local officials, and

Table 1.1: Modes of Environmental Mobilization in the MENA

Mode of engagement	*Degree of institutionalization*	*Typical participants*	*Activities*	*Environmental foci*
Informal and widespread: "encroachment" and wildcat protests	Low	Farmers, community residents, fishermen, miners	Petitions and complaints to local officials, direct action (blocking roads, government offices, bridges, squares), marches, sit-ins	Inadequate public services; lack of access to water and resources; pollution; land use and facility siting decisions
Environmental organizations and NGOs	High	Staff, lawyers, middle-class professionals, expert activists	Provision of science/expert input; service delivery and projects; coordination with international environmental organizations	Conservation, reforestation, rural development and urban improvement projects, environmental laws and regulation
Popular resistance campaigns (*hamlat*)	Medium (varies)	Community activists, journalists, local politicians; may scale up to get support from labor unions, human rights networks, opposition parties, official NGOs	Lobbying, direct action, media coverage, lawsuits, expert and scientific input, use of social media/internet to coordinate	Industrial and energy land use decisions; pollution and public health; may expand to broader critique of corruption, lack of democratization, accountability, and decentralization

generally pressure state authorities through these illicit yet vocal actions. These actions are often spontaneous, generally engaging local state or firm agents through small-scale disruptions to force those responsible for decision-making to negotiate and sometimes accommodate demands. While these forms of activism often generate small changes in state and corporate behavior, adequate documentation of these small-scale protests is generally lacking. Moreover, because officials tend to capitulate on highly visible environmental problems with cheap, short-term measures, the deeper drivers of environmental degradation often remain unaddressed. Local officials may sometimes accommodate the demands of wildcat and informal protest, precisely because informal actions are easily contained, and thereby prevent more sustained challenges to existing distributions of power and resources.[25]

Environmental voluntary organizations

The spread of environmental non-governmental organizations (ENGOs) in the Middle East and North Africa represents a more institutionalized form of mobilization. Almost all governments in the region require associations to seek official government registration and permission to operate. Government agencies may deny registration, as the so-called "Ministry of Social Solidarity" in Egypt has often done for human rights, labor, and environmental associations. In many cases, registered environmental organizations consist of a few individuals who are often experts in specific environmental or health fields. Overt government sponsorship has also been common in the more interventionist states, as in Iran and Egypt. In Turkey, for instance, environmental associations are subject to greater state supervision regarding membership, funding, and external cooperation than Islamic foundations.[26]

Not surprisingly, the relatively more open institutional contexts of Lebanon, Turkey, Israel, the West Bank, and Tunisia saw significant growth in formal environmental associations over the past few decades. In Lebanon, the number of ENGOs grew rapidly after the 1991 Ta'if Accords ended the civil war; eighty-five new associations were created in 1991 out of a total of 138 registered with the Ministry of Environment by 2009.[27] In Iran, numerous environmental associations were founded once the reformist Mohammad Khatami was elected to the presidency.[28] Israel's environmental movement included ninety-seven active environmental associations as of 2010, over half of which were established after 1999.[29] As in Egypt, environmental activism in Israel has grown rapidly, not only in major cities but also in provincial regions where mining and polluting activities are concentrated.[30] In 2002, a European Commission reported 72,800 environmental associations in Turkey, although only a few were national in scope.[31] In the Persian Gulf, the dire air pollution unleashed by oil fires set by retreating Iraqi troops in 1991 prompted the creation of the first Kuwaiti ENGOs to monitor health and environmental impacts.[32]

Despite fragmented territorial control, internal factionalism, and the ongoing limitations imposed by a lack of political solution to the Israeli–Palestinian conflict, Palestinian ENGOs have also proliferated. A 2012 mapping analysis found sixty-four active associations in East Jerusalem, the Gaza Strip, and the West Bank.[33] These organizations worked on community initiatives, campaigns, consultancies, and service provision. However, only seven organizations were identified as key players, employing more than 55 percent of the total employees of ENGOs.[34] Palestinian associations with some focus on environmental issues—including water, sanitation, and solid waste—represented only a small percentage of the 2,225 voluntary organizations registered with the Palestinian Ministry of Interior.[35]

The spread of associations, however, does not necessarily translate into public awareness of their work or policy effectiveness. A 1998 survey in Istanbul found that 58 percent of respondents were unable to name correctly even one NGO working on environmental issues in Turkey.[36] A later comparative study of the four largest and most influential environmental organizations in Turkey found that while it appeared that they had gained increased access to policy-making processes, this access was "only in appearance and discourse, rather than ensuring their genuine participation."[37] Of the four studied, only Greenpeace-Med had a mass membership base that sustained the organization through small-scale donations, making it relatively autonomous from both corporate interests and governmental pressures.[38]

Some ENGOs focus on a single environmental issue or a particular community, while others work across multiple issue areas and forms of activism. In Egypt, several well-known associations focused on the environment and urban heritage in Alexandria (*Asdiqa'a al-bi'ah*, Friends of the Environment), and services and community upgrading among the Coptic garbage collectors (*zabaleen*) in Cairo (the Association for the Protection for the Environment). Some associations took the model of legal aid and advocacy developed in human rights organizations in the 1980s and 1990s, and applied it to environmental issues, such as Egypt's *Markaz al-Ard lil-Huquq al-Insan*, the Land Center for Human Rights, which focuses on rural issues including land ownership.

The Land Center provides an unusual example of how environmental issues, economic livelihoods, and community mobilization can be integrated into an environmental justice strategy in the region. Since 1996 the Center has provided legal aid for small agricultural producers, migrant laborers, children, women, and tenant farmers. After the 2011 uprising, the Land Center sought to help small producers form independent cooperatives. Despite assurances from post-Mubarak cabinets that independent unions were to be allowed, however, attempts to register legally both unions and cooperatives encountered numerous delays and obstacles.[39]

As mentioned previously, nature conservation, biodiversity, and habitat protection are often the focus of elite, state-supported ENGOs. Conservation scientists and protected-area advocates often participate in larger transnational networks of expertise, and can sometimes leverage international attention and funding. In Egypt's South Sinai, efforts to safeguard protected areas combined pressures from international environmental advocates, European Union-funded projects, and local diving and tourism operators.[40] A significant number of ENGO activities documented by a local monthly publication (*Al Marjaa-Cassander*) in Lebanon between 1994 and 2002 were devoted to conservation and reforestation.[41] In neighboring Israel, a well-developed ENGO sector has long focused on nature protection and open spaces, as well as addressing environmental hazards and public health.[42] The movement remains hindered in reaching out to Palestinian Arabs with Israeli citizenship, however, in part because of the historically tight link between reforestation projects and land acquisition for Jewish settlement.

Environmental campaigns

The popular resistance campaign (*hamla*) has emerged as the most publicized and flexible form of activism in the Middle East. Environmental activists have learned from other regional solidarity campaigns how to frame concerns broadly, build alliances across scales, establish local coordinating committees, and combine tactics of protest, media outreach, and lobbying to achieve limited successes. At the same time, however, campaigns often gradually lose momentum as they encounter police repression, complex bureaucracies, and official promises that often fail to materialize. Sustaining campaigns requires organizers either to make use of existing NGOs and networks or to create new organizational infrastructures. Meanwhile, regimes use a variety of tactics to demobilize and disempower activists, including smear campaigns in the media, arrests, and firing employees from public and academic employment. Demobilization and de-escalation are thus likely outcomes even for highly publicized, well-organized campaigns.

To gain traction in such unpromising political contexts, environmental campaigns in the Middle East often share several common features that allow them to organize against significant odds. First, campaigns typically frame specific environmental issues in terms of their direct impacts on public health, economic livelihoods, and local/regional identity. These issues resonate with much larger constituencies and are particularly effective when responsibility for environmental harm can be clearly attributed to one firm or state agency. As we shall see, foreign multinationals in particular make for populist targets. State-owned enterprises, despite their dismal pollution records in many sectors, are more difficult to challenge.

Second, when such movements begin to scale up and attract broader constituencies, the discourse around environmental claims becomes more encompassing and politicized. Many local campaigns seek to build upon widespread concerns with privatization, dictatorships, corruption, cultural authenticity, and lack of accountability.[43] Campaigns on the periphery may highlight how local concerns among *al-sha'ab* (the ordinary people, the popular classes) living in provincial towns, poorer urban neighborhoods, and rural areas are overlooked by state elites, corrupt businesses, and political leaders in the capital. Scaling up, however, may risk association with broader oppositional currents and invite heightened scrutiny and repression.

Third, relatively successful campaigns typically include participation from middle-class professionals, environmental experts, journalists, and others with specialized expertise and experience in navigating state institutions. These participants help to publicize the campaign and use their expertise to engage the legal avenues of state to document grievances and put forward policy alternatives. Legal cases, parliamentary hearings, fact-finding commissions, and other routes to engagement are important in making a convincing case for changing existing practices.

Fourth, the transformed communications landscape of the past few decades has played an important role in broadening the ability of local environmental campaigners to reach out across borders to transnational advocacy networks and migrant diasporas. In the case of protests against the proposed construction of the Ilisu Dam on the Tigris River in Turkey for instance, local activists connected with global networks of activists to pressure foreign multinationals and European export credit agencies to pull out of the project in 2009. The

Ilisu Dam is only one of the twenty-two dams that constitute the pillars of the Turkish government's Southeast Anatolia Development Project (GAP) designed to "modernize" the largely Kurdish south-eastern region. The transnational campaign around Ilisu sought to shift the venues of activism from those of an inhospitable Turkish state to European policy-makers and credit agencies that had pledged to adhere to global norms for dam planning and consultation.[44] Global activist networks argued that the Ilisu Dam imposed unacceptable costs to local ecologies and communities by flooding 199 settlements as well as many cultural heritage sites and abandoned villages depopulated by the decades-long conflict between the Turkish government and the Kurdistan Workers' Party (PKK). In 2012, then-Prime Minster Erdoğan exempted the Ilisu Dam from environmental impact assessments. Although Turkey's highest administrative court ruled against the decree, construction eventually continued using domestic financing and construction firms.[45] GAP dams were also contested by diaspora communities living abroad. "Hometown" (*hemşire*) organizations founded by Alevi and Kurdish migrants in major cities across Europe, Australia, and western Turkey helped to sustain environmental mobilization in the Munzur Valley against GAP-proposed dams and in support of eco-tourism and nature preservation.[46]

The last shared feature of prominent environmental campaigns is that they make use of direct action rather than simply engaging in lobbying or media outreach. These direct actions are highly public affairs, designed to occupy public spaces, block roads and ports, confront police forces (often nonviolently), and demonstrate outside government offices and company headquarters. Both the numbers of protesters and their targets of protest matter for making an impact; in China, a common slogan is that "a big disturbance leads to a big solution."[47] Where activists directly interfere with energy and transport infrastructures, block access to industrial sites or forests, or stage sit-ins, national centers of power are often drawn into responding. Where development decisions and public services are decentralized to sub-national government units, as in China, protesters may seek to involve the central party-state in overturning unpopular local decisions.[48] However, in the Middle East and North Africa, where large-scale industrial and infrastructure projects are often decided by central governments, and implemented as joint ventures between multinationals and large state-owned enterprises, local opposition often directly targets decisions taken by the national government.

State responses to environmental activism

How do Middle Eastern states and firms respond to popular environmental campaigns and other modes of environmental activism? As elsewhere, harassment, detention, torture, and long prison sentences have been periodically used to deter dissent. MENA countries also impose tight restrictions on foreign funding of environmental organizations, successfully cutting most of them off from international ENGOs, with the exceptions of Lebanon, Israel, Palestine, and Turkey. Egypt, for instance, has detained activists, raided their offices, and filed lawsuits against prominent environmental and social organizations for accepting foreign funding. Regimes also act pre-emptively to deter activism from materializing. State security forces in the region conduct extensive surveillance of activists, tracing their family backgrounds and alleged political affiliations, and monitoring foreign travel, meetings, and routine activities.

Regimes and business groups have also become savvy about conducting negative public relations campaigns against activists, using new media platforms and the internet. While Vladimir Putin's Russia has received the most publicity for its extensive propaganda operations regarding Crimea, the Ukraine, and the 2016 US elections, Egyptian President al-Sisi and Turkish President Erdoğan also demonstrate how the media can serve as an echo chamber for polarizing populist appeals to national security over environmental concerns. These media attacks often emphasize national "unity," particularly when seeking to discredit movements based in provincial areas with large minority populations, such as the Alevi and Kurdish areas of Turkey.[49] Environmental campaigners often struggle to refute allegations circulated by state security forces that activists are foreign agents, hooligans, or out for personal gain.

Repression and negative public relations campaigns are not the only regime responses. All three modes of environmental activism also provoke accommodation, negotiation, and occasionally concessions. Indeed, wildcat strikes, petitions, and sit-ins are often used to engender responses from local authorities. Conflicting decrees and judicial findings from various state agencies also open up opportunities for continued social contestation by providing a variety of bureaucratic venues, even as these also wear down activists facing state fragmentation and competition.

The range of common state responses in the region is summarized below in Table 2. In the next section, I demonstrate the interplay of activist strategies

Table 1.2: State responses to environmental activism

State responses to environmental activism	*Typical features*	*Actors*	*Outcomes for environmental activism*
Production of counter-discourse to discredit	Activists "threaten" security, economic development, national identity, and are "agents" for external interests	State-owned and private media, officials, nationalist-right parties and networks, military and intelligence services	Weakens movements and NGOs, generates backlash to environmental claims
Harassment and repression	Lawsuits against movement leaders or NGOs; arrest and detention; keeping or expanding legal restrictions on civil liberties; restrictions on travel and participation	Internal state security, judiciary, administrative and executive decrees	Increases risks to environmental activists and organizations, promotes demobilization and disillusionment
Co-optation and clientelism	Selective registration/recognition of NGOs, selective corruption/foreign financing charges; selective inclusion/exclusion in planning processes and government commissions	Administrative agencies, judiciary, state-supportive media, state security services	Promotes divisions and fragmentation through selective distribution of benefits and punishments
Negotiation and accommodation	Formal policy changes; cancelling land use decisions; extending services or access to resources	Prime minister, president, governors, mayors, urban planning commissions/processes	May embolden environmental actors and claims; changes in planning/consultation processes possible

and state responses through vignettes of environmental campaigns in three very different Arab countries.

Egypt: port cities protest industrial siting

The environmental campaign conducted against several fertilizer plants in the Egyptian port city of Damietta, prominent from 2008 to 2012, exhibited the state responses of repression, counter-discourses, and co-optation.[50] Over time, the protests attracted an increasingly diverse cross-spectrum of participants, including local popular organizations (*jam'iyyat ahliyya*), journalists, parliamentarians, members of professional associations, local landowners, and university faculty and students. This diverse coalition was fueled by shared outrage that Cairo cared more about investing in fertilizer plants than the broader economic well-being of the city and its environs. Activists undertook their campaign first against a proposed Canadian-owned fertilizer plant, and later against an existing state-owned fertilizer company, arguing that such industries negatively impacted Damietta's economy as a fishing town and a coastal summer tourism resort for many Egyptians.

Although the initial campaign succeeded in getting approval for the Canadian plant withdrawn, the Egyptian government sought to compensate foreign investors by promising to expand the adjacent state-owned plant and offering them a stake in the new production lines. After the Supreme Council of the Armed Forces took power in the wake of the January 2011 uprising, it acted ruthlessly against renewed protest about the plant's expansion. When residents of a nearby village blockaded the road to the industrial zone and cut off power to the port, the military sent in troops, attacking protesters and shooting dead a young man. Local residents poured into the streets for the funeral, castigating the then-ruling military junta as well as the planned plant expansion.[51]

Environmental campaigns in other cities followed suit in the heady political atmosphere that prevailed for a few years after the 2011 uprising. Frustration with Cairo's lack of concern for provincial cities and their citizens' well-being was a central motif of these environmental campaigns. Marginalized communities, including the Bedouin of South Sinai and the Nubians in the south, also organized to make more formal claims for access to land and water resources.[52] The post-revolutionary withdrawal of security and police forces for months after January 2011, however, also produced significant environmental damage: significant encroachments on protected areas, an explosion in hunting and trapping of migratory birds and endangered mammals, and rampant construction in agricultural lands near Cairo and other cities.

Many environmental campaigns subsided in the comprehensive crackdown on protests that followed the military coup of June 2013. The circles of urban activists who catalyzed the 2011 uprisings turned their attention to grassroots initiatives and local development projects, and moved activism off the streets and back into the press and online. Several groups from the "Tahrir networks," for instance, conducted a campaign against the government's announcement that it would import coal to power a variety of industries in the face of natural gas shortages.[53] The anti-coal groups focused on the air pollution impacts of burning coal on human health, as well as increased carbon emissions and risks to climate change. However, the campaign did not attain the clout or reach of the Damietta campaigns; it attracted fewer participants, did not mobilize local constituencies, and could not undertake direct action given the repressive political climate and popular exhaustion with street action.

Lebanon: solid waste mismanagement in Beirut and its hinterland

Widespread protests gripped Beirut in August 2015 over the shutdown of trash collection and disposal services in the capital, catalyzed by the closure of the Na'ama landfill outside Beirut by local villagers. Small demonstrations, organized initially by the group "You Stink" to protest against the rising piles of refuse and garbage in Beirut, cascaded into much larger protests after Lebanese police responded with rubber bullets, water cannon, sound grenades, and batons.[54] By late August, several other cities in Lebanon saw garbage-related protests as well.

Before the Lebanese civil war, trash collection was the responsibility of municipalities. After the war ended with the Ta'if Accords in 1989, the government under Prime Minister Rafiq Hariri privatized trash collection, treatment, and disposal for all of Beirut and Mount Lebanon into the hands of Sukleen, a firm with close ties to Hariri. Thus, the You Stink protesters framed the government's inability to develop an adequate solid waste plan as part of a broader critique of privatization, corruption, and the inability of the state to meet the basic needs of its citizens. As one journalist observed, "The protests were triggered by the trash crisis, but the people we've been speaking with say that was the straw that broke the camel's back ... they point to power shortages, water shortages, and inherent corruption within the state."[55]

The trash crisis in the capital was precipitated by protest on the part of villagers living adjacent to the Na'ama landfill. Designated as a temporary site for trash in 1997, it had been continuously used as a dumpsite since then and continuously contested by nearby inhabitants. In 2013, villagers formally declared the launch of a "Campaign to Close the Na'ama Dumpsite."[56] They blockaded roads leading to the landfill in 2014, prompting the government to assure them that the landfill would be closed. Protesters returned to shut down the roads again in the summer of 2015, once it became clear that the government had made no progress. This prompted Sukleen to stop collecting trash throughout the capital as it had nowhere to dispose of it.

The You Stink campaign viewed the state's failure to develop viable landfills as the consequence of a factionalized and paralyzed central government. One of the slogans chanted by protesters made the connection succinctly: "Our waste should be recycled, our leaders thrown in the trash." Lebanon's leadership, however, outlasted the campaign, which subsided once Sukleen began collecting and exporting garbage outside the area. The government to date, however, has failed to propose a long-term plan for creating landfills, while local communities and campaign organizers contest proposed sites.

The You Stink campaign also highlights the exclusionary boundaries of some popular campaigns when it comes to inclusion of marginalized communities and non-citizens. Palestinian refugee communities living in informal areas of southern Lebanon have long suffered from garbage crises, which became particularly acute in 2012, but they have been unable to conduct formalized protest campaigns given their precarious status in the country. Their garbage issues were noticeably not part of the Beirut campaigns. Excluded from formal waste collection systems and forced to negotiate with informal powerbrokers, these communities instead resorted to illegal dumping.[57]

Algeria: protesting hydraulic fracturing in a rentier state

Revenue accrued from the sale of fossil fuels and minerals has long sustained state expenditures in a number of oil-and gas-exporting MENA states. Yet protest around extractive industries, and our knowledge about such activism, has been limited by several factors. Extraction of oil, gas, and minerals in the region often takes place in relatively remote locations with sparse human settlements. Decision-making around energy resources is highly centralized; regimes, national energy companies, and multinational oil firms typically negotiate contracts without soliciting input of subnational units or local communities. Local inhabitants in rural and provincial areas have had few avenues to engage in dissent or publicize it, and thus our knowledge of historical protests around extractive industries in the region is incomplete.

Globally, conflict between extractive industries and impacted communities has been endemic and costly, as the well-known case of the Niger Delta, among many other examples, has shown.[58] Regimes and extractive firms have long argued that revenues from extractive industries funded national subsidies for food, housing, education, and health care for citizens; typically, however, national redistribution has been skewed toward major cities far from centers of mining and extraction. Natural resource revenues also allowed states with small domestic populations of citizens and large expatriate workforces—as in the Persian Gulf city-states and Libya—to create intrusive systems of surveillance, buy political acquiescence, and promulgate state ideologies focused on modernization, national consolidation, and restrictive citizenship.

Rentier states with larger domestic populations, such as Algeria, have faced greater fiscal pressures, more poverty and inequality, and consequently more political unrest. Algeria relies on hydrocarbon revenues for roughly 97 percent of its hard currency export earnings and 60 percent of total government revenue.[59] The youth led widespread riots in 1988, sparked by government austerity measures and rising unemployment. A brutal civil war between the military-dominated regime and a range of Islamist groups—marked by mass atrocities on both sides—ensued during the 1990s. The regime remains dominated by the army and internal security apparatuses and riven by continuous competition between various elite factions, hindering long-term planning and policymaking around natural resource governance.[60]

In the wake of the 2011 Arab uprisings, the Algerian government increased its spending on social subsidies, on public employment, and on the security services in an attempt to ward off mass protest—as did fellow monarchs in the Persian Gulf, Morocco, and Jordan. Faced with low oil prices and increased spending, however, the Algerian 2015 budget deficit was estimated at $52 billion, while the country's hard currency reserves—essential to the import of food and goods—dropped to $159 billion by early 2015.[61] By 2016, the government was seeking to curb expenditure by 9 percent, with the International Monetary Fund (IMF) pushing for even greater spending cuts.[62]

The Algerian government was thus eager to explore new avenues for hydrocarbon extraction, notably hydraulic fracking techniques that had taken off rapidly in the United States. In 2014, the state-owned oil and gas company Sonatrach signed agreements with the US multinational corporation

Halliburton to drill a number of pilot wells in and around the southern provincial oasis town of Ain Salah, in the central Saharan region of country. In neighboring Tunisia, the government signed a similar contract in 2012 for exploratory drilling of wells using hydraulic fracking, sparking a strong reaction from several Tunisian environmental organizations.[63]

As in Egypt's Damietta, local activists in Ain Salah became concerned about the environmental impacts of a new industrial activity: in this case, the impacts of hydraulic fracturing on groundwater quantity and quality. Ain Salah, like other Algerian southern oasis towns, relies on fossil (i.e. non-renewable) groundwater aquifers for an estimated 96 percent of its total water supply.[64] The aquifer system spans much of Algeria, Tunisia, and Libya, and escalating withdrawals exceed minimal recharge flows. With current technologies, hydraulic fracturing is a highly water-intensive process, with potential for significant contamination of groundwater sources.[65] In addition, anthropogenic climate change has contributed to unprecedented heat waves in the area, meaning that more water is used to sustain local agriculture.[66]

Protesters contended that Halliburton's pilot fracking activities had contaminated several local wells around Ain Salah, sickening several local residents and generating immediate concern. The anti-fracking campaign that emerged in this remote area included local residents and several middle-class professionals with experience in running local associations. For instance, an engineer with Sonatrach who helped to organize the campaign already ran a local environmental NGO, Shems, which provided the campaign with an existing organizational infrastructure.

The protests in Ain Salah spread quickly to several surrounding towns in the south, drawing on widespread feelings that the southern desert areas remain economically and politically marginalized.[67] Violent clashes with the police ensued when young activists took direct action, spraying the walls of the Halliburton base camp near Ain Salah with slogans including "Dégagez, Halliburton!" (Leave, Halliburton!). This slogan was a clear echo of the slogan that protesters across the Arab world chanted in 2011 to incumbent regimes: "Irhal! Irhal!" (Leave! Leave!). These anti-fracking campaigners were largely on their own, however, without connections to the emerging global movement concerned about the environmental impacts of hydraulic fracking.

The anti-fracking campaign gradually expanded its discourse, from focusing on the digging of pilot wells to calls for a national dialogue around non-conventional techniques for oil and gas extraction and increased transparency over revenue distribution. This broader framing helped the organizers reach out to the media as a nonviolent, popular campaign mobilizing against centralized and unaccountable decision-making.[68] As in Damietta, the involvement of multinational firms allowed the campaign to frame its opposition to fracking in nationalist as well as environmental terms. Several opposition parties signed on, helping to coordinate a joint protest in the capital Algiers, a space where the central government usually prohibits demonstrations. However, as in Damietta, challenging the authority of an important state-owned enterprise—in this case, the state-owned energy firm that generates a significant portion of government revenue—meant that protesters were targeting an opaque web of elite and regime interests tied to the generation of economic rent.

The central government had incentives to negotiate with campaigners, however, and dampened protests rather than engaging in repression. Informal and wildcat protests take place regularly outside the capital throughout the countryside; one politician estimated between ten and twelve thousand protests a year.[69] However unreliable, his estimate speaks to the frequency and scale of protest actions. The central government also faces significant security challenges in the Sahelian and Saharan regions, particularly in the regions adjacent to Libya, Mali, Mauritania, and Niger, where collusion and corruption among state security forces, jihadist movements, and local smuggling networks are rampant.[70] Thus, while the regime can physically contain protests in the south, it is wary of simply repressing discontent.

The Algiers government responded to the anti-fracking campaign with several inducements to the protesters, while also seeking to undermine their central claims. The army was sent to negotiate and the government announced various ad hoc economic and social development projects for southern towns.[71] However, government officials, led by President Abdelaziz Bouteflika, also launched a counter-narrative, arguing that the exploitation of Algeria's non-conventional fossil fuels reserves was essential for the country's national security and economic development.

Challenges and opportunities for environmental activism in the Middle East and North Africa

As the three disparate cases explored above illustrate, social mobilization around environmental issues has spread significantly over the past few decades in the Middle East and North Africa, as ecological conditions have worsened and possibilities for activism have increased. This chapter argues that the principal modes of environmental activism in the region have consisted of informal encroachment and small-scale, wildcat protests; the growth in formal environmental associations; and, most prominently, popular resistance campaigns. The popular campaign has proven more flexible than other modes of engagement in terms of building organization, influencing public opinion, and scaling up into larger cross-class coalitions. Often launched by local residents or youth activists, campaigns that gain traction with transnational networks and state agencies often elicit cooperation from environmental experts, civic aid organizations, scientists, journalists, and expatriate communities.

Environmental mobilization in the Middle East and North Africa shows a clear spatial patterning reflecting developments in the region's political economy. While environmental protest in capital cities often emerges around issues of air and industrial pollution, garbage and solid waste problems, and conversion of parks and green spaces, vibrant environmental campaigns have emerged in provincial cities and rural areas as well. The peripheries increasingly attract environmentally hazardous activities, whether gold mining in the Turkish city of Bergama or hydraulic fracking in Algeria's southern oasis towns.[72] Extractive industries and related pollution-intensive activities abut on rapidly urbanizing areas, creating contention around pollution, noise, and health impacts. In contrast, nature conservation per se has largely been pursued by international conservation organizations, monarchical regimes, and aid donors seeking to preserve marine and territorial habitats.

Anthropogenic climate change is another challenge for environmental activists in the region, with significant impacts on Middle Eastern environments and communities already evident in flood events, heat waves, and unusually intense periods of droughts. Higher temperatures and decreased precipitation are evident in the drought that has gripped much of the Mediterranean since the late 1990s. A recent study using tree ring records and historical documents found that the ongoing drought is the most severe observed in the 900-year record, significantly exceeding natural patterns of climate variability.[73] As in the industrialized countries, however, social mobilization has been in its nascent stages, given the more complex and less clearly attributable linkages to public health, livelihoods, and quality of life. There are incipient signs, however, that climate change is emerging on the environmental agenda. In Egypt, some youth activists driven from the streets have joined transnational climate networks such as 350.org, or established international organizations such as Greenpeace. Others have worked with donor agencies to facilitate discussion among technocrats, scientists, and citizens, such as the

Cairo Climate Talks sponsored by the German Embassy.[74] Regional climate networking and awareness was further facilitated in fall 2016 when the 22nd Conference of the Parties (COP22) for the United Nations Climate Change Conference was held in Marrakesh. COP22 was notable in part for highlighting the role of youth in leading climate change activism and for the outspoken advocacy of a coalition of forty-eight countries considered most vulnerable to climate change.[75]

Environmental mobilization in the Middle East and North Africa will intensify, as ecological challenges increase with population growth, resource scarcity, and tightened restrictions on migration outside the region. The structural social, economic, and demographic transformations that underpinned widespread popular uprisings in 2011 remain drivers of social contestation, as do networks of activists with significant experience in conducting popular campaigns. This chapter has focused on environmental contestation in relatively stable states of the region. However, the wave of wars in Syria, Libya, and Yemen, which devastated public services and generated massive refugee flows to surrounding states, will exacerbate these socioeconomic and environmental challenges. Modes of environmental activism will continue to evolve in response to these new circumstances, drawing on the actors, tactics, and forms of engagement already prevalent in the region.

2

TUNISIAN PHOSPHATES AND THE POLITICS OF THE PERIPHERY

Francis Ghilès and *Eckart Woertz*

The Arab uprisings started in December 2010 in Tunisia, a country that until then had been hailed as a role model of economic development and resources management by European governments and international institutions like the IMF and the World Bank.[1] Cracks below the surface escaped the attention of these development planners. The Ben Ali regime combined economic liberalization and export orientation with an increasingly suppressive state apparatus.[2] While Tunisia achieved robust macro growth rates, wealth only trickled down unevenly to the general population, and at the time the periphery faced neglect.[3] Unemployment rates in the disadvantaged regions in the west and south were almost double the 15 percent that characterizes the capital Tunis and the coastal areas.[4] It was here that the vegetable vendor Mohamed Bouazizi set himself ablaze and the Tunisian revolt started. Similar social unrest before, such as the bread riots of 1984 and the revolts in Tunisia's phosphate mines in 2008, had also started in the Tunisian hinterland. A successful transition in Tunisia can only be achieved if the economically disenfranchised population in peripheral areas gets a fairer deal—which, crucially, implies developing an alternative social contract and restructuring the socio-ecological formations that have generated prosperity for a transnational elite while causing extensive environmental degradation.

The phosphate mines around Metlaoui have played a pivotal role in the economic development of Tunisia's periphery and have been a bone of contention in social protests and trade union politics. In what is otherwise an arid region of high plateaux, the discovery of phosphate ore in the late nineteenth century brought undreamt-of wealth for a few. During the colonial period, these few were the phosphate companies that developed the mines, and the colonial authorities for whom phosphate was a precious source of tax income. Tunisia's independence in 1956 and the subsequent development strategy of "import substituting industrialization" (ISI) saw further expansion of phosphate mining, which was used to provide the finance for any number of infrastructure projects outside the region. Tunisian leaders decided to develop the coast first, where levels of education and infrastructure were better than inland; then they hoped to leverage that development to shift the policy inland. That shift, however, failed to materialize in the 1970s and 1980s. Neglect of the hinterland was entrenched and accelerated during the economic liberalization of the Ben Ali years.

After 2011, production of phosphates and fertilizers, one of Tunisia's key exports, collapsed in the wake of successive occupations of the plant entrances by job-seekers who pretended to be strike pickets and refused to let bona fide workers in.[5] New social actors and semiautonomous groups, such as young people who connected via social media, emerged from the structures of a partly liberalized autocracy and launched the Tunisian revolt.[6] On the one hand, Tunisia has had a tradition of autonomous expression and constitutionalism that Ben Ali could not suppress. On the other hand, he left the army marginalized in order to control it and prioritized the police and internal security apparatuses. These were used to suppress the lower classes and the peasantry who—unlike the middle classes—were not offered avenues to prosperity in a liberalized economy. The isolated position of the army within the regime and its broad-based nonsectarian recruitment brought with it a mixture of professionalism and relatively low levels of loyalty toward the leadership. This would prove crucial during the uprisings, when the army refused to shoot demonstrators and turned against the police and security services. Only partly corporatized and with a degree of leeway, the country's trade union, Union Générale Tunisienne du Travail (UGTT), became an important actor in the country's democratic transition when it manifested itself as a voice of secularism against the autocratic aspirations of emergent Islamist groups. Under Zine el Abidine Ben Ali's presidency of 1987–2011, the leaders of UGTT were increasingly co-opted into power, but the local branches remained restive. They did not initiate the December 2010 revolt, but played an active part in supporting it when it was underway.

Using underexplored grey literature and personal interviews with officials, experts, and businessmen, this chapter discusses the constitutive role of phosphate mining and trade unions in the politics of the periphery in Tunisia—politics that have been crucially affected by post-independence development agendas, the transformation of national elites in the crony capitalism of the Ben Ali era, and its interplay with international donor and development institutions. First, the chapter gives an historic overview of Tunisian phosphate mining and its role in regional development. Second, it analyzes the politics of Tunisia's periphery, UGTT's role within it, and the emergence of new social actors. Third, it takes a detailed look at how such conflicts played out during the strikes in the phosphate mines in 2008 and after 2011. It concludes with an outlook on possible future developments.

Tunisian phosphate mining and development

Colonialism

A French army officer made incursions from neighboring French Algeria in the 1870s and discovered phosphate ore in Tunisia. The mines were put into production in 1897, sixteen years after the French occupied Tunisia. Metlaoui became a model company town, imagined as an outpost of civilization, benevolently planted in a harsh environment to tame nature and natives alike.[7] It lies in a spectacular lunar landscape in the rugged mountains north of Gafsa, the capital of the Djerid region. The Djerid has been famous for its *deglet nour* dates, but the mountainous region around Metlaoui was desperately poor. The traditional tribal confederations had held sway until the French arrived in 1881, at which point they were seriously upset by a centralized colonial power structure run by civil servants. Their allegiance to the Bey of Tunis had traditionally taken the form of levying taxes, but conflicts between the people, the tax-farming tribes, and the ruler in Tunis were frequent, particularly during times of drought when harvests failed but fiscal pressures remained.[8]

Authority and privilege in Metlaoui were allocated along ethnically segmented lines in order to control the workforce, similarly to other settlements associated with extractive industries worldwide.[9] Workers from as far away as Morocco, Algeria, and Libya sought employment in the mines. To the members of the Ouley Bouyahia tribe, who lived around Metlaoui, were added members of tribes from the Djerid region. Meanwhile, all the engineers and managers were Europeans, mainly French and Italians, the latter being the largest European group in colonial Tunisia. Workers from the Maghreb were usually single, while engineers and managers often had their families with them. This produced a typical colonial society with any number of social and class distinctions: Metlaoui boasted a swimming pool, tennis courts, and celebrations for the French National Day, *le 14 juillet*, which attracted the colonial upper crust from Tunis. French officials would travel with their wives once a year, in what was an exotic outing into the unknown and slightly dangerous south, and quaff vintage wines—a civilian form of *beau geste*.

Phosphate mining became coterminous with prosperity and even civilization itself. Phosphate companies owned the houses, the local general store, and the pharmacy, and provided free electricity, water, and medical care to the managers and engineers. Working conditions for the miners, by contrast, were harsh, but after independence they were also provided with the same range of free services. Proper homes were built for them from the 1960s onward, and a decade later they were all decently housed. Throughout these years, a job in the mines was very sought after because of the relatively high wages; besides, there were no other alternatives aside from herding. Metlaoui and its satellite mining towns remained quintessentially company towns, in which the government and regional authorities hardly intervened. There were some local police to provide broader security, and even they would get their petrol free from the local pump, courtesy of the phosphate companies.

The colonial period produced infrastructure decisions that would foreshadow the later development path of Tunisian phosphate mining. A railway line was built in the late nineteenth century to ship the ore to the eastern port of Sfax, from where it was exported; hence one of the most important mining companies was known as La Companie des Phosphates et du Chemin de Fer Sfax–Gafsa. After the Second World War, the first large fertilizer plant was built in Sfax. Others were added after independence in the late 1960s and 1970s further down the coast in Gabès. Between the two ports, a third export center was built at La Skhirra in 1985, where an oil export terminal had already been built in the 1950s, initially for oil from French Algeria and later from the El Borma field in the south of Tunisia.

Independence, import substituting industrialization (ISI), and its crisis

By the time Tunisia achieved independence, phosphate mining was well established as a major source of revenue for the state. From 200,000 tons in 1900, production rose to 3.5 million tons by 1976, when all companies in the sector were brought under the same umbrella: la Compagnie des Phosphates de Gafsa (CPG).[10] In the first two decades after independence, phosphates were an important source of income; this was long before oil—starting from the second half of the 1960s—produced dramatic revenue growth during the boom of the 1970s, before peaking in the early 1990s.[11]

Like many other developing countries Tunisia embarked on a course of import substituting industrialization (ISI) during its post-independence period. During the time of state-led inward growth in 1961–9, the state was relatively autonomous. However, most of the party leadership came from Tunis and other cities along the coast. A tradition of populist authoritarianism and patronage was established. During the early beginnings of the labor movement in the 1920s, unions were too weak to form an independent political force because of the limited size of the working class.[12] Now, urban workers of the formal sector belonged to the winners of the ISI development strategy.[13]

This also applied to the workers in the phosphate sector, which was nationalized five years after independence. The income of those employed by the CPG was four to five times the minimum wage.[14] Employment by the company was seen as a ticket to a decent life in an otherwise harsh environment. The two main sources of labor were tribal groups around Metlaoui, and others further south around Gafsa. Balancing the claims from both groups required a deft political hand. CEOs who came from the region, such as Mohammed Fadhel Khalil or Kais Daly, understood the complex ties of family and tribe, which helped them manage the company successfully. Some of the CEOs who hailed from Tunis or the coastal region, however, showed contempt for southerners and ignorance of the complexities of local politics. Many of those who had graduated from the Grandes Écoles in Paris thought of themselves as quasi-Europeans. They viewed the phosphate region as the back of beyond.

By the early 1970s, as in so many post-colonial states, the shortcomings of ISI became apparent. The infant industries of ISI never matured and merely shifted import dependence from manufactured goods to capital goods. The inefficiencies of the founded industries led to an increasing balance of payments crisis. As a result, the minister of planning, Ben Salah, was ousted in 1969 and there was a subsequent shift to liberalization.[15] The government adopted a more liberal economic policy that welcomed foreign investment in newly set up manufacturing units, mostly textiles. The head of the Central Bank, Hedi Nouira, was appointed to implement the new policy.

Initially gradual, the policy of liberalization accelerated under Hedi Nouira's successors, especially after 1986 when the IMF assisted in a formal Structural Adjustment Program (SAP). It became a cornerstone of economic policies during the reign of President Ben Ali (1987–2011), the former minister of interior who came to power in a bloodless coup against the aging and incapacitated founding father of modern Tunisia, Habib Bourguiba (1957–87).[16] Economic liberalization in Tunisia achieved appealing GDP growth on a macro level with inflation adjusted by 4.6 percent on average between 1987 and 2010.[17] In contrast to other countries in the region such as Jordan, Egypt, and Morocco, the Tunisian government did not disengage as much from social provisioning. Poverty rates declined from 9.6 percent in 1985 to 4.1 percent in 2000.[18] Yet, unemployment remained stubbornly high, around 15 percent, and inequality manifested itself along geographic lines: the peripheral regions of Tunisia's interior where the phosphate mines lay, and others along Tunisia's frontiers with Algeria to the west and Libya to the south, were neglected at the expense of the capital and other coastal regions.

Most of Tunisia's manufacturing and tourist industry created wealth along a narrow coastal strip around Tunis. By the late 1980s, even among regime insiders, the feeling was growing that, despite a rise in salaries, too much of the wealth of the region was accruing to the coast where the phosphoric acid and fertilizer plants were based.[19] As the population in the phosphate basin increased, jobs became scarcer and competition for them ferocious. Some CEOs were quite happy to play tribal politics with recruitment, which made matters worse. After all, phosphate mining accounted for 70 percent of added value in the region.[20] The vast majority of young people were forced to leave Metlaoui and surrounding towns to seek jobs on the coast or in Tunis.

Restructuring and environmental impact

Until the late 1970s, mining was carried out in galleries dug into the hills. Open pit mining was introduced in 1978 at Kef Schafaier and was subsequently started in nine other locations. More modern methods of extracting ore resulted in a rapid rise in production and exports. Production more than doubled from 3 million tons in 1970 to 6.3 million tons in 1990. Phosphate exports as a share of total exports mostly ranged between 6 and 11 percent between 1995 and 2007, reaching a peak of 13.9 percent in 2008, and declining thereafter to 5–6 percent after the revolt of 2011.[21] By the turn of the century, Tunisia was the fifth-largest producer in the world after the United States, Morocco, China, and the USSR; its phosphoric acid and fertilizers were recognized as being of excellent quality. However, Tunisia has slipped to eighth rank since 2011, and could slip further if production levels fail to rise in the years ahead; this is worrying and could compromise growth perspectives in the post-revolutionary transition of the country.[22]

In 1994, the upstream and downstream sectors were merged to build a stronger overall strategy for the whole sector. In the process, fertilizer industries based on the coast became more important in phosphate value chains compared to the mines in the hinterland. Le Groupe Chimique Tunisien (GCT), which in the late 1970s had been put in charge of downstream activities such as the production of phosphoric acid and fertilizers, was put together with the CPG under the same CEO and board of directors. Investment in downstream activities was concentrated on the coast in the ports of Sfax, where plants had already been built in 1952 and 1964, and later in Gabès and La Skhirra. This left inhabitants of the mining area with the impression that their wealth was being siphoned off, a perception reinforced in the 1990s when prices of ore rose sharply while jobs in the mines were cut as the introduction of open pit mining increased mechanization and reduced the need for labor.[23] Only one plant was built in the phosphate basin, at M'dilla in the early 1980s. This appeasing gesture was possibly prompted by a preceding attempt by dissident Tunisians to take over the regional capital of Qafsa in January 1980; they were backed by the Libyan leader Muammar Qaddafi and hard-line elements within the Algerian secret service. This prompted King Hassan of Morocco, the American sixth fleet, and the French military to offer to help control the situation.[24]

In the late 1970s and early 1980s, the CEO of the GCT and CPG, Ali Boukhris, brought in Kuwaiti, Abu Dhabi, and French equity partners. The range of products increased to include fertilizers and aluminum fluoride. Tunisian patents to make phosphoric acid were (and still are) used in China and Romania. Some of these equity partners remain today, but do not play as active a role as before. Meanwhile, *Khaleeji* investors rather turned to tourism, property, banking, and telecommunications: sectors that were also more in line with regime preferences.[25] In the 2000s the Tunisian phosphate sector teamed up again with foreign partners to modernize its production, this time experts from India. Tunisia's main export markets are India, Iran, and Indonesia.[26] Two Indian companies, which were long-standing customers, emerged after 2000 and took a 30 percent share in the $500 million investment to produce phosphoric acid in a plant opened at La Skhirra in 2013.[27] The two Indian partners undertook to buy the plant's entire output at world-market prices for thirty years, thus guaranteeing the long-term viability of the project.

Increased impact of pollution from open pit mining and the CPG's neglect of the environment added to the grievances. Health risks incurred by the miners include silicosis and cancer. Before the phosphate rock is moved to Sfax and La Skhirra, it is washed. Agriculture accounts for 80 percent of freshwater withdrawal in Tunisia, followed by municipal (15 percent) and industrial uses (5 percent). Phosphate mining withdraws 20 million cubic meters of water a year, about 14 percent of the country's total industrial water withdrawal.[28] This is considerable in a predominantly arid area. Some of the water is pumped from deep fossil aquifers of nonrenewable water and then disposed of partially treated. It was only in 1995 that the first sludge storage ponds were built. Until then, mud sludges from washing plants invaded dry riverbeds. Sheep that were grazing the sparse grass would get hurt or stuck, a considerable inconvenience for a region where semi-nomadic lifestyles are still found and where many families engage in sheep rearing as part of their livelihood. Even with storage ponds, there are reports of muddy water seeping into depressions on the northern edge of the palm groves further south, around the oases of Nefta and Tozeur, putting tourism and the date industry at risk.[29] A century of negligence will take both time and money to clear up.

Fluor has contaminated large areas, the worst of which are around M'dilla, ending any hope of developing agriculture. In the words of Lakdar Souid, a journalist who knew the region well and felt passionately that its inhabitants deserved a better deal, "For the past 115 years, the CPG has acted as a milk cow which leaves its dung in Gafsa, whose milk goes elsewhere, and which allows its calves to go hungry."[30] For decades, the dust from the phosphates has badly affected the health of all the inhabitants, not just the miners.

The Ben Ali liberalization

In the 1980s the phosphate sector was liberalized at an increased pace, with negative consequences for the local population. In 1986 the World Bank assisted in a restructuring plan for Tunisia's economy. The CPG had already started a program of early retirement on full pay, with the idea that new employment would be found for them with the help of regional development projects. This brought the number of employees in 2006 down from 14,000 to less than half.[31] The challenge, however, was to find new employment, not only for those who had been retired, but also for others in a region where birth rates remained above those on the coast. Tourism developed around Gafsa in the 1980s and 1990s, but other new jobs were not forthcoming, as the state never produced a serious development plan for the region and failed to deliver badly needed public infrastructures. The early retirement schemes soon fell prey to complicated bargaining between the management, the unions, and local tribal clans. Unemployment continued to rise inexorably, and reached 38.5 percent in some mining towns, way above the national average of around 15 percent.[32]

The mid-1980s also witnessed the growth of sub-contracting companies, whose workers did not enjoy the security of employment, social advantages, and levels of pay of the CPG workers, whose privileges were deeply resented. By the time the phosphate region rose in revolt against the regime in January 2008, the secretary general of the regional union of UGTT, Amara Abbassi, owned several of these sub-contracting companies, employing 800 workers. He was both a deputy and a member of the ruling party's Rassemblement Constitutionnel Démocratique central committee (the RDC had replaced the Socialist Destour Party in 1989). He had been hired by the CPG as a trade union representative for a managerial position in the early 1990s.[33]

By 2008, the Tunisian political system had "effectively confiscated all the rights of the population: the right to express its choices, the right to decide about its environment, and the right to decide about its future generations."[34] As the Ben Ali regime became harsher and more predatory, Tunisians were increasingly less able to speak out and voice different opinions from the prevailing orthodoxy. Tunisia was hailed as a role model by international institutions. Together with Morocco, Jordan, and Egypt, it was seen as a possible alternative to past state-led, import-substituting industrialization in the Middle East.[35] The cheerleading by the World Bank and Western aid donors of the Tunisian "example" made it even more difficult for the periphery to articulate its demands, as Gilbert Achcar has pointed out.[36] Only in recent years, the World Bank has modified its stance. A policy research paper published three years after Ben Ali's fall noted:

> The World Economic Forum repeatedly ranked Tunisia as the most competitive economy in Africa, and the IMF as well as the World Bank heralded Tunisia as a role model for other developing countries. Yet the Tunisian model had serious flaws; unemployment and corruption were high over the period and contributed to Ben Ali's downfall.[37]

The politics of rural neglect

The liberalization policies of the Ben Ali era happened in a broader context of rural neglect and wealth stratification along geographical lines. The eleven provinces of inland Tunisia account for 70 percent of the country's landmass and one-third of Tunisia's 10 million population. They hold 50 percent of the country's oil, gas, and water resources, support 70 percent of durum wheat production, and 50 percent of olive oil and fruit output.[38] Yet these regions are disadvantaged, average income is only one-third of the national average, and their inhabitants have accumulated very little capital since independence. The youth either despair or are driven away, while 80 percent of internal labor migrants come from the hinterland. Even the local elites have moved to the coastal towns, which has hollowed out regional decision-making capacity and reduced the weight of the periphery in national political processes even further.[39]

The development strategy of the regime prioritized tourism and offshore manufacturing along the coast, which enjoyed privileged access to finance.[40] Many hotel projects have been disguised land and property speculation. The result of such cronyism is a debt hangover of the tourist sector that has increased the cost of credit to every other sector, which is particularly discouraging for small- and medium-size enterprises; bad loans amount to 20–24 percent of GDP, and Tunisia ranks 96th among 103 countries worldwide for non-performing loans.[41] Yet a reform of the Tunisian banking system is impeded by the strength of the tourist lobby. The tourism sector was used for decades to burnish the image of "an open country" and Ben Ali being a benevolent dictator.[42] No government dares to shut down any state bank behemoth, force speculators to take their losses, and redirect the funds to the eleven poorer provinces. Half of the country's hotels are closed, but the hotel lobby carries a lot of weight.

In contrast, nobody advocates for the hinterland. Over the past twenty years, no effort has been made to set up a regional bank, promote irrigation, build a cement plant, or set up teleworking. International phosphate prices spiked almost tenfold in 2007–8 before falling back to levels that were much reduced, but still well above long-term averages.[43] This sent profits of CPG and GCT soaring, but few of these profits were reinvested in a region where the rates of literacy and the number of young people going to university were among the lowest in Tunisia. Tunis never stopped promising investment to alleviate the rising rate of unemployment, which reached 38.5 percent in some mining towns, but nothing ever came of such talk.[44] Nor has anything been done since the revolt of 2011; the problem is very deeply structural, not just the offspring of one particular government or regime.

This leaves the people of the region, especially its youth, with few options. They can either migrate, move into the informal sector, or they can join the smuggling networks of the region, which have become a serious challenge to the authority of the state and a threat to its security. The mining towns of Metlaoui, Moulares, Oum Laarayes, and Redeyef lie close to the country's southwestern border with Algeria, a region which has, since the downfall of Ben Ali and Qaddafi, seen both a boom and a diversification in smuggling. In addition to cheaper (subsidized) Algerian coffee and sugar, they smuggle petrol (also subsidized) and cannabis. Worse, the collapse of state authority in Libya following the civil war and the fall of the ancien régime there have opened the gates to a flow of modern weapons, synthetic drugs, and manufactured goods from Asia that are pushing Tunisian industries out of business. Until 2011, smugglers were known to the border police who turned a blind eye as this activity provided desperately needed employment for younger people. Today's gangs running this trade are heavily armed, equipped with four-wheel drives, and communicate by satellite telephones. Some mutate from smugglers to Islamist rebels all the more easily, as tribal and family connections bestride Tunisia's frontiers with both its neighbors. The security threat they pose to the state—as witnessed by their attack on the town of Ben Guerdane close to the Libyan boarder in March 2016—is far more serious than that posed by the smugglers of old.[45]

The Tunisian armed forces, strongly supported by the watchful and well-resourced Algerian army, are engaged in a tough fight against hard-line *salafi* groups, which have dug into the Jebel Chambi mountains north of Gafsa. The situation is even more fraught around Medenine on Tunisia's border with Libya, which was closed in November 2015 following a terrorist attack in Tunis. This black economy presents a challenge to the traditional power of Tunis, as many local people in these traditionally poor regions are determined to get their own back on what they consider as decades of neglect by the richer north and coastal towns.

The politics of the periphery and the UGTT

Trade unions have been the stepchildren of political economy analysis in the Middle East; yet in some countries, such as Egypt and Tunisia, they have carried considerable weight in political contestation, either as corporatized institutions with the capacity to maneuver or in the form of independent protest movements when the corporatized institutions have not been able to channel and suppress discontent.[46] The UGTT has played a key role in Tunisian politics since it was founded in 1949, a few years before independence. Trade union activists were closely involved with Tunisian nationalism.[47] Tunisia has the second-oldest trade union movement in Africa, which boasts more than 500,000 members today and has acted either in unison or in competition with the Neo Destour Party and its renamed successor parties, which dominated Tunisian politics from the 1930s until 2011.[48]

UGTT Secretary General Ferhat Hached was murdered in 1952 by the French right-wing La Main Rouge underground special forces during the fight for independence. Since 1956, the UGTT has held an ambivalent position with regard to social conflicts in Tunisia. On the one hand, it has acted as the strong arm of authoritarian regimes; on the other hand, it channels workers' demands for better working conditions and higher salaries. Miners have been among its key constituents, along with teachers, dockers, and railway workers. Many leaders of the UGTT hail from the Gafsa region. In many ways it has represented a labor aristocracy of steadily employed workers, but never farm workers or part-time workers, whose ranks have grown steadily and who represent a majority of the working class today. In the mining basin, where unemployment rates have been about twice the national average, this has resulted in UGTT losing credibility and authority. The informal sector represents about half of Tunisia's economic activity. Those who work in it neither articulate their demands as a group nor pay taxes.[49]

UGTT's relation with the ruling PSD—and from 1989 the RCD Party—has fluctuated between co-optation and contestation. Leading UGTT officials have been members of the ruling party and of parliament, and its higher ranks were offered opportunities to participate in the crony capitalism of the Ben Ali era. Until the revolution of 2011, the UGTT also enjoyed the endowment with captive membership fees that came with the legally stipulated monopoly of the organization as a single trade union. The UGTT had been more autonomous before the 1980s and even led a general strike in 1978. Its local sections were more willing to articulate local grievances, whereas the headquarters in Tunis and its senior members were far more co-opted into the power structure. Yet local UGTT structures had only limited room to maneuver and could not, for instance, declare strikes by themselves, as this would have contradicted the union's internal procedures and hierarchy. UGTT has not contributed much to the debate on regional development and how to develop the periphery. That debate has only opened up since the fall of Ben Ali, but no government since has dared to put the issue center stage, where it belongs.

In the 1970s, as the populist authoritarianism of Tunisia's ISI period retreated and left its beneficiaries in the rain, the working class started to call for political reforms. The UGTT organized rank-and-file opposition in 1969, already gaining strength in the early 1970s. To appease the UGTT and bring it back into the government's fold, a new collective bargaining system was introduced in 1973 that made the UGTT an equal partner alongside the Union Tunisienne de l'Industrie, du Commerce et de l'Artisanat (UTICA), and the state. The new arrangement led to higher wages and provided a number of additional benefits and bonuses, but failed to achieve the social peace the government was hoping for as social inequality rose.[50]

In January 1978, the first general strike since independence resulted in riots in Tunis, which were brutally repressed by the army. The UGTT played an active role in this revolt, led by its charismatic leader, Habib Achour, who openly challenged the power of Bourguiba. At the same time, the role of Islamist opposition movements grew. By 1981, the umbrella organization Mouvement de la Tendence Islamique was established, which changed its name to the Ennahda Party in 1989. Yet the Islamists were still marginal to national politics in the 1970s and lacked the power of the UGTT and the students' organizations in terms of mobilization. To gain ground they sought common cause with the unions in 1978 and added a social agenda of labor and social rights to their demands, which hitherto had mainly focused on complaints about so-called anti-Islamic policies of the government. The ousting of the charismatic head of UGTT, Habib Achour, in 1978 made UGTT more compliant to the government. Its agenda for democratization was put on the back burner. By 1984, the UGTT had been tamed. It did not play a prominent role in bread riots during that year, which occurred after the government had doubled the price of bread. The riots started in an oasis south of the mining region in late December and spread through the Gafsa province further north before engulfing the coast and Tunis. This resulted in the measure being cancelled within a matter of days.

By the late 1980s, Islamists were the dominant opposition movement. Escalating tensions brought the country to the brink of civil war in 1987 and led to the disposal of President Bourguiba in a bloodless coup. The new head of state, Zine el Abidine Ben Ali, announced a "new era" agenda that ostensibly favored democratic transition. Islamists were the main challenge to the rebranded ruling party, the RCD. They took 14 percent of the nationwide vote in highly managed elections in 1989.[51] In large cities their support was even higher, reaching 25 percent and more, according to estimates.[52] Meanwhile, the economic crisis and neoliberal reform weakened the UGTT. By 1989, it had dropped its democratization agenda and acquiesced to a new set of corporatist institutions in which it participated.[53] Major agreements with the UTICA were signed in 1990 and 1992.[54] Authoritarianism hardened and the alignment of the UGTT with government politics prevented the formation of socialist or social democratic parties that could have provided alternatives to the ruling party and challenge it in a multiparty system.[55]

As the Ben Ali regime got harsher, public discussion of economic and social issues became more and more difficult. The UGTT leadership increasingly toed the line. Tunisia was hailed internationally as the success story in Africa and the Arab world. The regime meanwhile was becoming increasingly predatory, even as living standards for poorer Tunisians were beginning to fray. By 2008, when the mining region revolted, there were the steadily employed workers who formed a labor aristocracy, sub-contracted workers, and a growing mass of unemployed; the two latter categories were in no way represented by the UGTT.[56]

The revolt of the phosphate basin in 2008

The phosphate-mining basin rose in revolt against the regime in January 2008, protesting against corruption, cronyism, and lack of job opportunities. In contrast to 1984 and 2010, the revolt did not spread to other regions, and the government was successful in preventing media coverage of the events. It was put down with brute force after six months of an increasingly bitter confrontation between local inhabitants and the security forces. The background to this revolt and the forms it took bear retelling, because the challenges they threw up have not been answered.

By the turn of the century, young Tunisians were finding it ever harder to get jobs. The unemployment rate ballooned in the three central Maghreb countries from the mid-1980s, and in Tunisia the problem was exacerbated by regional disparities for which the mining basin offered a perfect illustration. The indicators of poverty compiled by the World Bank and the International Monetary Fund were "highly dubious," according to the Arab Human Development Report 2003, the second in a series published by the United Nations Development Programme (UNDP). It unpicked the differences in methodology, which had led the World Bank to underestimate levels of poverty, pointing to high levels of social exclusion, wealth inequality, and poor services despite ostensibly modest levels of income inequality.[57]

Conspicuous consumption was abounding. Tunisia is a small country and any visitor to Tunis or the coastal resorts of Sousse and Hammamet could hardly miss the behavior of the Tunisian elites, whose new villas got bigger by the year. The arrogant behavior of the presidential family made matters worse, the sheer vulgarity of the Ben Ali clan lifestyle contrasting vividly with the traditions of the older ruling elites of Sfax and Tunis. As new plants and hotels in the coastal region and Tunis mushroomed and provided jobs there, younger people in the phosphate basin and the western uplands of Le Kef and Jendouba were finding it impossible to gain employment unless they migrated. In the mining area, frustration was further fueled by the sharp rise in phosphate prices in 2007–8, where the benefits did not seem to trickle down to the general population.[58] It is hardly surprising in such circumstances that the feeling of being left behind rose in a region where average unemployment rates were stuck between 26.7 and 38.5 percent.[59] Frustration reached boiling point in January 2008, aggravated by the divisions between the haves and have-nots. The CPG was by then run by someone very close to the ruling Ben Ali family, Abdelhafidh Nessiri, who initiated a policy of early retirement among senior cadres and engineers—to the utter disbelief of all his predecessors.

The trigger for the revolt was the announcement on 5 January 2008 regarding the result of a hiring contest for 380 workers, technicians, and managerial staff by the CPG. This was perceived to be all the more unfair as there had been no hiring for six years, a result of CPG's policy of non-replacement of those who were retiring.[60] Starting in 1986, an agreement between the managers of CPG and the regional leadership of UGTT had drawn up the rules for the hiring of new staff. In 1993 it was decided that the quota of 20 percent of all new jobs from early-retired workers would be reserved for young people from the mining towns. By 2000, this system had degenerated as the regional UGTT leader, Amara Abassi, and other local union leaders favored their own families. By 2008, the population could stand the system no more.[61]

The following day, four unemployed graduates started a hunger strike in Redeyef. They belonged to the new Regional Committee of Unemployed Graduates (RCUG) that was copied from similar committees set up in Tunisia and gained support among some UGTT members as well.[62] Their hunger strike was followed the next day by a march and a sit-in in front of the CPG headquarters by hundreds of high school students and unemployed people. Similar marches took place in Moulares, during which the demonstrators proclaimed their right to work and denounced corruption. There was no repression from the security forces for three months, but as hunger strikes spread, a negotiating committee was set up, headed by Adnan el Hajji. He was a primary school teacher and a UGTT member, but untainted by the bad reputation of the local UGTT mining officials who were perceived as corrupt because they sought to get members of their families recruited on a privileged basis by the CPG, regardless of their qualifications. El Hajji tried to get a dialogue started with the local *sous-préfet*. In other mining towns such as M'dhila, protests turned violent and tires were burned. An attempt was made to set fire to a service company belonging to UGTT leader Amrane Abassi. The tracks of the phosphate railway were torn up and trucks transporting ore were stopped.[63] As the crisis worsened, the local branch of the ruling RCD Party attempted to divide the protesters by playing on tribal allegiance, while Adnan el Hajji denounced the nepotism of the local UGTT and RCD leadership. The government cracked down on the protests. As the movement gained momentum, shopkeepers and local doctors joined the strike. This prompted renewed arrests by the police, among them people who had become emblematic in the protests, such as Adnan el Hajji and some of the members of the RCUG.

Faced with rising tension, the arrival of unemployed protesters from outside the mining region, and the support of the Tunisian League of Human Rights (TLHR), the police retreated from the center of the towns. Every time they tried to come back and intervene to disperse demonstrators, sheer numbers overwhelmed them. Women played a prominent role in this. They were present in the street demonstrations and among the tents set up outside the headquarters of the CPG: "The Eleven Widows tent was to become a symbol of the movement. This tent, set up by the wives of former CPG workers who had died following a work accident, became the heart of the various tent camps. They would relentlessly demand that their children be hired by the CPG."[64]

Meanwhile, production at the mines and the washing plant were brought to a standstill and the railway line was blocked. The death of a young demonstrator by electrocution from the electric generator in the village of Tabbedit provoked revulsion and another wave of violence. Throughout June and July, the authorities regained control, but at the cost of many wounded and one demonstrator killed. A wave of arrests put dozens of leaders, not least from the Committees of Unemployed Graduates, behind bars. Heavy sentences fell on the emblematic leaders of the revolt at a trial in December 2008.[65]

But as they were waving the stick, "the authorities were also waving the carrot: in order to calm the tension, President Ben Ali dismissed the governor of Gafsa and the Director General of the CPG."[66] The president committed himself to allocate "a percentage of the income on the export of phosphate towards the construction of a new cement factory and new infrastructures."[67] He promised to accelerate small projects linked to cleaning up the environment and to hire young graduates to work on the municipal construction sites. Local people, however, felt that these were empty promises.

The significance of six months of unprecedented social and labor mobilization made the position of the national and regional leadership of UGTT untenable. The union's leadership in Tunis did not intervene with events in the mining area, which were a revolt against the system of which UGTT was part. UGTT was further discredited because the education, health, and postal sections of the trade union movement remained silent. Worse, the education section of UGTT took Adnan El Hajji's name off their list, thus easing the moves to prosecute him. Guilty silence was the only reaction of UGTT headquarters to what were unprecedented events. The TLHR had tried to help, but the police throughout the country mercilessly harassed its members. The conflict had not spread to other poor regions, however, and it was hardly reported in the international media—the few exceptions being in France, not least among certain Tunisian immigrant associations. The result was that many observers misread its importance for the future of the country. Few saw it as the red warning light of further trouble to come.

Among the political conclusions that could be drawn from these events, three stand out. First, the regime reacted by tightening their security screws ever more, which was a sign of weakness rather than strength; second, future change would come from the bottom, i.e. popular revolt; third, the internal contradictions of UGTT could act as a paradoxical lightning rod to social protest.[68]

The unprecedented crisis in the mining basin underlined the limits of the corrupt patronage system. The World Bank failed to appreciate to what extent the ruling family had captured the "economic rent," as it recognized in two unusually frank reports published in 2014.[69] In the private words of one senior EIB official who asked not to be mentioned, and who knew Tunisia well, "we Europeans, not least the French, were happy to have stability and cared little for the political cost."[70] Regional security after 9/11 was the overriding consideration, even if it came at the cost of being accomplice to a ruling clan that was ever more predatory on Tunisia's wealth.

Back in the capital, no one alerted the aging president, who by then was more interested in sharing Tunisian spoils among his large clan than worrying about the mounting crisis in the mining area. Western leaders and members of international donor institutions averted their eyes from the looming symptoms of trouble, and seldom travelled to the poorer regions.[71]

The legacy of Tunisia's revolt and the role of the UGTT

The stage was set for an explosion. In the twenty-eight months before Bouazizi's suicide in 2010, troubles were limited to minor riots by unemployed graduates in La Shkirra and Ben Guerdane, but a palpable sense of fear gripped Tunisia's middle class. The situation blew up on 17 December 2010 in Sidi Bouzid, after Bouazizi's self-immolation, and spread like wildfire through the poorer regions of Tunisia. Finally, protests engulfed the capital at the end of the first week of January 2011. It took four weeks for the "political component of the power elite, civilian and police officials alike, as well as members of the ex-dictator's immediate entourage in the power elite's capitalist component ... to be sacrificed."[72] The dictator had become too great a liability and was abandoned by the power elite. This was a revolution *in*, not *of*, the system. Because there was no outside factor, nor an Islamist one for that matter, the US did not interfere. Ennahda, the political party vehicle of Tunisia's Islamic movement, only entered the picture after the fact. When it came to power it preferred to ensure a piece of the pie for its clientele, in terms of public sector employment and subcontracts, rather than replace the old elites. The oldest ally, France, was caught completely unawares. As long-standing grievances bubbled up and strikes spread, the production of phosphates more than halved in 2011, and exports of phosphoric acid and fertilizers declined.[73] Five years later, strikes continue to bedevil the mining region north of Gafsa centered on the mining town of Metlaoui. The government has failed to come up with a bold strategy to deal with Tunisia's many economic and social problems, in particular those of the mining basin.

UGTT, for its part, has played a much more important role politically since the fall of Ben Ali. Its relations with the Islamist Ennahda-led government, which came to power after the first free elections held in the country in December 2011, went from bad to worse. In February 2012, thousands of union members protested against the Islamists' tactic of having truckloads of rubbish dumped in front of UGTT branches in an attempt to stop them protesting against deteriorating social and economic conditions.[74] Trouble was brewing on 4 December 2012, when Ennahda militias (called the Comités de Protection de la Révolution) attacked the UGTT headquarters at Place Mohammed Ali in the heart of the capital, just as the union was celebrating the anniversary of the death of its founder, Ferhat Hached. This was symbolic of a broader incapacity of the Islamists to engage in dialogue with key sections of civil society. A further escalation happened in 2013, when jihadist militants assassinated two prominent left-wing members of parliament.

UGTT and its influential leader, Houcine Abassi, also had to contend with the endless strikes that followed in the wake of the fall of Ben Ali. Ever since then, local UGTT leaders have gained more power and often pay scant attention to headquarters, once again exposing the internal contradictions of the union. Many factory owners have accused it of making excessive wage claims in what has been a steadily worsening economic climate, when a number of foreign investors have closed down their operations in Tunis.[75] The UGTT also played a major role in the country's democratic transition. In the summer of 2013, it joined forces with three other organizations—the TLHR, the Tunisian Order of Lawyers, and the Tunisian Confederation of Industry, Trade, and Handicrafts (UTICA)—to broker a deal between the government and the opposition coalition Nidaa Tounes, at a time when Tunisia looked as if it might descend into civil war. The Quartet, as it came to be known by the time it was awarded the Nobel Peace Prize in 2015, managed to convince the government to step down in December 2013, and make way for a technocratic administration that ran the country in the run-up to its first free presidential and second free general election in the autumn of 2014. The leader of Nidaa Tounes, Beji Caid Essebsi, won against the incumbent interim president, Moncef Marzouki, and his party won more seats than Ennahda a few weeks later in the general elections. Tunisia thus preserved its options towards establishing a lasting democracy.

Conclusion and outlook

Almost a decade after the revolt, the country's economy has stalled; the income from two of its most important economic engines—tourism and phosphates—has fallen. The second government, led by Habib Essid since January 2015, has failed to address some of the key economic challenges confronting Tunisia, but it has improved overall security. Facing up to the complex mix of problems in the phosphate and fertilizer industries is arguably a priority for the government. Before recent falls in production, phosphates contributed 4 percent of GDP and 10 percent of Tunisia's exports in 2010.[76] Gabès' importance for employment cannot be understated, as it accounts for

8–12 percent of salaried jobs in various parts of the province.[77] As wages are vastly higher than in other sectors of the region, the contribution to livelihoods is even higher.

Modernizing the industry is a multifaceted challenge that faces commercial, social, and environmental exigencies that can be mutually exclusive. First, real managerial skill must be brought in and allowed to get on with running a large industry. Those who run the GCT and the CPG are beholden to interference by the central government and behave more like civil servants at the beck and call of the minister of mines than free managers of an important industry. Second, economic development and jobs within or outside the mining industry need to be part of the process, as the social malaise of the hinterland continues and the absorption capacity of the coast to host labor migrants from the interior is limited for lack of opportunities and housing. Third, the longstanding environmental grievances of the phosphate basin must be addressed. That will cost money—615 million Tunisian Dinars are budgeted for depollution of the GCT's plants by 2020, according to the Ministry of Mines.[78] The fallout from pollution needs to be dealt with in a much more up front fashion. Agricultural land has been damaged, and date palms are affected by fluoride emissions that seep into the water system. In the coastal towns of Sfax, La Skhirra, and Gabès, gypsum deposits in the shallow seawater has destroyed the fishing industry.[79] In Sfax, Tunisia's second-largest city, the pollution has affected the health of many. Its inhabitants have asked for compensation from the state and are desperate to see the outdated phosphoric acid plant of SIAPE, a subsidiary of GCT, replaced by more modern plants in the vicinity that are being built in cooperation with Indian joint-venture partners. The SIAPE plant, built in 1952, has polluted parts of the city and 18 kilometers of coastline. Its mere presence is delaying many other investment projects. Pollution in Gabès, which is home to one of the four fertilizer plants in Tunisia, has destroyed the oasis, the once-thriving fishing industry, and agriculture. In damning articles on the legacy of pollution and ill health in Gabès, Eric Goldstein of Human Rights Watch and Tunisian journalist Moez Jemai reported that the GCT continues to dump 13,000 tons of phosphogypsum into the Mediterranean every day.[80]

Most of Tunisia's phosphoric acid and fertilizers are exported and serve as a precious source of hard currency for a troubled economy. Export income has been cut in half by the inability of the Tunisian government to bring the mines back to work and production back to the levels it reached on the eve of the revolt. In such a context, talk of developing new phosphate seems a classic case of putting the cart before the horse. Joint ventures could be brought in, but only after the legal framework of CPG and GCT with the government are modernized, and the companies put in the hands of a strong CEO and a board comprising a more diversified and experienced group of people than mere civil servants.

Tunisia has fallen behind its competitor Morocco, which has more reserves and produces far greater quantities of ore. In Morocco, the Office Chérifien des Phosphates (OCP) is the top exporter of ore in the world today. Over the past ten years, the percentage of ore that it transforms into phosphoric acid, diammonium phosphate (DAP), and trisodium phosphate (TSP), has nearly doubled, from 45 percent to 85 percent.[81] It has overhauled its management methods, bringing in a number of US advisers. It has been able to do this because it has had only one CEO in the last decade who reports directly to the king. Meanwhile in Tunisia, CEOs come and go—four in the last five years, in a game of musical chairs—which prevents any single one of them from implementing a long-term strategy.

The composition of the two companies' boards is symptomatic of the contrasts between the two countries. In Morocco, OCP's board includes high-level representatives of different ministries, not least foreign affairs, industry, and finance; in a way, it is a powerful inter-ministerial steering committee chaired by a CEO whose international experience is considerable. By contrast, Tunisia became ever more bureaucratized under Ben Ali, and the prime minister's office sought to control the higher echelons of the civil service ever more tightly. Those who sit on the board of the GPG and GCT are often second-tier civil servants being rewarded for their diligence. This state of affairs is not conducive to bold and quick decision-making, the essential ingredient of a modern company with international interests. Back in 2000, OCP faced challenges and lost money, while the smaller CPG and the GCT seemed more efficient. Matters took a turn for the worse when Ali Boukhris was forced out in the late 1980s. Instead of letting the CPG and GCT be managed autonomously, government ministers started interfering. Years after the fall of Ben Ali, Tunisian leaders are still grappling with an economic and security situation that remains very difficult countrywide, especially in the mining basin, and a company structure that does not allow the two companies to be nimble international players.

In this debate, the Ennahda Party, which is in coalition with the larger Nidaa Tounes, has little to contribute so far. Like other parties that are linked to the Muslim Brotherhood, Ennahda has yet to elaborate any in-depth economic thinking that addresses the complex problems of a developing economy. Whatever the solution, there is general agreement that if the disparity between poorer and richer regions is not reduced, the next crisis risks becoming a revolution *of* the system, not just *in* the system. In focus-group interviews with Tunisians, the most frequent expectations of constitutional reform were jobs and economic development, right after a reform of the security sector.[82] Tunisia has a well-educated population, constitutional traditions, a sizable middle class, and some industrial culture.[83] It also has a demographic window of opportunity. Even though the youth bulge is petering out as fertility rates have fallen below replacement level, this large young population is now entering the workforce. Successful transition to democracy can only be assured if the disenfranchised population in peripheral areas, such as the mining basin, gets a fairer deal, and if past excesses of crony capitalism are not repeated.

3

THE SECURITIZATION OF OIL AND ITS RAMIFICATIONS IN THE GULF COOPERATION COUNCIL STATES

Jill Crystal

This chapter examines the political construction of a new understanding of how natural resources and security are linked in the Gulf Cooperation Council (GCC) states. It begins with the role of oil in state and class formation, and next examines its broader securitization in the Gulf, a trend of particular salience in the last ten to fifteen years. I document the driving forces and motivations behind this process, both regionally and locally. The chapter concludes with some reflections on the links between natural resources, development trajectories, and political outcomes.

Oil differs from other natural resources, notably in its economic importance and in the ways it has structured politics in the Middle East. Its early centrality to solidifying the power of Gulf monarchs, its role in creating a more unequal relationship between rulers and the population, and in creating an ideology to support that relationship, both structured and diminished opposition in many other realms, among them environmental activism.

Fighting the environmental degradation associated with hydrocarbons (e.g. the 1991 oil fires that darkened Kuwait's skies lowered air quality and contaminated groundwater and Gulf water feeding desalination plants) was claimed early on as the state's preserve, leaving environmental activists to seek out less overtly political ways to express opposition.[1] Yet subsequent developments would lead to a further closing of the space to dissent, framed by the state as protecting resources and people.

The 2006 al-Qaeda attack on Saudi Arabia's Abqaiq oil facility was a watershed and led to rapid securitization of oil, first in Saudi Arabia, then in the other GCC states. Because of the economic centrality of hydrocarbons, governments faced no resistance in applying a security framework when oil facilities were at risk. With the onset of the Arab uprisings in 2011, then the fall in oil prices in 2013–14, Gulf regimes deepened their authoritarian tendencies. The securitization rhetoric, developed initially around oil, could now be deployed against any opposition, around any issue: governments viewed all dissent through a terrorism lens. Once on the same page, GCC rulers were more willing to link their domestic policing to a regional security framework long favored by Saudi Arabia. The discursive framework of terrorism gave a sense of urgency to a range of problems, reducing the apparent need for public scrutiny. When oil prices fell, governments reduced popular subsidies. The historical trade of political quiescence for wealth was now off the table as governments offered a new bargain: political obedience in exchange for security. Governments had now created an all-purpose securitization discourse that could be deployed in a variety of situations. By 2017 Saudi Arabia was able to dispense with emphasizing the economic vitality of hydrocarbons altogether; it could now invoke a very broadly defined era of terrorism to launch an embargo on its regional rival, Qatar, which deprived it of overland access to food and water. This chapter explains what happened to make this possible.

Regime security

The GCC states owe their existence and continued security as a distinctive monarchical regime type to the interwar discovery of oil. The freedom that oil revenues provided fundamentally restructured the relationship between the rulers and merchants—the business elite of that era, shifting political power from the merchants and into the hands of the rulers and ruling families. No longer dependent on merchants for tax revenues, rulers had no need to respond to their political demands. Oil revenues allowed rulers to develop instead a new system of rule in which rulers distanced themselves from the business elite and developed a new state bureaucracy dominated by key ruling family members placed in the most important, or sovereign, ministries. To placate the merchants, rulers worked out a new arrangement: a trade of wealth for access to formal power. The merchants largely withdrew from formal politics. State formation in the GCC was thus closely tied to oil.[2]

Energy infrastructure security

Oil also brought the attention of outsiders, in the form of threats and of protective umbrellas. Oil meant that the world's most powerful states, dependent on petroleum, would pay close attention to the GCC. It also meant that neighboring states would look closely at the wealthy, but poorly protected, oil wells that these states possessed. Such dangerous attention culminated in 1990 with the Iraqi invasion and occupation of Kuwait. Fortunately for Kuwait, powerful oil-importing states were watching, and its independence was restored when US-led forces defeated Iraq, making the US itself an important regional player. Foreign forces secured Kuwait's sovereignty, but not before withdrawing Iraqi forces set fire to most of the country's oil wells. Those fires, which took several months to extinguish, brought home clearly the importance of two factors. The first was oil security—both the literal infrastructure and key global alliances. The second was the importance of the nexus between oil and the environment; one immediate consequence of the fires was months of darkened skies, and deterioration in air quality with consequent respiratory problems for residents. Oil spills also contaminated the sand, threatening the groundwater and the Gulf waters, and contaminating the water desalination plant intakes.[3] The Iraqi departure thus brought home the importance not only of securing alliances with powerful external forces, but of literally securing the critical energy infrastructure, beginning with the oil wells.

The Gulf states' more recent concern with oil security dates to a February 2006 attack on the Saudi facility at Abqaiq. This facility includes one of the world's largest oilfields, able to process over 7 million barrels of oil a day. It contains some forty-six pipelines, including nearly 400 miles of pipeline running to Ras Tanura, the world's largest oil export terminal.[4] About two-thirds of Saudi Arabia's oil is exported from Ras Tanura.[5] This facility is so important that the 2006 attack, although immediately thwarted, prompted an oil price spike of $2 a barrel.[6] Suicide bombers driving two Saudi Aramco vehicles attempted to ram the facility's outer gate. Saudi security forces fired at the attackers' vehicles, prompting the drivers to detonate their explosives at the facility's outer perimeter, killing themselves and two guards. Although there had been previous attempted attacks on oil company offices and housing compounds, this was believed to be the first direct attack on Saudi oil production facilities. The following day an al-Qaeda website claimed responsibility.[7] Authorities arrested several connected with the attacks, sentencing one to death, others to prison.

This event prompted the Saudi government to focus on oil security and terrorism: the failed attack might well have succeeded. As Saudi Interior Minister Muhammad bin Nayef noted in a cable sent on 22 August 2008, "We did not save Abqaiq, God did."[8] A wave of attacks had begun in the kingdom in 2003, already raising concern over terrorism. Now terrorism was linked to oil. The Abqaiq attack focused attention on an important vulnerability. Although the facility itself is gated, its pipelines run close to major highways and residential areas and thus pose a security threat. Pipelines are not only more vulnerable to hit-and-run attacks, but are also more attractive targets than oil facilities to attackers interested in overthrowing the government (thus inheriting oil facilities functioning and intact).

This concern with oil security was reinforced in 2007 when the government arrested members of an al-Qaeda cell for planning to hijack civilian aircraft and fly them into Abqaiq and Ras Tanura.[9] After the 2006 attack, the government took measures to strengthen energy infrastructure security. It built a 35,000–40,000-person Facilities Infrastructure Force dedicated to oil security, soliciting help from the US government, which sent a team to assess security and help develop the new force.[10] The US ambassador to Saudi Arabia, Ford Fraker, was put in charge of the program. Although training and advising missions date back to the 1950s, this mission marked the beginning of a new type of security relationship between the two governments and US defense manufacturers. This relationship was formalized in 2008, and in the following years US Department of State records showed a dramatic increase in direct commercial sales to Saudi Arabia around energy infrastructure, including a $1 billion contract to Northrop Grumman to build and install a perimeter surveillance system.[11]

Improving security proved challenging. One problem, according to the WikiLeaks cables, was the differing assessment and concomitant infighting between Saudi Aramco and the Interior Ministry. The Interior Ministry was concerned that Iran might work with local Shi'a citizens to attack the facilities. Saudi Aramco worried that the Interior Ministry employed members of suspected terrorist groups. They found the staff sent by the Interior Ministry incompetent: acting carelessly, smoking cigarettes close to combustible material, and moving their vehicles dangerously close to equipment. American officials suspected that Aramco's perimeter surveillance system was intended to keep Saudi security forces as much as terrorists away from Aramco facilities.[12]

For understandable reasons, governments are reluctant to reveal much about how energy resources are protected, but protected they are. By the time Abqaiq was attacked again, in September 2015, Saudi authorities were prepared. When a gunman approached the facility, he was immediately killed by security forces.[13] The government had taken several measures to enhance security further in previous years. These included fitting pipelines with more emergency shut-down valves, putting security teams at intervals along the pipelines, increasing the amount of material needed for pipeline repair, and installing more security cameras.[14]

Other GCC states were also concerned about energy infrastructure security, and Western firms were anxious for the work. Kuwait created the Oil Sector Services Company, a subsidiary of the Kuwait Petroleum Corporation, to handle oil security overall. The government was less interested than Saudi Arabia in securing US assistance. In November 2006, US government officials met with Ali Al-Obaid, Deputy Chairman of Kuwait's Oil Sector Services Company. He said that Kuwait was primarily interested in long-term strategic planning and intelligence sharing.[15] Kuwait turned first to a British firm, Global Village. In August 2015, Kuwait signed an agreement for new telecommunications and security systems for the Kuwait National Petroleum Company's large Mina al-Ahmadi Refinery with a Japanese firm, NEC.[16] NEC would also add a biometric dimension to security with a new ID card authentication and authorization system.[17]

A more recent security concern for the oil industry has been cybersecurity. An annual survey by Gulf Business Machines in 2013 found that about 45 percent of GCC IT professionals reported that their organizations had experienced at least one IT security incident in the previous year.[18] When the original energy infrastructure was built, cybersecurity was not something the oil industry worried about. Oil companies did not seriously protect the software and the sensors and controllers that operate the system. But as cybersecurity became a growing concern, all the GCC states hired more information security officers and improved cybersecurity on several levels. This threat was brought home dramatically in August 2012, when the Iranian government launched a cyberattack on Saudi Aramco.[19] In that incident, a virus removed data from three-quarters of Aramco's corporate computers, replacing them with a burning US flag. The attack forced Aramco to shut down its internal corporate network to halt the virus' spread. The attack was relatively minor because the oil production operation computers are separate from the internal communications network. Nonetheless, the hard drives of tens of thousands of PCs had to be replaced. To help, Aramco brought in a dozen US computer security experts. This attack was thought by some to be in retaliation for the US–Israeli Stuxnet virus that destroyed centrifuges at an Iranian nuclear facility in 2010.[20] In the days following the attack, Saudi Aramco was without functioning phones and email, and was forced to use typewriters and paper. Resources proved critical. Saudi Aramco used its company fleet to fly employees to Southeast Asian factories, buying so many hard drives that they affected the market price of PCs and hard drives into 2013. Once again in the aftermath, Aramco expanded its cybersecurity operations.[21]

The other GCC states also stepped up cybersecurity. Officials in Qatar blamed Iran for an attack on Qatar's RasGas two weeks after the Aramco attack, which crashed the company's website and office computer systems. In May 2014, Kuwait's oil minister raised concerns about the dangers of cybersecurity in the energy infrastructure, announcing that Kuwait was increasing its attention to this issue.[22] The United Arab Emirates created a National Electronic Security Authority (NESA) to handle cybersecurity. The Abu Dhabi Company for Onshore Oil Operations hired Booz Allen to analyze its cybersecurity risk.[23] Today, cybersecurity is a central part of energy infrastructure security.[24]

Securing natural resources

Energy resources are critical to the region's economy. But other resources, such as food and water, are central to Gulf states' very existence. The GCC is oil-rich and water-poor.[25] Public understanding of the importance of securing access to water and food has taken longer to materialize, in part because the threats have been subtler. In 1973, when the Organization of Arab Petroleum Exporting Countries states boycotted oil sales to the US, there were rumblings of a retaliatory food embargo.[26] The implication of this dependence was revealed starkly when differences between Saudi Arabia and Qatar over the latter's support for the Muslim Brotherhood culminated in the withdrawal of Saudi, Bahraini, and Emirati ambassadors from Doha in March 2014.[27] In the heat of the moment, rumors swirled about possible Saudi border closure and sanctions that could have deprived Qatar of imported food and water. These threats were realized in 2017 when Saudi Arabia did close its frontier, sending Qatar scrambling for new food sources.

Like much of the Middle East, the GCC states are heavily dependent on imported water and food, virtual water, and they are susceptible to any disruption in the global food supply. Qatar, for example, imports 90 percent of its food and maintains only two days of water reserves. It receives about 75 millimeters of precipitation per year and is well below the World Bank's water poverty line. All the GCC states save Oman suffer from absolute water scarcity, with the situation particularly pronounced in Kuwait.[28] Most are largely dependent on desalination for drinking water and have emergency reserves of only a few days.[29] They also have high consumption rates.[30] A 2015 report by the World Resources Institute listed Bahrain, Kuwait, and Qatar at the top of a list of countries facing an "extremely high water risk" by 2040 (with the other GCC states not far behind).[31] Heavily subsidized water has hidden this dependence from consumers. Nonetheless, states have taken efforts to address it. Abu Dhabi has been at the forefront of efforts to address climate issues, beginning in 2006 with the Masdar Initiative. The Dubai Water and Electricity Authority is the only such Gulf authority that runs a profit on water and electricity sales, largely by not subsidizing the expatriate population.[32] Perhaps the boldest recent strategy is the UAE's putative plan to build a mountain to increase rainfall using cloud seeding.[33] This policy is oddly reminiscent of a decades-old plan to import oil by towing icebergs.[34] Authoritarian governments have a short-term advantage in responding to environmental challenges, but only if the leader chooses to act. The evidence on popular attention to environmental issues is mixed. There is some evidence that people are increasingly realizing the vulnerabilities independent of government concern. One survey in Abu Dhabi noted a considerable rise in environmental awareness and sense of responsibility.[35] Still, lifestyles throughout the GCC indicate that this preference does not always translate into practice.

The GCC states' lack of water in turn limits agricultural production, forcing states to import food. The two strategies for dealing with this problem—growing food locally and acquiring continued access to harvests elsewhere—both present challenges. Saudi Arabia tried for years to expand domestic agricultural production, but is now abandoning that effort, having depleted much of its groundwater.[36] After the food crisis of 2007–8, Saudi Arabia began to shift to investment in foreign agriculture. Qatar, however, is considering growing more food locally and hopes to use solar energy to produce water for some local farming.[37] The government wants to produce up to 70 percent of its food by 2023.[38] Investment in foreign agriculture has been a primary response to dependency on imported food.[39] Gaining access to land and harvests in other areas, notably Africa, presents other challenges.[40] These strategies have not been very successful.[41] Other countries compete with the GCC for crops. And, as the GCC states are well aware, these strategies will not guarantee food imports in times of crisis, when political pressure will likely prompt food growers to restrict exports, a concern that has led some to recommend a strategic food reserve.[42] This concern became more pronounced in 2008 when some suppliers imposed export restrictions on food.[43] The GCC continues to import massive amounts of food (including nearly $3 billion worth from US producers), with Saudi Arabia recently overtaking the UAE as the largest market for US food products in the GCC.[44]

Climate change will make access to water and food still more problematic. As the world moves away from fossil fuels, the GCC will see revenues fall further. Climate change will make the GCC a more difficult place to live. Rising temperatures may make much of the GCC virtually uninhabitable by the end of the century.[45] This could result in elite migration, as nationals, building on the tradition of nomadic pastoralism, take to moving abroad for much of the year, returning in the winter months to maintain a claim to their land and national identity. Saudi Arabia would face the daunting challenge of handling a summer hajj. The Gulf states are incentivized both to avoid this crisis, and to maintain the status quo of a world dependent on the fossil fuels they possess. Some at the 2015 Paris climate summit accused Saudi Arabia of trying to undermine the summit in order to protect its future as one of the world's largest oil producers, an accusation previously launched at Saudi Arabia.[46] The GCC states did not set specific emission reduction targets at the Paris conference, but merely promised to develop renewable energy.[47] Even before the fall in oil prices, the GCC states, led by Saudi Arabia, opposed internationally driven mitigation efforts that could potentially reduce reliance on oil.[48] Nonetheless, all the GCC states ratified the Kyoto Protocol and the United Nations Framework Convention on Climate Change.

Luomi attributes the GCC's present "natural unsustainability" to three factors: the rentier state, persisting authoritarianism, and the ruling bargain that brings the first two factors together.[49] Regime survival, she argues, drives rulers to create the "illusion of abundance," which sustains a lifestyle of wasteful water and energy consumption and, more broadly, a disregard for environmental sustainability. However, if this ruling bargain is no longer sustainable and the illusion of abundance is stripped away; if a transition away from a rentier state occurs; and if the population rejects a new bargain based on security by demanding limits on authoritarianism (and participation in exchange for taxation), then the factors that underpin Luomi's natural unsustainability will weaken and an agenda of natural sustainability might emerge. As discussed below, at current oil prices, the status quo is untenable. Ultimately the GCC states' deep dependence on imported food and water and exported energy leaves them vulnerable to outside forces, which risks destabilizing the domestic settlement.

Policing the people

In the years leading up to the Arab uprisings, the GCC states increased energy infrastructure security. They were fortunate in having the resources and state capacity to do so; attacks on such infrastructure can be devastating.[50] By the time the Arab uprisings arrived, not only a security infrastructure, but also a security discourse was in place around oil, ready to be deployed in new contexts. Following a 2015 suicide bomb attack in Kuwait on the Shi'a Imam al-Sadiq Mosque by a Saudi national with ties to ISIS, the Kuwaiti government very publicly announced that it was increasing security around oil installations, although there was no obvious connection between oil and the mosque attack.[51] Where once oil was discussed in the language of resource nationalism, it was now discussed in the language of security. Resource nationalism originally fitted well with the language of Arab nationalism. But in the Gulf, Arab nationalism over time had given way to state nationalisms and to a broader *khaleeji* identity. This occurred in part precisely because of oil; other states could use Arab nationalism to launch a claim to the oil wealth of the Gulf.

With the rise of al-Qaeda, and attacks on oil facilities, oil became cloaked in the language of anti-terrorism: a terrorism–energy nexus had been created. That anti-terrorism framing could be imposed on any domestic challenge. This discursive framework was important because it gave a sense of urgency to any issue to which it was applied, reducing the apparent need for public scrutiny. As Barry Buzan argues, like other writers from the securitization literature, when an issue is securitized, it "is presented as an existential threat, requiring emergency measures and justifying actions outside the normal bounds of political procedure."[52] When the Arab uprisings occurred, all the GCC leaders began moving in varying degrees in a more authoritarian direction. This discursive strategy now proved useful. When a language was needed to accompany new modes of authoritarianism, one was on hand. Because attacks on oil installations came from people whom the state had clearly established as terrorists in the public eye, it was easy for states to use the existing securitization discourse to create a connection between energy security and opposition.

The Arab uprisings created a completely new policing context. The GCC states were more successful than the region's single-party regimes in surviving the Arab uprisings, although the reasons for this are debated.[53] All were shaken, but all survived and none—save Bahrain—survived by relying primarily on the heavy use of force, although all relied more heavily on force and its threat than in the past. Each GCC state saw some popular mobilization. Even Kuwait, the most politically open, with preexisting institutions for channeling discontent, saw demonstrations in the tens of thousands—massive for Kuwait.

At first the GCC states responded by doubling up on existing practice: spending more money and less infrequently applying force. Largely wealthy and benign, none of the Arab Gulf states, save Bahrain, possessed a police state of the sort seen in single-party regimes. Their leaders responded with techniques that had proven effective in the past: raising wages and generally deploying money through clientele networks.

As the Arab uprisings deepened, the responses of GCC leaders began to change and diverge. As Steve Heydemann argues, "path dependence matters, but at moments of crisis, regime adaptations can and do move governance beyond the boundaries of current practices."[54] This moment of crisis caused the regimes in the GCC to move beyond tweaking historically successful practices and toward new modes of authoritarianism. New laws were introduced that focused on dissent, particularly on social media.[55] In each country, government forces responded more quickly with force or its presence, regardless of whether the opposition resorted to force. Ordinary police forces, the first line for public protest, responded in a more heavy-handed way to opposition. Security forces, tasked with political policing, were expanded. And militaries, which in the GCC were, as Springborg points out, "parade ground forces," now were strengthened to deal with threats at home and abroad.[56] The more authoritarian trend in the GCC following the Arab uprisings was part of a regional trend. It was also part of a long-standing pattern within the GCC of studying what worked in other GCC states, and was consistent with a simultaneous movement toward greater GCC cooperation.[57]

Variations in policing practice also emerged. Regime reaction varied from all but ignoring the Arab uprisings (domestically) in Qatar, to launching a fiercely repressive response in Bahrain. Qatar responded by handing out revenues, at first in the form of public sector raises, a move that reached nearly every Qatari.[58] It also upgraded its modest security state. Opposition was muted, and so too was the government's response. It imprisoned some online protesters, but did little more to stifle opposition.[59] Instead, in an extraordinary move for the GCC—where rulers typically maintain power (or at least their title) for life (or in Qatar's case, until overthrown)—Qatar's ruler Sheikh Hamad bin Khalifa pre-emptively overthrew himself in 2013, handing power to his son Tamim. Another factor setting Qatar apart was the government's decision to use the opportunity of regional chaos to leverage its position by actively supporting dissidents in Libya and supporting the Muslim Brotherhood throughout the Arab world, a policy that set it on a collision course with its Saudi neighbor. As Ulrichsen points out, "uniquely among regional states, Qatari officials saw the outbreak of unrest in Tunisia, Egypt, and Libya in the early months of 2011 as an opportunity to be seized, rather than a challenge to be contained."[60]

The government's response in the UAE stood in stark contrast to Qatar. The UAE, like Qatar, faced little opposition during the Arab uprisings, yet it responded with criminalization and crackdowns aimed largely at social media activists.[61] In July 2015, the emir issued a broad royal anti-discrimination decree aimed at countering terrorism and outlawing religious or racial discrimination.[62] Part of the explanation for the differences lies in the fact that, although historically the UAE had lacked a large police presence, it had grown one shortly before the Arab uprisings, by buying a police force "off the shelf," and hiring mercenaries initially largely from Colombia, then South Africa, from Reflex Responses (R2, owned by Erik Prince, formerly owner of Blackwater), a US-based private security company dogged by controversy because of excessive use of force in Iraq.[63] The first R2 contingent arrived in the summer of 2010, and the group's job included preparation for special operations missions both domestically and abroad, and defending oil pipelines.[64] In a WikiLeaks document from January 2007, Abu Dhabi's Crown Prince Mohammed bin Zayed Al Nahyan specifically linked the hiring of mercenaries to his lack of confidence in his own army and security forces.[65] In early 2010, the government augmented R2 by creating a Presidential Guard with today an estimated 5,000 soldiers, dominated by Australians. In 2014, the government announced that it would pay US Marines to train the guard.[66] The government also created a panoptic state, flooding its cities with so many security cameras that it could watch activity in the capital in real time. Finally, it added a touch of "security theater" with the announcement in January 2016 that it would appoint a minister of happiness. Security was becoming a performative act.

Part of the explanation for the different response lies in the UAE's decision to link domestic opposition to the Muslim Brotherhood, thus aligning itself closely with Saudi Arabia. Dubai Police Chief Lieutenant General Dahi Khalfan spoke publicly of what he saw as the dangers of the group, asserting that "my sources say the next step is to make Gulf governments figurehead bodies only without actually ruling. The start will be in Kuwait in 2013," citing "leaks" from Western intelligence.[67] In 2012, the foreign minister called on fellow GCC members to launch a coordinated crackdown on the organization.[68] Trials in 2013 convicted fifty-five of plotting to take power in the UAE and coordinating with foreign groups.[69] Among them were many prominent Emiratis. Finally, as Greg Gause argues, part of the difference lies simply in the personal preferences of Gulf rulers, who possess so much autonomy that national interest is whatever they say it is.[70]

Between Qatar and the UAE stood Kuwait. Kuwait has long had a highly participatory parliament. Part of the reason lies in domestic politics: Kuwait's first attempts at formalizing participatory politics date back to the interwar period. Kuwait's National Assembly provided a natural focus for grievances. Other explanations lie in Kuwait's international vulnerability. Michael Herb argues in *The Wages of Oil* that a key factor explaining why Kuwait developed a more robust parliament than the UAE lay in the recurring threat to Kuwaiti sovereignty emanating from Iraq, both at Kuwait's independence in 1961 and again in 1990.[71] With the Arab uprisings, Kuwait retained its practice of participatory politics, but began to develop a hybrid security state, which it increasingly deployed following the onset of the Arab uprisings, notably following large protests in 2012 over changes in the election law. This was a significant divergence from historical practice, when Kuwait had a police force far more attuned to maintaining law and order than to maintaining a particular order.[72] In 2015, Amnesty International published a report which, while praising Kuwait for its long record of political freedom, nonetheless criticized the erosion of those freedoms since the Arab uprisings, noting that "since 2011, in the face of increased criticism and amidst a volatile regional context, the authorities have taken a series of steps which have seriously eroded human rights, with the right to freedom of expression among the main casualties."[73]

The rise of ISIS in Iraq enabled the government to frame opposition increasingly in the language of terrorism.[74] Hundreds of Kuwaitis may have traveled to join ISIS, with many returning to Kuwait; others gave ISIS financial support. In 2014, a former MP, Khalid al-Shatti, wrote a piece in the *New York Times* warning that "Kuwait has been overtaken by a wave of extremism that has made it a center for terror financing."[75] In March 2014, the government dismissed Nayif al-Ajmi, minister of *awqaf* (religious endowments), following US criticism that al-Ajmi had a history of promoting terrorism in Syria.

Unlike Saudi Arabia, Kuwait was more reluctant to use a sectarian frame in a country where Shi'a, perhaps a third of the national population, lived peaceably amid a largely Sunni population. Similarly, Kuwait was reluctant to embrace Saudi hostility for the Muslim Brotherhood, also represented in Kuwait's National Assembly. Indeed, Kuwait had welcomed Saudi Shi'a in the early part of the twentieth century when radical Saudis were attacking them, even building a *hussainiyyah* for those fleeing persecution.[76] A brief period of sectarian tension, largely the result of government discrimination against Shi'a following the 1979 Iranian Revolution, was soon regretted, and remembered. The government also relied on Shi'a MPs at times to balance other parliamentary blocs. But as Kuwait moved closer to Saudi Arabia, even that became impossible. In January 2016 a Kuwait court ruled against twenty-five Kuwaiti Shi'a and one Iranian for belonging to a terror cell linked to Iran, an act that came not long after a government statement of solidarity with Saudi Arabia after the Iranian attack on the Saudi embassy in Tehran. This prompted all nine of Kuwait's Shi'a MPs to boycott the Assembly.[77]

An anti-terrorism framing posed fewer problems. In April 2013, Kuwait passed legislation aimed at limiting terrorist financing and established an independent financial intelligence unit to monitor such activities. In February 2014, shortly after Saudi Arabia had issued a decree imposing prison terms for membership of a terrorist group, a pro-government MP, Nabil Fadhl, called for similar legislation in Kuwait. In 2014, the government stripped three dozen people of their citizenship and deported them for threatening government security. It also began moving against dissenters largely on social media. In June 2015, Musallam al-Barrak, head of the Popular Action Movement and former MP, began serving a two-year sentence following a conviction related to a 2012 speech criticizing the emir at a rally that was met by Interior Ministry forces who cleared the crowds with tear gas.[78]

A turning point came with the suicide attack on the Shi'a Imam al-Sadiq Mosque in June 2015, by a Saudi national with ties to ISIS, which killed twenty-seven people and wounded over two hundred—the worst terrorist attack in Kuwait's history. Kuwait's emir visited the bombing site shortly after the attack and attended the funeral procession the following night. In July 2015, the government announced that it had arrested twenty-nine suspects and would seek the death penalty for eleven (seven were later sentenced to death).[79] Following the mosque attack, the government deployed "unprecedented security measures" at Shi'a mosques around the country for Friday prayers.[80] Thousands of Shi'a and Sunnis held joint prayers at Kuwait's Grand Mosque, which the emir, crown prince, and several cabinet ministers attended. In July 2015, the National Assembly passed a series of stringent laws. One was a law put forward by the Interior Ministry allowing for the creation of a DNA registry of all Kuwaiti nationals and residents.[81] The Assembly also approved an additional $400 million in emergency funding for the Interior Ministry. It approved a cybercrime law that severely restricted online speech, prompting criticism from Human Rights Watch.[82]

In Oman, a state lacking its neighbors' wealth, the Arab uprisings came with a list of demands for economic and social justice; the opposition called for higher wages, the removal of corrupt government officials, and more power for the Consultative Council. Path dependencies guided the government's initial response: it tried to placate the opposition with cabinet reshuffling, promises of new jobs, increased unemployment benefits, and more legislative power to the Consultative Council. New security measures were also introduced.[83] Riot police ended peaceful protests. Protesters, journalists, and human rights activists were arrested. The government increased its police presence and expanded police powers. In 2011, a new cybercrime law was issued. Although force was used at times against crowds, along with heightened security measures, a police state did not emerge.

Bahrain alone responded to the Arab uprisings with massive force. Bahrain combined a terrorist and sectarian framing to separate the Sunni pro-democracy protesters from their Shi'a counterparts. It then framed the uprising as part of an Iranian conspiracy. While there was no evidence to support this, it resonated with Saudi Arabia's view. This framing in turn facilitated the decision to allow Saudi forces to intervene and put down the uprising with force. Saudi Arabia came to the decision early on that if a war for regime survival had to be fought, it would be fought in Bahrain, not at home. The Bahraini government now bolstered its security state. In July 2013, following a car bomb explosion, the government expanded anti-terrorism legislation to cover inciting violence, threatening social cohesion, and using social media to convey false information or threaten national interests. The government also targeted activist leaders. In June 2015 it sentenced Shaikh Ali Salman, head of the leading Shi'a opposition organization al-Wifaq, to four years in prison for inciting disorder and sectarian strife. Other arrests followed.

Bahrain was the outlier for several reasons. Alone among the GCC states, it had a well-developed security state on hand to deploy. This was partly because of the larger British police presence in the colonial era. It was also part of a conscious decision by the newly independent government to retain that structure, often by hiring former colonial police officers, and to direct that structure largely at the Shi'a population. For Bahrain, deepening existing authoritarianism was simply doubling up what it had always done. The sectarian framing favored by the government at home resonated effectively with the regional sectarian framing which Saudi Arabia had imposed on every regional conflict that involved Shi'a. Iran had to be behind it, whether it was or not.

Saudi Arabia's response was initially modestly more authoritarian. At home, Saudi police had long targeted certain groups: Shi'a, women, some expatriates. Its performative police presence at the hajj aimed to instill a sense of security.[84] But these elements notwithstanding, the government had been slow to develop an actual security state. Even after the 1979 Grand Mosque attack, the government, although ruthless toward those involved, relied more heavily on concessions to and co-optation of those more generally sympathetic. It responded in the following years by conceding to many opposition demands, along with strengthening its security apparatus.

Saudi Arabia only developed the rudiments of a security state following domestic terrorist attacks in 1995, after which a Special Forces unit was created to combat terrorism. Following the 11 September 2001 attacks, and most notably after the 2003 Riyadh bombings, the government began relying more heavily on its security services. Initially the use of force against jihadists was tempered by a concomitant reliance on jihad rehab, an approach not offered to other dissidents. But by 2016 the gloves were off. In January, Saudi Arabia executed forty-seven people in one day, the largest mass execution since the 1980 executions of those involved in the 1979 Grand Mosque attack.[85]

As the Arab uprisings dragged on, Saudi Arabia began developing more robust anti-terrorism legislation. In December 2013, new anti-terrorism laws criminalized a wide range of behaviors, including acts that damaged the state's reputation.[86] In February 2014, royal decrees criminalized fighting in Syria and Iraq and publicly endorsing or sympathizing with any group that the Saudi government deemed extremist. As its critics feared, such legislation was used to target a range of political activists. Among the first to be tried was a human rights activist, Waleed Abulkhair, for criticizing the regime. In July

2015, the Saudi government announced that it had arrested over 400 ISIS members, mostly Saudi; some of whom were believed to be behind the bombings in the Eastern province.[87] Human Rights Watch reported that Saudi Arabia was sentencing peaceful activists to long jail terms—and even death—on vague charges.[88]

The Arab uprising was the first step in attempting to change the historical ruling bargain between the government and its citizenry throughout the GCC. Political quiescence was still expected; what the government would offer in exchange was security from what it marketed as an ambient terrorist threat. This resonated as well with the discourse of the GCC's US ally; the war on terror was the primary concern. If people would not accept the government's securitization framing of this new arrangement, there was the deepened authoritarian state ready to engage.[89] This was a dramatic securitizing move, a radical reframing of a long-standing social contract. Initially it was tempered by a continued degree of state largesse; when the Arab uprisings began, the government responded with financial concessions. But once oil prices began to fall, this was no longer possible.

Falling oil prices

Falling oil prices intensified the problems laid bare by the Arab uprisings. By January 2016, prices had fallen below $35 a barrel, the lowest in eleven years. The historical bargain of material wealth for political quiescence was beginning to fray. The emir of Qatar was blunt about this, warning in 2015 that the government can no longer "provide for everything."[90]

The ruling bargain now in peril had its origins in the early years of oil. Oil revenues, as noted above, allowed rulers to distance themselves from the old business community. And when the Arab uprisings occurred, most of the demands came from ordinary citizens. The merchants remained largely quiescent; that part of the bargain remained intact.

In the early days of oil, however, governments not only created new arrangements with business elites, but also developed new coalitions with the national population by extending state employment and generous welfare benefits. The working class, which in the 1950s scared governments with labor agitation—often in the oil industry—was now transformed into a more docile middle class. Foreign labor was imported to replace them. Initially, as Chalcraft argues, foreign labor energized the emerging labor movement. Laborers from Palestine, Yemen, and elsewhere brought pan-Arab and leftist ideologies and organizations, and joined local labor in popular protest.[91] The regimes adapted by hiring labor from the subcontinent, and encouraging spatial and sartorial (and other symbolic status markers) distance between nationals and foreign workers, who could be deported.

The new national middle class became much less politically challenging. However, this peace came at a cost. Maintaining an expanding welfare state was expensive and predicated on higher oil prices.[92] The bureaucracies that provided jobs to nationals were typically fragmented, unwieldy, and inefficient.[93] There was also a political component to the ruling bargain. Beginning in Kuwait, governments also began to allow a degree of political participation to the national population, consolidating their coalition with the new middle class by giving them limited political rights, typically in the form of partially elected consultative bodies.

When oil prices fell, the GCC governments made clear that the new bargain previewed in the Arab uprisings would remain. Governments would now cut at the core of the original bargain: they would limit state employment, cut benefits to citizens, and even introduce taxes.

Alternatives were possible. GCC rulers did not seriously consider cutting infrastructure and other capital spending.[94] They did not consider expanding political participation to bring more stakeholders into the decision-making process. In Saudi Arabia, they did not rein in an expensive and ineffective foreign policy adventure in Yemen. Rather they focused on cutting subsidies and introducing taxes: policies that would fall heavily on the middle class.

The UAE, with perhaps the least political participation and the most money, was the first to start, in July 2015, when it announced a reduction in fuel subsidies.[95] The others quickly followed, apart from more participatory Kuwait, whose Assembly rejected a similar proposal.[96] Cuts in other subsidies were next, followed by announcements about the introduction of taxes. In December 2015, the GCC states agreed to roll out a common value-added tax.[97] Taxes on nationals, expatriates, and businesses were also explored. GCC governments were using the crisis as an opportunity to introduce structural reforms. In May 2015, Oman announced that it would cut benefits for employees in state agencies (including health, life, travel and car insurance, loans, bonuses, school fee allowances, and housing) as part of an austerity drive,[98] later followed with cuts in gas subsidies and electricity. Gengler and Lambert attribute the choices to four factors: the emergence of a younger generation of neoliberal elites, international pressure pushing for energy reform, the attraction of a Dubai model (where expatriates generate significant state revenues), and regional instability.[99]

The boldest move came from Saudi Arabia. In April 2016, following the collapse of talks on an oil-production freeze in Doha, and facing a growing deficit, the government laid out a new initiative, Vision 2030, to help the kingdom rapidly diversify into a post-oil era. The proposal included a major subsidy cut and a limited public offering of Aramco shares, with revenues to fund new investment in tourism and mining.[100] In April 2016, the government announced that it would establish a government-owned military company to oversee the development of the local military industry, and would make 50 percent of its military purchases local (Saudi Arabia is the world's third-largest military spender).[101]

The practical challenges are many. The Vision's speed is breathless, its goals ambitious. It aims both to reduce unemployment and to increase women's labor force participation. It assumes that foreign direct investment (FDI) and local capital will create substantial job growth for nationals. It was drafted largely by Western consultants, understandably less attuned to the domestic consequences, especially second and third order, of its proposed changes. Diversification away from oil presents its own dangers, as Dubai experienced in 2008 when it was severely shaken by the global financial crisis. The enthusiasm for neoliberalism seems inattentive to the disintegration of the neoliberal compact across the region in the years leading up to the Arab uprisings.

The consequences of these decisions are just beginning to unfold. There is some evidence that, given regional insecurity, nationals value security more than they once did. Gengler and Lambert cite survey data indicating that the percentage of Qatari nationals who value stability is both high and rising. In Qatar, 37 percent of nationals identified "maintaining order and stability" as their top priority in 2011; by 2014 that proportion had risen to 75 percent. The percentage who valued "giving people more say over important decisions" had fallen to 8 percent.[102] But Qatar may well be the exception; its extraordinary wealth insulates the population more.

Elsewhere, the early signs were that this new deal would not be easily accepted. Whether the national population accepts it, and the concomitant need to remove many issues from the realm of public debate, or instead asks for more representative participation especially in the economic decisions shaping their lives, remains unknown.[103]

An early sign occurred, as it had in the past, in the oil industry. In April 2016, Kuwait's oil union announced a three-day strike over changes in pay that would adversely affect industry workers. Some 7,000–13,000 of the 18,000 Kuwaiti nationals in the oil sector participated in the strike, according to union estimates (expatriates are not permitted to strike). In the end the union concluded the strike with no concessions. But this was likely only round one—sending a message. While the strike did cause a production cut from 2.8 mbd to 1.5 mbd, Kuwait National Petroleum Company reported that increased production prior to the strike had given the country sufficient oil to weather the strike.[104] While the other GCC states had moved ahead with austerity measures in late 2015 and into 2016, Kuwait, with its parliament and mobilized population, particularly in the unionized oil industry (banned or controlled in the other GCC states), had moved more slowly, with reforms still under discussion at the time of the strike. As Shafeeq Ghabra put it, "The oil strike was a showdown between a welfare government and a civil society fearful that the government will solve its problem ... at its expense."[105] Kuwait's history of trade union activism and parliamentary participation made austerity measures a challenge for the government. As one headline put it, "Kuwait freedoms make austerity drive tricky for government."[106]

Opposition also appeared in Saudi Arabia. In 2016, one of Saudi Arabia's largest employers, the Binladin Group, was forced by low oil prices and a moratorium on government contracts to lay off over two-thirds of its Saudi employees and perhaps 77,000 foreign workers (many of whom were refusing to leave in protest over unpaid back salaries).[107] In protest, angry workers set fire to several buses in front of the Binladin offices in Mecca.[108] In April 2016, the king fired the water and electricity minister, criticizing him for rate increases and cuts in energy subsidies. In May, the oil minister of twenty years was fired amidst a cabinet reshuffle.

In January 2016, when the Bahraini government announced a significant increase in gas prices, several MPs in a decidedly pro-government body (since most Shi'a boycotted the 2014 parliamentary election) walked out of the Assembly in protest.[109] The session was adjourned amid shouting, and this was in a country where the government had demonstrated its willingness to crack down on opposition. While Qataris did not take to the streets, when citizens were asked in 2015 how they felt about paying more for their electricity and water usage, their responses were quite negative, with more than half the respondents saying they should pay nothing.[110]

The grievances that propelled the Arab uprisings, even in the GCC states, have not lessened. Unemployment, especially youth unemployment, remains quite high.[111] Throughout the GCC, most employed nationals work in the public sector and most private sector workers are expatriates, despite decades of trying to increase the national employment there. Anticipated cuts in public sector employment will thus fall most heavily on an already politicized youth population. Likewise, subsidy reductions will be felt most keenly by the middle class. Protecting the poorest from government actions is a goal, but largely aspirational. The very absence of an income tax makes it administratively more difficult for the government, both to identify accurately and to help the most vulnerable.

There is a potential environmental upside to the reforms. Reductions in oil and energy subsidies will likely reduce consumption. Insofar as governments are able reduce the expatriate population by increasing national employment (an effort tried with mixed success in the past), that would reduce the demand for imported food and water. But if the new arrangement is not accepted, the alternatives are deepened authoritarianism or a radical restructuring of the ruling bargain that allows for more participation.

Securing alliances

Several factors have led the once-reluctant GCC states to strengthen regional cooperation on security matters in recent years. These include the shared challenges of the Arab uprisings, the subsequent civil wars, the rise of ISIS, the growing power of Iran, the fear of waning US commitment to the region, and a concern with regime survival provoked by these changes. Saudi Arabia drove the trend toward greater GCC cooperation. What is different today is the greater, although still tempered, willingness of the smaller GCC states to follow Saudi Arabia's lead.

The force behind this change occurred when regime survival became the primary driver of foreign policy, evidenced by the GCC states' decision to form a military alliance with the distant monarchies of Morocco and Jordan, and even invite them into discussions (even if fruitless) on GCC membership.[112] Similarly, the fear of Iran flows less from a concern with its military threat than with its perceived ability to support dissidents abroad. Regime vulnerability was a driving force bringing the GCC monarchies together.

The fear that they were increasingly on their own also led the smaller GCC states to set aside their concern over Saudi domination and close ranks to work more toward closer regional integration. The central security alliance for the GCC states has historically been with the US. That alliance remains intact, but it has been tested in recent years: first, with the fall of Hosni Mubarak in Egypt, which indicated to the GCC that the US might not stand behind all its allies; and second, with the 2015 US–Iranian nuclear deal which prompted concerns over both rising Iranian power (and the occasional bellicosity of Iran's hardliners, notably its Revolutionary Guard, toward the US following the nuclear deal), and perceived weakening American commitment to the GCC.[113] This also hastened efforts to build pipelines bypassing the Strait of Hormuz.

Saudi Arabia historically led efforts to create a regional security structure. This began in 1981—following the Iranian Revolution and the onset of the Iran–Iraq War—in response to threats to regional security, but also to contain domestic opposition to the shared monarchical regimes, to which the Islamic Republic offered an initially attractive alternative. Although security cooperation was not clearly articulated in the GCC's founding documents, shortly after its establishment in 1982, the Peninsula Shield Force, based in Saudi Arabia, was created and became operational in 1984. Today it consists of roughly 10,000 personnel.[114] This force was insufficient to deal with a significant regional threat, such as Iraq's 1990 invasion of Kuwait, but it could be used effectively in the service of regime security, to subdue a domestic uprising, as occurred in Bahrain in 2011.

Saudi Arabia began pushing for a new regional security framework following the Arab uprising. It convinced the GCC states (except Kuwait) to sign the joint security agreement adopted at the December 2012 GCC Summit in Bahrain. The GCC secretary general, Abdullatif al-Zayani, said that "the security pact will empower each GCC country to take legal action, based on its own legislation against citizens or residents or organized groups that are linked to crime, terrorism, or dissension." Human Rights Watch expressed concerns that the agreement, which allowed governments to share citizen information at the discretion of the Interior Ministry, would provide GCC states with another mechanism to clamp down on dissent.[115]

The GCC intelligence services, ordinarily wary of cooperation, also began working together at unprecedented levels, engaging in intelligence-sharing about known dissidents, blocking visas for foreigners critical of GCC regimes, and arresting GCC nationals on each other's behalf. Kuwait, for example, arrested a social media activist for criticizing the Saudi-led war in Yemen and for insulting the Saudi royal family.[116] Bahrain likewise arrested a man for online insults of Bahraini troops in Yemen.

In 2013, at the summit meeting in Kuwait, the GCC also decided to establish a Unified Military Command with a substantially larger force, aiming for 100,000, with half provided by Saudi Arabia (where it would be headquartered). While this force faced several practical challenges, among them interoperability, it was another step toward working together on security issues.[117] In 2014, the Council announced the creation of a regional police force based in Abu Dhabi.[118]

Other joint efforts launched by Saudi Arabia were more problematic. When the Arab uprisings began, Saudi Arabia evidenced a new willingness to project itself militarily, as head of a Saudi-led GCC project, and to do so more or less independently from the US. The first such effort was the intervention in Bahrain in March 2011, where Saudi Arabia was joined by modest forces from the UAE under the umbrella of the Peninsula Shield Force. The next was the ill-fated Saudi intervention in Yemen, launched in 2015. While these efforts were not fully embraced by the GCC states, Qatari, Emirati, and Bahraini forces did join the fight in Yemen, while in December 2015 Kuwait also agreed to send troops.[119] In 2014, Qatar and the UAE introduced conscription, and Kuwait announced that it would reintroduce it in 2017.[120] Perhaps the strangest Saudi initiative came in December 2015, when Saudi Arabia announced that it had formed a coalition of thirty-four countries to fight terrorism, an announcement that came as a surprise to some named in the group.[121] Running a close second was the Saudi government's stated willingness to prepare to deploy ground troops to Syria to fight ISIS.[122]

Oil made the GCC states vulnerable to unwanted outside attention, causing them to band together. Dependence on imported food and water had a similar albeit less dramatic effect. As Fahad al-Attiyah, in charge of Qatar's food security, put it, "a country that has no water has to worry about what happens beyond its borders."[123] At the regional level, the GCC member states have worked cautiously together on issues related to resources—an initiative that goes back to 1986 with the UAE in the lead, creating the Abu Dhabi Global Environmental Data Initiative and working with global partners on a range of environmental issues.[124] In 2005, the GCC agreed to establish a regional environmental disaster and crisis center. For the Gulf states, cooperation on energy and climate change is, as Wehrey and Sokolsky point out, a relatively low-cost enterprise.[125] Gengler and Lambert argue that the new interest in cutting energy subsidies is linked in part to rising concerns over climate change.[126] While this concern may have originated in an international agenda, it has now been internalized by GCC governments. The United Nations has singled out the GCC states as the worst offenders in per capita energy usage. This international concern led to open questioning of Qatar's suitability as a venue for the 2012 UN Climate Change Conference ("COP 18").[127] The IMF has repeatedly called for the GCC states to end their inefficient energy subsidies. Perhaps the bright side of falling oil prices will be new efforts toward sustainability.

Conclusion

When the GCC's energy infrastructure was threatened by terrorism, governments created a discourse of securitization of resources to frame the problem—an intuitively straightforward response with far-reaching (and for many, unanticipated) consequences. With the onset of the Arab uprisings, and the fall in oil prices, Gulf monarchies developed new modes and instruments of authoritarianism to apply this discursive framework more broadly. While they have not gone as far as Egypt's government, which declared security a "religious necessity," mandating imams to invoke the "blessing of security" in their Friday prayers, the GCC governments have normalized the language of anti-terrorism to buttress their domestic control.[128] When the GCC was created, in 1982, it viewed security through a realist, state-centric frame, defined by military threats to the state; following the 2011 uprisings, regime, not state, survival became more important. The historical trade of political quiescence for wealth was replaced by political quiescence in exchange for security. However, the intervening fall in oil prices and concomitant cuts in services made this offer much less attractive.

While oil was the vehicle prompting the GCC to band together and create a discursive framework for challenging terrorism, this framework could be applied quite broadly. Saudi Arabia proved this in 2017 when it invoked terrorism, loosely, to place an embargo on Qatar, depriving it of access to the overland food and water. Qataris, having turned their environment over to the government, now found themselves vulnerable. This was reminiscent of what had happened earlier in Kuwait, as al-Nakib argues, where the government redeveloped the downtown through a series of masterplans, creating an unlivable city. Al-Nakib ends on an optimistic note, however, suggesting that with the government's failure, the oases of revitalization today come, as they had originally, not from the government but from Kuwaiti citizens. She takes us through a dialectical dance between government and opposition for control over the city's public spaces, with each move and countermove changing the physical space.[129] Finally, during the Arab uprisings, demonstrations were held in the space around the National Assembly. Perhaps, as in Kuwait, the discursive process of securitization will generate a more subtle and iterative process between governments and citizens.

4

GREENING GULF LANDSCAPES

ECONOMIC OPPORTUNITIES, SOCIAL TRADE-OFFS, AND SUSTAINABILITY CHALLENGES

Ali El-Keblawy

Environmental issues are complex in that they are both intra-connected and interconnected with social, political, and economic problems.[1] Water availability, in particular, is at the center of development: all economic and social processes, ultimately, depend on water for sustainability. The 2002 World Summit on Sustainable Development in Johannesburg highlighted the linkages between water management and agriculture and industrialization; health and pollution; and sustainability and power generation.[2] These "hydro-interconnections" are of an existential nature across the Arab world. Yet despite the grave scarcity of water in the Arabian Peninsula, very limited groundwater reserves, and extremely high evapotranspiration,[3] the Gulf Cooperation Council (GCC) states have for decades invested significantly in the "greening" of their landscapes. This chapter examines the process of greening landscapes from inception to completion.

The term "greening" is linked to the development of green party politics in Europe, increasingly impacting other countries around the world.[4] Greening, and environmental awareness more broadly, refers to new lifestyles as well as brand images.[5] Yet the concept is operationalized here as an active and integrated approach to the appreciation, stewardship, and management of living elements of social and ecological systems. Greening takes place in cities, towns, townships, and informal settlements in urban and pre-urban areas.[6] In my understanding, it covers any active attempt to improve sustainability, from recycling in households to the adoption of environmental philosophies in corporations.[7] In urban landscaping, Krusky et al. used the term "greening" to refer to the process of restoring landscaping and blighted property, promoting growth, and maintaining natural areas, such as parks, gardens, and residential yards.[8] Here, the term "greening" refers specifically to the sustainable use of natural resources to grow plants and vegetation in the Arab states of the Persian Gulf. The types of landscapes that are covered in this chapter include agricultural lands, cities, and degraded natural habitats.

Prior to the discovery of oil, *Khaleejis* lived in a harsh environment with an extremely hot and dry climate.[9] Their economic activities ranged from farming and fishing to pearl diving and camel grazing. The livelihoods and quotidian habits of *Khaleejis* were directly embedded in interactions with the natural resources in their surroundings. Traditionally, agriculture had only been possible in the form of cultivation of land near oases and in the mountains. Today, however, the GCC states have transformed large swaths of their deserts into rural production zones through intensive irrigation schemes and technologies. This transformation process required the devotion of enormous water resources to agricultural development, park landscaping, and nature reserves. However, given the harsh climate conditions in the Arabian Peninsula, landscaping practices are under scrutiny for their contested sustainability, particularly due to limited water resources. Irrigation in the GCC states depends heavily on groundwater that is non-renewable. In addition, over-pumping of groundwater may lead to environmental and political problems. Environmentally, it causes salinization and depletion of wells, and saline water intrusion.[10] Politically, the overuse of natural resources risks causing tensions within and between GCC societies using the same sources of water that are hydrogeologically connected. Over-pumping from one country may affect the productivity of aquifers in other countries. Groundwater pumping should, therefore, be practiced within a framework of an integrated groundwater policy in the region. In addition, some countries have constructed dams to store rainwater. Consequently, the new dams have reduced water flow to neighboring countries. To address the risk of conflict, the GCC states have cautiously started to work together on issues related to sustainability of natural resources. For example, they agreed to establish a regional environmental disaster and crisis center in 2005.[11] This is a start, but these efforts fall short given the magnitude of the challenge. The Gulf states urgently need to address the devastation of the region's ecosystems; ultimately, the well-being of all *Khaleejis* is dependent on moving away from intensive and uncontrolled exploitation of resources.

Elhadj reports that the GCC states rely heavily on freshwater for growing crops and greening desert landscapes.[12] He concludes that money and water can green a desert until either of them runs out. The main source of wealth in the GCC states is fossil fuels. As fuels and freshwater are nonrenewable resources, new strategies for food production and greening landscapes should be explored.

Most of the literature covers the problem of agricultural development and sustainability from the perspective of sustainable use and diversification of water resources.[13] Only limited studies examine technical solutions for reducing water demands of plants used in greening landscapes. In this chapter, the sustainability of greening landscapes in cities and deserts of Arab states of the Persian Gulf is examined; it explores ways to work with nature rather than against it, by suggesting an approach to conserve the very limited water resource while ensuring sustainability of current and new landscapes.

Many of the existing landscapes rely on the introduction of exotic crops or ornamental plants that cannot adapt to the local environment. Therefore, the GCC states are exerting ever greater efforts to diversify freshwater sources, such as desalinated seawater and treated sewage water, to sustain the huge water demands of these plants. The impracticality of using exotic and ornamental plants in landscaping shows the advantage of using native plants as a viable alternative. Native plants are well adapted to the local environment, and consume a fraction of the freshwater guzzled up by exotic plants. This chapter explores the advantage of using native plants, ways of restoring degraded landscapes, and using unconventional water sources, such as seawater, for irrigation. Moreover, using native plants in greening deserts and restoring degraded landscapes would help in reducing carbon dioxide emissions as part of the global mobilization against climate change.

Challenges for sustainable greening landscapes

Water shortage challenges

According to the United Nations World Water Assessment Programme, management of available water resources and provision of access to drinking water and sanitation are twenty-first-century global problems.[14] In addition, Arab countries, which cover about 10 percent of the Earth's surface, receive only 2 percent of the world's average annual precipitation, and contain as little as 0.3 percent of the global annual renewable water resources.[15] Insofar as the GCC states are concerned, they have arid and hyper-arid climates that make the problem of water scarcity even more severe.

The lack of renewable water resources is a critical hindrance to sustainable development in the GCC states, as it undermines national plans for human, industrial, and agricultural developments. The shortage of renewable water resources is becoming more pronounced due to the tremendous increase in human population over the last few decades. In addition, the quality of the available water is deteriorating. Water shortage is likely to approach crisis levels in these arid countries.[16]

Groundwater, which is the main water source in the GCC states, is severely and increasingly threatened. Groundwater reserves in the deep aquifers of the Arabian shelf are estimated at 2,330 billion cubic meters, while the average annual recharge rate is estimated at 2.7 billion cubic meters.[17] In Abu Dhabi, for example, groundwater extraction is twenty-five times faster than can be naturally replenished.[18] If the current, unsustainable approach to water use continues across the United Arab Emirates, organizations and individuals would face stark economic, social, and environmental impacts.[19] With the depletion of groundwater reserves and the increase in water demand, the use of desalinated water will increase significantly. However, desalination is far from a sustainable solution, and presents significant economic and environmental challenges in its own right.

One problem is overreliance from a strategic point of view. On average, the GCC states rely on desalination plants for 65 percent of their freshwater needs.[20] Saudi Arabia and the UAE are the two largest producers of desalinated water in the Middle East. Saudi Arabia's desalinated water alone exceeds 30 percent of global production, while all other GCC states are almost totally dependent on their desalting plants for freshwater supply.[21] A second issue is that desalination plants consume vast amounts of energy. Therefore, GCC states must increase electricity output, which is currently dependent on non-renewable fossil fuels. Consequently, a long-term solution could be developing nuclear power and solar energy. The GCC states need energy diversification to operate energy-intensive water desalination facilities effectively to meet urgent human and agricultural needs.

Oil and gas production constitute the major economic strength of the Arab states of the Persian Gulf. Hydrocarbons have underpinned expanding living standards and the use of scarce natural resources. In Saudi Arabia, for example, the total water consumption in 1990, 1992, 1997, 2000, 2004, and 2009 was reported to be approximately 27,000, 31,500, 18,500, 20,500, 20,200, and 18,500 million cubic meters, respectively.[22] Taking into consideration that the effective annual recharge of groundwater is 886 million cubic meters, the consumption ranges between twenty-one and thirty times the recharge of groundwater. At these rates, available resources will run out in the near future.[23] Similarly, in Abu Dhabi, groundwater withdrawals total over 3,400 million cubic meters per year, but natural groundwater renewal accounts for only 300 million cubic meters per year.[24] The Ground Water Assessment Project of Abu Dhabi estimated that 7 percent of groundwater in the Emirates is fresh, and 93 percent is brackish water. This is a serious problem as groundwater is depleting.[25] In addition to the current water shortage in GCC states, the future of water availability is predicted to decline as a result of global warming. Water balance modelling indicates that total internal renewable water resources, such as run-off and groundwater recharge, will decline significantly as a combined effect of the changes in precipitation and evapotranspiration.[26]

Despite its scarcity, water continues to be misused. New technologies help farmers to extract groundwater at rates greater than it recharges, which results in depleting aquifers to exhaustion. Groundwater depletion complicates the situation through creating other serious problems such as desertification and land degradation in dry areas. Another environmental problem that exaggerates the issue of groundwater depletion and desertification is climatic variation and change, which leads to depletion of the vegetative cover, and loss of biophysical and economic productivity through the exposure of soil surface to wind erosion and shifting sands. Although these are global problems, they are especially severe in the dry areas of the Arabian Peninsula.[27]

Water scarcity and greening landscape

Arab states of the Persian Gulf have transformed significant areas of their desert environment into green landscapes with enormous resources devoted to agricultural development, park landscaping, and natural reserves. For example, in Saudi Arabia, the cultivable land was estimated to be 52.7 million hectares. In 1971, the total cultivated land was less than 0.4 million hectares. In 1992, the cultivated land was expanded to approximately 1.62 million hectares.[28] Most of the cultivated lands were used for wheat, fodder crops, fruit, date, and vegetable production.[29]

The UAE has pursued "desert greening" more than the other GCC states. Emiratis recognized the importance of this concept to attract highly skilled expatriates and investors. Enormous desert lands of the UAE, particularly in Abu Dhabi, have been transformed into green landscapes. It has been reported that around 80 percent of water consumption in the UAE is used for different greening projects.[30] The Environmental Agency of Abu Dhabi has reported that nonrenewable groundwater constitutes 70 percent of the total water demand of the UAE.[31] Moreover, the lifetime expectancy of groundwater aquifers is estimated to be between sixteen and thirty-six years.[32]

It has been reported that the average rate of annual increase in cultivated land in the UAE reached 14.9 percent during the period 1985–2000: increases of 137 percent from 1985 to 1995, and 700 percent from 1995 to 2000. The actual area of cultivation increased from 68.3 thousand hectares in 1985, to 161.7 thousand hectares in 1995, and 546,500 hectares in 2000. By the year 2000, cultivated land had reached 6.5 percent of the total area of the country.[33] The area of artificial forest increased from 40,000 hectares in 1985, to 100,000 in 1995, and 300,000 hectares in 2000.[34] The Dubai municipality has greened 3 percent of the emirate's area, expecting to increase this figure further to 8 percent.[35]

Unsurprisingly, water consumption by the agricultural sector in the UAE increased from 950 million cubic meters per year in 1990 to 3,320 million cubic meters per year in 2011.[36] Around 709 million cubic meters of the annual water consumption is fulfilling the requirements of afforestation and other landscaping purposes, such as the street and park plantations.[37] This was mainly achieved by using groundwater aquifers, which covered at least 82 percent (above 579 million cubic meters) of the water requirements of the forestry sector. The remaining irrigation water requirements are covered by treated domestic wastewater, which contributes to irrigating around 130 million cubic meters (18.3 percent) of the irrigated lands.[38]

Future of green landscape depends on water resource diversity and management

Soaring urban populations and the associated increase in greening activities in the Arab states of the Persian Gulf, mainly in agricultural and urban landscaping, are underlining the urgency of developing more sustainable foundations for these economic and aesthetic gambits. Consequently, GCC governments have started to establish new strategies for reducing the dependence on groundwater, increasing water use efficiency in greening, and using alternative water resources, such as treated wastewater and seawater for landscaping. I highlight the current efforts in these strategies.

Improving water-use efficiency and management

Despite the essential and valuable nature of water, most GCC states continue to supply it for agricultural production at low, highly subsidized cost.[39] The Arabian Peninsula is exhausting strategic groundwater reserves to produce crops that could be imported at a lower price. In the 1990s, the Saudi government reduced subsidies for wheat production in order to reduce water consumption and sustain the limited freshwater resources. Consequently, productivity was reduced by 62 percent in two years, nearly from 5×10^6 t in 1994 to 1.9×10^6 t in 1996.[40] In addition, Saudi Arabia reduced its cultivated lands from 1.11 million hectares in 2005 to 1.07 million hectares in 2006.[41] The obvious incentive for farmers to restrict their use of water is reasonable water pricing. However, this concept is seriously challenged in many countries of the region and considered a political no-go. Farmers' pressure for subsidized inputs for agriculture makes it difficult for decision-makers to implement water pricing.[42] One alternative option, in the face of political resistance from below, is therefore trade.

Water in the global trading system is known as "virtual water." It is the water embedded in key water-intensive commodities such as wheat and animal fodders. The trade of "virtual water" through agricultural products and its appropriation through foreign direct investment in food production has emerged as a potential strategy for water-scarce countries seeking food security.[43] In Saudi Arabia, where domestic agricultural enterprise remains a state priority despite extreme water scarcity, a shift to overseas food production to meet domestic demand could have significant implications for water and energy use as well as local labor markets.[44] The international wheat trade—a crucial artery of the world economy—is a very effective and highly subsidized global trading system which operates to the advantage of water-scarce and food-deficit countries.[45] Consequently, economic systems, not the evidently inadequate hydrological systems, could solve the water supply problem for the region through importing water-intensive commodities. Virtual water has significant potential to minimize groundwater pumping for food production in arid environments. For example, the production of every cubic meter of a food commodity such as wheat requires a water input of about 1,000 cubic meters.[46]

Trade provides one way to deal with the crisis of permanent water scarcity, but cannot and should not be considered a panacea. Domestic changes in production and consumption patterns are inevitable. To maximize the benefit from the available limited water resources, every drop of water must be used carefully and in an economically sound way. As water demands differ significantly among various crops and types of irrigations, Saudi Arabia has tried switching to crops with less water demand, such as date palms, instead of water-intensive crops, such as wheat; one hectare of land for wheat production requires approximately 13,713 cubic meters of water, while one hectare of land for producing dates requires approximately 9,100 cubic meters of water.[47] Culture and economics sometimes complicate difficult measures to boost sustainability, but can also facilitate them. Palm trees are considered part of Emirati cultural heritage, but the UAE also has the largest number of palm trees in the world. It has been reported to have more than 40 million date palm trees and a minimum of 200 cultivars, 68 of which are most important commercially,[48] according to the most recent information from the UAE Ministry of Culture and Information. The Emirates might even be home to more than 100 million trees. Because palm trees are thus such a part of the sustainability challenge, the Abu Dhabi Food Control Authority (ADFCA) has initiated a big project for reducing the use of water irrigation for palm trees. With an estimated cost of $133 million, the initiative seeks to modernize irrigation systems in all the farms in the western region of Abu Dhabi through the Farmers Service Center. A total of 2,333 out of 8,000 farms have been provided with modern irrigation networks that are expected to help reduce water irrigation consumption by 50 percent in some farms.[49]

The Emirati efforts do not just stop at palm trees. Grain production requires significantly less water than meat production: 1 kg of grain requires 1,000–2,000 liters of water, but the production of 1 kg of meat requires 4,000–15,000 liters of water.[50] In this context, the government of Abu Dhabi had reduced the number of farms producing Rhodes grass, a fodder that consumes too much water, from 16,000 farms to about 10,500 farms by the end of 2011. Simply put, the huge amount of water that is currently used by fodder plants could be saved by importing meats. To sustain the groundwater use, the government of Abu Dhabi is working on increasing agricultural output, while significantly reducing water use and protecting the important cultural aspect of agriculture. In addition, Environment Agency—Abu Dhabi (EAD) has enacted a law that regulates access to groundwater by licensing the drilling of groundwater wells, as well as underlining that the drilling of new wells without a permit would be illegal. Despite these regulations, the practice of illegal drilling continues in Abu Dhabi.[51]

Whether in the Emirates, Saudi Arabia, or elsewhere, these initiatives are important but insufficient. Hundreds of billions of cubic meters of rainwater in the dry environments are lost every year. This loss occurs mainly through lack of proper management for rainfall water. The development of water harvesting systems in the dry areas can save substantial amounts of water that is otherwise lost. ICARDA has demonstrated that over 50 percent of this water can be captured and utilized for agricultural production if integrated on-farm water-use techniques are implemented properly.[52]

Investment in new technologies that improve the use of available water must become a priority for improving water-use efficiency. It has been claimed that existing technologies of irrigation may double the amount of food produced from present levels of water use.[53] The water productivity of the available resources could be improved through using proper harvesting techniques. It is crucial to implement and transfer these technologies. There is a need to provide farmers with economic alternatives to the practices that lead to wastage of water, and with incentives that can bring about the needed change.[54]

Using treated wastewater

Treated wastewater could be a good substitute for freshwater in agriculture and industry. The present gap between water demands and available water resources has led GCC states to consider domestic wastewater as an integral part of their water resources. At present, GCC states recycle no more than 35 percent of their total treated wastewater, which contributes 2.2 percent of their total water supply. This water is used mainly for landscaping, fodder crop irrigation, and some industrial uses. The main handicaps for reuse expansion are both social (psychological repugnance and religion) and technical (microbiological pollutants, potential heavy metals accumulation in irrigated soil, and industrial waste mixing). However, major plans for water recycling exist in most of these countries.[55]

Planned water reuse for agriculture and irrigation is emerging as an established water management practice in several water-stressed countries. For example, urban areas of Abu Dhabi generate roughly 550,000 cubic meters of wastewater daily, which are treated in twenty wastewater treatment plants. All facilities are equipped to treat effluent for reuse in irrigation. There is an expected increase in urban wastewater associated with the increase in urban growth in populations. To accommodate increased wastewater flows, the Abu Dhabi government has embarked on the Strategic Tunnel Enhancement Program, which will construct a new 40-kilometer wastewater tunnel. This could further increase the opportunities for reusing wastewater in agriculture.[56]

Use of reclaimed water is an attractive option and entails a number of benefits, including reduction of surface water pollution commonly resulting when wastewater is discharged into the environment. In addition, nutrients in treated wastewater can reduce the need for applying chemical fertilizers, thereby reducing costs and potentially adverse effects associated with fertilizers. However, there are also risks associated with water reuse that warrant specific attention in agriculture. These hazards impact on the health of agricultural workers who are exposed to untreated or inadequately treated wastewater during irrigation; and on the health of consumers of agricultural goods produced from this low-quality wastewater. Chemical pollutants found in inadequately treated wastewater could also contaminate soils, plants, and ground and surface water.[57]

Natural and anthropogenic environmental challenges for landscape greening

Several environmental and anthropogenic environmental factors have hindered the recovery of natural vegetation and success of artificial greening. Among the anthropogenic factors are livestock grazing; off-road vehicle use; urbanization and its attendant, oil exploration; production activities; and introduction of exotic species. In this section, I outline the main environmental factors that hinder natural vegetation recovery and lead to desertification, which make landscape greening a challenging process.

All GCC states fall within the boundaries of arid or hyper-arid regions, where land degradation, primarily desertification, reduces the ability to green landscapes. Drought, which means that water precipitation is less than water evaporation, happens when rainfall is less than average and/or groundwater resources are depleted. Drought alters plant community composition and habitat structure. An analysis of 9,500 sites across the central United States confirmed the tremendous importance of water availability to plant productivity.[58] As rainfall is the most important factor that affects plant productivity in arid deserts, severe drought substantially reduces plant cover and productivity and consequently the opportunity for landscape greening.[59] The frequency and magnitude of extreme drought will increase as the global climate changes. Regular, severe droughts will cause a decline in plant water potential, which alters their functions to increase the efficiencies of water uptake and utilization.[60]

Agriculturally productive lands in the Arab world are fragile systems prone to degradation and highly vulnerable to desertification.[61] Desertification, as defined in the UN Convention to Combat Desertification, is "land degradation in arid, semi-arid and dry sub-humid areas resulting from various factors, including climatic variation and human activities."[62] Several reports have considered desertification as one of the main types of land degradation in the GCC states. It threatens environmental conservation efforts and the sustainability of rural livelihoods. Typically, desertification of sandy areas, driven by wind erosion, results in the dominance of a few shrubs and grasses, while most of the land is devoid of vegetation.[63] Deterioration in soil and plant cover has adversely affected nearly 50 percent of the land areas, which is mainly the result of human mismanagement of cultivated and natural rangelands.[64] Desertification reduces the ability of the land to support life, thus affecting wildlife, domestic animals, agricultural crops, and humans. It has been suggested that desertification can be an irreversible process when the degraded state becomes stable.[65]

Soil erosion, salinization, and desertification could result in loss of soil fertility, soil compaction (i.e. soil porosity is reduced), and soil crusting, which eventually would lead to vegetation deterioration. Urbanization, mining, and recreation also have adverse effects on rangelands, dry farming, and irrigated lands. The reduction in plant cover that accompanies desertification accelerates soil erosion by wind and water. For example, South Africa is losing approximately 300–400 million tons of topsoil every year. The deterioration in vegetation cover and soil layers increases the impact of rainfall run-off on soil properties and their ability to store water.[66] Combating desertification can be achieved successfully by using biotic techniques, but the cost in the GCC context would be high, and success is not always guaranteed. For example, the harsh environmental conditions in the Arab states of the Gulf, especially temperatures that can reach up to 50 degrees Celsius, hinder the applications of several beneficial soil microbes.

Natural processes interact with human activities to wreak havoc on the natural ecosystems of dry lands and consequently retard their ability to recover the natural vegetation. Key anthropogenic factors include conversion of land for agricultural use, the expansion of forestry plantations, habitat fragmentation (brought about by urbanization and road construction), the ceaseless extraction of groundwater, the increase in soil salinity, encouraging overgrazing, and the spread of damping pollutants and solid wastes.

Many researchers have reported that overgrazing, in particular, is considered a major impediment to dry land sustainability and the maintenance of biodiversity.[67] Most of the studies on the GCC states indicate that grazing can affect plant community composition and structure, and consequently alter natural landscape. Under long-term intensive grazing, palatable species are replaced by unpalatable plants. For example, in the UAE, overgrazing, mainly by camels, resulted in a significant reduction in the abundance and cover of the palatable *Stipagrostis plumosa*, *Crotalaria aegyptiaca*, *Indigofera articulata*, *Pennisetum divisum*, and *Panicum turgidum*, but a significant increase in the unpalatable *Haloxylon salicornicum*.[68] Similarly, in the arid rangelands of Saudi Arabia, overgrazing caused a reduction of palatable forage plants such as *Rhanterium epapposum*, *Ochradenus baccatus*, and *Lasiurus hirsutus*.[69] Historically, small antelopes grazing in the UAE had resulted in the dominance of many palatable plants, such as *Limeum arabicum*, *Dipterygium glaucum*, *Moltkiopsis ciliata*, *Crotalaria aegyptiaca*, and *Heliotropium digynum*. However, camel grazing caused the dominance of unpalatable plants such as *Calotropis procera*, *Haloxylon salicornicum*, *Heliotropium kotschyi*, and *Aerva javanica*.[70] Sustainable use of rangelands will keep a balance between nature and humankind. By achieving this balance, life and development of both present and future generations could be maintained without deteriorating natural rangelands.[71]

Grazing effects can produce a significant change in vegetation composition and productivity, which is primarily augmented directly by water stress and secondarily by additional factors that accompany drought.[72] In a study conducted in the Dubai Desert Conservation Reserve (DDCR), irrigation enhanced the establishment and growth of twenty-two species in the absence of grazing; none of these plants were recorded in the irrigated grazed sites. Ten of these species are chamaephytes, three hemicryptophytes, three phanerophytes, and six therophytes. Most of these species are palatable for animals. The most important palatable plants that were regenerated in the irrigated enclosures are *Tribulus pentandrus*, *I. intricata*, *Limeum arabicum*, *Haloxylon salicornicum*, *Stipagrostis plumosa*, *Eremobium aegyptiacum*, *Monsonia nivea*, *Pennisetum divisum*, *Heliotropium digynum*, *Chloris virgata*, and *Rhanterium epapposum*.[73]

In Arab tradition, rangelands were managed through a system called *Hima*, in which a reserved pasture is set aside seasonally to allow plant regeneration.

According to *Hima*, the animals are allowed to graze the rangelands in a sequential system of every other or every two to three years. *Hima* has contributed positively to saving and protecting natural resources, rangelands, and forests for over 5,000 years.[74] However, no country is applying the *Hima* system now as a tool for the management of the grazing system. Consequently, a management system based on the calculation of carrying capacity (i.e. proper stoking rate) should be established in the different fragile, arid rangelands of the Arab countries, where rainfall is very scarce and temporally and spatially unpredictable.

Artificial forest in the UAE: a case study for greening landscape

Forests, artificial or natural, are believed to be appropriate sites to conserve local flora, especially in desert sandy areas where biodiversity is suffering. Commercial afforestation of natural ecosystems is increasing worldwide,[75] not least because forests can offer several valuable ecological services. Afforestation in arid and semi-arid regions has been considered a method for ecological revival in terms of vegetation enrichment and soil amelioration.[76] In addition, afforestation in different sandy areas can control sand movement.[77] Furthermore, large-scale afforestation in arid and semi-arid land is one of the most promising countermeasures for fixation of carbon dioxide, which is chiefly responsible for the global warming problem.[78] Unfortunately, improper management of artificial forests can also lead to serious irreversible damage to the local environment, because the abundance of understory plants is sensitive to changes in management treatments.[79]

The UAE has developed many programs to promote afforestation of large areas of the deserts. The main goals of afforestation in the UAE have been to develop the wildlife habitats and reduce the impact of sandstorms. Several newly introduced trees and a few native trees have been used in an afforestation program to combat desertification, reduce run-off and soil erosion, and provide several other biological and ecological services. El-Keblawy and Ksiksi evaluated the role of artificial forests in the UAE in protecting floral diversity.[80] They assessed the effect of forest trees on species diversity and abundance of perennial plants in six forests. They also assessed the impact of artificial forests on physical and chemical characters of the soil. Their results showed that artificial forests helped in vegetation enrichment and improvement of soil fertility. Forests in the UAE provided a refuge for desert birds and mammals during the extremely hot days of summer. Many of these birds use forest trees as nest sites. However, El-Keblawy and Ksiksi also found a significant reduction in species diversity and abundance of forests planted with exotic trees, compared with native trees.[81] This suggests that native trees should be used instead of exotic trees.

El-Keblawy and Ksiksi reported a significant increase in the levels of salinity and total sodium ions in the soils, which indicates a deterioration of the quality of irrigation water and soils.[82] The high levels of salinity in irrigated waters and groundwater usage are issues that need to be addressed through an integrated and strategic research and development program. As a management option to enhance plant diversity in artificial forests in the UAE, El-Keblawy and Ksiksi suggested reducing crown size through timely pruning.[83] The reduced parts from plants will save a great amount of water lost in evapotranspiration, especially during very hot summer days. In addition, the cut parts could be used as forage for some animals, especially wildlife species that represent an important part of the UAE heritage, namely Arabian oryx and gazelle.

One of the major serious outcomes of the afforestation program in the UAE is the introduction of *Prosopis juliflora* (honey mesquite). During the last three decades, this species has escaped the forests and is currently considered a weed. In different habitats of the UAE, *P. juliflora* is highly aggressive and coppices so well that it crowds out native vegetation.[84] The high competitive ability of *P. juliflora* is threatening some important native plants of the UAE, including the important *Prosopis cineraria*. El-Keblawy has assessed the impact of *P. juliflora* on the associated flora in the natural habitats of the UAE and concluded that this exotic tree significantly reduces the evenness, richness, and density of the associated plants beneath, compared with open places beyond their canopies.[85] In addition, many farms, especially in the northern Emirates, have been invaded by *P. juliflora* and already ruined. Furthermore, the very deep root system of *P. juliflora* extracts the precious limited water resources in the UAE (Figure 4.1).

P. juliflora is growing densely even in residential areas, which make it a potential source of respiratory and skin allergies.[86] Allergy to *P. juliflora* pollen antigen has been reported from several countries, including the US, Mexico, Saudi Arabia, South Africa, India, Kuwait, and UAE.[87] Bener et al. report that 45 percent of the patients they tested in the UAE were sensitive to this species.[88] *P. juliflora* is known to flower most of the year, but with two main seasons, each of three to four months.[89] This evidence makes *P. juliflora* a potential contributor to allergic diseases in most of the Arab states of the Gulf in which it has been introduced.

Figure 4.1: Satellite images show the invasion of *P. juliflora* across sand dunes next to Sharjah Airport, UAE. Without the invasion of *P. juliflora*, these sandy dunes are almost barren of vegetation.

Opportunities for future sustainable greening in the GCC states

Any green landscape requires good soils and water supply to be sustainable. In the Gulf, there is little land available of high quality. Using lower-quality lands for green landscaping could result in several environmental problems. In addition, high temperature, water scarcity, and repeated drought are already challenging landscape greening. Consequently, specific kinds of plants should be selected to withstand such a complicated set of harsh conditions. Those plants could be genetically modified crops or native plants that have evolved to grow and tolerate all the current environmental challenges facing the GCC states.

Genetically engineered crops

There are two ways of increasing global food supply: using more land and raising yields on existing farms. The major food crops require high-quality soils and enough water supply to achieve high yields. Introducing lower-quality lands for food production is usually associated with more environmental problems, such as desertification, salinization, and exhaustion of aquifers that have been used for irrigation.[90] Consequently, increasing the yield on the currently available area suitable for agriculture could be a more feasible option for reducing the problems associated with using low-quality soils, which usually lead to environmental and biodiversity degradation. This has happened several times through several green revolutions, which were achieved largely through improved genetics through conventional breeding, coupled with enhanced agronomy and crop protection.[91]

Plants usually resist abiotic stress reactions by the production of stress-related osmolytes like sugars, sugar alcohols, amino acids, and certain proteins, such as antifreeze proteins.[92] Genetic engineers can genetically modify plants by triggering genes for the production of one or more of these compounds that show increased tolerance for environmental stresses.[93] Abiotic stresses that plants should resist under desert conditions of the Gulf include heat, drought, salinity, and intense light. These environmental stresses result in the destruction and deterioration of crop plants, which leads to low crop productivity.[94]

The harsh conditions of the Arabian Peninsula make plants more adapted to high temperatures, salinity, and drought. Over the centuries, these extreme conditions have applied stringent evolutionary selection pressures, resulting in a unique biodiversity and breathtaking genetic variation. Identifying and isolating genes of tolerance of salinity, heat, drought, and high light intensities could help in transferring such genes to some economic crops that could be grown in the deserts of the GCC states.

Some of the most tractable methods to improve photosynthetic efficiency (and consequently crop yield) include systems/synthetic biology, genetic engineering, and computational modelling strategies as part of a new green revolution. In the last four decades, genetic engineering techniques have offered the prospect of directly altering the genomes of higher plants to change their metabolism and improve growth and yield under adverse environmental conditions, in the service of human requirements.[95] For example, genetic modification can decrease the water requirement of several crops by selecting traits that could increase the rate of photosynthesis and depth of root structure, as well as decrease the rate at which water is lost through transpiration.[96] Interestingly, genetic engineers can select for certain phenotypes, such as drought, salinity, and heat tolerance stresses without having to undergo selective breeding within a population. Consequently, genetic engineering takes less time than selective breeding, and in some cases is able to carry out genetic changes that would not occur naturally.[97]

For decades now, the safety of genetically modified organisms has been an intensely controversial topic, debated around the world. Published results are contradictory, due to the range of different research methods employed, the inadequacy of available procedures, and differences in the analysis and interpretation of data.[98] In many of these studies, no effects on human health have been detected after the general population has consumed genetically modified foods. Indeed, genetically modified foods currently available on the international markets have passed safety assessments and are not likely to present risks to human health. To convince the local society and decision-makers in the GCC states that genetically modified food is safe to eat, national authorities need to execute rigorous case-by-case assessment of each modified crop to determine the safety of each. If genetically modified foods are broadly cultivated in high-quality soils that are suitable for growing conventional non-genetically modified crops, it would be more acceptable to grow such genetically modified crops in hyper-arid desert lands that could not be sown with any conventional crops.

Seawatered landscaping

Several halophytes have evolved naturally under the harsh environmental conditions of the Gulf. These plants are hardy, as they have adapted to the local harsh conditions.[99] In the GCC states, halophytes grow in a wide variety of saline habitats such as coastal regions, salt marshes and mudflats, inland deserts, salt flats, and steppes. They play an important role in protecting habitats and maintaining ecological stability, and also have huge potential to aid agricultural development and habitat restoration in areas affected by salinity.[100] In order to survive in saline habitats, halophytes have evolved a range of adaptations to tolerate salinity effects. Therefore, halophytes could be perfectly suitable for greening the coastal zone and could be irrigated directly with seawater.[101]

Sea-watered agriculture is defined as growing salt-tolerant crops on land using water pumped from the ocean for irrigation. Glenn et al. have tested the feasibility of sea-watered agriculture and found that it works well in the sandy soils of the coastal desert habitats.[102] In 1978, Glenn and his colleagues conducted trials on the most promising halophytes grown in the coastal desert at Puerto Peñasco on the western coast of Mexico. They irrigated the plants daily by flooding the fields with high-saline, forty parts per trillion, seawater from the Gulf of California, continuously watering the same sandy fields with seawater for over ten years. Strikingly, this did not affect the soil quality. In addition, plants grew well as there was no build-up of water or salts in their root zone.[103] In their review on sea-watered agriculture, Glenn et al. indicate that halophytes can maintain high productivity of useful agricultural products up to a root-zone salinity of 70 grams/liter TDS, double the salinity of seawater.[104] To achieve this result, frequent irrigation was required to keep the shallow-root zone at field capacity and to ensure continuous leaching to prevent accumulation of salts.[105]

It has been reported that many halophytes in several parts of the world could be used as ornamental plants in urban landscaping because of their beautiful flowers and several leaf forms and growth patterns. For example, 172 halophytic plants (thirty-four species from Chenopodiaceae), which naturally grow in the Mediterranean area, were categorized as potential ornamental plants.[106] Similarly, Khan and Qaiser have identified thirty-four halophytes of Pakistan as potential ornamental plants.[107] In their review of the potential halophytes that could be used in native landscape, Khan et al. reported several other examples in different places around the world.[108] For example, *Paspalum vaginatum* and *Sporobolus virginicus* were considered as suitable candidates for lawns and golf courses. Other examples of potential halophytes in landscape include *Aster tripolium*, *Limoniastrum monopetalum*, *Batis maritima*, *Tamarix nilotica*, *Tamarix amnicola*, *Cistanche fistulosum*, and *Noronhia emarginata*.[109]

In the GCC states, large numbers of terrestrial halophytes grow and complete their life cycles exclusively on seawater or in hyper-saline salt marshes. For example, Boer and Al Hajiri have identified a total of forty-nine plant species as halophytes in Qatar, including twenty-nine as tolerant or highly tolerant to salinity.[110] Similarly, in a survey conducted in the coastal zone of Abu Dhabi, Boer and Gliddon recorded twenty-two halophytes; nine of them are tolerant to inundation by seawater.[111] Many of the halophytes of the Arabian Peninsula are growing even in hyper-saline Sabkha, salt marshes, where salinity reaches several folds greater than the seawater salinity.[112] Yet, these plants are growing in appealing shapes, colors, and textures and could potentially be used in landscaping the coastal zones of the urban regions.

Using native desert plants in urban landscaping

The expansion of urbanization and the demand for green spaces in GCC cities increase the pressures on already stressed water resources.[113] In addition, GCC states prefer to use exotic species as landscape plants, selected and cultivated for their aesthetic value. However, such exotic ornamental plants have not developed life-history traits that help them cope with the prevailing environmental conditions of countries of introduction. The use of native desert plants in landscaping GCC cities could, therefore, be a feasible approach for sustaining the limited water resources. In addition, Bill Adams reported four aesthetic reasons to landscape with native plants.[114] These are uniqueness, authenticity, subtlety and refinement, and historical context.

The types of exotic plants that are commonly used to landscape the cities of the Middle East are almost always the same set of species and varieties. In most cases, plant nurseries and the plant sections of home-improvement stores are not organized by region of origin of the plants they sell. In fact, the plant labels rarely mention the native region of the plant. As a result, landscapes in urbanized areas across the region look much alike. In contrast to landscapes of exotic plants, native plants create unique landscapes.

The aesthetic argument is important, but the environmental case for indigenous plants is even stronger. Most introduced ornamental plants rely heavily on unsustainable inputs of synthetic fertilizers, toxic pesticides, fossil fuels, and exotic plants. They are not adapted to the local environment and, consequently, lose great amounts of water through evapotranspiration. In addition, they regularly need maintenance and are at risk of infection by local pests. By contrast, native plants do not require much water, pesticides, herbicides, or mechanical maintenance. Hence, using native plants would contribute to cities' sustainability efforts. Moreover, there is no specific infrastructure needed for growing native plants. Yet, there is a need to build the capacity of horticulturalists and architects for growing and using native plants in their design.

The greatest challenge facing the use of native plants in landscaping is their propagation; it is not easy to propagate native desert plants. This is largely because of a lack of propagation information for most of them.[115] In addition, finding seeds or other propagules, such as vegetative cuts, is not an easy process. In the GCC states, little information is available for most of the native plants on time of fruiting, ways of fruit/seed collection and cleaning, seed dormancy, germination requirements, seed viability and longevity, and propagation under nursery and urban conditions. Desert plants could respond positively or negatively to irrigation water, but this could depend on the kind of plant species, amount of irrigation, irrigation system (drippers, sprinklers, etc.), substrate (soil) type, and time (season) of irrigation. We simply do not know enough at present.

The author had the chance to secure a sizeable fund from Qatar Foundation for achieving innovative approaches that could reduce the demand for freshwater resources in urban landscapes in the GCC states. A total of ninety-six plant species were propagated under shade-house conditions (eighty-five propagated from seedlings and eleven from vegetative cuts). Many of the plants grew well under wet conditions, compared to dry conditions, but the reverse was true for other plants. According to the amount of water used for the ornamental plants with regular irrigating, native plants saved 70 percent of the water used by ornamental plants, even in the wet treatment.[116]

Greater knowledge of indigenous plants and their benefits, as well as the connection between ecological sustainability and cultural revival, are both critically needed. The concept of "xeriscaping" needs to gain traction among *Khaleeji* societies. A "xeriscape" integrates garden design, irrigation methods, and plant selection for defining the potential native plants that could be used for this purpose. Historically, *Khaleejis* maintained deep links to nature, especially native plants. Previous generations used native plants as sources for food, medicine, biofuel, etc. *Khaleejis* from different ages used to spend much of their time, especially during holidays and weekends, in desert and coastal habitats. Bringing native plants to cities will help in conserving this part of the natural as well as cultural heritage. This will also increase the awareness of new generations about the interconnections that are at the heart of sustainability.

In order to spread the concept of xeriscaping, it is important to create some demonstration sites landscaped with native plants. This could convince the general public, as well as those specifically active in the agricultural sector, of the importance of using native landscaping. Additionally, it is important to provide horticulturalists and architects with practical training about the propagation of potential native plants under nursery and urban site conditions.

Providing information about native plant propagation in nurseries and in urban habitats would encourage the development of private and governmental nurseries for the production of native plants. Development of such information would also encourage people to grow native desert plants in their backyards and around their homes. Consequently, there is a real need for a professional guide which could illustrate the different steps for dealing with native plants from seed collection, germination and breaking dormancy, growing under nursery and open site conditions, and their maintenance and water requirements. Furthermore, horticulturalists and architects should be provided with practical training about the propagation of potential native plants under nursery and urban site conditions. As extensive collections of native plant seeds from natural habitats might threaten their existence, it is important to establish maternal sites for the mass production of seeds from different plant species under controlled environmental conditions. This will make seeds of the different species available for any agency or person interested in using native plants in urban landscapes.

Conclusion

The landscape and natural vegetation of the deserts of the Arabian Peninsula have been significantly altered during the last fifty years by a variety of factors. Many of the Arab states of the Persian Gulf have put too much effort into greening their cities, agricultural lands, and deteriorated natural habitats. As I have argued in this chapter, many such initiatives are misdirected and sometimes even counterproductive. Most of the greening programs are carried out with exotic plants that are not adapted to the local environment and consume too much scarce freshwater. Such activities represent real dangers for local habitats that have very harsh weather and extremely limited storage of groundwater. Historically, most greening, especially in deserts, failed and proved to be unsustainable. Such failures are directly attributable to the deterioration of natural resources and simplistic notions of greening. For example, over-pumping of limited, nonrenewable groundwater led to drying and salinization of most of the wells. In addition, irrigation from salinated wells led to the accumulation of salts in the soils, which eventually led to their desertification and loss of productivity.

During the last few years, the GCC states have begun to recognize the importance of working with, not against, the harsh conditions of the local environment to sustain their green landscapes. Several projects, many of them in the UAE, have started using native plants, instead of exotics, to reduce the demand for freshwater and to sustain the cities and artificial forests. Using native plants in landscaping cities provides a beautiful, hardy, drought-resistant, low-maintenance landscape while benefiting the environment. As native landscaping does not need permanent irrigation, and requires little or no pesticides and fertilizers, their use should sustain the growing GCC cities. In addition, little attention has been paid to salt-tolerant plants (halophytes) as fodder and biofuel crops. More research should be directed toward incorporating halophytes in greening the cities, especially in regions that border the coasts, as they could help conserve scarce freshwater resources. There should be a collaborative regional research program between the GCC states to intensify the research that could produce genetically modified crops. Such engineered crops could tolerate the great abiotic stresses of the regional environment, such as salinity, heat, drought, and high light intensities. The key point in sustaining the local habitats and cities is to use and mimic local plants. As this chapter has consistently argued, we should learn from local plants how to design crops that can survive and reproduce under harsh weather conditions and which could probably be irrigated with seawater. Local plants in the Gulf have unique genes, even if their potential remains underexplored. This combination of genetic diversity and ecological resilience should be considered as the region's real future wealth, rather than depleting hydrocarbon reserves.

5

BURNING SOMALIA'S FUTURE

THE ILLEGAL CHARCOAL TRADE BETWEEN THE HORN OF AFRICA AND THE GULF

Ilya Gridneff

The February 2017 presidential election of Mohamed Abdullahi Mohamed, or "Farmaajo" as he is commonly known, sparked wild jubilation across Somalia. But despite the nation's optimism about the new leader and a peaceful handover of power, Somalia remains in the midst of a complex and protracted transition more than five years since the Somali Federal Government (SFG) was first formed in August 2012.

While there has been some progress toward establishing effective political and security institutions, formal governance structures and the rule of law remain absent in a weak state struggling to legitimize itself in and outside the capital Mogadishu. Powerful interests, some of them in government, militate against an end to the violence and the construction of an open, well-regulated economic system that could offer prosperity to Somalia's estimated 10–12 million citizens.[1]

Figure 5.1: The charcoal trade between the Horn and the Gulf

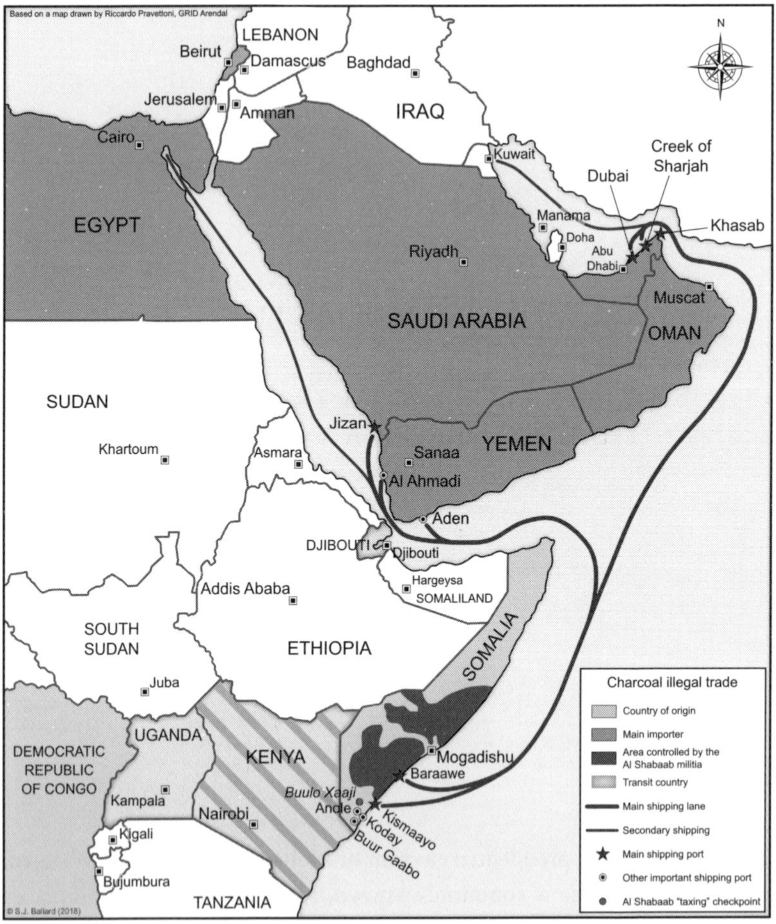

Source: Riccardo Pravettoni, GRID Arendal, 2014.

Somalia's war economy has made the illicit charcoal trade one of the country's few lucrative revenue streams. This natural resource, albeit destructive and illegal to export, funds a collection of security forces and earns a handful of individuals the needed revenue to manage their own fragile and tumultuous political environment. The trade, in an incredibly complex and evolving state, illustrates the status quo for Somalia. It symbolizes a nation mired in uneven or limited development while retarded by extreme violence and malfeasance. The industry's negative consequences, from its environmental impact to funding the resurgent jihadist group Al-Shabaab, undermines the SFG's rhetoric of development and ignores broader governance issues.

This chapter argues that the charcoal trade exposes Somalia's political economy as a driver of persistent conflict fueled by competing local, regional, and international interests. Of particular note is the tendency of Gulf Cooperation Council (GCC) states to buy Somalia's charcoal, whether licit or illicit, for domestic use: such commercial activity contributes to the country's regressive imbalances. At the same time, GCC states jockeying for geopolitical influence across the Horn of Africa increase the uneven spread of resources and access to finance for Somalia's leaders. This process has fed the political elite's insatiable appetite for personal patronage, and has produced a nexus of competing rivalries that further destabilizes Somalia and the broader Red Sea region.

While Alex de Waal posits that Somalia's collapse began with the thawing of the Cold War and a decreased strategic importance, the catastrophe really moved into higher gear with the fall of Somalia's military dictatorship, the regime of Siyaad Barre (1969–91).[2] Subsequent decades of civil war and foreign intervention have placed Somalia at the bottom of all United Nations indicator tables and ranked it as one of the world's most corrupt countries.[3] In view of this instability, Somalia faces immense international scrutiny due, in part, to Western interests pursuing the post-9/11 paradigm of a Global War on Terror. Since 1991, and with fears increasing after 9/11 that Somalia is a so-called failed state, the international community has spent an estimated $55 billion in aid and assistance.[4] These international efforts have repeatedly failed to achieve their objectives or have caused unforeseen consequences—often due to Somali fears that they might resuscitate a repressive and abusive state apparatus which they rejected in 1991.[5] Furthermore, Somalia's lack of cohesion and development is at the same time exploited by external forces pursuing their own agendas for regional or broader aspirations. GCC states, Turkey, and interventionist neighbors like Ethiopia and Kenya are all supporting and funding differing Somali groups or individuals in pursuit of their own commercial, religious, or political agendas. While the Western-led "international community" urges Somali leaders to work together for the common good, proxy wars and regional feuds play out in a scramble for resources, influence, and prestige.

This chapter will study the use of one natural resource, charcoal, and its trans-boundary trade as a vehicle to illustrate how Somalia's ties to the GCC states—and the broader Islamic or Arab world—are being strengthened.

I contend that this growing proximity is both offering beneficial forms of assistance and support, as well as proving to be a factor for destabilization at a time when Somalia is becoming of increasing strategic concern for Western and emerging powers.

Charcoal: Africa's power and fuel

Wood charcoal production is a dirty, low-energy resource relied upon by millions of East Africans, and hundreds of millions across the continent. More than 80 percent of urban households in sub-Saharan Africa use charcoal as their main cooking and heating source.[6] It is a common sight throughout African cities, regularly sold by the roadside or in rural markets as bundles of black charcoal bricks. Known to burn hotter than firewood, it is also lighter to carry and easier to store. The total quantity of this ubiquitous natural energy source used in Africa in 2012 was estimated to have been approximately 30.6 million tons, valued at $9.2–$24.5 billion annually that year.[7] Charcoal is not just for Africa's domestic use. It is also used in less-developed Western economies that have not updated their infrastructure to accommodate energy sources like gas or solar. In Europe, more than 800,000 tons of charcoal is used every year, with an estimated 40 percent imported from Africa. Nigeria, Africa's largest economy and population, supplies approximately a quarter of all charcoal to Europe.[8]

While it is a lucrative international trade, African charcoal is essentially a fuel for poor people made by poor people. The process usually begins with an uneducated, rural population that produces charcoal in small-scale, artisan-style networks. The preferred tree for charcoal production in East Africa is *Acacia bussei*. However, other types of *Acacia*, like *Senegalia*, *Acacia tortilis*, and *Terminalia* are also commonly used. As the trees are locally sourced, charcoal is usually the community's main form of income. It has become a lifeline for the people it employs directly or indirectly across the continent and Somalia.

The production process follows several simple methods. Wood is collected and then burned in an open fire. The charred remains are used as small charcoal bricks to be sold with the buyer reigniting it for cooking, warmth, or light. Another method employs kilns constructed from mud or dirt that restrict the supply of air during carbonization to make a better charcoal product. Producers simply dig a hole in the ground and put the wood inside the large kiln-like pit. Once burned down, the remains are bagged and distributed in villages, urban centers, or trucked to major cities. In Somalia, the timber is usually covered with iron sheets, buried in sand, and left to burn slowly for a week.[9]

Charcoal's popularity is due to it being such a convenient and easily accessible fuel. At the same time, it must be noted that it is also an ineffective and wasteful energy source. From the chopped tree's wood—in the Somali context, usually *Acacia*—it is estimated that only 30–40 percent of the wood is actually converted to usable charcoal.[10] Its popularity in Africa is, in part, due to rapid urbanization and the prohibitively high cost of sustainable, environmentally friendly, or more efficient energy sources like solar, natural gas, and electricity. Despite the popularity and the industry's huge monetary value, charcoal remains a predominantly informal sector that intersects with criminality and rapid deforestation. It is an industry steeped in serious environmental and health concerns, along with ethical dilemmas and criminal elements. Yet the charcoal trade generally operates in the absence of government policies or formal taxation regimes. If there are any regulations, they are loosely based around producer cooperatives and are easily corrupted due to the trade's informal nature. Official data are limited, except for a handful of environmental agencies and non-governmental organizations (NGOs) whose research provides the basic outline for the industry, and this chapter.

Environmental groups have repeatedly called for a ban on charcoal use, but to little effect. Attempts to ban the trade in Tanzania and Chad dramatically failed, as have recent international bans on its export from Somalia. In 2009, when Chad banned charcoal, media outlets reported that families already struggling with high food prices resorted to burning furniture and rubbish in order to cook.[11] In Tanzania, the 2006 ban was reversed two weeks later due to a dramatic increase in the illegal trade. Repeated calls to ban the trade in Nigeria failed to gain traction until May 2016, when the government officially banned the export unless traders planted two trees for every one they cut down.[12] However, internet trading sites selling charcoal still openly offer Nigerian charcoal at around $200–$300 per metric ton.

In the Democratic Republic of Congo, rebel groups fund their fight against the central government by trading charcoal while destroying lush forests and endangering wildlife in Africa's oldest national park, Parc National des Virunga. The illegal trade in eastern Congo has become one of the most lucrative enterprises for the insurgents of the Democratic Forces for the Liberation of Rwanda (FDLR). In Goma, where 1 million people live, it is estimated that more than 105,000 tons of charcoal are burnt every year, at a total value of about $55.9 million.[13] A recent report from the Washington-based NGO, Enough Project, estimates that the FDLR generates $35 million a year through charcoal sales run by mafia-like cartels that control the business.[14] The report, which recommends sanctions and an International Criminal Court investigation, highlights the broader networks of police, politicians, and businessmen who all benefit and perpetuate the trade. The illegal charcoal trade and its violent kingpins are symptoms of a broader system of theft, corruption, and exploitation that has become systemic in Congo. This trade is not an isolated case, but it is uniquely damaging—not only to one of the world's most biodiverse places, but to human security and the rule of law.[15]

In Sudan, the export was first banned in 1960 but reversed in 1995 to eradicate the invasive species *Prosopis chilensis*. Sudan, unlike most East African countries, has developed policy and legislation regarding charcoal. A regulatory system of planting and harvesting for charcoal production has been established, as well as professional charcoal groups that have formed self-regulatory associations.[16] Several agroforestry bodies—like the Nairobi-based World Agroforestry Centre (ICRAF)—have promoted the Sudanese model as a framework for East Africa to formalize the trade and reduce environmental damage, while improving revenue flows for all involved.

Somalia's black economy

Somalia's population of approximately 12 million is one of the poorest nations in the world.[17] The government only collects revenue in the range of 1–2 percent of the country's $5.95 billion GDP, whereas other countries in the region collect on average about 13 percent.[18] The country is beholden to $5.3 billion of external debt, and has few prospects in the foreseeable future for paying it back.[19] Livestock export of goats, sheep, and camels, mostly to GCC and other Arab states, remains the biggest industry, estimated to be worth $384 million a year.[20] Overall, Somalia's economy relies heavily on direct budget support, foreign aid, and diaspora remittances; in 2015, for example, it was estimated that a total of $1.4 billion was sent back to Somalia, the equivalent of 23 percent of GDP.[21] The prime minister's office reported that official development assistance, excluding military and peacekeeping spending, was $1.3 billion in 2015.

The GCC states have become major benefactors to the Somali economy. Between 2010 and 2014, the United Arab Emirates contributed $60 million in specific humanitarian and development aid to Somalia. In June 2015, a maternity and children's hospital was opened in Mogadishu, paid for by the UAE. At the same time, the UAE trained Somali army commandoes for graduation in January 2016 and provided police equipment and payment to soldiers across the country.[22] Qatar is offering similar support with direct budget financing and a host of humanitarian packages. In May 2013, for example, Qatar announced $18 million for infrastructure projects in Somalia.[23] Rumors abound that the actual sums of GCC money flowing to the country are much higher still, but are not coming in via official, formally registered channels.

The decline of Somalia's economy began with the collapse of Major General Mohamed Siyaad Barre's regime in 1991. Siyaad, who came to power through a coup in 1969 promising a socialist revolution, was initially popular, owing to his education reform programs, empowering women with new laws, and efforts to move Somalia away from being a clan-based society. However, Siyaad's dictatorial rule, high levels of military spending, and favoring of his Marehaan co-ethnics (a sub-clan of the Darod) sparked growing disquiet across Somalia and ultimately exploded in inter-clan conflict. After a variety of rebel factions failed to topple Siyaad, the United Somali Congress, a Hawiye clan guerrilla group formed in 1987, took control of the capital and played a key role in the overthrow of the weakening government in January 1991.

The subsequent purge of Darod clans linked to Barre and the desertion of tens of thousands of soldiers launched two decades of fierce fighting to control Mogadishu and swaths of Somalia. It also inspired the breakaway region of Somaliland in the north, which claimed independence in 1991 although it gained no official international recognition.[24]

The civil war's effects were immediate. Somalia's once-prosperous banana industry—the country's biggest agricultural industry and second-largest export at the time, with strong links to the Italian colonial period—began to struggle and by the mid-1990s became nonexistent.[25] Up to 10,000 hectares of land in Somalia's Middle Shabelle, Lower Shabelle, and Lower Juba had produced bananas that in their prime earned the country approximately $1 million a month. The industry made a slight recovery from 1993 to 1997, with exports to Europe and the Middle East, but devastating El Niño floods and reduced access to European markets saw trading end in 1997.[26] As the economy crumbled, destitute rural communities increased their reliance on the charcoal trade as a vital source of income. Many banana growers moved to charcoal production. But it was not just economic desperation that propelled the trade. Somalia's charcoal shipments to GCC states coincided with the UAE banning logging in the 1990s, which put a stop to their domestic industry and created a need for timber and charcoal imports.

In 1996, the estimated charcoal output for northeast Somalia, now known as Puntland, was 120,000 to 144,000 tons a year.[27] Producing this volume required cutting about 2.1 million *Acacia nilotica* trees, with an average density of sixty trees per hectare, which translates into a deforestation rate of 35,000 hectares of land per year.[28]

If we rely on these figures, the 10 million sacks of charcoal produced in southern Somalia during 2011 would equate to an estimated 4.375 million trees cut, or clearing 72,916 hectares of land.[29] A joint study using Google Earth satellite imagery from 2006 to 2012 found "worryingly high" areas of southern Somalia affected by the charcoal trade, with an estimated loss rate of 7.2 percent over the five-year period.[30] World Bank data show Somalia's forest coverage has steadily declined, from 83,000 square kilometers in 1990 to 64,000 square kilometers in 2015.[31] With such alarming exploitation rates, Somalia's charcoal trade is literally destroying the country's opportunities from the ground up. Most of the forest in Somalia's south, known as the Jubaland region along the Shabelle and Juba rivers and the inter-riverine areas, has been cleared for agricultural use and the charcoal trade over the past two decades.

Limited revenue from informal taxation systems or ad hoc tariffs at major ports has forced Somalis to compete for control over what finite resources or revenues are available—including charcoal. Competing warlords and militias purporting to represent clan interests have ruled a violent landscape that made Somalia, in James Fergusson's book title, the "world's most dangerous place."[32] Successive Somali governments, and even warlords like General Muhammad Farah Aideed, who controlled Mogadishu and whose militia was responsible for the infamous "Black Hawk Down" incident in which eighteen American marines died, have at times banned the charcoal trade based on environmental grounds. However, Aideed's son, who took power when the general died in 1996, did not impose such restrictions.[33]

The main reason for Somalia's thriving charcoal trade is that, as an export, it fetches low-income sellers four times the domestic price.[34] In 2007, charcoal in Somalia was priced at $3–4 per bag, while in the GCC states the same bags sell for $10 each.[35] In Jubaland markets, in May 2016, a bag of charcoal was sold at around $7–11 dollars and peaked at $14 when reserves were low.[36] The higher export price for Somalia's charcoal, predominately from *Acacia* trees, is because it is the most popular type for GCC states users.

Khaleeji traders and consumers prefer Somali charcoal for the longer-lasting burn and strong aroma when cooking or smoking *shisha*, a popular pursuit seen in cafés across the Middle East.[37] It is simply a better product compared to other charcoal products, and the demand drives the price up and perpetuates the export.[38]

Traditionally the export follows a simple pattern. The shipping route has been firmly established through centuries of trade with Arabs along the East African coast. The starting point is the *Acacia* trees in Somalia, which are cut down and burned; then the blackened remains are bagged and trucked east to the ports of Kismayo, and previously Barawe. From the Somali coast, it travels north by small boats (dhows) that are at sea for more than 4,000 kilometers en route to hubs in the GCC states.[39] Charcoal is bought and sold predominantly from Dubai's port and is usually stored in warehouses in the nearby industrial zones. Destinations also include Oman, where it is often taken overland and put into new bags and sold to traders in Dubai.[40] Due to the illegal nature of Somalia's charcoal, forged paperwork is regularly used to disguise the goods as originating from another destination like Ethiopia, Djibouti, Sudan, or even as far away as Ghana in West Africa, where the trade is not illegal. Corrupting shipping or customs officials is critical to the trade, although GCC states have repeatedly denied a whole range of allegations associated with buying illegal Somali charcoal, and the implication of their nationals—as officials or private businessmen—in the trade. Once the smuggled supplies reach Dubai, the charcoal is sold via middlemen who then sell the charcoal in smaller quantities to retailers, who use it to heat the sweet-smelling tobacco resin smoked through *shisha* water pipes. Restaurants also buy it for grilling meat.

Environmental impact

The most obvious environmental effect generated by Somalia's charcoal exploitation and trade is large-scale deforestation in the Lower Juba and Lower Shabelle regions. This, in turn, exacerbates associated environmental problems like drought and flash flooding. Soil erosion, due to deforestation, diminishes the effectiveness of planting crops, especially mango trees, which take three decades to bear fruit. In 2011, during the Horn of Africa's worst drought in sixty years—which killed 50,000–250,000 people and forced hundreds of thousands to flee to neighboring countries,[41]—more than 10 million people were adversely affected.[42] Chronic poverty, armed groups, and failed crops all contributed to the devastation, but industrial levels of charcoal production (and preceding and subsequent deforestation) also added pressures. In these regions, the context of chronic scarcity of resources and general impoverishment has led to ongoing disputes between locals who cut the trees for charcoal and nomadic pastoralists who need the trees to feed their livestock. As the Somali Environment Ministry reported to the United Nations:

> The *Acacia* species were originally a source of grazing for goats and camels, nitrogen fixation to enhance soil fertility, fencing of livestock in night enclosures and the traditional use of only dead trees for cooking. Such local use was sustainable, but logging of living trees for charcoal export resulted in extreme deforestation and is leading to desertification.

Some efforts are being made to counter the nefarious effects of the industry, to change behavior, and to stem the outflow of charcoal harvested from deforested land, but so far the results have been limited. In April 2013, then president of Somalia, Hassan Sheikh Mohamud, launched the UN-sponsored Somalia Program for Sustainable Charcoal Production and Alternative Livelihoods (PROSCAL). At the event, Philippe Lazzarini, the UN's resident coordinator in Somalia, said: "the charcoal trade is directly linked with instability and is a major impediment to the peace process." He stated that the joint program "will trigger local economic opportunities" and create alternative sources of livelihoods. Only an effective and comprehensive set of interventions will be able to counter the destructive short-term logic of exploiting Somalia's *Acacia* groves.[43]

Apart from press releases on two UN websites, there is no further information about the initiative. There is no information about the project's success or results after its launch amid fanfare and officialdom.[44] In the same month, the UN's Food and Agriculture Organization (FAO) launched a tree-planting campaign in Mogadishu that aimed to plant 4,000 trees around the capital. "Every Somali should plant a tree today. Every family should have some trees in their homes," President Hassan is reported to have said while inaugurating the scheme.[45] Similarly to PROSCAL, the FAO was unable to explain the program's success or any wider environmental impact.[46] The broader security and political concerns facing Somalia have clearly taken precedent over grassroots environmental issues that are affecting large sections of the population.

Charcoal terrorism, environmental terrorism?

It is not just Western NGOs and international civil servants that have shown increasing concern about the debilitating effects of the nexus between deforestation and the charcoal trade in and from Somalia. Letters discovered after the death of al-Qaeda supreme leader Osama bin Laden in Pakistan in 2010, revealed that the Saudi-born radical held grave concerns about climate change as part of his antagonism against the West, which he blamed for global warming. In some of these uncovered documents, mostly penned in 2009, bin Laden chides al Shabaab leaders for not taking climate change and ecological concerns seriously enough and urges them to stop cutting down so many trees for short-term gain. While al Shabaab is not extensively discussed in the cache of letters, there are enough references that show bin Laden's displeasure with the group's style of governance.[47] Al Shabaab's monopoly over the charcoal trade and its harsh taxation on locals went against bin Laden's thinking, and the letters reveal misgivings about al Shabaab not doing enough to empower the local population, as required by bin Laden's interpretation of the Shari'a.[48]

In the letters, publically released by the US Department of Justice in March 2015, bin Laden writes specifically about the folly of al Shabaab's reliance on charcoal. Rather than chopping down scarce trees for economic gain, bin Laden suggested planting other kinds of trees that would encourage economic growth and reduce deforestation:

> The brothers need to be alerted that cutting down trees in big numbers for commercial reasons like making coal without replanting others during the rainy season is dangerous for the environment of the region. They should cut down just enough to supply the needs of the people in Somalia. Cutting the trees for export is very damaging.[49]

Climate change was also a prominent theme in an eleven-minute recorded voice message of bin Laden released in 2010. It was the second time that year that environmental concerns were revealed as part of bin Laden's ideological framework.[50] Some counterterror experts described these concerns as publicity stunts to appear humane in the context of a jihad waged against the West. But whether or not Osama bin Laden was sincere, one thing is certain: neither the letters by the al-Qaeda leadership nor its public messages released via the media persuaded al Shabaab (officially affiliated to al-Qaeda and its representative in the Horn of Africa) to stop exploiting and profiteering from the charcoal trade.

To understand why the jihadists matter to the trade and why the trade matters to them, it is important to remember how they burst onto the Somali scene and how they organize their sacred war. Al Shabaab came to prominence after splintering as a radical faction from the more moderate Union of Islamic Courts (UIC). The UIC had for approximately six months ruled Mogadishu and southern parts of Somalia, but was ousted by a US-backed Ethiopian invasion in December 2006, which opened an opportunity for jihadist resistance against the foreign aggressor.[51] Since then, al Shabaab has morphed into a decentralized force with various layers, groupings, and operational elements. Its title means "youth," and al Shabaab has been al-Qaeda's nominal affiliate since February 2012: a disparate force of approximately 13,000, out of which only 6,000–7,000 are actual combat soldiers.[52] They are a resurgent force capable of carrying out deadly and sophisticated attacks in major centers or on army camps in rural areas. Crucially, the movement is now a threat beyond Somalia: their reach spreads throughout the Horn of Africa, with identified networks in Kenya, Uganda, Ethiopia, and Tanzania, as well as a track record of terror. The first foreign attack blew up a bar in Kampala during the 2010 World Cup Final; al Shabaab's most notorious strike was undoubtedly the siege at Nairobi's Westgate Mall in 2013, during which at least sixty-seven people were murdered. While the African Union peacekeeping force, known as AMISOM, has made some progress in forcing al Shabaab out of key towns in Somalia and protecting government infrastructure, large parts of the countryside remain under the jihadists' control and lethal attacks are commonplace. They have been a dominant force in Somali politics for a decade now, and are unlikely to wither away anytime soon.

In parts of Somalia, al Shabaab retains influence and support through its ability to provide security and dispute arbitration, and it takes advantage of local grievances against government authorities or rival clans. While a jihadist group, al Shabaab's populist ideology appeals to the marginalized, destitute, and aggrieved, capitalizing on the Somali government's failure to propagate a persuasive political narrative or at least offer hope of a viable alternative.[53] Their guerrilla tactics have consistently outmaneuvered AMISOM's 22,000 troops, a force originally deployed on a six-month mission more than a decade ago. Regular US drone strikes have killed al Shabaab leaders and senior officers, but a well-stocked, mid-level tier quickly provides new leadership. At the heart of this militant organization is a sophisticated financial management system that perpetuates their operations via imported financing and fundraising capabilities, often from members with international experience.[54]

Al Shabaab's reliance on charcoal for financing its core political and military activities can be compared to the usefulness of the opium poppy trade for Afghanistan's Islamic Taliban. In 2009, the UN Office on Drugs and Crime reported that, since 2005, the Taliban and other insurgents in Afghanistan earned around \$90–\$160 million per year from taxing opium production and trade.[55] Similarly to Somalia, as the Afghan state dissolved during years of civil war, local warlords took control of territory and relied on the opium trade to fund militias. The Taliban, who originally sought to stamp out drug trafficking when they were the dominant armed group in Afghanistan between 1996 and September 2001, pragmatically lifted their ban on poppy production after the US-led invasion in October 2001.[56] And despite the US spending approximately $7 billion over the past fourteen years to fight the trade, there are signs that a local narco-state administered directly by government officials—and not just the Taliban—has emerged as a firmly entrenched business in Afghanistan.[57]

Somalia's charcoal industry has been estimated to be worth $250–$384 million annually.[58] More recently the trade is estimated to be worth $135–$180 million wholesale, and $171–$228 million retail, in the United Arab Emirates, the principal export market.[59] In 2011, it was reported that charcoal earned al Shabaab $25 million through taxes, tariffs, and fees from those producing charcoal or transporting it to shipping centers, whence it makes it way to the GCC states. Al Shabaab's control of Somali ports, especially Kismayo and Barawe, was vital to establishing a grip on the trade, and gained it the most considerable amount of tax along the transnational supply chain. UN investigators repeatedly identified individuals based in the GCC states acting as middlemen to the trade and directly linked to al Shabaab; they labeled them "terrorist financiers." In 2012, the UN Security Council implemented resolution 2036, which banned direct or indirect imports of charcoal from Somalia due to its direct funding of al Shabaab. In October 2014, after President Hassan Sheikh's written request, the UN Security Council authorized international navy fleets in the Indian Ocean to interdict any boat suspected of carrying charcoal.[60] The main concern for the Somali government, and the international community at large, was that the charcoal business funded al Shabaab's core activities and continued despite the UN resolution and ban. The jihadist group would extract *zakat* (Islamic tax) at roadblocks and checkpoints from charcoal traders and transporters taking bags of charcoal to port. In 2011, the UN Monitoring Group even stated that "charcoal is the single most important source of income" for al Shabaab. However, the UN reports also exposed a complicated network of traders and benefactors and a trade-based money laundering scheme that also included local politicians and business leaders, some of whom were the very representatives that the Western-led international community had been investing in as part of the joint effort to rebuild state institutions. Despite Somali government denials of the extent of the trade, satellite imagery of areas that the militants controlled clearly shows the countryside decimated by the charcoal business. The images show large black patches that are charcoal stockpiles or the residue from previous stockpiles, still visible outside Kismayo town. Al Shabaab transformed a subsistence-level economic activity into a trade on an industrial level, and their sophisticated and functioning tax system relied on its trade. Now, as the charcoal trade declines, al Shabaab focuses their taxation methods on targeting NGOs, individuals, businesses, and transporters across the territory that they control. It is not just charcoal that is taxed, but all aspects of life, business, or even humanitarian aid and development operating in areas that they control. One of the emerging ironies from this research is a persistent admission that al Shabaab's organized, albeit brutal and deadly, taxation methods provide more structured governance systems than Somalia's central government. According to a confidential report for a United Nations agency in Somalia: "With its wide reach and sophisticated accounting methods, Al-Shabaab's tax system parallels that of many a small nation state."[61]

Attacks against major hotels and restaurants in Mogadishu, including the Liido beach restaurant attack in January 2016, are largely believed to be consequences of noncompliance with al Shabaab's demand for payment, or blackmail or illicit taxation, ranging between $15,000 and $30,000 from these business establishments in the capital city.[62] Humanitarian agencies and international NGOs grapple with the realities on the ground, that is, the need to pay *zakat* to operate in areas of vulnerable communities controlled by al Shabaab. Since 2012, as al Shabaab has been pushed into more remote rural areas, it is morphing into a group devoting more of its energies to extortion than jihad.[63] Some sources suggest that in recent years charcoal has declined as a staple income, but what is clear is that the trade provided al Shabaab with an economic platform from which to continue their violent campaign of destabilizing Somalia.

The charcoal trade is not black and white

The international dimension of the charcoal trade is not limited to the implication of *Khaleeji* businessmen and consumers; key players closer to home are similarly vital to the importance of the commerce in charcoal. Kenya, and the Kenyan army especially, are deeply implicated; its presence was initially established for security reasons, but quickly acquired a commercial dimension. The Ethiopian National Defense Force had moved in during the 2006 invasion, and officially withdrew from most parts of Somalia in February 2009. This was followed by the forging of a new alliance between a local militia, the Ras

Kamboni Brigade, and al Shabaab for joint administration of the port of Kismayo in southern Somalia. The arrangement quickly broke down, and by late 2009 the two groups were at war with each over control of the town and port. A senior figure in the UIC, one-time al Shabaab leader and staunch opponent of Somalia's then Transitional Federal Government, Ahmed Madobe, subsequently steered the Ras Kamboni group into an alliance with Addis Ababa and Nairobi, essentially inviting the Kenyans to help him establish his local authority. In September 2012, in a joint operation with the Kenya Defense Forces (KDF), Madobe's militia ousted al Shabaab from Kismayo. The KDF has not left Somalia since.[64]

The official justification for the KDF's incursion into its neighbor was the kidnapping of foreigners and aid workers, but diplomatic cables from February 2010, released by WikiLeaks in 2011, highlight US officials offering a variety of reasons for why any Kenyan invasion was a bad idea and was unlikely to result in an improvement of the security situation back home. One cable shows US officials encouraging the possibility of capturing Kismayo port in response to Kenya repeatedly urging the US to support their move to create a security buffer zone via their so-called "Jubaland initiative."[65] This, however, appears to have been a convenient excuse, given Kenya's domestic military aspirations and the regional political dynamics. Kenyan officials also failed to highlight acts of violence committed by al Shabaab, and refused to participate in any international or regional efforts to defeat Islamist militant groups, raising questions about the validity of their security concerns.[66]

The KDF launched Operation Linda Nchi ("Protect the Country" in Swahili) in October 2011, which saw 2,000 soldiers deployed into Somalia. The partnership with Madobe and his Ras Kamboni movement was critical to Kenya's ultimate success. While al Shabaab in 2010 had signaled its intent to attack, there was never a direct threat to Kenya, but the aim was, with the help of the Ras Kamboni, to neutralize al Shabaab and to wrest control of the Kismayo port. In February 2012, the KDF rehatted its expeditionary contingent to be integrated into the AMISOM mission, boasting that they had "liberated" close to 100,000 square kilometers since the launch of Linda Nchi and stressing that Kenyan troops provided humanitarian support and were not an occupation force.[67]

Once al Shabaab had fled Kismayo, the KDF and Ras Kamboni took effective control of the port and its surroundings. High-ranking military officials, along with Kenyan government officials, have since been accused of using the port as their personal revenue stream.[68] According to the Kenyan-based

Journalists for Justice, a civil society project administrated through the International Commission of Jurists, the KDF are an integral part of the "seamless cycle" of lucrative smuggling networks that are protected and assisted by political leaders at the highest level of government. Journalists for Justice accused the KDF sector commander of Kismayo, Brigadier Walter Koipaton, of overseeing a network of soldiers who benefit from the trade, including senior ranks working with the port authority. The report alleges that the KDF made an estimated $1–$2 million a month from charcoal, and similar figures for levies put on importing sugar.[69] Put differently, what transpired in Kismayo was nothing less than a transfer of control of the illicit trade from al Shabaab to KDF and Ras Kamboni, which facilitated and collected the fees for the import of low-quality, unprocessed sugar and the export of charcoal.

The KDF alliance with Ras Kamboni forces, which went on to populate senior ranks in the nascent Jubaland administration and security apparatus, requires a realpolitik of accepting charcoal export as significant revenue with which to build a security and political architecture in a post-conflict state. Similar to allegations surrounding CCTV footage of KDF soldiers looting during the Westgate Mall attack, Kenyan government officials privately make the distinction between an officially sanctioned looting scheme and corrupt practices by individual officers in various locations.[70] In southern Somalia, al Shabaab's strategic shift away from producing and facilitating the charcoal trade since mid-2015, can be traced to a breakdown in a revenue-sharing agreement with Jubaland's President Ahmed Mohamed Islam, or "Madobe," that had constituted a significant share of its income from charcoal.[71]

Numerous industry sources claim that sugar and consumer goods leave the port to travel west through al Shabaab-controlled areas to the Kenyan border town of Dhobley.[72] Kenyan border officials and police are bribed before the cargo makes its way to the world's largest refugee camp, Dadaab, 470 kilometers east of Nairobi. Networks of Somali traders rebag the sugar and sell it locally or for distribution across Kenya; the Kenyan sugar industry's failure to meet consumer demands has opened up a market that smugglers are keen to take advantage of. Following a similar route, although in the opposite direction, charcoal makes its way from the Somali interior to the coast before sailing north from Kismayo to the Arab states of the Persian Gulf.

Kenya's intervention in Somalia might have been highly rewarding from a financial viewpoint for KDF officers, but it has generated increasing domestic skepticism and blowback. Al Shabaab has launched hundreds of cross-border raids, including in the aforementioned carnage in Nairobi's Westgate Mall, the assassination of scores of civilians at Mpeketoni, and the brutal murder of more than 140 faculty, students, and staff at Garissa University in 2014. In January 2016, the el Adde attack overran a KDF camp on Somali territory and killed up to 180 soldiers, arguably the KDF's biggest military defeat in its history.[73] Neither AMISOM nor the KDF ever provided the public with a full explanation of what happened or how many soldiers were killed, or how the attack was even possible in a supposedly well-protected military camp. History repeated itself in January 2017 when al Shabaab overran the KDF's Kulbiyow base in Jubaland, and officials denied the severity of the attack despite widely distributed al Shabaab propaganda videos highlighting the carnage. It comes as no surprise then that since the launch of Linda Nchi, Kenyans have increasingly questioned their armed forces' role in Somalia. A Kenya-wide survey, published in July 2016, found that 44 percent of respondents approved of their Somalia policy when only given a "remain or withdraw" option, but 29 percent chose "remain in Somalia" when given a choice of four deployment possibilities.[74]

Kenya's foreign policy in Somalia remains opaque, but it has been a keen ally of the US in its Global War on Terror. Kenya and Tanzania were, of course, the targets of the al-Qaeda-orchestrated US embassy bombings in 1998 that killed 200 people, as well as a Mombasa tourist attack on an Israeli-owned hotel in 2002. Now al Shabaab is a regional threat operating in at least six East African countries and is responsible for a spate of attacks between 2013 and 2015 in Kenya that claimed over 350 lives.[75] The discourse on terrorism and anti-terrorism seems to serve other purposes and interests. Kenya's moves to close Dadaab refugee camp by the end of 2016 and its April 2014 "Usalama Watch" operation, which resulted in an estimated 4,000 people being harassed and detained by police, along with the police's widespread use of extrajudicial killings, have all been excused based on security grounds.[76] Extortion, corruption, and bribery go hand in hand with these "security" pursuits. However, these types of allegations are routinely denied by officials: Kenyan Defense Cabinet Secretary Raychelle Omamo and KDF spokesman David Obonyo vehemently disagreed with the UN Monitoring Group's 2014 report, but they must be seen in the context of the country's long-standing poor reputation for fraud, bribery, and misgovernance.[77] Kenya has repeatedly ranked among the world's worst in index tables on perception of corruption; and its political system, which has been blamed for indirectly helping al Shabaab, is regularly rocked by huge bribery scandals, especially in the security sector.[78]

Despite the illegality of the business and its link to al Shabaab, flows of charcoal have continued as KDF controls Kismayo port. The UN Monitoring Group in July 2013 estimated a 140 percent increase in the trade since the 2012 ban. The KDF "continues to play a substantial role in the illicit export of charcoal from Somalia," and at $2 a bag they are estimated to have received $12 million from the trade in 2016.[79] That initial growth in 2013 is linked to the illegal export of charcoal stockpiles in Kismayo, but over the following years the trade significantly decreased. While continuing their illegal activities, Kenyan security officials simultaneously lobbied the UN in 2011 and 2012 to allow the legalized sale of the massive charcoal stockpiles sitting in Kismayo's warehouses. Kenya faced a real dilemma: the Jubaland authorities relied on the trade to finance their takeover of Kismayo, so the KDF would have risked a confrontation with their most valued on-ground military ally if they had prevented the trade.

However, Kenya's proposal for the legal sale of charcoal stockpiles was rejected in New York on the grounds that it further encouraged the trade by disguising the continued or increased illicit commerce.[80] This leaves unresolved the conundrum of what to do with the charcoal stockpiles. The European Union's naval force operating in the Indian Ocean, Operation Atalanta, is expected to interdict vessels carrying charcoal. But what is to be done following the interdiction and where the charcoal is to be impounded are significant hurdles posing ongoing dilemmas for the contributing European nations. Operation Atalanta commanders have been resisting the push to include charcoal in their mandate, which has focused specifically on anti-piracy activities in the Horn of Africa. At the peak of the piracy crisis in 2012, Somali piracy cost the global economy between $5.7 and $6.1 billion. It was almost halved to $3.2 billion the following year and has been in decline since, due mostly to the deployment of an EU mission.[81] So far, the role of international naval forces stopping charcoal flows has been minimal. This has become a political problem rather than one of security or environmental protection. Behind the scenes, EU diplomats and UN investigators pressure GCC state officials to improve their own policing of the trade, which they see as more crucial to stopping illicit flows than naval patrols.

For its part, AMISOM, the African Union force deployed in Somalia, is a peacekeeping security mission with little interest—or clear legal mandate—to stop the charcoal trade. It is rife with a mixture of competing interests and a lack of coordination and cooperation that keeps the mission floundering. Kenya and Ethiopia are at once Somalia's neighbors, and also possess overt political—and some say financial—objectives that clash with the presumed common goal to impose military defeat on al Shabaab. Troops attached to AMISOM get significantly higher salaries than they do when serving at home, which gives African states incentives to see peacekeeping as a cash cow for rent-seeking militaries.[82] On average, an AMISOM soldier earns $1,028 per month, with $200 going to their respective government for administration costs.[83] For a low-ranking Kenyan soldier, that is about four or five times more than the regular salary. Such skewed incentives help explain the skepticism or outright hostility that many Somalis feel toward AMISOM, which is supposedly a neutral force, while in practice comprising the regional states that have a considerable amount to gain financially from the country's enduring instability. AMISOM has received €1.08 billion between 2007 and the end of 2015 from the European Union, via the African Peace Facility, for troop salaries, allowances, and some operational costs.[84] The mission's limited achievements have become a profitable business for contributing nations, despite being one of the world's most deadly peacekeeping missions. In the words of one critic, the mission has created a "militarized status quo where each player in the conflict has learned how to maximize its interests while losing sight of the overall goal of nation-building."[85]

Finally, of course, the dynamics of the charcoal trade cannot be fully grasped without reference to the involvement of a third (local) force in the business. The local administration of Jubaland Regional State, which consists mostly of ex-Ras Kamboni cadres, is in charge of collecting customs duties levied at the Kismayo port; such income is a major source of revenue, used to run the town by the regional authorities. Using the UN's numbers, of 1 million bags a month leaving Kismayo in 2014, it is estimated that more than $1 million a month was flowing to the administration through port taxes. An important chunk of this sum maintains Jubaland's security apparatus, in particular those troops protecting the state president, Ahmed Madobe, elected in 2013 and re-elected in 2015. The supposed public revenue thus pays for the security and interests of a private citizen with a highly questionable human rights track record. As Menkhaus aptly described, politicians—who are at once clan leaders, gangsters with private militias, and respectable international partners holding local communities in their grip through the use of violence—have colonized Somalia's security apparatus.[86]

One of the grave ironies here is that two nominal enemies—al Shabaab on the one hand and the KDF and Madobe's Jubaland forces on the other—collude in the charcoal trade. Such implicit relationships between government officials and al Shabaab are typical of Somalia's political economy today, in which the state relies on actors who are often the very agents of chaos destabilizing it. Kismayo may be producing less charcoal now due to greater scrutiny and pressure on GCC states, but new departure points and stockpiles have emerged along the south coast in places like Buur Gaabo, 50 kilometers north of the Kenyan border and in proximity to KDF troops attached to AMISOM. The trade has seen a shift whereby tax collection points are disparate rather than consolidated at one exit point. Having lost Kismayo and other ports, al Shabaab collects taxes on transport and charcoal producers in remote parts of Jubaland.[87] From conversations with Jubaland locals and officials, the trade has become "a tug of war in between al Shabaab and societies in Badhaade district," a region south of Kismayo and north of the Kenyan border. The trade continues with tensions around who "controls" the supply to coastal communities and "locally arranged points where boats transporting charcoal from Somalia are met and loaded in the water by smaller local boats from the shore."[88] Often al Shabaab crackdowns on charcoal occur in retaliation for Ogaden communities or other clans in Jubaland refusing to join their ranks.[89] Nevertheless, Jubaland officials continue to deny that any charcoal is traded in their region; several Somali politicians in Mogadishu maintain that UN claims for the trade were inflated.[90] Jubaland President Madobe mostly seems unbothered by the accusations and continues to consolidate power and run a regional state. He knows that the EU, US, and UN consider him a vital figure for Somalia's future and a pillar of regional stability. One external actor, the United Arab Emirates, has shown particular interest in intensifying ties with him; the UAE trains troops and provides equipment as well as monthly stipends to soldiers in the Somali National Army, based in Jubaland. It is to the role of the GCC states that we now turn. Control of Kismayo port would be a lucrative acquisition for the UAE's DP World, which has an increasing presence in the region, including Somaliland's Berbera port and the semi-autonomous region of Puntland's Bosaso port.[91]

Tectonic plates: the regional geopolitics of Somalia

While charcoal links Somalia to the GCC states and beyond to the Middle East, historical ties with the Arab world date back more than a thousand years. Many of these connections were forged through the trading ports of Zeila, in the north, and in Mogadishu, where Arabian tomb inscriptions were found dating back to the eighth century. Mogadishu's Fakr ad Din mosque was built in the thirteenth century.[92] Commerce with the Arabian Peninsula went hand in hand with the spread of Islam. Arab links to the north of Somalia, a short boat ride across the Gulf of Aden, facilitated waves of migration and trade from Yemen and further afield. The proximity between "Africanness" and "Arabness" has fostered fierce independent "Somalianess" that is neither and both. In a strategic location geographically, politically, and culturally, straddling these identities has built opportunism and opportunity. In the same year that Somalia joined the Arab League, 1974, it also hosted and chaired the Organization of African Unity Heads of State meeting.[93] During the Cold War period, Somalia was propelled to significance as a Soviet Union proxy, competing against US interests in the region. This relationship ended in 1977, when Somalia invaded its neighbor Ethiopia, another, albeit more important, Soviet proxy. Somalia then turned to the US for support during the 1980s. In 1990 Somalia was forced to pick a side when the Arab League split over Iraqi President Saddam Hussein invading Kuwait. Somalia's military regime aligned with the US-led alliance in support of Kuwait and Saudi Arabia. But the Siyaad Barre government was already on its last legs, beset by domestic insurgencies, and in early 1991 it collapsed and Somalia descended into civil war.

Somalia now finds itself caught in the shifting alliances of post-Arab-uprising politics. The UAE's increasing focus on Somalia is, in part, competition against its regional rival Qatar, which directly supports the Muslim Brotherhood. Saudi Arabia in March 2014, and then the UAE that November, declared the Muslim Brotherhood a "terrorist" organization that threatens their national security. Such rivalries between GCC states can be seen with Qatar and the UAE locked in a bitter proxy war in Libya in the post-Muammar Qaddafi era, where each side provides weapons to rival militias.[94] The UAE's aversion to political Islam, seen as a threat to hegemonic kingdoms in the Arab states of the Persian Gulf, drives their foreign policy in the Middle East and Somalia. These competing ideologies further burden a Horn of Africa that is already dealing with proxy wars, internal divisions, and poor governance. The European Union's special representative for the Horn of Africa, Alex Rondos, wrote in early 2016 that the Muslim world's internal conflict has led to a realignment of loyalties in the Red Sea region, where "the aftermath of the Arab spring and the confrontation between the Sunni and Shia communities in the Middle East now have direct impact."[95] Europe's concerns lie with increasing refugee flows and rising terrorist threats from jihadist groups. These fears align with those of Ethiopia and Kenya, homes to millions of refugees, most of whom are destitute; and to millions of Muslim citizens, many of whom feel ignored or neglected by their national governments.

Not only is the return of the GCC states to Somalia ideological, but it is also related to their economic growth. The Emirati economy has grown from $50 billion in 1990 to the Arab world's second largest after Saudi Arabia, with an output of $400 billion in 2015, almost double Qatar's $203 billion.[96] In 2013 the UAE contributed about $48 million a year in monthly installments to the Somali government—money not registered by the Central Bank in Mogadishu. Similarly, Qatar donated $60 million to the authorities in Somalia; and of that sum, only $6.7 million was accounted for through the Central Bank.[97] Often the money allegedly went directly to chosen political figures and their network of supporters. Qatar financially supported Somalia's Transitional Federal Government president, Sheikh Sharif, up until 2012 and his resignation, when Doha then switched financial support to the new president, Hassan Sheikh, and the Damul Jadeed, or "new blood" group, a splinter group of the al Islah or Muslim Brotherhood in Somalia.[98] Qatar reportedly gave $7 million to President Hassan's 2013 election campaign.[99] The UAE provided financial support to both Sheikh Sharif and to former finance minister and transitional government speaker, Sharif Hassan Sheikh Adan.[100] As stated in a confidential United Nations report: "The UAE support to the opponents of (president) Hassan Sheikh indicates Abu Dhabi's intention to counter the influence of the *Damul Jadeed*."[101] In addition, "To counter the Muslim brotherhood in Somalia should be seen as part of a bigger game played by different Muslim countries in several world stages."[102]

Frequent presidential visits to UAE or Qatar are integral parts of the election cycle, as Somalia's political landscape remains fixed on buying support with cash or lucrative key positions in government. In November 2016, Somali regional leaders flew to Abu Dhabi for a top-level meeting to discuss the 2017 presidential election. When contacted, the Somali president's office declined to discuss GCC and Arab states' financial support.[103] World Bank efforts have made some progress in building Somalia's public financial management structures, and private enterprise drives minor growth, yet large gaps remain in domestic revenue collection, and there is no new industry or job creation on the horizon. These external influences are aggravating Somalia's political sphere and fight to control scant resources. GCC state financial aid is of no broad benefit to Somalia; rather it perpetuates a spiral of cronyism and corruption, fueling the need for impoverished communities to rely on low-income pursuits like charcoal. The charcoal trade, a small facet of the regional integration or interdependent economies, illustrates how the GCC states have adopted an approach of clientelism in Somalia, based on disbursement of financial and political support, while choosing to tolerate the charcoal trade in defiance of UNSC resolutions. Meanwhile, those very GCC states compete politically and financially for prestige and influence by giving humanitarian assistance to Somalia and funding different political leaders. This suboptimal scenario infects Somalia's development. It derails continuity and international efforts as the benefactors pursue personal gain over governing a developing nation-state.

One of the most controversial actors in Somalia, apart from Qatar and the UAE, which uses its petrodollars to compete for influence in Somalia, has been Saudi Arabia. More than four decades ago, Riyadh began aggressively funding Salafist scholars and Sunni Muslim organizations in the Horn of Africa to counter the Iranian Revolution in 1979.[104] Now private Saudi-funded madrassas and mosques operate throughout East Africa. Somalia is no different. Saudi Arabia's government offers finance to the Somali government, but figures, however rudimentary, are hard to find. Former Prime Minister Ali Ghedi listed a $32 million donation from Saudi Arabia as expenditure during his tenure of 2004–7, even if this sum was not registered in the Central Bank of Somalia. Apart from senior politicians, the educational sector has also been a major recipient of Saudi largesse. Saudi scholars and imams, as individuals, have built a quasi-education system to fill the gap left by the lack of formal schooling or a national curriculum.[105] Scholarships for young Somalis to study at the Islamic University of Medinah, popular since the 1980s, and funds for graduates to continue their work in their homeland or abroad have had a significant impact in Somalia. Al Medinah International University has official links to at least four Somali universities.[106] Saudi individuals fund charities and NGO-type organizations in Somalia, a form of soft power that might well be more effective than giving individual leaders or senior politicians support in cash.[107]

Another sphere of Saudi influence comes from the kingdom's hiring of up to 50,000 Somali workers every year as domestic help, drivers, and laborers.[108] Labor migration to Saudi Arabia dates back to the 1970s and despite regular allegations of abuse, in particular toward women, this pursuit has become an economic lifeline for hundreds of thousands of Somalis. One noted effect is that Somali citizens return having embraced a more puritanical version of Islam after spending time in Saudi mosques.

Saudi ongoing efforts to thwart Shi'a, or more specifically Iranian, influences in the Red Sea region have seen a radical shift of opportunistic support from Horn of African nations, including Sudan, Eritrea, and Somalia.[109] Fierce competition between Iran and Saudi Arabia has led them to support opposite sides in the Syrian and Yemeni protracted civil wars, and to seek support in Africa for their cause.

Somalia cut diplomatic relations with Iran in January 2016, after a top Shi'ite cleric was executed in Saudi Arabia and Iranian protesters responded by torching the Saudi embassy in Tehran. On the same day, a $50 million aid package from Saudi Arabia was sent to Mogadishu.[110] Sudan, home to Osama bin Laden between 1991 and 1996 before he left for Afghanistan, also ended its diplomatic ties with Iran after three decades of strategic relations. Sudan joined the Saudi-led fight in Yemen in March 2015, and Riyadh allegedly deposited $1 billion in Sudan's central bank in July and August that year.[111] General Ahmad Asiri, a military advisor to the Saudi government, in a Voice of America radio interview said that peace and stability in the Horn of Africa are "very important" to Saudi Arabia. "This is why we coordinate with Eritrea, with Djibouti, with Ethiopia, with Somalia, with the legitimate governments of Yemen and Sudan, to make sure that this area is controlled and secured."[112]

A great deal of Qatar's aid and assistance flows through individual charities or support to hospitals and Islamic schools. Qatar's benevolence to Somalia began in 1996 when its foreign policy was in its infancy. Qatar chose Al Islah, Somalia's official branch of the Muslim Brotherhood, to be the local implementing partner. As Somalia's turmoil continued over the next decade, Qatar's involvement deepened.[113] Qatar seized an opportunity when Mogadishu's business leaders, who suffered from warlords' violent rule and stifling trade, supported the UIC's Islamist agenda. The state's dynamic foreign policy, of dealing with those whom others would or could not, filled the void left by Ethiopia, Kenya, and the US. As the international community worried about the implications of the growing Islamic presence, Qatar engaged with "non-state actors" and was thrust to the diplomatic center stage. Qatar directly engaged with the UIC leadership, which had taken control of much of southern Somalia by the end of 2006. Qatar regularly invited to Doha its leader and future president of Somalia, Sheikh Sharif, for meetings and peace talks. Despite criticisms, Qatar's flexibility to engage with all stakeholders saw them successfully bring Somali's numerous warring factions together to form the fragile transitional government of 2009, which included former members of the UIC. During this period, however, Qatar's close relationship with Eritrea, which gained independence from Ethiopia in May 1991, caused significant friction with negotiations. Ethiopia cut diplomatic ties with Qatar in April

2008, due to its perceived support of al Shabaab via Eritrea. While Qatar denied the charges, diplomatic cables released via WikiLeaks show that US Ambassador Susan Rice echoed Turkey's concerns regarding Qatar's support of al Shabaab.[114]

As a further complication to the mix of agendas, it is not just GCC states that look to Somalia for wider geostrategic importance or foreign policy prestige. Access to ports is a major interest for Turkey, which also competes for primacy in the Horn of Africa, and has a particular focus on Somalia. In February 2014, Somalia's then governor of the central bank, Abdusalam Omer, told Reuters that as part of Turkey's direct budget support, the ambassador would deliver $4.5 million every month in boxes of cash.[115] Turkey has spent $400 million on projects and direct budget support in Somalia since 2011, while recording bilateral trade volume worth $72.3 million in 2015. Somalia has become the largest recipient of Turkish aid in Africa.[116] In parallel, or possibly as a result, Turkish companies have gained lucrative contracts to run Somalia's airport and seaport, where an estimated 80 percent of Somalia's revenue is made. In September 2013, the Turkish company Favori took the management contract of Mogadishu airport from UAE firm SKA Arabia. Somalia's World Bank-sponsored Financial Governance Committee raised a number of concerns about the "secret contracts" and the lack of an open tender process. However, the companies have continued operating. Turkey's highly visible projects, including President Recep Tayyip Erdoğan's well-publicized visits, have made them popular in Somalia.[117] The Mogadishu embassy is their largest in Africa and their "no questions asked, can-do attitude" of building roads and a hospital appeals to Somalis, who have tired of decades of international NGOs and UN bureaucracy. In part, Turkey's apparent soft power among the Somali population seems to lie with the explicitly Muslim identity of the ruling Justice and Development Party in Ankara.[118] Turkey's third way in Somalia appears as a middle ground to the GCC states—and, crucially perhaps, seems unconnected to the illicit charcoal trade that has wreaked so much damage in the country.

Conclusion

As argued in the preceding paragraphs, Somalia might be one of the world's poorest countries, but key political, security, and commercial interests have put it at the center of regional geopolitics. Almost all the maritime trade between Europe and Asia, about $700 billion each year in monetary terms and 4.7 million oil barrels,[119] sails through the narrow Bab el-Mandeb on the southern entrance to the Red Sea, en route to the Suez Canal.[120]

It is within this context that the charcoal trade, with its strong transnational character, must be situated. This chapter has provided an overview of the nature of the trade, and the multiple local, national, and international actors involved. It has argued, repeatedly, how this type of commerce is not just environmentally destructive, but also politically destabilizing. While Somalia's charcoal trade is a small and illegal link between the GCC states, it is a huge symbolic bridge between two worlds competing and coalescing in Somalia's burning future.

Somalia's charcoal trade will continue regardless of international pressure, laws, and bans. There is a need for a pragmatic approach to formalize the industry to benefit a wider group than just the handful that are presently benefiting. As the trade directly supplies the markets of the GCC, greater pressure must be applied on end users to invest in reforestation or regeneration programs in specific locations in Somalia. To avoid al Shabaab taxation and control, charcoal initiatives should be run close to urban centers that are under the control of government forces—for example, in Jubaland on the outskirts of Kismayo, where the support of the Kenyan soldiers could be employed to protect traders or producers in legitimate business. Money earned from the formal trade could be earmarked for specific community-based programs like environmental education and protection to security initiatives. Such integrated initiatives, provided they are supported by GCC states, could see the emergence of a formally regulated charcoal development program in Somalia, which could address climate change concerns, deforestation, and poverty. It is a view already shared by the World Bank: "Clarifying the regulations that govern the sector in one coherent framework would facilitate all subsequent reform steps toward making the charcoal sector more environmentally, economically, and socially sustainable."[121]

Finding ways of bringing local charcoal traders to pay tax or formal fees will be an incredible challenge fraught with obstacles, both with internal stakeholders and externally. Bringing the illicit networks into a formal framework is difficult, but experiences with small-scale reforestation programs and regularization of the trade elsewhere in Africa have shown promising results. In the Democratic Republic of Congo, the World Wide Fund for Nature, an environmental NGO, has run a sustainable charcoal program that produced 16 tons of charcoal from 9,000 hectares of reforested area to undermine the illegal trade that had been wreaking havoc on the Parc National des Virunga.[122]

The program worked directly with local communities and Congolese authorities, and offered incentives and lower direct taxation regimes benefiting producers. Another part of the program, while focused on the domestic market, saw the wide-scale production of energy-efficient charcoal stoves for cooking; they are estimated to have saved about 14,000 tons per year of charcoal, or about 4,200 hectares of forest.

Many approaches to pulling Somalia out of the quagmire have failed or faltered, due in part to a lack of coordination or continuity, but also because efforts have been misdirected and problems misdiagnosed. While reforestation schemes may be difficult, considering the scale of such an effort and the associated security issues with developing an on-the-ground approach, the alternative of tolerating the illicit trade with all its nefarious consequences for people and planet is simply not an option. Underdevelopment and environmental degradation are among the root causes of the intractable instability in Somalia—an insecurity that affects its neighbors, the greater Middle East, and Western states. The charcoal trade may not appear to be the most pressing problem facing this troubled African nation; but understanding it and regulating it properly would go a long way towards improving the lives of ordinary Somalis and putting state-building efforts on a much firmer and more ethical footing.

6

ILLEGAL FISHING AND PIRACY IN THE HORN OF AFRICA

THE ROLE OF THE MENA REGION

Afyare A. Elmi

The Red Sea, Gulf of Aden, and Indian Ocean have always been vital routes for world navigation and traveling.* These waters are particularly important for most of the countries in the Middle East and North Africa. More than 20 percent of world shipping, including 70 percent of the world's petroleum products and 80 percent of Europe's maritime shipments, transit through the Gulf of Aden.[1] The rising economic powers of India and China rely particularly heavily on this route.[2] The majority of the oil products originating from the Gulf region destined for Europe transit through this important route.[3]

* This research was made possible by NPRP Grant 5–1275–5–196 from the Qatar National Research Fund, a member of Qatar Foundation. The statements made herein are solely the responsibility of the author. I would like to thank Said Mohamed and Ruqaya Abdirahman; the research assistance and comments they provided have significantly improved the chapter.

Maritime piracy, illegal, unreported, and unregulated (IUU) fishing, and legal commerce in the MENA region are closely linked in multiple ways.

This chapter examines the geopolitics of maritime piracy and IUU fishing in the Horn of Africa waters. First, the chapter provides historical background on maritime piracy in Somalia, arguing that this is a new phenomenon in the region. Second, it discusses the extent of illegal fishing in Somali waters. Third, it revisits and reassesses the political and economic explanations for clandestine maritime activities of statelessness, illegal fishing, toxic waste dumping, and poverty. Fourth, the chapter analyzes the implications of piracy and illegal fishing for the region. On the security front, pirates have attacked and hijacked many ships from MENA countries. On the economic front, the MENA region has lost valuable trade and paid high insurance premiums. Moreover, during the peak of piracy (2005–12), the fishing and tourism industries of the countries in the piracy-affected areas declined. The chapter concludes by assessing the contributions of the MENA countries in addressing maritime insecurity and environmental destruction, arguing that these countries play a nominal role in the efforts to control piracy, while at the same time perpetuating illegal fishing in the waters of the Horn of Africa.

Piracy in the Horn of Africa waters: historical background

Piracy has for centuries been a threat to world sea trade, and it was thus historically branded as "the enemy of mankind." Across the ages and across borders, it has been considered a universal crime that requires collective and immediate suppression. Recent incidents of world piracy have largely been concentrated in the Horn of Africa.[4] This has prompted scholars to explore the early history of the area to explain the scourge of modern piracy—a classic strategy of historiography where there always seem to be ancient precedents for any modern phenomenon. Historians noted that seafarers departing from Aromata in the land of God (Punt) or "Holy Myrrh-land" were afraid of the sea robbers in the "land of the Trogodytes ... and Koloboi" (current Eritrea).[5] Yet in the writings of early European travelers and historians, the Somali-inhabited areas (500–1,500 km southwest of the land of the Trogodytes and Koloboi) were not listed as pirate-infested waters. Rather, among early Greek and Roman travelers, the region was known for its high-quality frankincense and myrrh—entirely legitimate and legal commerce.[6]

The tenth-century Arab geographer Al-Muqaddasi (al-Maqdisi) wrote: "the island of Usqutrah (Socotra) rises like a tower in the dark sea; it is a refuge for the pirates, who are the terror of the sailing ships in these parts; and not till the island is cleared do they cease to be a cause of fear."[7] Later in the thirteenth century, two Arab and European travelers and geographers, Ibn Al-Mujawir and Marco Polo, also identified Socotra—a four-island archipelago 250 kilometers east of the African continent and current Somalia—as the center of pirates, mostly from India. In different but related incidents, in the fifteenth century, the maritime forces of the Portuguese and Ottoman empires confronted each other in the Horn of Africa waters as they battled for regional supremacy. The Portuguese navy carried out trans-global looting and destruction in the cities on the Indian Ocean and the Red Sea, and it captured or annihilated its enemies. During this time, the Portuguese navy systematically destroyed the Somali cities of Barava and Zaila.[8] It also dispatched troops to Abyssinia to fight alongside the Christian highlanders against the Muslim sultanates in the Horn of Africa in the 1490s.[9] Historically, the inhabitants of the Horn of Africa were victims of foreign pirates. During the era of the nineteenth-century steamships, the slave trade with Europe and the Arabian Peninsula increased, along with Africa's interaction with Europeans more generally. Although there is evidence that suggests Somalis were involved in the slave trade, piracy was nonexistent on the Somali coast. The treaties that the British Empire signed with Somali elders contained articles requiring "the abolition of the slave trade" in Somali territories.[10] For this reason, these multiple treaties do not include any reference to piracy whatsoever (there was simply no need for British representatives to raise the issue), while agreements with the Persian Gulf sheikhs explicitly included articles that called for the "cessation of plunder and piracy by land and sea on the part of the Arabs."[11]

However, after the British brig *Marianne* (or *Mary Anne*) was wrecked in 1825 near the Berbera coast and two lascars were lost, the British navy blockaded Berbera in the trade season. The Berbera wreckage triggered the first commerce treaty with Somali clans on 6 February 1827, in which they "agreed that any vessels bearing the English which may come to the port of Berbera (or any other port under the authority of the Habr Owal tribe) for the purpose of trade shall not be molested or injured but shall receive every protection and support from the said Sheikhs." In this treaty, the British demanded that the Habr Owal pay "equivalent for the value of the British Brig Marianne and her cargo, which was plundered in the port of Berbera," estimated to be "the sum of fifteen thousand Spanish Dollars."[12] Besides protecting the ships, the Somali elders also agreed to help stop trafficking slaves. Moreover, some of the British warships were even stationed in Somali waters to suppress the slave trade to the Arabian Peninsula.[13]

Britain and Italy were mostly concerned with Somalis with large herds of animals confronting each other in and around water wells, which resulted in some clan warfare and risked destabilizing the colonial settlement in British and Italian Somaliland respectively.[14] For this reason, Somalis have always been identified as people with livestock. Few were fishermen who depended on the sea for their livelihoods. Cruttenden, a British officer investigating one of the British shipwrecks, wrote that some Somalis "possess upwards of a thousand she camels, which may be valued at two or three dollars each."[15] Somalis were characterized as Bedouins tending their camels, sheep, and goats. Prior to the establishment of an independent Somali nation-state in 1960, Somalis, for some reason, were not engaged in piracy. Moreover, during 1960–91, Somalia had a sovereign government that was able to control the country and police its coastline and maritime waters.

In short, unlike other parts of the world such as North Africa and the Gulf countries, piracy is actually a new phenomenon on the Somali coast. There is simply no record of Somalis boarding and capturing ships and demanding ransoms before the 1990s. The presence of the colonial empires in the area and the Somali people's inward-looking nomadic culture are some of the reasons given for the lack of piracy in the region.[16] However, there were about forty shipwrecks on the Somali coast between 1801 and 1960 with victimized Somalis onboard. Sometimes, however, they rescued and took care of the sailors.

When the Somali state collapsed in 1991 and rival warlords battled each other in the absence of a central government, the security situation on the coast started to deteriorate. According to the International Maritime Bureau's comprehensive database, from 1991 to 2015 more than 1,100 ships were attacked and about three hundred of those were hijacked. However, compared to the 20,000–30,000 ships that transit the Gulf of Aden every year (500,000–900,000 over the last twenty-five years), the hijacked ships are negligible in numbers. What makes the threat of piracy detrimental to world trade is not the number of ships, but the type of ships hijacked and the importance of the geostrategic "chokepoint" under threat. Pirates captured the Ukrainian MV *Faina* freighter in 2008, which, had they succeeded in unloading the weapons it was carrying, could have destabilized the region. The hijacking of the Saudi oil supertanker MV *Sirius Star* in 2009 caused oil prices to rise.

Another interesting point is that the ransoms collected in the same time period are worth about $400–$600 million, while the goods that transit through the region are worth trillions of dollars. Despite the limited monetary value of the actual pirate activity, piracy has had huge economic and security implications for global trade. The United Nations Security Council invoked Chapter 7 of the UN charter and called for all nations to employ "any means necessary" to stop piracy in the Horn of Africa. As a result, the international community has identified as a High Risk Area (HRA) about 2.4 million square kilometers of the Western Indian Ocean, the Arabian Sea, and the Gulf of Aden. Over thirty warships from the multinational navy forces of the Combined Task Force (CTF)-151, the EU Naval Force Operation Atalanta, NATO's Operation Ocean Shield, and individual countries constantly patrol the area. The HRA affected more than twenty countries, including Pakistan, India, Iran, Oman, the United Arab Emirates (UAE), and even as far south as Mozambique and South Africa.[17]

Illegal fishing in the Horn of Africa waters

Unlike piracy, illegal, unregulated, unreported (IUU) fishing has been ongoing off the coast of Somalia for a long time. Even during the powerful military government of Siyaad Barre (1969–91), the Somali navy was still too small and weak to protect the longest coastline in Africa, a formidable 3,300 kilometers. In addition, the 1982 Law of the Sea introduced the Exclusive Economic Zone (EEZ): 200 miles that each state has the right to control for its own economic development. Although Somalia ratified the United Nations Convention on the Law of the Sea (UNCLOS), and in 1989 prepared and passed a bill that was consistent with the treaty, the process was not completed properly. For unknown reasons, these instruments were not deposited with the Division for the Ocean Affairs of the Law of the Sea (DOALOS), the United Nations agency that handles the law of the sea.[18] This created a legal debate; some argued that Somalia did not have a legally defined EEZ, and therefore its waters were free for all. However, others contended that international customary law protects the Somali seas. For example, the special advisor on Somali piracy to the UN secretary general, Jack Lang, wrote: "[in] the absence of delimitation in accordance with international law, Somalia is legally deprived of a territorial sea and an exclusive economic zone."[19] Others disagreed. A longitudinal report on the issue concluded: "all foreign fishing in Somali waters is unregulated, most of it is unreported to Somali authorities, and unknown amounts of it are illegal."[20]

IUU fishing is a global phenomenon, which has disrupted the fish ecosystem, ocean sustainability, and the lives of millions of local fishermen living in coastal areas. While there are multiple definitions in the literature, the Food and Agriculture Organization (FAO) provides the most comprehensive definitions of IUU fishing. According to the FAO, illegal fishing refers to activities "conducted by national or foreign vessels in waters under the jurisdiction of a state, without the permission of that state, or in contravention of its laws and regulations."[21] Additionally, the FAO defines unreported fishing as fishing activities "which have not been reported, or have been misreported, to the relevant national authority, in contravention of national laws and regulations."[22] Finally, the organization characterizes unregulated fishing as "fishing activities in the area of application of a relevant regional fisheries management organization that are conducted by vessels without nationality, or by those flying the flag of a State not party to that organization, or by a fishing entity, in a manner that is not consistent with or contravenes the conservation and management measures of that organization."[23]

Interestingly, of the yearly $110 billion fishing industry globally, IUU fishing represents $23.5 billion, about one in four fish caught from the oceans.[24] The main reason behind IUU fishing is its profitability. Put simply, for those engaged in IUU, the benefits outweigh the costs, and so far the international community has failed to address this challenge.[25] The Environmental Justice Foundation report authored by Trent, Williams, and Buckley explained how the IUU fishing vessels exploit a number of loopholes in the system. These include flags of convenience, lack of effective monitoring, and the availability of ports of convenience.[26] Flags of convenience are sold by states to fishing vessels without any questions about how or where they capture their fish. This gives them enough capacity to exploit the ocean and sell the illegally captured fish in international markets. Another technique is "flag hopping," where IUU vessels change their flag of convenience several times during their activity.[27] Changing flags allows fishing vessels to flag-hop between shipping registries, which makes them potentially untraceable. Moreover, vessels engaged in IUU take advantage of the lack of effective monitoring and the availability of ports that do not scrutinize their illicit activities.[28]

After the Somali state collapsed, many countries exploited the post-1991 legal uncertainty, and many ships from different parts of the world came to fish illegally in the Somali seas. At one time, FAO reported that more than 700 vessels were fishing in Somali waters.[29] The United Nations Monitoring Group reported that 180 vessels from Iran were engaged in illegal fishing in Somalia in 2013. The authors relied on various sources of information, including the Somali authorities.[30] Previously, trawlers with the flags of

France, Italy, Japan, Korea, Pakistan, and Spain were fishing illegally in Somali waters.[31] The "Securing Somali Fisheries" report identified many countries engaged in IUU fishing. Of the top four countries that fish illegally from Somali waters, three are from the MENA region: Iran, Yemen, and Egypt.

Somalia's "marine capture" is small compared to other countries that fish from the Western Indian Ocean. The "Securing Somali Fisheries" report estimated that foreign vessels captured 3,100,000 metric tons of marine life between 1981 and 2013, while Somalia's domestic capture was one-third of the above figure (1,404,125 metric tons) over the same time period.[32] In 2013, foreign vessels caught 132,000 metric tons, compared to Somalia, which caught only 40,000 metric tons. Iran caught 45,000 metric tons of fish in Somali waters in 2013, while Somalia caught 29,800 metric tons in the same year.[33] Scholars provide estimates about the value of the marine resources that Somalis lose to foreign fishing of around $300–$450 million every year.[34]

Some academics and activists characterize IUU as "fish piracy" and use the two terms interchangeably. For instance, according to Greenpeace International, fish pirates destroy the global environment by diminishing ocean life.[35] Hagan agrees with this characterization and writes, "A major contributor to the feeble state of the global fish inventory is Pirate Fishing, or Illegal, Unreported, and Unregulated (IUU) fishing."[36] Others broaden this concept and call IUU fishing "resource piracy."[37] In this case, those engaged in IUU fishing are after resources other than fish. The motivation behind the use of the "piracy" label is to expose the magnitude of the crime of IUU fishing. In addition, activists and academics that often use the "pirate fish" concept want to raise consumer awareness in developed countries. However, most of the literature on this issue distinguishes between piracy and IUU fishing. Piracy is equivalent to slavery, and it has a precise legal definition. Pirates are considered the "enemy of mankind." IUU fishing is considered a separate crime and therefore is dealt with separately in the literature. For this study, I consider these two concepts distinctly.

Officially, Somalia—with a transitional government supported by the UN, African Union, and Western countries—closed the legal loophole and proclaimed its EEZ in 2014.[38] Yet, many who are engaged in the illegal fishing business ignore the existence of the legally delimited Somalia EEZ that is consistent with UNCLOS. Illegal fishing is still ongoing along the Somali coast.

Political economy of piracy and IUU fishing

Some piracy experts link the Somali piracy phenomenon to a very complex network, like transnational organized crimes.[39] This approach argues that some Somali authorities and other military or commercial actors have collaborated with others in neighboring countries, like Kenya and Yemen, to perpetuate piracy in the region. In fact, some UN agencies advanced this perspective and branded many Somali actors as spoilers.[40] This approach had unintended consequences, as it has inadvertently criminalized some legitimate Somali businesses. Scholars have provided political and economic explanations for the scourges of piracy and illegal fishing. State collapse is the most frequently employed political explanation of piracy in Somalia. This view argues that pirates are exploiting the power vacuum, since there is no functioning state that can enforce its laws. The statelessness explanation points out that pirates organize their criminal enterprise freely from cities within the country. There is no authority that hinders their movement. In fact, the general public sees pirate leaders extravagantly spending their money in the major cities, purchasing cars and properties paid for by the crime. More importantly, when pirates hijacked ships they brought them to the shores of one of the four cities of Eyl, Hobyo, Gara'ad, and Haradere.[41] Sometimes it takes months to negotiate the ransom, which is spent on legitimate and illegitimate businesses alike.

Many scholars argue that because of the statelessness, illegal fishing and toxic waste dumping have also increased on the Somalia coast since 1991. Many ships from different parts of the world have taken advantage of the lack of authority in Somalia. Those engaged in illegal overfishing harassed and sometimes killed Somali fishermen.[42] Illegal fishing vessels from Iran, Yemen, South Korea, Egypt, Spain, and other countries use more sophisticated ships, thus making it difficult for the poor Somali fishermen to fish freely from their own waters.[43] Additionally, stories of toxic waste dumping were reported as early as the 1990s.[44] This further fed into the widespread grievances that Somalis developed against illegal fishing, thus contributing to the spread of conspiracy theories. Therefore, pirates politicized these issues by arguing that they were coastal guards fighting against illegal fishing and toxic waste dumping.[45]

Others provided a different political explanation to illegal fishing. Some argued that since Somalia hadn't claimed its EEZ in the past and there was no functioning state, Somali seas were free for all.[46] These politicized legal opinions made the predatory behavior of the ships that were engaged in illegal overfishing look legitimate. Some had obtained illegal licenses from a local chief or a warlord who cannot issue legally binding documents.[47] It is alleged that "pirate gangs have sought new sources of revenue, such as selling fishing licenses to foreign fishing trawlers and providing armed, on-board security."[48] These illegal activities provided them with the means to keep their criminal entities intact. Additionally, some scholars provided an economic rationale as to why piracy has proliferated in the Horn of Africa. Somalia's gross domestic product (GDP) per capita fell to $97 in 1991. The economic condition of the country got worse, even prompting the December 1992 US-led humanitarian intervention of Operation Restore Hope. A new Somali generation matured amidst chaos and the prolonged stateless condition. The Somali youth, the primary recruitment target of the pirates, have grown up amidst civil war and economic despair. The argument is that piracy emerges from poverty, which forced pirates to take up arms and attack ships transiting the Gulf of Aden simply because they had no other legitimate means of surviving.[49]

However, a critical look at these explanations reveals that there are three deficiencies with the political and economic explanations given above. First, there are 3,300 kilometers of coastline in Somalia, the longest in Africa. There are many cities and coastal settlements throughout the country. Yet, strikingly, piracy has been concentrated in only four cities along the coast of Central Somalia: Eyl, Hobyo, Gara'ad, and Haradere. Though the whole of Somalia has not had a functioning state since 1991, pirates have not used all coastal cities; in fact, most of these cities have never seen a pirate. The four chosen as pirate bases do not differ from other cities in any major way. They are not poorer, nor is their local governance any different. Moreover, illegal overfishing has been reported throughout Somalia. So, these arguments are limited in explaining the causes of piracy in the Horn of Africa. Instead, as proposed elsewhere, the crime of opportunity is a better explanation for the behavior of pirates.[50] Pirates could attack a ship, hijack it, bring it to the coastline, and negotiate a ransom (sometimes) for months and then go unpunished. This is an organized criminal enterprise. Therefore, pirates were driven by potential economic incentives and the low risks associated with their crimes.[51]

Pirates have successfully employed the grievance narrative—that they were protecting Somali seas from illegal fishing and toxic waste dumping.[52] Pirates argued that they were protecting Somali waters from intruders coming from as far away as France and Spain and fishing illegally in Somali waters.[53] For them, it is fair game. They can capture illegal fishing boats and collect a ransom. In fact, pirates understood that the grievance narrative would help them to get the support of the coastal communities that were angered by the illegal fishing that was making their lives difficult.[54]

However, that grievance narrative could not be sustained because of the behavior of the pirates. Close observation of the ships that pirates hijacked showed that less than 20 percent were fishing vessels. The overwhelming majority of ships captured were tankers and bulk carriers.[55] In addition, pirates hijacked ships sailing as far as 1,300 nautical miles from the Somali coast.[56]

Therefore, illegal fishing can only help us understand the initial incidents and the tolerance of the coastal communities for pirates. Initially, the general public naively believed the pirates' rhetoric of protecting the Somali seas. As such, the public welcomed and at times protected them. However, within a short time, the general attitude toward pirates changed. Many questioned their hijacking of all kinds of ships and taking the crews hostage. When they collected ransoms, pirates spent the money on alcohol, drugs, and prostitution. Thus, religious scholars, civil society, and elders campaigned to reverse the attitude of the public toward pirates.[57]

The role of the Middle East and North Africa region in illegal fishing and piracy

The MENA region is critical for global trade and security. It affects and was affected by the illegal fishing and piracy in Somalia in multiple ways. First, several MENA countries are implicated in illegal fishing in Somali waters: Iran, Yemen, and Egypt. Iran is number one on that list. The "Securing Somali Fisheries" report estimated that vessels from Iran have caught 1,032,000 metric tons of tuna fish from Somali waters since 1981.[58] Moreover, the UN's monitoring group reported that 180 Iranian vessels were illegally fishing from the Somalia coast in 2013.[59] According to a Somali government official, Iranian diplomats did not deny this, but argued that Iranian fishing vessels were being targeted and discriminated against at the same time as many other countries were also illegally fishing in the area but did not receive equal criticism.[60]

Yemen and Egypt have also engaged in IUU fishing since the 1980s. Yemen's physical proximity to Somali shores, advances in fishing technology, Somali statelessness, and historical relations between Yemenis and Somalis have given it almost unlimited access to Somali territorial waters. Moreover, the Yemeni fishing industry, operating from Aden and Al-Mukalla, has always been the biggest market for Somali fishermen. The UN Monitoring Group reported that 300 Yemeni boats fished from Somali waters every year. It has been estimated that Yemeni fishermen caught 29,000 metric tons of fish from Somalia's EEZ every year.[61] Moreover, Egyptian trawlers took advantage of the lack of authority in Somalia with thirty-six Egyptian trawlers fishing from Somali waters in 2005.[62] The "Securing Somali Fisheries" report estimated that Egyptian trawlers catch 13,000 metric tons every year from the Somalia coast. Other studies have identified several Middle Eastern culprits, such as Oman, Saudi Arabia, and the UAE, with Spain, France, Italy, China, South Korea, Taiwan, Thailand, Japan, and India also named as fishing illegally in the region.[63]

Besides the impact on Somalia's people and coast, illegal overfishing degrades the environment, which might affect other countries in the region. Commercial fishing trawlers involved in illegal fishing are "the single biggest threat to the biodiversity and marine environment in the Somali waters because of the unorthodox fishing practices they employ."[64] If this industry is not regulated, overfishing could threaten endangered fish and other forms of marine life, particularly on the sea floor. Sarah Glaser's "Securing Somali Fisheries" report concluded that "foreign fishing vessels have encroached on Somali waters for years, harvesting over one million metric tons of fish in the last decade, destroying habitats, and harming the ecological balance of the marine environment."[65] Connected to the Gulf of Aden and the Arabian Sea, Somalia's devastated marine habitat could negatively impact the adjacent Arab countries, whose questionable reputation for environmental sustainability and conservation is already under heavy scrutiny. Climate change, caused by industrialization and unbridled urbanization, has already negatively impacted the GCC.

Furthermore, because of maritime piracy and its connections to illegal fishing, MENA countries have faced mounting security risks when transiting the Somali coast and the broader maritime space: the Arabian Sea, the Gulf of Aden, and the Western Indian Ocean. The Horn of Africa waters are commercially and geopolitically important as they connect Europe, Africa, and Asia. Most of the oil products that originate from the Middle East to Europe transit the Gulf of Aden. Around 3.8 million barrels of oil passed through the 18-mile-wide strait of Bab el-Mandeb daily in 2013.[66] All the other routes are much longer and thus too expensive. Middle Eastern countries depend on this chokepoint for their trade with other parts of the world. Moreover, with their use of "mother ships," pirates have threatened the wider area of the Arabian Sea and the Western Indian Ocean. They capture a ship, use it as a mother ship and go out to sea and capture more vessels. Somali pirates have attacked more than 1,100 ships and hijacked more than 300 since 1991.[67] Many of those attacked and/or hijacked have been carrying products originating or going to the MENA region.

These developments led the international community to declare more than 2.4 million square kilometers of the sea a "High Risk Area." These waters included those maritime territories under the sovereignty of Middle Eastern states, including some of the GCC countries' coasts. If a ship enters those waters, it has to pay a high insurance premium and/or hire private security guards, significantly increasing the cost of economic activity.[68] Oman has been campaigning to remove its coastline from inclusion in the high-risk area since 2012.[69] In the Working Group 3 (WG3) "Maritime Counter-Piracy and Mitigation Operations" of the Contact Group on Piracy off the Coast of Somalia (CGPCS) London meeting in 2013, Oman, India, and Egypt requested the revision of the HRA. A group of shipping and oil industry organizations represented by the Baltic and International Maritime Council (BIMCO), the International Chamber of Shipping (ICS), the International Association of Dry Cargo Ship-owners (INTERCARGO), the International Association of Independent Tanker Owners (INTERTANKO), and the Oil Companies International Marine Forum (OCIMF) reviewed and reduced by 55 percent the high-risk area on 7 October 2015.[70] When the high-risk area reduction went into effect on 1 December 2015, India, Pakistan, Mozambique, and South Africa were removed, although the ships entering the old high-risk areas are still required to report to UK Maritime Trade Operations (UKMTO) and Maritime Security Centre–Horn of Africa (MSCHOA). Most of the coastlines of the Middle East countries are still within the high-risk area.

Many of the ships that have been hijacked were flagged, managed, or owned by Middle Eastern countries. One ship paid a ransom of $9.5 million, while another paid $3 million. Legally, a captain can refuse to take a ship into these high-risk waters. Pirates are involved in other criminal activities, such as transporting migrants from Somalia to Yemen and smuggling weapons and drugs. Boats used for human trafficking on their return to Somalia either bring weapons or carry out piracy activities.

Piracy in Somalia has affected 60 percent of MENA countries and 23 percent of sub-Saharan Africa (SSA) countries.[71] Most of the hijackings occurred in the places that fishing fleets operate. Moreover, according to the World Bank report, Somali pirates hijacked forty-four fishing vessels.[72] Some of these vessels were not close to Somalia's territorial waters or its EEZ. In fact, they were in international waters—an astonishing 650–800 kilometers beyond Somali territorial waters.[73] As a result, many of the fishing fleets had to relocate to the eastern side of the Indian Ocean. Consequently, the tuna catch dropped by 26.8 percent annually.[74] For example, Yemen claimed that it lost $150 million because of Somalia-based pirates in 2009.[75] For the MENA region, the fish export has significantly declined. Mbekeani and Ncube concluded, "The threat of pirate attacks has prompted many vessels to avoid some of richest fishing spots in the Indian Ocean."[76] As time progressed, the amount of ransom paid to pirates increased. In the 1990s, pirates collected the cash available onboard the ship, which was often under $20,000. In the 2000s, the ransoms increased as pirates developed networks that allowed them to keep the ship while they negotiated for a better deal. The One Earth Foundation estimated that the average ransom was $150,000 in 2005, but this shot up in 2010. For example, pirates charged $7 million before they released the *Samho Dream*, a South Korean tanker, and $9.5 million for the MV *Maran Centaurus*, a Greek supertanker.

Somali pirates succeeded in hijacking the Saudi-owned supertanker *Sirius Star* on 15 November 2008, which was carrying more than 2 million barrels of oil worth close to $100 million.[77] This was the biggest ship the pirates had ever hijacked. Because of the amount of oil, 25 percent of Saudi daily output, and the unprecedented sophistication of the pirates' capacity to hijack such a ship more than 450 nautical miles off the coast of Somalia, the hijacking sent shock waves around the world, creating greater fear in the shipping industries transiting the high-risk area.[78]

The cost of shipping insurance skyrocketed between 2005 and 2012. The industry purchases four types of insurance: war risk, kidnap and ransom, cargo, and hull. The industry classified the area where pirates were operating as a war-risk area. Ships transiting through the high-risk area had to buy war and kidnap and ransom insurance. As a result, "the cost of war risk premiums have increased three hundred fold from $500 per ship, per voyage; to up to $150,000 per ship, per voyage in 2010."[79]

The World Bank report (2013) estimated that Somali pirates cost the world $18 billion every year from 2008 to 2012, though the ransom they collected was between US$315–$385 million from 149 hijacked ships. The report further estimated that piracy has heavily impacted countries in the MENA region, arguing, "almost sixty percent of all MENA countries and twenty-three percent of all SSA countries are considered to be affected."[80] Furthermore, these countries, since the shortest route is through Somalia, lost "7.4 percent in the value of their yearly trade."[81]

In turn, piracy has had a negative impact on Somalia in multiple ways. Most directly, it has impacted the ability of ordinary Somalis to access urgently needed relief assistance. Between 2005 and 2009, Somali pirates hijacked at least six ships carrying humanitarian aid for the needy Somali people. Humanitarian agencies including the World Food Programme could not secure ships that were interested in taking food to Somalia. This further worsened the humanitarian situation in the country in 2011—a particularly sensitive time as famine was engulfing large swaths of the territory and killing thousands. The cost of living in Somalia also increased when pirates hijacked many ships carrying business goods to the country. Most importantly, piracy permanently damaged the image of the Somalis, as they were seen as people who tolerated the torture and ransom of peaceful seafarers, and were therefore unworthy of international charity or global humanitarian assistance. According to the UN Monitoring Report, some leaders of the pirate groups "carry out piracy operations with complete impunity, even seeming to enjoy access to high-level Federal Government of Somalia politicians in Mogadishu."[82] In another instance, there was an accusation that "senior Transitional Federal Government officials [shielded] a notorious pirate kingpin from prosecution, providing him with a diplomatic passport and describing him as a 'counter-piracy' envoy."[83] The same is true with officials working for the autonomous region of Puntland. In short, pirates have corrupted the nascent Somali institutions, thus preventing them from becoming effective.[84]

Since there was ambiguity on what to do with captured pirates, a catch-and-release practice was common in the beginning. To end this impunity, the European Union signed a third-party agreement with Kenya, the Seychelles, Mauritius, and Tanzania. Oman, Yemen, and UAE have captured pirates and brought them to their territories. There is no unified, anti-piracy law agreed upon by either the GCC or MENA regions. Somali pirates in MENA regions face different legal systems that result in various sentences. For example, when pirates attacked the UAE-flagged ship MV *Arrilah-I*, the UAE captured and brought back ten Somali pirates and sentenced them to life imprisonment.[85] There are also a number of Somali pirates in prison in Oman. Some of these countries do not have anti-piracy legislation. Unlike Western countries that captured pirates, these countries do not have third-country agreements that would allow them to hand pirates to Kenya or the Seychelles to be tried and then transferred to Somalia.

As explained above, there is no question that Middle Eastern countries are affected by piracy in the Horn of Africa. In addition, these countries contribute to the problem through their illegal fishing activities, which is linked to piracy. The question, therefore, is: what are the MENA countries doing about these interlinked issues? MENA countries nominally contribute by sending their navies to participate in the counter-piracy operations. There are various naval efforts to counter piracy in the region including EU-NAF, which is European Union-led. Another is NATO-led and the third is CTF, led by the United States. Saudi Arabia, Bahrain, Iran, and Turkey participate in patrolling the Horn of Africa waters. However, this is mostly a nominal contribution, because the three main fleets consist largely of European and North American vessels. Therefore, even though these countries are signatories to the Djibouti Code of Conduct and participate in patrolling the high-risk area, most of them have not been doing anything substantive.

The UAE has been the most active member of the MENA and GCC when it comes to ending piracy in the Horn of Africa. It is also one of the most affected countries outside Somalia, because of the commercial activities between Dubai's port and other countries. Other than the navies on the high seas, private security guards onboard ships have played the most important role in the reduction of piracy. Although most are from the United Kingdom, many operate from the UAE's strategic ports. In fact, a recent World Bank report claimed that these private security guards were more effective than the navies in reducing piracy in Somalia.[86] But as noted by Affi, Elmi, Knight, and Mohamed, there were legal, humanitarian, and practical challenges that come with the use of private security guards.[87]

The UAE, at the peak of piracy in 2011, convened the first international counter-piracy conference in Dubai. At the opening of this conference, the UAE minister of foreign affairs, Abdullah bin Zayed al Nahyan, called piracy a "criminal growth industry of the twenty-first century" that "could slip toward piracy economies" in many other countries. The UAE advocated the long-term onshore solution for piracy problems and further hosted four more counter-piracy conferences in Dubai.[88] The last counter-piracy conference communiqué in October 2014 called for the international community "to foster coordinated efforts to effectively combat maritime piracy at sea and regional threats on land."[89] Helping tackle the piracy problem onshore, the UAE funded an onshore counter-piracy project in Puntland that trained about 400 members of the coastguard.

The response by MENA states is a necessary but insufficient condition to get to grips with an increasingly trans-continental problem. IUU fishing is not limited to Somali waters, nor are the fishermen operating illegally solely coming from Iran, Yemen, Egypt, and Oman (though many do). Vessels from all corners of the world are involved in IUU fishing: this is a global problem. The upper estimates suggest that close to one quarter of the fish in the global market fall under IUU fishing practices.[90]

There are four major explanations regarding the reasons for the rise of illegal fishing in general and in Somalia in particular. Andrews-Chouicha and Gray, in their Organisation for Economic Co-operation and Development (OECD) report, argue that increased market demand, over-capacity, and poor social/economic conditions of fishers are the main drivers of IUU fishing globally.[91] There is high market value for fish and the price has been on the rise. Those engaged in IUU fishing target certain types of high-value fish such as tuna. Moreover, overcapacity is another driver of IUU fishing. Overcapacity means that the size and ability of fishing fleets exceed the amount of fish available for harvest in a given period.[92] Finally, many fishers who are engaged in IUU fishing come from developing countries, including the MENA region. The three MENA countries that are most actively involved in illegal fishing (Iran, Egypt, and Yemen) fit this profile.

Second, factors unique to Somalia facilitate IUU fishing in the Horn of Africa waters. For instance, Somalia has a long coastline of 3,333 km in strategic and accessible waters. It is estimated that the EEZ of Somalia is 830,389 sq km.[93] Vessels from different parts of the world—Europe, China, and Middle East—can easily access the Western Indian Ocean and the Red Sea that border Somalia. Additionally, Persson et al. contend that seasonal monsoons result in upwelling that make the Somali coast rich with highly sought tuna and billfishes. According to the "Securing Somali Fisheries" report, spiny lobsters that are commercially important are also found in Somali waters.[94] Interestingly, although these environmental conditions create a large number of fish for those sophisticated ships from overseas, Somali fishermen with poor equipment cannot fish here in the most productive season. In other words, unfavorable weather, lack of harbors, and poor equipment prevent Somali local fisherman from taking advantage of the available fish in their own EEZ.[95]

Third, for far too long, Somalia's state has not been functioning at all. This has further made its territory more vulnerable. Somali parliaments have struggled to establish legislation to protect Somali waters, and even if there are some laws, Somali governments are not able to enforce them. As noted above, Somalia ratified the international law of the sea treaty and enacted national legislation consistent with it in 1989. Yet, Somalia has not declared and deposited its EEZ with the United Nations. As a result, some, including former advisor to the UN secretary general, Jack Lang, argued that since the country did not declare its EEZ and did not deposit the instrument, Somali waters were not protected.[96] Many vessels, including those from MENA countries that were engaged in IUU fishing, took advantage of this legal loophole for a long time. However, as of 2014, Somalia again declared its EEZ and deposited it with the UN. It also passed fisheries legislation in 2014 that outlawed IUU fishing from Somali waters, perhaps only for the books. More importantly, Somalia ratified the Port State Measurement Agreement (PSMA) in 2015.[97] This is the most comprehensive treaty that attempts to address IUU fishing globally. However, only Oman has ratified the PSMA treaty when it comes to the states in the MENA region.

Finally, like many developing countries, Somalia cannot practically monitor and control its territorial waters and its EEZ. Somalia's state has not yet "monopolized the use of legitimate violence" and therefore cannot control the country physically to enforce whatever laws it has enacted. The country does not have well-equipped and well-trained coastguards. Besides having to contend with the threat of the jihadists of Al Shabaab in South-Central Somalia, there are various regions where the authority of the federal government means very little. Somaliland has seceded from the rest of the country, and therefore is a de facto state with its own laws and institutions that are at times more effective than the Mogadishu government. Puntland is autonomous and it rarely follows Mogadishu's instructions. Moreover, there are many entities (clan leaders, warlords, and sometimes pirates) that issue illegal licenses to foreign fleets. Recently, according to a report presented to the Indian Ocean Tuna Commission, Somalia's federal government identified several ships that had illegally fished from Somali waters.[98] Some of these ships were from Iran and they did not have legal permit to fish within the EEZ of the country. Others produced illegal licenses issued by competing authorities in the coastal towns.[99] In other words, some Somali entities play a role in the illegal fishing in Somali waters by issuing fake licenses. The Iranian and Yemeni fishing industries deal directly with some members of the coastal clans. By giving money to middlemen and hiring armed militias from sub-clans, armed fishing vessels are regularly seen in Somali territorial waters.[100]

Recently, Somalia complained to the Indian Ocean Commission, which regulates the fishing industry. To date, countries from the MENA region have not addressed this issue publicly. To prevent further militarization of fishing vessels in Somali territorial waters, and to prevent or reduce illegally caught fish easily being taken to the MENA region, regional states need to develop integrated and coordinated policy addressing these issues. As Pramod et al.

argue, IUU fishing "distorts competition, harms honest fishermen, weakens coastal communities, promotes tax evasion, and is frequently associated with transnational crime such as narco-traffic and slavery at sea."[101] The international community's efforts to eliminate IUU fishing have evolved over the last decades. Hagen explains several phases that these efforts passed, culminating in the establishment of a new treaty: the Port State Measure Agreement (PSMA). For Hagen, although PSMA has its shortcomings, the treaty is a "ground-breaking instrument as it targets 'economic incentives' that motivate IUU fishing."[102] However, most of the MENA countries are not signatories to this important treaty that would help eliminate IUU fishing.

Conclusion

The persistent problems of piracy and illegal fishing are a crucial, but under-examined dimension of Africa–MENA relations. The development of piracy in the Horn of Africa waters is chronic and highly costly, though not an old headache as some historians have readily claimed. On the contrary, I have shown that although many shipwrecks took place off the Somali coast, piracy is a new phenomenon and needs to be understood in the context of state collapse in Somalia and changing cost–benefit ratios for organized criminals with transnational operations. Crime is the vital link between piracy and the development and expansion of illegal fishing in Somalia, a much older phenomenon. Contrary to conventional accounts, I have argued that while statelessness, illegal fishing, toxic waste dumping, and poverty are useful in explaining aspects of the rise of the piracy phenomenon, in fact it is primarily greed that motivates the pirates. They have attacked and hijacked all types of ships navigating far beyond Somali waters, and have kidnapped crews for ransom. Finally, the chapter concludes with an analysis and evaluation of how the MENA countries affect and are affected by piracy and illegal fishing. I have assessed the role that they play in resolving these issues, arguing that very few countries from the region contribute to counter-piracy activities, while some perpetuate IUU fishing in Somalia. Needless to say that this passivity—or active complicity—further complicates the efforts of the fragile Somali state and the international community to tackle the two most important problems threatening the livelihoods and lives of ordinary Somali fishermen and, more broadly, those of all creatures inhabiting Somalia's territorial waters.

7

LEARNING GEOPOLITICAL PLURALISM

TOWARD A NEW INTERNATIONAL OIL REGIME?

Clement M. Henry

The Middle East can be viewed as Hell's kitchen, depository of most of the world's most cheaply accessed oil that accounts for much of our global warming.[1] Given its environmental impact, somehow containing its omnipresence must surely be a priority for any political ecology of the region. The Middle East is also viewed by many as a geopolitical prize astride three continents, now sharply fragmented by proxy wars in Libya, Syria, and Yemen. While these conflicts are not about oil and have important local drivers, the imputed strategic value of the commodity has reinforced the region's geopolitical significance as an arena for competition among great powers.

Political ecology (the third paradigm proposed in the introduction to this book), particularly in its more constructivist interpretations, may suggest, however, that oil be viewed as just another commodity without any special strategic value. Was "securing oil" not simply a construct to buttress the US military industrial complex and to legitimate the United States protecting the Free World and pressuring potential adversaries?[2] Yet overemphasizing this narrative risks overlooking not only how oil has been a key material factor in state formation and nation-building in the last century (as explained in the volume's introduction), but also how, under the shadow of Anglo-American hegemony, the oil producers managed to control production first in Texas and then in the whole of the non-Soviet world. In response to an oil glut in the early 1930s, when the price of oil dropped to under 10 cents a barrel, the Texas Railroad Commission acquired the authority to prorate production. Subsequently the major oil producers developed other means among themselves of managing the production of Middle Eastern oil so as to avoid gluts and financial catastrophes.

In the absence of any state government, the major transnational corporations developed other forms of governance that liberal internationalists (following the first, mainstream paradigm discussed in the introduction) define to be "regimes." Underpinning their institutions, rational self-interest may also be seen at work, in the form of iterated prisoners' dilemmas. Resolutions of dilemmas of common interest require actors who set greater value on their expected profits over the long term than the quick gains to be had by defecting. As discussed in this chapter, the "strong hands" of major oil producers supported a self-governing oligopoly that kept control over production. Indeed, Texas export prices subsequently served as a marker for international oil pricing. Until 1959, when the United States slapped import controls on cheaper Middle Eastern oil, crude petroleum was a truly fungible commodity (albeit of many varied grades), traded in a single global market.

Whatever lay behind its construct as a uniquely strategic resource at different points of time in the twentieth century, this chapter proposes to view oil merely as a commodity, but one of a special sort requiring lumpy investments, long lead times, and hence ingenious measures needed to match supply and demand: the properties of oil have important consequences for the kind of institutions that can be built around it. The construct of its strategic value, however, offers a useful forum for teaching the great powers, who probably still believe in the construct, the practice of geopolitical pluralism.

"Geopolitical pluralism" is a term used by former US National Security Advisor Zbigniew Brzezinski in *The Grand Chessboard: American Primacy and its Geostrategic Imperatives* to convey tactics for containing Russia. Although the concept is not yet part of the American foreign policy establishment's official discourse, it should be, but for a different purpose. It conveys hopes of a new international order. This chapter addresses the problem of assembling a new geopolitical pluralism by focusing on the international management of crude petroleum resources. It will argue that key state actors may learn to practice geopolitical pluralism in this clearly defined sector of international political economy, with potential spillover into related sectors. Accordingly, this chapter will first discuss the evolving nature of geopolitical pluralism, notably with respect to the Middle East, and then focus on a possible evolution of the international oil regime.

The expanding location of geopolitical pluralism

At the time Brzezinski published his *Grand Chessboard*, the United States appeared to be the world's "first and only global power," towering above Russia, the European Union, Japan, and China.[3] This dominance was visible both globally as well as in the macro-regions of the earth, with one important exception. Writing from the standpoint of the hegemon, he identified "geopolitical pluralism" as the situation then prevailing in the "black hole" of Central Asia after the break-up of the Soviet Union, and he insisted on reinforcing this pluralism by active US involvement in the region to fence in Russia. He even whetted US strategic interest by advertising its reserves of natural gas and oil, but his focus was on containing Russia.[4] Brzezinski argued that geopolitical pluralism would steer Russia away from its tsarist imperial traditions toward a democratic future in alignment with an expanding Europe.[5] He more broadly envisioned an American regency, "to foster stable geopolitical pluralism throughout Eurasia" for coming decades, until emerging powers grew up to share its power and responsibilities—America's civilizing mission, so to speak.[6]

Geopolitical pluralism in Brzezinski's hands was a whip for preserving America's "liberal" hegemony. Harking back to Sir Halford Mackinder's worries about any one power controlling the "heartland" of the Eurasian "world island," Brzezinski insisted that geopolitical pluralism "has to be an integral part of [an American] policy designed to induce Russia to exercise unambiguously its European option."[7]

> In the short run, it is in America's interest to consolidate and perpetuate the prevailing geopolitical pluralism on the map of Eurasia. That puts a premium on maneuver and manipulation in order to prevent the emergence of a hostile coalition that could eventually seek to challenge America's primacy, not to mention the remote possibility of any one particular state seeking to do so.[8]

In the two decades subsequent to Brzezinski's book, the United States has lost much of the soft power associated with hegemony, but has paradoxically succeeded in implementing the *Chessboard* strategy so successfully—by extending NATO to the Baltics and encouraging the EU to embrace Ukraine—that it has catalyzed a potentially hostile coalition of Russia and China. Unleashed from its whip hand, unruly geopolitical pluralism has expanded the "black hole" of Central Asia to the Middle East and beyond.

Geopolitical pluralism in the Middle East

Richard N. Haass, president of the Council on Foreign Relations, got it right when he announced in 2006 that after "less than 20 years ... the American era in the Middle East ... has ended. Visions of a new, Europe-like region—peaceful, prosperous, democratic—will not be realized. Much more likely is the emergence of a new Middle East that will cause great harm to itself, the United States, and the world."[9] In other words, the American hegemony presumed by Brzezinski no longer prevailed a mere decade later, after the fiasco of the US-led invasion of Iraq in 2003. In 1997, Brzezinski had carefully distinguished between the "power vacuum" of the "Eurasian Balkans" and the Middle East, which was also unstable but where "American power is that region's ultimate arbiter."[10] For Haass, that distinction made little sense when American power was waning, globally as well as regionally. Not only had the United States defied the United Nations requirement of a second resolution to authorize military intervention in Iraq; it also preempted the inspection of Hans Blix for weapons of mass destruction, only subsequently to discover that there were none.

Finally in 2011 Brzezinski, too, recognized major changes in the distribution of global power and, presciently for some of the studies in this book, wrote, "As American hegemony disappears and regional competition intensifies, disputes over natural resources like water have the potential to develop into full-scale conflicts."[11] Interviewed in 2014, he fully laid to rest any idea of American hegemony. "The fact of the matter is that the redistribution of global power has produced a situation in which the US is no longer the sole hegemon."[12] Geopolitical pluralism, originally the condition of a "black hole" in Central Asia, now extended to the entire hemisphere.

Late-twentieth-century America's other geopolitical rockstar, Henry Kissinger,[13] points to a significant source of underlying global instability. Stable geopolitical pluralism, like the pluralism of a liberal or consociational democracy or some form of corporatism, would presuppose a set of generally accepted norms of behavior; but for Kissinger, the world stage is a cacophony of norms. In his *World Order*, Kissinger moved a step beyond Samuel Huntington's classic *Clash of Civilizations*—with as its main argument the emergence of religious and cultural fault lines that spelled doom for any attempts at building a consensual global order—and sought to specify the norms most vigorously put forward by the principal protagonists on the international stage.[14] Agreement on any common denominator such as Europe's Westphalian order seems distant; there are no commonly accepted scales or procedures for balancing the national interests involved in global pluralism. Kissinger recognized that the post-World War II (liberal) order of the "Free World" no longer prevails, despite the collapse of the Soviet Union. The absence of a shared normative framework in global politics bodes ill for world order in this reading of contemporary international relations.

These pessimistic analyses by some of its veteran observers notwithstanding, much of the American foreign policy establishment continues to perceive the United States as the lone superpower, "indispensable" for holding the world together with its multiplicity of alliances and trade agreements. In Hillary Clinton's review of Kissinger's book, she observes, for instance: "No other nation can bring together the necessary coalitions and provide the necessary capabilities to meet today's complex global threats ... the United States is uniquely positioned to lead in the 21st century."[15] But how, in her words citing Kissinger, may America relate "power to [the] legitimacy" required of any new international order? Her answer is for the United States to use all of the diplomatic as well as military tools at its disposal, including "soft" and "smart" power, terms elaborated by Joseph Nye. The latter defines soft power as the ability to have one's way without exercising coercion or offering economic incentives.[16]

The substitutes of soft power and smart power still serve for many members of the foreign policy establishment to propel the "American Century," originally proclaimed in 1941, well into the twenty-first century.[17] In *Is the American Century Over?* Nye dismisses the pessimists, but unfortunately America's new "preponderance" (rather than hegemony or empire) seems primarily based on excessive military power, since the other principal forms of state power, economic, and ideological or soft power, are diminishing relative to other states.[18] The good news is that soft power is no zero-sum game: an increase in Chinese soft power does not entail a decline in America's, but might rather enable the two to work more effectively on global issues, such as climate change and energy conservation.

Nye hence lays groundwork for geopolitical pluralism, but underestimates how radically American soft power has declined in the Middle East and

North Africa. Like much of the American foreign policy establishment, he recognized the adverse consequences of the invasion and occupation of Iraq, but may miss the broader perception of America as "rogue nation." A rogue, as with a rogue elephant, is "no longer obedient, belonging or accepted, not controllable or answerable; deviant, having an abnormally savage or unpredictable disposition."[19] For Clyde Prestowitz, anticipating Mearsheimer and Walt, "America's differences with the world could be largely explained in four words: Israel, Taiwan, religion, and lobby."[20] Leaving Taiwan aside and focusing on the Muslim world, extending from Morocco across Central Asia and Northern Africa to Indonesia, uncritical US support for Israel, a colonial settler state, has steadily eroded the moral authority of mid-twentieth-century America.[21]

In truth, the United States had one major strategic interest in the Middle East in 1945, namely oil, especially Saudi oil. In President Roosevelt's historic meeting with King Abdel Aziz Saud, he cemented America's close ties with the kingdom and promised to consult him about the disposition of postwar Palestine. Without any consultation, however, President Truman went ahead, against the advice of his state and defense departments, to recognize the state of Israel in 1948. US diplomacy then attempted over many years to broker peace between the Israelis and Arab countries so as to insure continued friendly access to the region's oil. The fact that the management of oil was in the hands of private multinational corporations helped to insulate it from official American support for Israel. When President Dwight D. Eisenhower rejected the tripartite aggression of Suez against Gamal Abdel Nasser's Egypt by London, Paris, and Tel Aviv in 1956, the United States still appeared to be opposed to traditional European colonialism and ready to serve as an honest broker between Israel and Arab states. But it lost its benevolent image long before it invaded Iraq in 2003; one critical turning point was the 1967 Six-Day War. President Lyndon B. Johnson gave Israel a free pass for its surprise preemptive strike on Egypt.

Not only did the United States lose its credibility as an honest broker between Israel and the Palestinians over the years, it also gradually developed a military presence in the region that recalled earlier colonial occupations of Arab and Islamic lands. As the British withdrew their military presence from the Persian Gulf in the 1960s, the United States assumed its classic imperial responsibility to keep the sea lanes open, notably for the free flow of oil, while perhaps forgetting that the Muslim world had been the principal victim of European (including Russian) colonialism. The colonial empires depicted in bright colors in the early-twentieth-century maps were virtually coextensive with the Dar Al-Islam prior to the nineteenth century. Only a tiny sliver of it in the southern edge of the Philippines belonged to the United States. By the end of the twentieth century, however, American military forces were stationed in much of the Arabian Peninsula and were active in other parts of the Middle East and North Africa.

The first American military presence in Lebanon in 1958 paralleled the British return to Jordan, but was fortunately limited, as the Lebanese military rapidly took charge, allowing the US military to withdraw after three months. The second intervention there was less fortunate, as the United States, perhaps inadvertently, was perceived to take sides with the Israeli and (Lebanese) Phalangist forces in the internationalized civil war that erupted in 1975.[22] Ronald Reagan withdrew the two regiments of marines before the failure to bring peace to Lebanon could become an issue in his 1984 campaign for re-election. Meanwhile, however, the two-term Republican president had become militarily engaged with Qaddafi's Libya, first in 1981 over the Gulf of Sirte, then in 1986 with a major air raid and attempted assassination of the Libyan leader in response to an act of terrorism in a Berlin nightclub.[23]

As for other military intrusions, the Carter Doctrine (1980) had beefed up US commitment to Gulf security in response to the Iranian Revolution and the Soviet invasion of Afghanistan, but it was only with the end of the Cold War that a major US military build-up in the region became possible, now that the Soviet Union was no longer a deterrent. The consequences of Desert Storm—the US-led coalition operation which removed Iraqi troops from Kuwait in 1991 by deploying overwhelming force—were enormous. Prior to the invasion of Kuwait, many Saudi royals and clerics had deep misgivings about permitting the United States to build up its forces on Saudi soil. Security guarantees had hitherto been uncontroversial because they were "over the horizon." In retrospect, the key moment was in August 1990, after Saddam Hussein invaded Kuwait and annexed it as his country's nineteenth province. President George H. W. Bush determined, without any prompting (but with plenty of support) from British Prime Minister Margaret Thatcher, to prevent an Arab compromise and to punish Saddam for his transgression of the principle of national self-determination, resulting in a costly expenditure of US soft power.[24] He encouraged Egypt's Hosni Mubarak to torpedo any "Arab" solution that might extract Saddam from Kuwait without loss of face by attending to his grievances against Kuwait and the United Arab Emirates. The latter two were flooding international oil markets prior to the invasion and thus diminishing Iraqi oil revenues needed for reconstruction and debt repayment after the long war with Iran (1980–88).

The Bush administration's decision to rally unequivocally behind Kuwait and Saudi Arabia and to increase militarization of the crisis resulted in further military build-ups in the GCC from 1991 to 2002, displaying an ever more visible imperial presence, even before the invasion of Iraq. In effect, America lost much of its soft power in the Muslim world by converting it into hard military power, rather than making peace between Israel and the Palestinians. In 1990–91 the first Bush administration had managed to preserve at least some of America's soft power by maintaining a coalition consisting of Egypt, Morocco, and Syria, as well as many other countries. Standing up to Israel concerning loan guarantees for illegal settlements in occupied Palestine may have cost Bush the 1992 elections, but he retained America's standing in the region despite the use of hard power. Subsequent administrations forgot that the quid pro quo for any US military presence was enforcing a peace process upon Israelis as well as Palestinians.

Samantha Power, the US ambassador to the United Nations in the second Obama administration (2012–16), confirms the subsequent US loss of soft power in her very defense of American's selective interventions on behalf of democracy and human rights. She regrets that American diplomats, hidden away in "fortress-like embassies," are unable to develop local connections and urges "thicker involvement in—and knowledge of—the world beyond our borders."[25] Such efforts grow ever more problematic as public opinion in most countries—not only in the Middle East—has become more hostile, requiring ever greater security precautions for diplomats, and nowadays for scholars as well. A turning point came after Black September 1970, when Jordan suppressed the Palestine Liberation Organization (PLO), and the old American embassy beefed up its security. Eventually a new fortress replaced it. In Cairo, too, the American embassy underwent a major remodeling into a gigantic fortress surrounded by a high wall, just after official relations between the two countries dramatically improved. The pattern has been replicated across the Arab world.

Non-governmental organizations that in theory might promote American soft power also face increasing control and opposition from incumbent regimes. In Cairo, for instance, not only Human Rights Watch, but also the Carter Center closed down its offices. On one level the fate of these and many other NGOs could be ascribed to the comeback of Egypt's "authoritarian" regime backed by the military. But on a deeper level it was the US support for Sadat and Mubarak that had made them vulnerable. Sadat lost his life by enforcing Camp David agreements that betrayed the Palestinians, but Mubarak continued his pro-American policies against the bulk of Egyptian public opinion. As Jason Brownlee cogently argues, a US policy of "Democracy Prevention" systematically trumped any lip service to promoting democracy or human rights.[26] The two principal American objectives were to protect Israel and service good relations with the Arab oil producers. The United States supported dictators across the Arab East for the sake of oil and Israel.

As Prestowitz suggests, the underlying issue is uncritical support for Israeli settler colonialism by the American political class. The Israel lobby, which holds huge sway over the US Congress, repeatedly sabotaged efforts by the Obama administration as well as earlier ones to promote an Israeli–Palestinian peace.[27] Consequently much of Muslim and Christian Arab public opinion across the Middle East and North Africa views the United States as an accomplice of the Israeli occupation of East Jerusalem and the West Bank and its asphyxiating blockade of Gaza.

Polls of public opinion across the Arab world underscore how the United States is held in low esteem after years of misguided foreign adventures. Table 7.1 presents the findings of Pew polls from 2002 to 2015. People were asked whether they had very favorable, somewhat favorable, or unfavorable or very unfavorable opinion of the United States. Of those polled in Egypt, Jordan, Kuwait, Lebanon, Morocco, Palestinian territories, Tunisia, and Turkey, favorable majorities appeared only in Kuwait and Lebanon, and even in these countries opinion had turned against the United States by 2011. In Jordan, Lebanon, and Turkey, US approval ratings dropped respectively from 25, 36, and 30 percent to 1, 27, and 15 percent. After the Arab Spring in 2011, favorable views of the United States continued to drop across the world—in Egypt from 20 percent in 2011 to 10 percent in 2014, and even in Lebanon from 49 to 39 percent.

The soft power of the United States in the region in effect became negative, tarring American allies and recruiting more adversaries. As William Polk has argued on the basis of past experience, American involvement may further empower revolutionary forces such as al-Qaeda and the so-called Islamic State, known in the region by its Arabic language acronym "Daesh."[28] Indeed, both al-Qaeda in Afghanistan and Daesh in Iraq and Syria invited American retaliation so as to recruit more followers. Public opinion polls support the wisdom of such tactics. Majorities in most of the Arab countries surveyed by

Table 7.1: Percentages of people having favorable view of the United States

Country	*2002*	*2003*	*2004*	*2005*	*2006*	*2007*	*2008*	*2009*	*2010*	*2011*	*2012*	*2013*
Egypt	–	–	–	–	30	21	22	27	17	20	19	–
Jordan	25	1	5	21	15	20	19	25	21	13	12	–
Kuwait	–	63	–	–	–	46	–	–	–	–	–	–
Lebanon	36	27	–	42	–	47	51	55	52	49	48	–
Morocco	–	–	–	–	–	15	–	–	–	–	–	–
Palestinian ter.	–	–	–	–	–	13	–	15	–	18	–	–
Tunisia	–	–	–	–	–	–	–	–	–	–	45	–
Turkey	30	15	30	23	12	9	12	14	17	10	15	–

Full question wording: Please tell me if you have a very favorable, somewhat favorable, somewhat unfavorable or very unfavorable opinion.

Notes: Favorable combines "very favorable" and "somewhat favorable" responses. Unfavorable combines "very" and "somewhat unfavorable."

Source: Pew polls http://www.pewglobal.org/database/custom-analysis/indicator/1/countries/64,111,117,121,148,168,223,224/.

the Arab Barometer believe that "The United States' interference in the region justifies armed operations against the United States everywhere." Table 7.2 reports the findings in 2011 and 2013. In each survey more than half of the entire sample of Arabs surveyed agreed to the proposition. Only in Lebanon and Yemen for both years, and in Egypt and Tunisia in 2013, did small majorities reject the proposition.

Public opinion in the region clearly rejects unilateral American leadership. Geopolitical pluralism in the Middle East means that the United States must share any international responsibilities for order and security in the region with other interested outside parties, notably the permanent members of the UN Security Council, including China and Russia. By one measure (purchase power parity) China became the world's largest economy in 2014. It is also the largest importer of Middle East oil. Russia, which still enjoys nuclear parity with the United States, is one of the top three world producers of oil, along with Saudi Arabia and the United States. Russia also shares with the United States the dubious distinction of being one of the world's top two suppliers of military hardware.[29] Under Vladimir Putin, Russia has played an increasingly important role in the region, notably in Syria, and may also need to coordinate international oil markets with OPEC. The new geopolitical situation, for better or worse, will have a major impact on world energy markets and global warming. It is argued here that a new international energy regime could contribute significantly to a more stable geopolitical pluralism as well as to higher, less volatile prices for one of its key elements, crude petroleum.

International oil regimes

In the heyday of America's "liberal hegemony" following World War II, vast quantities of oil came on-stream from the Middle East to rebuild Western Europe. They caused barely a ripple in international oil prices, because an international regime was in place governed by multinational oil companies. In the language of international political economy, a "regime" was in place, consisting of "principles, norms, rules, and decision-making procedures… It is these intermediate injunctions—politically consequential but specific enough that violations and changes can be identified—that I take as the essence of international regimes."[30] They constitute a framework for managing a particular sector or policy arena of international political economy. In the case of energy security, defined as "the uninterrupted availability of energy sources at an affordable price," oil remains the principal source of global energy, and its

Table 7.2: War Against America

"The United States' interference in the region justifies armed operations against the United States everywhere."

Country of study	*Year*	*Number*	*% agree strongly*	*% agree*	*% disagree*	*% disagree strongly*
Algeria	2011	897	12.0	40.8	32.9	14.3
Algeria	2013	989	38.8	36.6	14.6	10.0
Palestine	2011	1,127	20.9	39.0	34.1	6.00
Palestine	2013	1,135	19.0	42.4	33.3	5.30
Iraq	2011	1,048	29.0	41.3	21.9	7.80
Iraq	2013	1,107	14.2	38.5	31.2	16.2
Jordan	2011	1,020	16.5	41.1	28.7	13.7
Jordan	2013	1,466	17.6	32.7	32.2	17.5
Kuwait	2013	963	12.5	47.0	28.6	11.9
Lebanon	2011	1,308	20.2	23.5	19.6	36.7
Lebanon	2013	1,112	22.5	26.3	17.9	33.3
Morocco	2013	1,002	12.5	41.9	27.6	18.0
Saudi Arabia	2011	1,042	28.4	31.3	17.4	22.9
Sudan	2011	1,337	34.6	26.9	22.7	15.8
Sudan	2013	1,143	18.8	34.8	28.0	18.4
Tunisia	2011	813	19.6	43.8	24.8	11.8
Tunisia	2013	966	12.8	29.7	28.1	29.4
Egypt	2011	1,092	19.4	43.0	25.3	12.3
Egypt	2013	961	11.1	37.0	26.1	25.7
Yemen	2011	1,004	16.2	30.9	30.7	22.2
Yemen	2013	1,042	16.3	21.2	29.9	32.5
Total sample	2011	10,688	22.2	35.4	25.5	16.9
	2013	12,977	17.8	34.3	28.3	19.6

international management—or "regime"—must assure its security of access, transit, and "affordable" pricing.[31] These three prerequisites may serve to define an international oil regime. The principal ones were a private sector oligopoly associated with the Seven Sisters; the Organization of Petroleum Exporting Countries (OPEC), founded in 1960; and the International Energy Agency, founded in Paris in 1974 by Organisation for Economic Co-operation and Development (OECD) countries in response to the oil shock of 1973–4.

The Seven Sisters (1928–70)

Whether US hegemony ended in the 2000s or the 1960s, it underwrote a remarkably effective oil regime until about 1970.[32] Despite huge surges in production and demand after World War II, an international cartel, the so-called Seven Sisters, kept oil prices steady and thereby underpinned the so-called "*trente glorieuses*," the nearly three decades of incredible economic reconstruction and prosperity in North America and Western Europe post-1945.[33]

In constant 2015 dollars, shown in Figure 7.1, oil prices moved from $13.58 in 1945, and a high of $20.15 in 1947, to a low of $10.98 in 1970. Access was not a problem, with most supplies in the hands of the multinational oil companies, whether in the Middle East or elsewhere, except Mexico, Romania, or the Soviet Union. US naval supremacy assured the free flow of oil across seas and through chokepoints such as the Straits of Hormuz in the Gulf and Malacca in Southeast Asia. It also enforced court orders such as

Figure 7.1: Spot Oil Prices 1861-2015

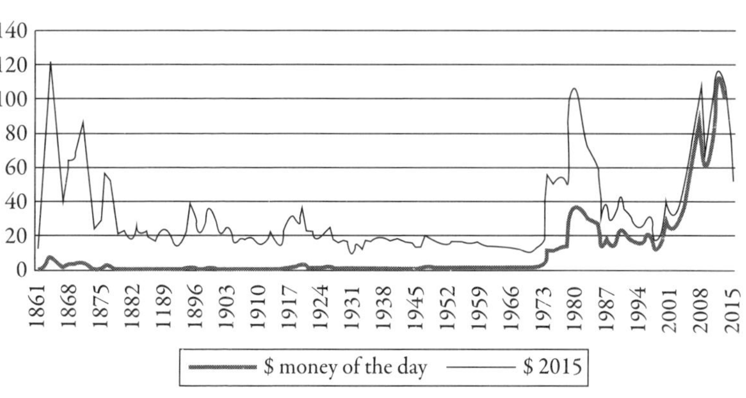

Source: BP Statistical Review of World Energy 2016.

Aden's quarantine of Iranian oil after Iran's Prime Minister Mossadegh nationalized it without agreement on compensation to the Anglo-Iranian Oil Company (now known as BP) in 1951. Indeed, the international legal system guaranteed the series of contracts signed between the major oil companies that transformed promises, such as the 1928 Achnacarry "As Is" agreement to respect each company's market shares—"ropes of sand" in oil magnate John D. Rockefeller's words—into enforceable commitments that sustained the market shares of the Seven Sisters.

The present account follows Theodore Moran in describing the analytic underpinnings of the sorority.[34] An Armenian trader, Calouste Gulbenkian, organized an original cartel in 1912 to exploit any oil discovered in the Ottoman Empire. After the First World War, he reorganized it with the corporate representatives of the victorious Allies to exploit any oil discovered in the successor states of the Ottoman Empire. The Red Line Agreement of 1928 included Turkey, the Levant, Iraq, and the Arabian Peninsula, but excluded Kuwait, a pre-war British protectorate. Gulbenkian bargained with the major companies, supported by the victors of World War I, Britain's Anglo-Iranian Oil Company and Royal Dutch Shell (60 percent Dutch-owned), France's Companie Française des Pétroles (CFP), and America's Standard Oil of New Jersey (Exxon), which also represented a group of smaller oil companies including Standard Oil of New York (Mobil). He exchanged his Ottoman concession for a 5 percent interest in a new Iraq Petroleum Company in which each of the four major companies or groups had a 23.75 percent interest.

These companies had different needs and expectations for new, eventually gigantic supplies of cheap oil. As explained by Moran, stronger companies such as Exxon had a greater interest in restricting supply to keep up prices for the long term, whereas weaker ones like the French, the smaller American companies, or Gulbenkian himself for that matter, had an interest in maximizing production of the cheap Iraqi oil discovered in 1927.[35] The stronger companies solved the problem of controlling supply by a system of weighted voting, whereby a supermajority of three companies or groups was required. And since Exxon always had one of the two American directorships, it only needed Royal Dutch Shell or BP—satiated with Iranian oil—to block any excessive production. These were the hard core of the cartel, controlling 71 percent of the market for crude petroleum in 1946.[36]

Other contractual arrangements, also analyzed by Moran, had similar outcomes for bringing Kuwaiti and Saudi oil online.[37] In Kuwait, BP teamed up with Gulf Oil Company, one of the smaller "Seven Sisters," and split production fifty–fifty, but sold it in long-term contracts to Exxon-Mobil and Royal Dutch Shell respectively. In Saudi Arabia, Standard Oil of California (Chevron) included Texaco to form Caltex, and then eventually added Exxon and Mobil to form the Arabian American Oil Company (Aramco), once the latter two renegotiated the Red Line Agreement with Gulbenkian. Arrangements within Aramco again ensured that Exxon could keep Saudi production in line with market demand. Supermajority voting requirements gave Exxon and Mobil a veto over its smaller partners, and if Mobil joined them, Exxon received automatic compensation for underlifting.

In Iran, too, the hard core of the cartel could control output once a CIA-sponsored coup in 1953 put the shah back on the peacock throne and opened up the Iran National Oil Company to an international consortium of the Seven Sisters, CFP, and nine independent American oil companies. Saturated with oil in 1954, the "strong hands" could prevent an oil glut through a system of weighted voting that gave them effective veto power over any additional production favored by the weaker sisters and independents.

Eventually new, unregulated Libyan oil—Colonel Muammar Qaddafi had taken power in Tripoli in a coup in 1969, flying the flag of anti-imperialism—unraveled the oil oligopoly as one of the American independents, Occidental Petroleum, broke ranks and consented to increased prices imposed by the host government. Not to be outbid, the shah of Iran ratcheted up oil prices, but it was the sight of the United States re-arming Israel in plain daylight—on 14 October during the Yom Kippur/Ramadan War of 1973—that produced the final break. On 17 October, the Organization of Arab Petroleum Exporting Countries (OAPEC) met in Kuwait and decided to boycott the United States and Holland and gradually to reduce total production. While the majors controlled shipping and downstream distribution, offsetting the boycott, the gradual cutbacks in production led to skyrocketing spot prices for crude petroleum.

OPEC (1973–present day)

The founders of the Organization of Petroleum Exporting Countries (OPEC), one of whom had studied at the University of Texas at Austin, were inspired by the Texas Railroad Commission (TRC), which is headquartered in the Texas capital. In the 1930s the TRC acquired the authority to set production quotas, ostensibly for conservation, but in reality to balance supply with demand and thereby regulate prices.[38] Once the oil-producing countries gained control of the companies and were able to set prices, the founders of OPEC aspired to emulate the TRC.[39] But OPEC is an association of sovereign states, whereas the TRC is an arm of state and federal government authorized to regulate the production of individuals and corporations.

Theodore Moran has argued that OPEC would need a system of weighted voting to achieve the balances between supply and demand and steady prices achieved by the Seven Sisters oligopoly. Power to determine OPEC allocations, like those of the Seven Sisters, would have to be in the "strong hands" of producers taking the long-term view of maximizing oil revenues rather than wanting quick returns. For instance, to simulate the decision-making structure of the Iraq Petroleum Corporation in the Red Line Agreement of 1928: "Imagine the OPEC governments leaving the exporting governments' decisions about production and price to an OPEC voting structure in which Saudi Arabia, Kuwait, and the UAE had four votes each, with one vote for the other ten members, including Iran, Iraq, Venezuela, and Nigeria."[40]

As it was, OPEC set the oil prices in Vienna in October 1973, just after Saudi Arabia and other Arab members of OPEC had agreed to cut production. As demand exceeded expected supply, OPEC could barely keep up with spot prices, and after 1980 it could do little in response to an oil glut. Only in 1982, as prices kept falling, did OPEC agree to allocate production among its members, and many of the states exceeded their quotas. In 1983, OPEC gave up any pretense of setting oil prices, and in 1986 Saudi Arabia, tired of serving as the swing producer losing market share, flooded the markets to discipline the cheaters who were suddenly faced with price drops and revenue losses. One of the big losers turned out to be Saddam Hussein's Iraq—a predicament that, as shown above, had major geopolitical consequences when he invaded Kuwait in 1990.

Due to nationalizations by the host governments of most of the international oil companies' concessions in the Middle East and elsewhere, upstream production of crude oil was disconnected from downstream refining and sales still controlled by the companies. For instance Exxon, which had been a totally integrated company, was subsequently in the 1980s and 1990s producing upstream about one-quarter of the product sold in its gas stations. Much greater volumes of crude oil were sold on international markets, primarily the New York Mercantile Exchange (NYMEX) and the London Metal Exchange. NYMEX and London's International Petroleum Exchange (now ICE Futures) eventually set forward market prices for West Texas Intermediate (WTI) and Brent, respectively. Traders and speculators in international commodity markets in effect replaced most efforts by the state oil companies to control prices, because OPEC could not enforce production quotas on sovereign states. One consequence was ever greater price volatility, with "financialization" compounding the impacts of geopolitics and business cycles on expected supply and demand.[41]

Part of then Vice President George H. W. Bush's mission (Bush himself, of course, was a Texan oil man) to Saudi Arabia in 1987, however, may have been to enlist the kingdom's help in propping up oil prices, which were impoverishing Texan as well as other oil producers. Figure 7.1 shows that prices bottomed out in 1986 and rose slightly in 1987, as the Saudis cut back production that year.[42] Possibly a "Saudi-American regime" was at work inside OPEC.[43] It would subsequently come to the military defense of those OPEC "strong hands" noted by Moran. Conversely, diminishing oil prices, due in part to Kuwait and the UAE exceeding their OPEC quotas, was one of Saddam Hussein's reasons for invading Kuwait in 1990. Iraq's invasion of Kuwait pushed up spot prices in 1990, once Kuwaiti and Iraqi oil were removed from international markets. They increased from a daily average of $18.23 in 1989, to an average high of $23.73 in 1990, with a peak of $40. OPEC, principally Saudi Arabia, increased production sufficiently to prevent another major oil shock like those of 1973–4 and 1979. As Figure 7.1 also shows, however, any Saudi-American oil regime had little steadying impact upon prices after 1997. From a low of $12.72 in 1998, they began their steady ascent due to understandings reached in 1999 between Saudi Arabia's Crown Prince Abdullah and Iran's reformist President Mohammad Khatami.[44]

However, improved Saudi relations with Iran were at cross purposes with America's Iran and Libya Sanctions Act of 1996. By then, Riyadh's relations with the United States were already under strain due to the prolonged American military presence in the land of Islam's holy cities of Mecca and Medina. After repeated US use of bases in Saudi Arabia to enforce no-fly zones over Saddam's Iraq, the Saudis found it convenient for the United States to transfer its forces to Qatar, whose rulers were less exposed to popular grievances expressed by religious leaders and themselves eager to enjoy the protection of the American security umbrella, giving them greater leeway in Gulf politics and paving the way for Qatar's post-2000 activist foreign policy.[45] And efforts of OPEC to control prices, with or without American prompting, no longer seemed possible for other reasons. The American-led invasion of Iraq resulted in a strengthening of Iranian influence that deeply unsettled the Saudi leadership, even if it stopped short of rupturing the Riyadh–Washington relationship. By removing Saddam and banning his Baathist Party officials from public life, the United States had dramatically diminished the influence of Iraq's Sunni minority in favor of the Shi'a majority, largely represented by political exiles returning from Iran, Saudi Arabia's traditional rival for regional leadership. This also explains King Abdullah's barely veiled meddling in Iraqi politics as sectarian violence increased, sometimes leading his agencies and the US Department of Defense and State Department to work at cross purposes, further deepening the political malaise in Iraq.[46]

Given the fundamental security and economic interests on both sides, Saudi ties with the Bush administration remained strong, however, and Saudi production again ramped up production by almost 2 million barrels per day, to a total of almost 10 million per day in March and April 2003, to alleviate geopolitical anxieties and keep oil prices steady. But the Saudis were unable to sustain such increases in production past May, and prices began their steep rise. By 2006, the Saudis no longer had the 2–3 million barrels in spare capacity needed to keep prices under control.[47] Subsequent increases in production did not keep pace with rising world demand until the economic crash of 2008–9, when Saudi Arabia cut its daily production by over a million barrels. The kingdom now needed more oil revenues to meet domestic needs of rising populations. The target range of $20–$30 per barrel in 2000 increased to $80 a decade later, and by 2011 the kingdom needed oil prices in this range in order to preempt the Arab Spring of popular uprisings and balance its national budget. But in 2014, with plenty of excess capacity, it opted to keep its share of the expanding market and put higher-cost US tight oil out of business (see below). Prices again plunged from all-time highs averaging $117 in 2011, to a low of $22.48 in January 2016 (Figure 7.2). Any OPEC or Saudi-American control of oil production and prices seemed out of the question. Not much was left of the once apparently impregnable oil-exporting regime, once state actors had replaced multinational enterprises.

The International Energy Agency (IEA)

The principal oil importers established their own rival international oil regime in 1975, in response to OPEC and to the first oil shock. In 1974, the major oil-importing countries had bid up prices against one another and were, in Robert Keohane's words, "unable to solve the dilemma of collective action" in the face of artificial shortages created by OAPEC cutbacks in production.[48] The IEA developed a set of rules and procedures for exchanges of information

Figure 7.2: Spot Prices 2003–2016

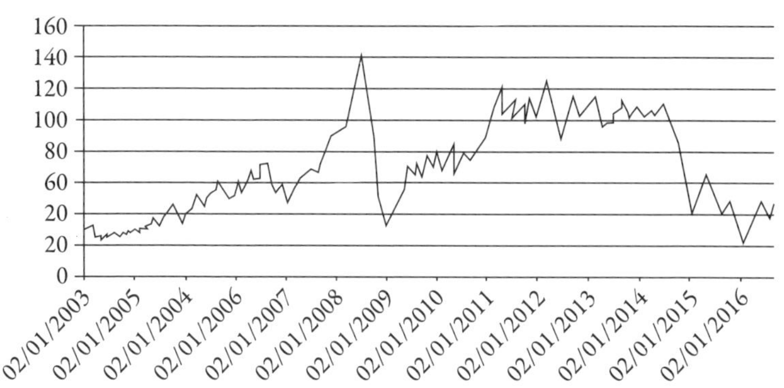

Source: OPEC database.

and emergency oil sharing to respond to any future crises. It also engaged in monitoring oil markets and long-range planning, including efforts to control pricing. To alleviate price volatility, it set a price floor in 1975 of $7 per barrel. The idea was to offer an incentive to producers to keep investing in capacity so as to prevent shortages and dramatic price hikes. But oil prices quickly bounded beyond the floor to new heights and higher floors.

Keohane gives mixed reviews of its responses to the oil shock of 1979 associated with the Iranian Revolution. Prices doubled despite the fact that production actually exceeded demand in the year as a whole, according to an IEA report.[49] Subsequently, however, the members were expected to accumulate strategic petroleum reserves (SPR) that enhanced the ability of the IEA to respond to future crises. Every member is now expected to hold reserves equivalent to ninety days of imports. With almost 700 million barrels in September 2016, the SPR of the United States almost met this requirement, as did the SPRs of other principal OECD members.[50] Although other major oil importers, notably China and India, are not members, they, too, are accumulating SPRs and are viewed as "partners" on the IEA's website. China is now the world's largest importer, but does not yet have plans beyond its goal in 2020 of accumulating a reserve of 500 million barrels, well below ninety days of expected imports.

If reserves are sufficiently abundant, some may be released to smooth prices. When the uprising against Qaddafi in 2011 disrupted Libyan oil exports, for instance, the United States and some European countries released some of their reserves, cushioning market instability. As Figure 7.2 shows, spot oil prices reached a high of $120 at the end of April 2011, but then quickly steadied to a range of $100–$110, until sharp ups and downs at the end of the year and spring of 2012. Many IEA members could then in subsequent years accumulate strategic reserves amounting to at least ninety days of expected imports, but the IEA would not prevent prices from plummeting in 2014.

Toward a new oil regime?

Classical theorists of international regimes, notably Robert Keohane, had hoped that their architecture would survive the loss of American hegemony; they were confident that the structures built over time would outlast the interests that initially gave rise to them. But there is another way of conceptualizing the relationship between global order and regimes than the former exogenously determining the latter. What is suggested here is that a (reworked) energy regime, building up from convergences of national interests, can actually contribute to the consolidation of a new world order—a much broader objective than merely governing energy markets. Chastened by its failure to bring peace to Afghanistan, Iraq, or Syria, the United States needs to redefine its national strategy in the new context of geopolitical pluralism. An oil regime including not only the Middle East and the OECD countries, but also China, the biggest importer, and Russia, one of the largest producers and exporters, could contribute to a more stable world order. How then might a new regime assure security of access, transit, and "affordable" pricing?

For starters, the International Energy Agency could be expanded to include all the principal consumers, not just OECD members. In 2015 more than half the world's consumption of crude petroleum came from non-OECD countries, and virtually all the substantial increase expected by 2040 was to come principally from non-OECD Asia. China and India need to become full members of the IEA, along with other "priority partner countries," such as Brazil, Indonesia, Mexico, and South Africa.[51] Since they are less developed countries, they should be exempted from the IEA's "demand-restraint program" for reducing national oil consumption. They need to join in IEA procedures for exchange of information and emergency oil sharing to respond to any future crises. For instance, were the Strait of Hormuz to be closed to traffic, they would need to coordinate alternative sources of supply with Japan and South Korea, the Asian members of the IEA, and the OECD.

Security of transit of internationally traded oil is currently assured by the US Navy. Alfred Thayer Mahan (1840–1914) was a prominent geostrategist and US Navy admiral who believed, unlike Mackinder, that "predominant

Anglo-American sea power in its broadest sense was the key to ensuring the geopolitical pluralism of Eurasia."[52] Today, even those who, like Barry Posen, urge "restraint" and ending the US role as world policeman nevertheless insist on an extensive US naval presence across the globe.[53] An effective international oil regime, however, requires full participation from principal consumers as well as producers. Consequently, close cooperation with rising Chinese and Indian navies will be needed to maintain security of transit along the Silk "Road" linking the South China Sea to the Persian Gulf.[54]

One sign of potential cooperation is the building in 2016 of a Chinese naval base only 8 miles away from a United States military base in Djibouti. Despite some US concerns about China's "aggressive" entry, the two naval powers will have to learn to live together.[55] Increasing its naval role in support of UN peacekeeping and other activities in the region is simply part of rising China's taking on larger global responsibilities, as with peacekeeping and other interventions in African affairs.[56] Indeed, Beijing and Washington have much to gain from recognizing one another's interests and from substantial cooperation, not least in terms of energy security. The more sensitive issue concerns the South China Sea. Just as Britain could compromise with rising American naval power in the Caribbean at the turn of the twentieth century, and thus ensured a peaceful transition in global maritime hegemony, so the United States and China must resolve their problem of freedom of navigation in these seas to buttress a peaceful new international order.[57] Strategic compromise is needed in the new world of geopolitical pluralism, of which securing a durable oil regime is only a small—but nevertheless vital—part.

In this new world, however, the upstream supplies of oil also need to be secured, and almost half of it exported to international markets comes from the Middle East and North Africa.[58] Much of it is at risk, especially since the Arab uprisings of 2011. Iraq and Libya have suffered extreme production losses, and the region's major producer, Saudi Arabia, has—successfully so far—defended itself against several attacks of the critical node of Abqaiq that might have removed up to 6 million barrels per day from international markets for several months.[59] Were an attack finally to succeed, how would markets respond? Worse, if the Saudi regime were to fall to Daesh or al-Qaeda, already active in Yemen, would the world still have adequate supplies of oil?

To prevent any one power from dominating the major oil supplies, the United States saw fit to intervene militarily in 1990, but any further interventions with boots on the ground seem out of the question, for both internal (fiscal and political) reasons and because of the external resistance that any intervention risks generating. Even a United Nations force would be highly problematic. To be effective, it would require the full backing of the Security Council, including all five permanent members—an unlikely prospect given the current geopolitical polarization. But a functional IEA could easily keep the world supplied—the ninety-day SPRs being able to compensate for half a year's supplies from the entire MENA region in the unlikely scenario of an entire region in flames. As for the United States, only 20 percent of its imports come from the Middle East, and increases in tight (shale) oil production could compensate for the loss within months.

The problem for any new oil regime is not to secure supply but rather to sustain an "affordable," relatively stable price. In the current situation of an oil glut, what may be affordable is a matter of greater concern to the producers than to the consumers. The producers of course need a price above their marginal cost of production. Many of them, including Russia, depend on the profits from their export of crude petroleum to balance their national budgets. Above the marginal cost of production, then, is another "fiscal break-even" price of oil; Figure 7.3 gives them for a number of oil-dependent economies. As noted above, Saudi Arabia, OPEC's classic "strong hand," has in a sense weakened because its break-even point increased to over $90 per barrel before diminishing as a result of vertiginous budget cuts in 2016 to $66.70.[60]

Figure 7.3: Fiscal Break-Even Oil Prices in 2015

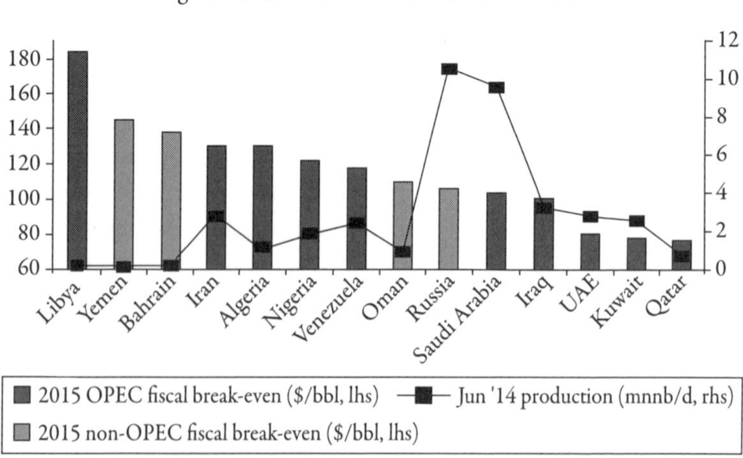

Source: IMF, Deutsche Bank, and Robert Scott, "Fiscal Break-Even Cost for the Top Oil-Dependent Economies," *Market Realist*, Jan. 7, 2016: http://marketrealist.com/2016/01/fiscal-break-even-cost-top-oil-dependent-economies/

Although slightly out of date, Figure 7.3 presents rough magnitudes of these fiscal break-evens for most of the principal oil producers, including Russia and Iran as well as Saudi Arabia. Across the bar chart a line traces their production in 2014, when Russia's slightly exceeded Saudi Arabia's.[61]

As international oil prices plummeted with increased US production and slower than expected demand caused by China's economic slowdown, Saudi Arabia opened its spigots. The kingdom surpassed Russian average levels of production in 2015 by more than 1 million barrels per day.[62] The Saudis (and UAE) had sufficient financial reserves to survive lower oil prices and were determined to preserve steady increases in market share. Perhaps, too, encouraged by the United States, they were not averse to creating fiscal difficulties for some of their geostrategic competitors, notably Iran and Russia. The official rationale was that they were determined to drive the American high-cost producers of unconventional "tight" oil out of business. Figure 7.4 presents the average marginal costs of production of various sources of crude petroleum. Assuming (conservatively) a total world production of 85 million barrels per day, it was supposed to be possible to increase the production of Saudi Arabia and some of the other low-cost producers on the left side of the graph so as to squeeze out the high-cost producers of tight (shale) oil at the right end.

The trouble with the strategy, of course, is that the new technologies for extracting "tight oil" are becoming ever less expensive. US production indeed

Figure 7.4

Average cost curve for the oil market $/barrel

Average cost ($/bbl)

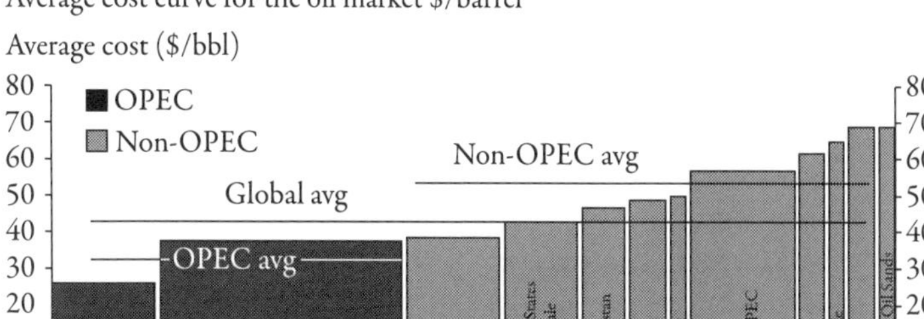

Production (mb/d)

Shale plays lie at the higher end of the non-OPEC marginal cost curve, as infrastructure build-outs, decline rates and high levels of rig activity keep costs high.

Source: Joseph Dancy, IEA: The Shale Mirage –Future Crude Oil Supply Crunch? In *Financial Sense*, Dec. 11, 2013, http://www.financialsense.com/contributors/joseph-dancy/iea-shale-mirage-future-crude-oil-supply-crunch

declined by about 1 million barrels per day in the year since its peak in May 2015, but marginal costs of production have dramatically diminished in some of the fields. There is considerable variation, from as high as $60 down to $23 per barrel in the Permian Basin, Texas. For the sake of comparison, Figure 7.5 presents a recent estimate of the marginal costs of production to the major conventional oil producers. At under $10 per barrel, Kuwait and Saudi Arabia are clearly the low-cost producers, but the other Middle East producers have only slightly higher costs. Costs in Russia are still well under $20 per barrel. But the country with the greatest reserves, Venezuela, is up to $23 per barrel, and its more expensive tar sands remain unexploited. They account for most of the reserves that Venezuela claims for the sake of negotiating production allocations with OPEC.

Might the biggest conventional producers, Saudi Arabia and Russia, come to agreements on production schedules that would meet their relatively high fiscal needs, as well as those of other potential "strong hands" in OPEC? Could Russia take the long-term view of "strong hands" and enforce a floor price that would be "affordable" to the producers as well as consumers? The trouble is that as fracking technologies become cheaper, the United States could join or replace Saudi Arabia as the swing producer, with an ability relatively rapidly to increase or decrease oil production. Might the Texas Railroad Commission also agree, "for the sake of conservation," to a floor price somewhere between $60 and $80 per barrel and tighten up its production allocations as in the good old days before 1970? Agreement between Russia, Saudi Arabia, and the United States would contribute not only to stabilizing oil prices but also to more stable practice of the new geopolitical pluralism.

Figure 7.5

Cost For Producing Crude Oil Per Barrel

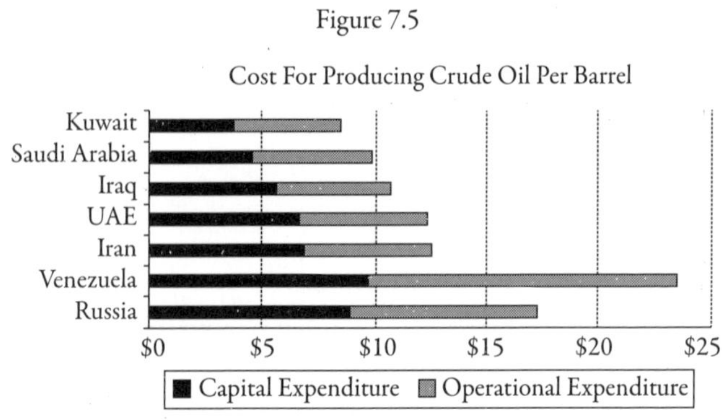

Source: CNN.com based on UCube by Rystad Energy.

Conclusion

This chapter has focused on a very small part of the overall problem of global energy in the context of global warming. The more urgent problem, as one reader of this chapter observed, is how to phase out hydrocarbons altogether if humankind is to avoid extinction like the dinosaurs 65 million years ago.[63] Despite new technologies of energy sources and delivery systems, however, world consumption of crude petroleum is still expected to increase slowly in the coming two decades, and its history has offered a rich diet of regulatory systems or "regimes." After the demise of the Seven Sisters in the early 1970s, OPEC and the IEA survived, but seem ever less able to control the volatility of oil prices that financialization has amplified since 1990s. But these institutions might yet become part of a learning process, teaching states how to navigate the shoals of geopolitical pluralism. Contentious negotiations no longer seriously concern access or secure supply, because vast SPRs, which continue to grow, are available to meet any serious shortages, such as the loss to world markets of Saudi production over several months. The "strategic" nature of the oil fetish can be demystified.[64] The only critical problem for a new oil regime is price volatility, a business problem over which superpowers can haggle and perhaps develop more trust in reiterated multi-player prisoners' dilemmas. Game theory is incisive in this regard and offers reasons for geopolitical optimism. When two players may expect to replay their game indefinitely, their options to cooperate with one another may yield expectations of gain greater than the gain of defecting immediately.[65] While the analogous "solution" for a game involving three or more players is more mathematically complex, they should be more resolvable than other dilemmas of common interest involving less measurable strategic stakes. Collective greed could keep prices high enough to control and eventually lower the global energy market share of liquid petroleum.

A new oil regime could work within the present global architecture. Pending revision of the United Nations Charter, the existing composition of the Security Council pretty well reflects the realities of global power, with China, Russia, and the United States being permanent members, along with the former colonial powers of Britain and France representing Europe (albeit weakened by Brexit). Three of them are also members of the International Energy Agency, in partnership with China and India, which are also beginning to fulfill their SPR requirements. OPEC also remains an important player, however ineffective its past efforts to control its members' production quotas. As the reserves of the price hawks among them dwindle, they may become more amenable to following the dictates of the "strong" hands, notably Saudi Arabia. The driving force supporting the price floor of the Seven Sisters until 1970 also still exists. The Texas Railroad Commission has not had to manage spare capacity in the United States since 1970, but the old institution is still very much alive.

Learning geopolitical pluralism will not be easy, however. Originally a part of Zbigniew Brzezinski's strategy to contain Russia, practicing it today involves major compromises with the permanent members of the Security Council. Clearly the behavior of the major players must change if the practice of pluralism is to define a new world order. Learning is bound to be difficult in the absence of political will on the part of the various ruling establishments, Texas included.

Epilogue

In the eighteen months since this chapter was drafted, Donald Trump was elected president of the United States and immediately cast aside any remaining pretensions of global American leadership and responsibility by withdrawing from the Paris climate accord. He also decimated the US foreign policy establishment that had upheld America's global mission and dissipated any vestiges of American soft power in the Middle East by unilaterally recognizing Jerusalem to be the capital of Israel. His National Security Strategy paper of December 2017 enshrines geopolitical pluralism—without using the term, tarred in any event by association with a former presidential advisor—as a doctrine of competition among the great powers.

In fact President Trump is already practicing global pluralism. He has enabled China, the world's leading petroleum consumer, to take the lead against global warming, launching the world's largest carbon market. Trump may not yet be aware of the dilemma of common interest shared by Saudi Arabia, Russia, and Texas oil men. His administration's affinities with billionaires offers this writer some hope, however, that the Texas Railroad Commission may rediscover its commitment to high oil prices, if only ostensibly for the sake of conservation, in the new context of "America First"—first especially for corporate America. Environmentalists could then hope that corporate greed would set floors to oil prices that would be high enough to lead to a gradual decline in world production of the devil's excrement.

8

SCARCITY DRIVES ECONOMIC DEVELOPMENT

THE EFFECT OF ENERGY SUBSIDIES ON EXPORT DIVERSIFICATION IN THE MIDDLE EAST

Wessel N. Vermeulen

The relative lack of sustainable development and economic progress in many Middle East and North Africa (MENA) countries is a problem that has been powerfully discussed by UNDP's Arab Human Development Reports and analyzed extensively.[1] The literature has highlighted a lack of competition between existing firms, and prohibitively high barriers for new entrants and competitors to gain a foothold in these economies.[2] Governments often privilege local companies against domestic and international competition through regulatory and trade barriers.

This question of dependency on a marketplace shaped by statist interference is, I contend, at the core of the developmental question in the Middle East and North Africa. Especially for the resource-rich countries in the MENA region, there are serious doubts about the economic sustainability of the non-resource sectors, in the absence of the rents and profits generated in the resource sector.

Therefore, natural resources have allowed resource-rich countries to sustain an economy that relies on firms that do not generally match the productivity, efficiency, and innovation present in other countries. In turn, this has consequences for a nation's ability to develop various non-resource industries successfully, i.e. economic diversification, which was and remains the key policy subject in MENA countries. Moreover, such dependence, lack of innovation, and inefficiencies are among the chief reasons why Gulf states especially are the world's biggest emitters per capita of greenhouse gasses (see also Clement Henry's Chapter 7). The Arab world contributes disproportionately to climate change because of skewed production and consumption patterns; there is thus both a severe economic and ecological price tag.

In this chapter, I look specifically at one policy tool: subsidies for energy. I am interested in the potential effect these have on trade-based measures of economic diversification and thus act as a crucial (dis)incentive for development in contexts of resource scarcity and abundance. This chapter sidesteps the question as to which political purposes these subsidies may serve. Instead, it uses a positivist approach to investigate the relation between subsidies and the international export performance of countries. This chapter fits in the liberal paradigm of theorizing the relationship between environment and development as described by Harry Verhoeven in the introduction. It explicitly aims to improve understanding of how state intervention has affected economic development in the MENA region. In the Middle East and North Africa, subsidies are an important part of the political economy and the social contract between state and citizens.[3] If a state chooses to change its subsidy policy, it will require a rekindled social contract.

Energy subsidies can affect trade diversification in two main mechanisms, with opposing effects. By making energy-intensive goods cheaper to consume or produce, subsidy policies can create an advantageous environment for industrial development through the artificially lower costs of inputs or through higher demand, even if the fiscal cost of the subsidy regime can be substantial. However, subsidized fuel may also help to explain the lack in the MENA region of a well-developed and dynamic private sector that generates jobs and stable economic growth.[4] Energy subsidies can discourage innovation and technological development, since the price of energy inputs is kept artificially low. Whereas the rest of the world is aiming to find solutions for increasingly expensive fossil fuel (due to taxation and the need to lower greenhouse gasses), companies in MENA are not equally incentivized to innovate, which may harm their potential to export. Which mechanism dominates is an empirical question that I aim to answer in this chapter, using regression analysis.

This study is the first to make an explicit empirical link between energy subsidies and trade diversification using trade statistics. In this way, it contributes to the literature that aims to model the effect of subsidy reforms on a global scale, including the effects on national GDP, trade accounts, and greenhouse gas emissions, and studies that document country-specific experiences.[5] Energy subsidies and the consequences of abolishing them have been studied mostly by using economic modeling frameworks.[6] These models aim to find the general equilibrium effect of energy subsidy reforms, for instance on GDP growth, while allowing for substitution between energy sources, sectors, and spillover effects from investments and trade. Instead, this chapter offers insights on how the various export industries in the MENA region have performed under different levels of energy subsidies, and on what is to be expected if further energy reforms are to be implemented. By focusing on MENA countries, rather than all middle- and low-income countries, I limit myself to a region in which countries share important political, demographic, and geographic features. The experiences of MENA countries have therefore a strong potential to be replicated, for better or worse, by their immediate neighbors.

The challenge of energy subsidy reform sits at the heart of debates about public finance, economic growth, and environmental policy. Some MENA countries are known for some of the highest levels of energy subsidies in the world.[7] However, volatile oil prices in recent years have forced various MENA countries to reconsider their energy subsidies, both for net resource exporters and importers, due to the increasingly prohibitive costs for government budgets. Numerous studies have looked at the impact or simulated effects in models of subsidy reform policies for specific countries.[8] Early evidence from case studies has suggested that subsidy reforms may on average have a very limited effect on economic growth.[9] In particular, the examples of Jordan, Morocco, and Tunisia are relevant for the broader MENA region in dealing with the issue of welfare distribution following subsidy reforms.[10] However, these studies are short on the effect of subsidy reforms on international commerce.

This chapter applies a different methodology and conceptual approach, offering an explanation through the mechanism of trade, of why subsidy reform may not be harmful to economic growth and could actually strengthen the economic base of MENA states. In the next section, I will set out how energy subsidies can affect the export performance of countries. Thereafter,

I derive measures of trade diversification and analyze quantitatively the relation between the levels of energy subsidies and export diversification.

Conceptual framework

The key concept here is economic diversification. For resource-rich countries, diversification is often coined as a policy to counter overreliance on natural resources in the economy. Due to the volatility of revenues and their exhaustive nature, natural resources may deliver more negative side effects through economic and political mismanagement than positive ones in terms of revenues and wealth, leading to what is commonly referred to as the "resource curse."[11] For instance, Venezuela, which has among the largest proven reserves of oil, is struggling to find a sustainable path between social policy and economic management. In Nigeria, tens of billions of dollars in oil revenue are wasted or stolen by local populations as well as corrupt government officials.[12] The fact that world leaders have repeatedly and legally pledged to reduce carbon emissions will also have implications in the medium term for those hydrocarbon exporters that had counted on selling oil and gas for decades to come. Economic diversification for such countries includes the shift away from industry reliant on cheap and abundant energy. For the non-resource-rich economies in MENA, the situation is often worse in the short term. Lacking natural resources, the income levels of the general population are lower compared to their oil-rich peers, and development must come from a stable economic and political environment in combination with growing productivity.

Another way of thinking about economic diversification is as an indicator of the level of sophistication of the economy. The ability to export a wide range of products to other countries is a function of international competitiveness and comparative advantage of firms, which is particularly relevant for manufacturing products. Richer countries tend to have a broader industrial base, producing a greater number of different goods in each industry, at a higher quality (range). Therefore, economic diversification is mirrored in the characteristics of the export portfolio of a country, especially when looking at the number of different goods and export destinations. Higher levels of technology tend to go together with a larger number of product varieties a country can potentially export competitively toward many different countries. For this reason, measures of export diversity can also be seen as a mirror image of domestic economic development and the state of the private sector. Moreover, the advantage of studying export data, rather than national economic variables or detailed industry statistics, is the public availability of fine-grained, high-quality, and internationally comparable statistics at an annual frequency.

Classical economic theory suggests that subsidies of any kind result in an inefficient allocation of goods and activities if not targeted to resolve market failures. However, subsidies are widespread across sectors and around the world, including in developed economies. They are often implemented for income support purposes, rather than for the correction of market failures. For instance, in the MENA region, apart from energy subsidies, governments often provide subsidized food and water. As noted in various reviews, energy subsidies tend to benefit the relatively better-off segments of the population rather than people in lower-income scales.[13] Therefore, even if the purpose is to redistribute and gain political support from the population, the picture looks muddled at best.

Government support for private energy consumption can be categorized into two items. State bodies either sell fuel and/or electricity below the cost price, or charge a lower price domestically than what they could obtain if they sold the product on world markets. The first item is mostly associated with net energy importers such as Jordan, Egypt, and Morocco. It requires that the government budget finances the subsidy measures with other revenue. The second item is mostly associated with net-exporters. Governments incur an opportunity cost from not selling energy on world markets at a higher price, but there is no direct fiscal budget implication. Saudi Arabia and Iran have notoriously low fuel prices that reflect not the world price of oil and gas but their low marginal cost to extract it. Notwithstanding this broad categorization, the actual policy instruments used to provide subsidies for fuel come in many different variants.[14]

This division also implies different responses to changes in world oil prices from net importers relative to exporters of natural resources. The direct cost of subsidies is the highest for importers when oil prices are high, forcing budget reforms on those countries either by lowering the provision of subsidies or by substantial international borrowing to finance subsidies. For energy exporters, fiscal reforms are more likely to occur when prices are low, since the remaining exports after domestic consumption are insufficient to cover imports. Lowering domestic consumption of fuel by increasing the domestic price may be the most suitable way to improve the balance of payments. A recent example is the reforms enacted by Jordan and Morocco in response to world oil prices between 2005 and 2008 surging above $140, while Saudi Arabia began tinkering with its subsidy regime after the price collapse of 2014.[15]

Given this context, it is important to understand how the private sector responds to changes in the levels of energy subsidies. There may be two mechanisms operating in parallel. On the one hand, if energy is priced domestically below world-market prices and energy is used as an input for the production of goods, producers may reap the benefit of this competitive advantage to price their goods below the level of a foreign competitor who faces a higher price for energy. On the other hand, there is a risk that subsidized energy may affect the direction of technological development and innovation of firms with long-term repercussions for competing in international markets.

The first mechanism follows from a standard model of production. When two firms produce the same good using the same technology and inputs while lacking the market power to set prices, they will charge a price equal to their marginal cost of production. When the costs of inputs are differentiated between the two firms, the firm with the lower input costs will reap the advantage to increase its sales.

Trade economists conventionally assume that trading between countries is costly due to the transportation and time involved. Therefore, if two firms are located in different countries, then they may each serve their home market, rather than compete for each other's market. Only if one of the firms is able to have sufficiently lower input prices will it export its products to foreign markets, since the lower average costs of production can cover the additional cost of shipping.

A further complexity may be introduced when thinking about products that are differentiated between the two producers, and consumers have a preference for more product varieties. Preference for variety allows both firms to sell in each other's markets, because they produce differentiated goods while price competition is maintained. In this case, a lower price of inputs will allow the firm with the lower marginal costs to charge a lower price for the final good, net of trade costs, and therefore reap a larger market share in both its home market and export markets. This mechanism extends to an economy with many firms in any two countries where each firm produces differentiated varieties of goods (but using the same inputs, such as labor, capital, and energy to produce those goods). This suggests that firms located in the country with relatively cheaper energy will be able to export more varieties to export markets, and the effect will be larger for those products for which the production process is relatively more energy-intensive. Note that if the subsidies are cut, the effect disappears and firms compete again on an equal footing.

In order to understand why subsidized energy may be detrimental to the export of goods, consider the field of environmental economics and the two mechanisms underlying "green growth" and the "Porter hypothesis." First, green growth pertains to how an economy can innovate and maintain economic growth while switching from legacy "dirty" technology and goods toward those that are environmentally sustainable.[16] Green growth studies postulate that a certain type of technological innovation may be biased in the wrong direction for long-term sustainability. The mechanism relies on the idea that innovation is costly, but small-scale innovation on top of existing innovation is relatively cheaper, given the benefits it yields in productivity compared to replacing the existing technology with a completely new and clean alternative. Nevertheless, the new clean technology would generate much larger benefits in the future once the costs of long-term damages associated with the use of dirty technology are taken into account.

In terms of energy subsidies for fossil fuels, the intensive use of fossil resources is clearly sub-optimal from an environmental viewpoint. The fact that prices for these inputs are lower in MENA countries discourages innovation in environmentally sustainable goods and production processes, locking in a socially detrimental status quo. Only public intervention seems able to reverse such negative path dependency. This could, for instance, be achieved through a combination of carbon taxes, to limit the benefits of innovation in dirty goods production and subsidies for the development of clean technology.[17] Because abolishing subsidies may not suffice to change the course of innovation, a proactive policy would be required to make the switch, for instance, to extensive fiscal penalization of fossil fuel consumption, as implemented in most European economies.

Second, the Porter hypothesis argues that gains from environmental regulation outweigh the direct cost of accommodating increasingly restrictive environmental regulation and reporting requirements.[18] There are various ways in which environmental regulation can be beneficial. First, there are gains from efficiency of production, in particular those that would not have been attained in the absence of regulation due to coordination failures or other externalities. Secondly, and crucially for trading economies, is the ability to gain access to more markets when regulation becomes harmonized with those of (potential) trade partners. For instance, firms in countries where fossil fuels are taxed will be making fast advancements in reducing the use of fossil energy and may block access for goods that are themselves not adhering to the environmental standards in energy use, or have been manufactured using "dirty technology."[19]

The same could be true if consumer preferences between countries shift. Public awareness of production processes in rich countries could affect consumers' preference for buying products from markets that prioritize high environmental standards in the production process.

I argue that the debate on directed technological innovation and the Porter hypothesis could be applied to the MENA region. Countries that subsidize the use of energy for firms effectively remove their incentive to innovate with regard to the energy efficiency of production processes. Firms in countries with low energy prices should produce at the same technology level as firms located in countries with high energy prices, in order to increase market share and profits. However, these firms are often not adopting these technologies. While this chapter does not aim to identify the reasons for this phenomenon in the case of the MENA region, its occurrence may be due to a combination of factors, including locked-in technology, protection from international and national competition, and rent-seeking. This implies that energy subsidies once implemented may have large detrimental effects on an economy if it fosters innovation toward products that are not in accordance with the preferences and regulations of the rest of the world and, consequently, limits access to foreign markets. Conversely, the reduction of energy subsidies, or even the taxation of fossil fuel consumption, may drive innovation in a direction that is compatible with other advanced economies and would thus foster "green(er) growth."[20]

Trade and energy subsidy data

In order to analyze the conjunction of export diversification and energy subsidies, I look at trade statistics using data available from the UN Comtrade database, and use this data to calculate the number of different varieties each country exports as well as the number of export destinations. These variables will subsequently be combined with various subsidy measures from the literature. As explained earlier, I take the development of exports as an indicator for the competitiveness and sophistication of development of a country vis-à-vis the world.

Trade statistics from the UN Comtrade database are harmonized and provide figures that are comparable between countries and available at a yearly frequency for an extended period. In relying on the UN Comtrade database, various characteristics of trade can be studied; apart from aggregate exports and imports value, bilateral trade flows of detailed product categories can be examined as well.

Although trade characteristics reveal many interesting dimensions of an economy, they—by definition—miss all economic activity that is not traded. Recently, work has been done with firm-level data in some of the MENA countries.[21] Such data sets can potentially offer more details on firm characteristics, including technology development and innovation, and do not limit economic production to exports only. However, such data sets are often limited to manufacturing firms only, so they do not include services; they are not as well harmonized or comparable between countries, which complicates cross-country analysis; and they are often not easily and publicly accessible or are limited in the number of countries and time periods.

Commodities dominate MENA countries' exports.[22] Exports also tend to be a small fraction of GDP relative to other economies of similar income level, especially when focusing on non-resource exports. This chapter goes beyond these aggregate statistics to leverage the detailed information available from decomposition by product category and destination. While earlier studies focused on export diversification using indices that capture both extensive (number of product varieties) and intensive margins (value of export per variety) of trade, I focus on the number of product varieties and the number of destination markets, ignoring the value of exports per variety.[23] The main reason for looking at this simpler measure is to have more intuitive and easily interpretable results relative to indicators that are more comprehensive but also more opaque.

From the UN Comtrade database I obtained import data at the 6-digit product level, the most detailed level available, between 1991 and 2014 for the 198 countries under investigation.[24] Rather than obtaining the export figures of MENA countries, I retrieved the import data from their trade partners to minimize any potential impact from how an individual statistics office reports its data. This resulted in around 7.2 million bilateral-product-year statistics (e.g. the value of "wood screws of copper and copper alloys" from Saudi Arabia to France in 2010). The analysis concentrates on two dimensions of the data: the number of exported product varieties (e.g. the number of different product categories from Qatar to the rest of the world in 2010) and the number of export destinations by MENA countries for each year (e.g. the number of countries to which Kuwait exported at least something in 2010) giving around 450 observations (19 countries times 24 years of data on average, depending on the data availability). I exclude all raw and lightly processed hydrocarbon product categories, since the focus here is principally on non-energy resource exports. Other raw commodities are included, such as phosphate, minerals, metals, etc.

One could argue that the relevant measure for trade is net exports rather than exports. The emergence of trading hubs in the Gulf (most prominently Dubai) has led some to argue that because such commercial hubs export many goods that were imported earlier, gross export figures are a poor representation of the capability of domestic economies. My reason for focusing on exports rather than net exports is that at the detailed product level, trade for a particular product variety often only goes in one direction.[25] The specificities of trading in Gulf countries is controlled for, since the analysis occurs within country groups so that those countries are compared with their comparable peers rather than with all the other countries in the region. My main indicator will be the number of different product categories that are exported by each MENA country to the rest of the world. The second indicator of interest is the number of trading partners each country has (for its exports). A high number for each indicator can be interpreted as successful diversification and ability to compete in world markets.

Data on subsidies were obtained from studies of the IMF, IEA, and two researchers, Maria Vagliasindi and Lucas Davis.[26] Since each of these studies has different methodologies of estimating subsidies and varies in scope, their figures are not necessarily directly comparable. The numbers from the IMF, IEA, and Davis are based on the method of comparing observed world prices and roadside price quotes of countries (price-gap approach). Davis's measure takes account of net taxation and therefore allows for negative figures. Vagliasindi relies strongly on individual country statistical offices and estimates by other studies.[27] The studies of IEA and Vagliasindi prioritize a specific country that is representative for their research purposes. The IMF and Davis data, by contrast, are nigh-exhaustive, including most countries in the world. The IEA data, when available for an individual country, range from 2010 to 2013. The IMF and Davis studies are for the years 2012 and 2014 respectively. Vagliasindi aims for a longer perspective, focusing on reforms over a ten-year period in the first decade of the twenty-first century, where data allow. Each method gives its figures in different measurements, namely percentage of GDP (IMF, Vagliasindi), aggregate dollar (IEA), or dollars per capita (Davis). In principle, it is feasible to transform each indicator to a common measure, but this may falsely suggest a greater comparability than is actually possible, since it is not always clear what population figures or type of international dollars are used to create the figures. Therefore, I simply take the figures as given and use the various measures and methodologies as an opportunity to infer the role of subsidies from different angles.

The dataset is combined with population and GDP (adjusted for purchasing power parity) figures and the Ease of Doing Business (EDB) rank of the World Bank Development Indicators. The EDB is a ranking that combines various indicators on the ease of setting up new and conducting private businesses, such as costs of establishments and permits, the time it takes to go through various procedures, e.g. tax and employment procedures, etc. This ranking is used to disentangle, to some extent, the correlation that may exist between energy subsidy policies and general business climate. If high levels of subsidies are observed in countries that do little to stimulate private enterprise, then the estimated effect of subsidies with regard to export variety may be too large when not controlling for this aspect. The EDB rank is used out of practical considerations, since it is available for all countries (although measured only in 2014) in contrast to other more detailed indicators.

The analysis is divided into three parts. Firstly, I discuss statistics on the diversity of exports of MENA countries in terms of export destinations and product variety. Secondly, I analyze how export varieties may coincide with the various measures on energy subsidies. Finally, the analysis of varieties, trade partners, and energy subsidies is statistically tested using regression analysis.

Descriptive statistics

Country groups

For the entire analysis, I make use of the categorization wielded in other studies, namely a division of MENA countries according to population and natural resource wealth: Resource Poor Labor Abundant (RPLA), Resource Rich Labor Abundant (RRLA), and Resource Rich Labor Poor (RRLP).[28] Two countries in the region, Turkey and Israel, are members of the Organisation for Economic Co-operation and Development (OECD). As members of an organization otherwise dominated by Western Europe and North America, they provide a convenient benchmark with which to compare the other countries.

For the descriptive statistics, I focus on the average over the years 2010–14. Table 8.1 gives an overview of the groups of countries and some summary statistics. With regard to exports analysis, I include only non-oil and non-gas exports.[29] I do this because otherwise the figures for the number of partners and trade volume risk being inflated for resource-rich countries, while this chapter specifically focuses on exports outside the hydrocarbons sector.

This grouping allows us to distinguish MENA countries according to resource-richness and population size, and has proved useful in other comparative studies. Note, however, that the grouping here does not impose anything on the data. Looking at Table 8.1 clarifies that the composition of each country group does not necessarily map the countries neatly together. While resource-rich countries have far more resource exports relative to the others, Saudi Arabia could alternatively be seen as a labor-abundant country, even if in terms of gross national income it fits more comfortably with the Resource Rich Labor Poor countries. The two OECD countries, Turkey and Israel, while implicitly taken as the benchmark for the region, differ greatly in terms of income per capita, resource exports, and population. Azerbaijan, usually not seen as part of MENA, is included owing to its historically close ties with Turkey and Iran.[30]

Table 8.1: Country overview

Group	*Country*	*GNI/pc*	*Oil exp. pc*	*Pop. (M)*	*EBI rank*	*Bus. reg*
OECD	Israel	31004	335.65	7.92	50.00	3.31
	Turkey	18174	58.61	74.11	51.00	1.02
	Egypt	9982	136.49	85.74	126.00	0.13
	Jordan	11420	8.01	6.32	107.00	0.72
RPLA	Lebanon	16724	0.54	4.44	121.00	–
	Morocco	6778	23.65	33.00	80.00	1.04
	Tunisia	10264	9982.00	136.49	85.74	126
	Algeria	13234	1693.54	37.46	161.00	0.46
	Azerbaijan	15432	2849.24	9.30	63.00	0.77
RRLA	Iran	17150	786.87	76.18	119.00	–
	Iraq	14298	2387.51	32.81	160.00	0.3
	Libya	19622	5888.37	6.27	188.00	–
	Syria	–	98.45	21.43	173.00	0.03
	Bahrain	35965	3621.79	1.32	61.00	–
	Kuwait	80972	26642.8	3.41	100.00	–
RRLP	Oman	35795	10242.01	3.57	77.00	1.44
	Qatar	125536	51041.91	1.99	65.00	1.95
	Saudi Arabia	48465	9622.10	29.49	84.00	–
	UAE	61378	11418.73	8.83	32.00	1.59

Source: WDI and COMTRADE, 2010–2014 figures. GNI figures in PPP, "Oil" is short for all hydro-carbon exports, EBI is World Bank Ease of Doing Business rank, Bus. reg is the number of new business registrations per 1,000 people.

Overview of varieties and destinations

In Table 8.2, I present data on the diversity of exports in terms of product variety and destination countries, again as averages over the years 2010–14. Destinations are aggregated in MENA (excluding Israel and Turkey), Europe (European Union member states, therefore excluding Norway, Switzerland, and Iceland), OECD members (excluding countries already in the Europe group), and the rest of the world in Other (which groups together countries not already included in the previous groups in Central and East Asia, including Russia, sub-Saharan Africa, Latin America, and the Pacific).

Table 8.2: Trade diversity in destination and product variety

Group	*Country*	*Trade value B$*	*MENA pct*	*Europe pct*	*OECD (*) pct*	*Other pct*	*Varieties*	*Destinations*
OECD	Israel	4.39	2	29	45	24	4081	125
OECD	Turkey	7.57	9	58	7	26	4665	132
RPLA	Egypt	1.2	28	35	12	24	3808	149
RPLA	Jordan	0.39	23	7	27	43	2572	136
RPLA	Lebanon	0.2	43	30	6	22	3003	140
RPLA	Morocco	1.55	4	66	7	24	3122	144
RPLA	Tunisia	1.12	5	81	3	11	2939	140
RRLA	Algeria	0.19	46	39	2	14	1305	113
RRLA	Azerbaijan	0.09	30	16	2	54	1609	94
RRLA	Iran	1.27	38	13	3	46	3270	145
RRLA	Iraq	0.04	36	5	35	14	715	81
RRLA	Libya	0.1	33	46	5	12	782	91
RRLA	Syria	0.21	62	21	2	16	2916	132
RRLP	Bahrain	0.35	37	14	21	29	1934	113
RRLP	Kuwait	0.34	24	10	9	58	2022	119
RRLP	Oman	0.46	25	9	14	52	1980	123
RRLP	Qatar	0.47	15	12	17	55	1738	120
RRLP	Saudi Arabia	2.71	23	16	8	53	4021	146
RRLP	UAE	2.81	34	20	4	41	4590	114

Source: COMTRADE, 2010–2014 figures, excluding all oil and gas exports.

Turkey and Israel stand out as having far larger export value, and predominantly exporting to Europe for Turkey, and OECD for Israel. They export both a large number of varieties to a scale only matched by Saudi Arabia and the United Arab Emirates. Also, most MENA countries export a large share to other MENA countries, and one other large share to one of the other three country groups. Only Tunisia and Morocco export a very small share to other MENA countries and have Europe as their main destination market. On average, the Resource Poor Labor Abundant countries export more varieties than the Resource Rich Labor Abundant, while the picture for the Resource Rich Labor Poor shows significant intra-group diversity. The number of export destinations does not vary strongly between groups; although resource-poor states appear to have more destination countries relative to their resource-rich peers, with the exception of Iran and, interestingly, Turkey and Israel.

Table 8.2 allows us to infer that the number of export varieties is correlated with the share of trade value exported toward Europe and other OECD destinations. Strikingly, a dominant share of exports toward fellow MENA countries correlates with a relatively small number of export varieties. Contrastingly, however, this pattern is not evident from the number of export destinations. A case in point is that Israel and Turkey number fewer export destinations than seven other MENA countries. These numbers suggest that firstly, there is heterogeneity in both trade destination and product variety among the MENA countries; and secondly, that the grouping of MENA countries according to resource wealth and population captures this heterogeneity to some extent.

Export diversity and subsidies

The trade figures are combined with energy subsidy data to allow further investigation of how energy subsidies may explain some of the variation in trade diversity observed among MENA countries. I focus on product varieties first, while the number of export destinations will be included in the regression analysis below. In order to make the number of varieties more comparable across countries, the number is divided by population. One can expect that a more populous economy will be able to produce more varieties independent of its income level. However, the population is reasonably predetermined with respect to export varieties, economic policy, and other country characteristics, while income level and export varieties are both an outcome from these.[31]

Figures 8.1–8.3 survey exported varieties per capita over time and the different measures of subsidies. The charts for Resource Poor Labor Abundant in Figure 8.1 indicate that Egypt, even though it has a large overall size of varieties (see Table 8.2), scores poorly relative to other group members, while it provides some of the most lavish energy subsidies. The EDB ranking

Figure 8.1: Resource Poor Labor Abundant

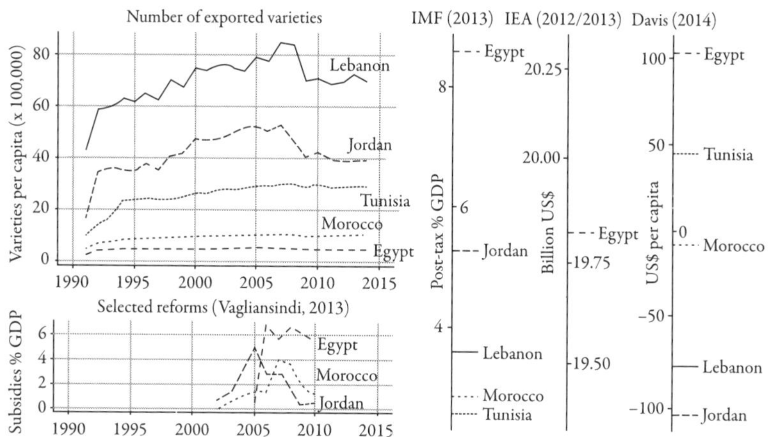

Figure note: Varieties based on UN Comtrade Data, data for subsidies as indicated in the text. The subsidy measure from Davis represents the mean of gasoline and diesel subsidies. Data from Vagliasindi for Egypt include a shift from implicit to explicit subsidies after 2005, which causes a jump in the subsidy figures.

indicates that Egypt is the worst performer in this category as well. By contrast, as indicated in the lower-left plot, both Jordan and Morocco went through significant energy subsidy reforms out of necessity as costs increased.[32] For Jordan, the drop in subsidies appears to pre-date the drop in export varieties, which coincides with the global financial crisis of 2008.

Figure 8.2 presents the results for the country group Resource Rich Labor Abundant. Azerbaijan appears to be an outlier, but it should be noted that the other countries score particularly low on the scale, also relative to other groups. Part of this difference between groups is due to the much larger variation in population figures compared to numbers of varieties, so that the relation is not really linear, i.e. it is relatively "easier" for smaller countries to obtain a high figure for varieties per capita than it is for more populous countries. Azerbaijan would be among the lower ranks in the other two groups. Among the rest of the group, Iran is clearly the more diversified country, but also has lavish subsidies. Generally speaking, resource-rich countries have higher levels of subsidies than resource-poor countries, although Azerbaijan was a reformer. Over the period 2005–8, Baku rapidly cut back on its subsidies, which is mirrored in the data of the IMF, IEA, and Davis. We also note the high subsidy levels in Iran and Iraq relative to the previous group.

Figure 8.2: Resource Rich Labor Abundant

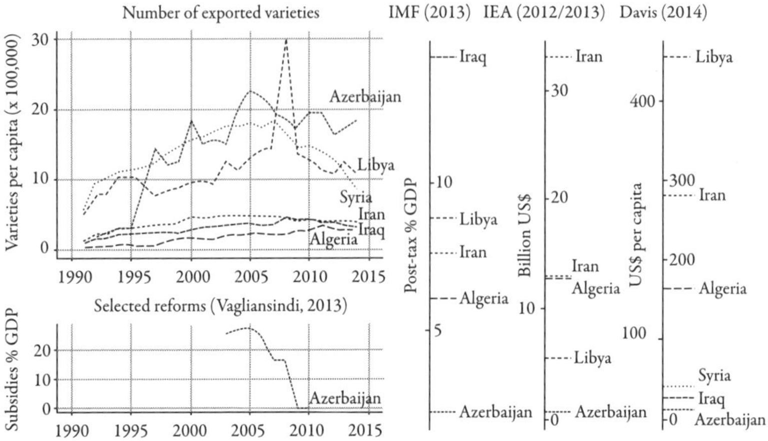

Figure note: Varieties based on UN Comtrade Data, data for subsidies as indicated in the text. The subsidy measure from Davis represents the mean of gasoline and diesel subsidies. Data from Vagliasindi for Egypt include a shift from implicit to explicit subsidies after 2005, which causes a jump in the subsidy figures.

Figure 8.3 focuses on the Resource Rich Labor Poor group. Saudi Arabia looks to be an outlier, more suitably placed in the Resource Rich Labor Abundant group, where it would fall just below Azerbaijan in most years. The other countries, due to their comparatively small labor force, perform exceedingly well on the exports measure. None of the countries of this group are included in the selection of Vagliasindi, while the measure of Davis indicates that these countries have the largest energy subsidies. The other two measures indicate more moderate levels of subsidies. Within the group, Saudi Arabia appears to be the country that most enthusiastically subsidizes energy, while the UAE seems to do the least.

Finally, data for the two OECD members of the MENA region are presented in Figure 8.4. In terms of varieties per capita, Israel and Turkey do not look as impressive as Table 8.2 initially suggested. The varieties per capita for Turkey are at the level of other labor-abundant countries, while Israel is more comparable to the Resource Rich Labor Poor countries. However, in terms of subsidies, the two countries are akin. Both have zero level of subsidies in the IMF measure, and significant negative levels in the measure of Davis. This is a strong difference relative to other countries. Comparing Turkey with Israel, the number of varieties per capita appears inversely related to subsidies. Both

Figure 8.3: Resource Rich Labor Poor

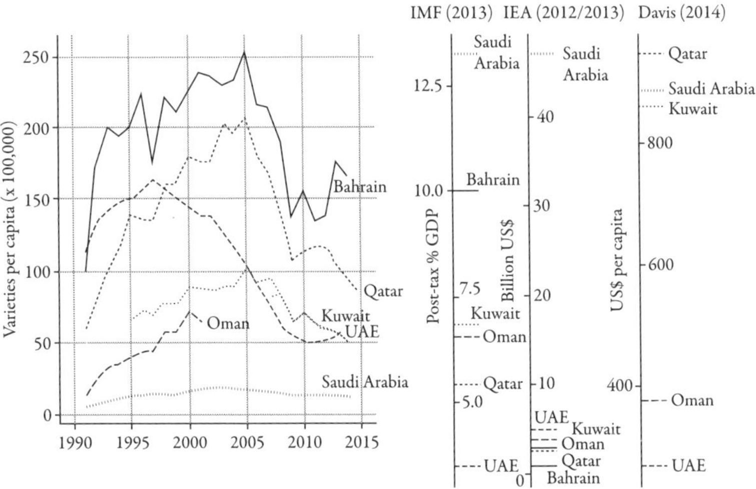

Figure note: Varieties based on UN Comtrade Data, data for subsidies as indicated in the text. The subsidy measure from Davis represents the mean of gasoline and diesel subsidies. Data from Vagliasindi for Egypt include a shift from implicit to explicit subsidies after 2005, which causes a jump in the subsidy figures.

Figure 8.4: MENA countries in OECD

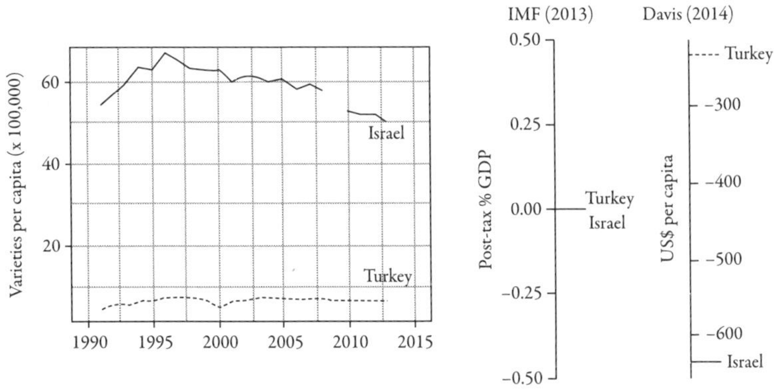

Figure note: Varieties based on UN Comtrade Data, data for subsidies as indicated in the text. The subsidy measure from Davis represents the mean of gasoline and diesel subsidies. Data from Vagliasindi for Egypt include a shift from implicit to explicit subsidies after 2005, which causes a jump in the subsidy figures.

countries are also ranked the highest in the business indicators of Table 8.1, after the UAE. While the IEA data include neither country, the lack of variation in the IMF measure makes this an uninformative indicator for comparing the two countries with respect to their energy subsidy situation.[33]

Regression analysis

The graphs presented provide mixed evidence about the relationship between subsidies and export varieties when looking between and across groups; depending on how one approaches the data, the relationship can be argued either way. To test statistically the hypothesis that energy subsidies may be detrimental to the development of a diversified export base, I conduct a regression analysis. This allows us to control for many country-specific and time factors that may be correlated with the outcome variables and hence muddy the particular relationship between subsidies and the outcome variable. In effect, a regression analysis allows a more structural investigation of the role of various measures of subsidies on the measures of export diversification, beyond the graphical analysis and tabulations.[34]

Econometric model

This chapter concentrates on the relation between energy subsidies and trade diversification. The pattern and characteristics of trade in goods for any country is a function of many external (global economic development, world commodity prices, trade agreements, etc.) and internal factors (industrial structure, business climate, workers' skills, etc.). In particular, subsidized energy appears implicitly to be a convenient measure for governments to shirk on good governance and democratization without facing the wrath of the wider population through public unrest.[35] In so far as energy subsidies are correlated with other public policies detrimental to economic development, one may expect that where subsidies are high, countries perform worse on economic development indicators. However, I want to identify as precisely as possible the effect of subsidies directly, excluding the correlation that may exist with other business environment aspects.

The variables to be explained are the number of varieties and the number of trade partners. The analysis is done in two ways. The first model can be stated as follows,

$$y_{i,t} = \beta_1 subsidy_i + \beta_x x_{i,t} + \gamma_t + g_i + \varepsilon_{i,t}, \quad (1)$$

where $y_{i,t}$ is the dependent variable, either varieties per capita or the number of export partners that varies across countries i and over time t. The coefficient of interest is β_1, which measures the partial correlation between dependent variable and the subsidy, for which I use one of the measures of the IMF, IES, and Davis. Additional control variables in the vector $x_{i,t}$ include the EDB rank, log(GDP per capita), and log(exports per capita) with their associated coefficients indicated by β_x. The first control variable measures the effect of subsidies while controlling for general business climate. The other two control variables define to a large extent the categorization of countries in terms of resource wealth and income levels.

The time-fixed effects, summarized by γ_t, control for general annual time variation common to all countries, such as world demand and trade developments as well as shifting technological frontiers. In Figures 8.1–8.4, there is clearly a common trend in the development of varieties, rising from 1991 to 2000 and declining thereafter for most. The time-fixed effects will filter out this common pattern.

Group fixed effects are summarized by g_i, which is effectively a dummy variable for each of the groups, RRLP, RRLA, and RPLA. Israel and Turkey function as the baseline against which the other groups are compared. These group fixed effects control for all time-constant factors between groups that are correlated with the dependent variable, such as historical and cultural links with export countries that group members have in common but that differentiate them from other groups.[36]

The inclusion of time-fixed effects and group indicators ensures that it is the relative level within each group that is used to identify the marginal effect of subsidy on export varieties, not the absolute level. Since subsidy indicators are not available as a time-series per country (and represent values measured in the period 2011–14), it is implicitly assumed that these relative levels of subsidy are representative for the entire period. Ideally, we would like to observe the average effect of implementing subsidy reforms on the development of exports in a more classic policy analysis set-up, but this is unfortunately not possible due to data limitations.[37]

Everything taken together, the coefficient on the subsidy measure is estimated as the average partial co-variance of an increase of a unit of subsidy with export varieties holding business climate, income level, and resource revenue constant, and controlling for the common time pattern and country group. Therefore, this regression set-up implies that this partial co-variance is estimated as the average effect over different sectors, between the country groups and toward different economic regions. However, much can potentially be learned from differentiating the effect of subsidies over these angles; I do so where data permit. Therefore, the second model will take into the account the export destinations,

$$y_{i,j,t} = \vartheta_{1,j} subsidy_i + \beta_x x_{i,t} + \gamma_t + g_i + h_j + \varepsilon_{i,j,t}. \quad (2)$$

The regression is similar to the first with one major difference. The subscript j now refers to the export regions EU, OECD, MENA, and others, exactly as defined in Table 8.2. Although the subsidy measure does not vary over the export destination, I allow the effect of subsidy on the outcome variable, now indicated by $\vartheta_{1,j}$, to emphasize the difference from β_1, to vary by export destination. The outcome variable $y_{i,j,t}$ now indicates the number of export varieties from country i to region j in year t, or the number of export destinations of country i in region j and year t. In order to capture the structural differences that exist between export regions, region fixed effects are also included in h_j.

Finally, in order to give a causal interpretation to β_1 or $\vartheta_{1,j}$, in the sense of a unit change in the subsidy causes export varieties, rather than merely a correlation or covariance, I need to assume that the model errors $\varepsilon_{i,t}$ and $\varepsilon_{i,j,t}$ are uncorrelated with their respective dependent variables. This assumption could, for instance, be violated empirically when there is an outside factor excluded from the regression model that affects both variables on the right-hand and left-hand sides. For this reason, it is crucial to include control variables and fixed effects. Another violation of the assumption on the model error occurs when export varieties affect the level of subsidies at the same time as subsidy levels affect export varieties. Using the above regression set-up, I cannot completely exclude the possibility of such violation. Therefore, unambiguous causality cannot be established based on this set-up. What we will learn instead is to what extent there exists a statistical relation as expected from the conceptual framework. With this caveat in mind, I will formulate the regression results as the subsidy effect on trade diversification.

Results

Table 8.3 presents the baseline results for equation (1). Each column represents the same regression model for each subsidy measure. The coefficients for the subsidy measures and the control variables are reported with a 95 percent confidence level in brackets. Year and group fixed effects are included in each model, but their coefficients are not reported for brevity. The measures of the

IEA and Davis indicate that an increase in subsidies is associated with fewer export varieties, while the measure of the IMF is positive but not statistically different from zero at the usual levels. The coefficients measure the effect of a unit change of the respective variable on the number of exported varieties. For instance, the coefficient on the IES measure indicates that an additional billion dollars of oil and gas subsidies decreases the number of exported varieties by 1.175 on average for every 100,000 people. The measure of Davis indicates that every $100 of additional subsidy per capita decreases the number of exported varieties by 2.4 on average per 100,000 people. This effect is sizeable. The average number of varieties per 100,000 people over all countries and years is around 45. Hence, 2.4 means a decrease of around 5 percent. However, as is visible in the figures, the level of exported varieties differs greatly between countries and therefore increases the effect for those countries that export fewer varieties per 100,000.

Table 8.3: Subsidies and export varieties

	Dependent variable: Varieties per capita (× 100,000)		
	(1)	*(2)*	*(3)*
Post-tax subsidies % GDP (IMF)	1.220 (-0.511, 2.951)	–	–
US$B oil+gas subsidies (IEA)	–	-1.175*** (-1.389, -0.961)	–
Subsidies US$/pc ×100 (Davis)	–	–	-2.408*** (-4.053, -0.763)
Ease of Doing Business idx	-0.510*** (-0.661, -0.359)	-0.316*** (-0.421, -0.211)	-0.327*** (-0.424, -0.230)
log(GDP/cap)	59.919*** (52.254, 67.584)	52.917*** (34.825, 71.008)	68.949*** (61.452, 76.446)
log(oil exports/cap)	-6.808*** (-8.536, -5.081)	-11.602** (-20.500, -2.704)	-3.786*** (-4.816, -2.756)
Year FE	yes	yes	yes
Group FE	yes	yes	yes
Observations	401	261	377
Adjusted R^2	0.586	0.681	0.796

Note: 95% confidence intervals in brackets, *p<0.1; **p<0.05; ***p<0.01.

With regard to control variables, coefficients indicate intuitive effects that are also consistent between the three models. An improvement in the general business climate such that a country's rank increases by three positions would be associated with an additional 1–1.5 varieties on average per 100,000. The coefficients for log(GDP per capita), allowing for a percentage interpretation, indicate that, *ceteris paribus*, a percentage increase in GDP per capita gives rise to a little more than half a variety ($ß_{log(GDP/cap)}/100$); or in other terms, a doubling of GDP per capita (100 percent increase) gives rise to an additional 53 to 68 varieties per 100,000. For log(oil exports per capita), the same method of interpretation holds. The coefficient indicates that resource exports are negatively correlated with export varieties, but given the size of the coefficient, the impact may be small.

Table 8.4: Subsidies and export varieties by sector

Sector varieties	*Subsidies US$/pc (Davis)*
All	-2.408*** (-4.053, -0.763)
Agriculture	-4.596*** (-5.449, -3.744)
Commodities	-3.810*** (-4.879, -2.742)
Raw chemicals	-4.260*** (-5.151, -3.368)
Processed chemicals	-1.378 (-3.795, 1.039)
Light manufacturing	-2.462*** (-4.077, -0.846)
Heavy manufacturing	-1.785* (-3.572, 0.001)
Machines and electric	0.410 (-2.825, 3.646)
Miscellaneous	-1.769 (-4.228, 0.691)

Note: 95% confidence intervals in brackets, *p<0.1; **p<0.05; ***p<0.01. Each row gives the coefficient a separate regression.

Table 8.4 gives the first decomposition of the effect using the measure of Davis. We may expect that certain sectors are more affected by subsidies than others, in the sense that the comparative advantage effect and innovation work differently in different sectors. As stated above, the production of energy-intensive goods might, in relative terms, benefit more from the provision of subsidies to fuels relative to other goods. For each sector, I calculated the number of varieties. The sectors were defined based on the first two digits of the product level and the definition given by the UN Comtrade.[38] Since some sectors include more product varieties than others, numbers were rescaled for the estimated coefficient to become comparable between sectors; this rescaling does not affect the variance of the coefficients. Using this number of varieties for each country, the model was estimated for each sector separately. The first row repeats the coefficient of Table 8.3 for reference, with the following rows reporting the coefficients for each respective sector. The regressions are only run for the measure of Davis, as it offers the best combination of country scope and variation in the levels of subsidies.[39]

The estimates suggest that the effect of subsidies is the strongest for agricultural commodities, basic chemicals, and light manufacturing, and that there exists no effect for the other sectors as the estimated coefficients are closer to zero and are less precisely estimated. This result is in line with the theoretical prediction that energy subsidies benefit the most energy-intensive industries and therefore compensates for the average negative effect observed for the other products.

In Table 8.5, I present results with the effect of subsidies differentiated by the four country groups. Note that the coefficients of the subsidies cannot be estimated for all four groups, due to the lack of information and variation for the different measures across country groups. This table explores to what extent the effect of subsidies on varieties is driven by a particular group of countries or is present among all. The inclusion of the group fixed effect controls for the level differences of the number of export varieties and the average level of subsidies. The coefficient on the subsidies is therefore estimated using the variation of export varieties and subsidies within each group. The IES and Davis measures indicate that the effect is present for all country groups, although the size of the effect is different between groups. For instance, in the Davis measure, the negative effect is strongest for the Labor Abundant Countries, while for the IES measure it appears stronger for the RRLP countries. The IMF measure yields different results as before. All coefficients are positive rather than negative, but statistically significant only for RRLA countries.

Table 8.5: Subsidies and export varieties by country group

	Dependent variable: Varieties per capita (× 100,000)		
	(1)	*(2)*	*(3)*
Subsidy measure (IEA)	Post-tax subsidies % GDP (IMF)	US$B oil+gas subsidies (IEA)	Subsidies US$/ pc×100 (Davis)
subsidy × OECD	–	–	-3.017*** (-4.742, -1.292)
subsidy × RPLA	0.602 (-0.814,2.017)	–	-8.945*** (-13.137, -4.753)
subsidy × RRLA	1.590*** (0.419,2.761)	-0.302*** (-0.484, -0.120)	-8.700*** (-11.739, -5.661)
subsidy × RRLP	0.967 (-2.586, 4.521)	-1.897*** (-2.245, -1.549)	-0.571 (-2.701, 1.559)
Ease of Doing Business idx	-0.511*** (-0.658, -0.363)	-0.280*** (-0.371, -0.189)	-0.298*** (-0.387, -0.209)
log(GDP/cap)	59.072*** (50.773, 67.370)	32.744*** (14.396, 51.092)	70.977*** (61.760, 80.193)
log(oil exports/cap)	-6.746*** (-8.471, -5.021)	-7.506** (-13.996, -1.015)	-2.064*** (-3.603, -0.526)
Year FE	yes	yes	yes
Group FE	yes	yes	yes
Observations	401	261	377
Adjusted R^2	0.584	0.727	0.814

Note: 95% confidence intervals in brackets, *p<0.1; **p<0.05; ***p<0.01.

As a final differentiation, consider how the number of exported varieties varies across different export regions. Table 8.2 gives an overview of the trade value toward different regions. Using the bilateral information of exports, I include the number of exported products from the country of origin to destination. Aggregating the destinations over country groups defined above gives a measure of exported varieties that varies over export regions.

The results of this model are presented in Table 8.6. There are two components in this table. Firstly, the first three rows indicate the average number of varieties that are exported to the indicated regions relative to the EU. For instance, the Davis measure indicates that each country exports on average

Table 8.6: Subsidies and export varieties by destination region

	Dependent variable: Varieties per capita (× 100,000)		
	(1)	*(2)*	*(3)*
Subsidy measure	Post-tax subsidies % GDP (IMF)	US$B oil + gas subsidies (IEA)	Subsidies US$/ pc×100 (Davis)
MENA	-4.297**	7.651**	-1.786**
	(-7.851, -0.744)	(1.390, 13.911)	(-3.338, -0.233)
OECD	-14.192***	-24.754***	-9.505***
	(-17.760, -10.625)	(-29.124, -20.384)	(-11.005, -8.006)
Other	7.116***	8.631***	4.247***
	(3.420,10.812)	(3.323,13.939)	(2.640,5.854)
subsidy × EU	0.381	-0.472***	-2.633***
	(-0.181, 0.943)	(-0.565, -0.379)	(-3.240, -2.027)
subsidy × MENA	1.402***	-0.594***	-1.407***
	(0.688,2.116)	(-0.723, -0.465)	(-1.965, -0.850)
subsidy × OECD	0.343	0.012	-3.719***
	(-0.107, 0.794)	(-0.059, 0.084)	(-4.194, -3.243)
subsidy × Other	0.080*	-0.556****	-1.734****
	(-0.470, 0.630)	(-0.649, -0.464)	(-2.420, -1.049)
Ease of Doing Business idx	-0.270***	-0.188***	-0.153***
	(-0.316, -0.223)	(-0.225, -0.152)	(-0.182, -0.125)
log(GDP/cap)	30.219***	27.561***	32.485***
	(27.327,33.111)	(22.510,32.613)	(29.998,34.973)
log(oil exports/cap)	-3.009***	-5.529***	-1.521***
	(-3.488, -2.530)	(-7.633, -3.424)	(-1.903, -1.140)
Year FE	yes	yes	yes
Group FE	yes	yes	yes
Observations	1,602	1,042	1,506
Adjusted R^2	0.550	0.628	0.707

Note: 95% confidence intervals in brackets, *p<0.1; **p<0.05; ***p<0.01.

9.5 varieties fewer to the OECD compared to the EU. This effect might be due to underlying factors, such as the on average greater distance to non-European OECD member states compared to the EU; the average level of income between the two regions; or historic cultural and political links that facilitate an easier access to the European markets relative to non-European OECD countries. Differences in the number of group members could also drive the effect: the more group members, the greater the likelihood of more varieties being exported toward the group as a whole.

Instead, the main point of interest is how the subsidy measure affects the exported varieties from the MENA countries toward various export destinations. I expect that subsidies are most detrimental for access to countries with the strictest environmental standards, in particular, those in the EU and OECD. In contrast, exporting to other MENA countries or the rest of the world might be relatively less affected.

I find evidence for this mechanism in the regression that uses Davis' measure. The coefficients on the subsidies indicate that the number of product varieties exported to the EU and OECD markets responds most strongly to every one-dollar increase of subsidies at the country of origin, with every $100 of subsidies per capita generating 2.6 to 3.7 fewer exported varieties per 100,000. The export destinations in MENA and other markets are also affected, but to a smaller extent. The IEA measure shows less variation between the coefficients on the different export regions, indicating that one variety fewer is exported with every $2 billion of additional subsidies. The OECD is the only exception with a measure close to zero.[40]

To some extent, the column based on the IMF measure confirms the hypothesis that the economically most advanced regions are harder to access for MENA region exports. The only coefficient that is significant is the one that indicates the effect for exports toward other MENA countries, which is in fact positive. The other coefficients are also positive, but not statistically significant.

Another way of approaching the ability to export to various regions is through counting the export destinations per country: instead of aggregating the number of different products, we count the number of export destinations. A country is an export destination for MENA countries if it has positive (non-resource) exports toward that destination in a particular year. The summary statistics of this measure (the average number over 2004–10) for each country were given in Table 8.2. The results of the regression using the three measures of subsidy are shown in Table 8.7 and disaggregated by world region in Table 8.8.

Table 8.7: Subsidies and export destinations

	Dependent variable: Export destinations		
	(1)	*(2)*	*(3)*
Post-tax subsidies % GDP (IMF)	0.739 (-0.156, 1.634)	–	–
US$B oil+gas subsidies (IEA)	–	0.758*** (0.686, 0.831)	–
Subsidies US$/pc ×100 (Davis)	–	–	3.386*** (2.382, 4.390)
Ease of Doing Business idx	2.492 (-2.247, 7.231)	11.999*** (7.103, 16.894)	1.442 (-3.258, 6.142)
log(GDP/cap)	0.618* (-0.011, 1.247)	-1.864* (-3.804, 0.075)	-0.347 (-1.113, 0.419)
log(oil exports/cap)	-0.086** (-0.168, -0.004)	-0.075*** (-0.118, -0.031)	-0.124*** (-0.194, -0.054)
Year FE	yes	yes	yes
Group FE	yes	yes	yes
Observations	401	261	377
Adjusted R^2	0.785	0.885	0.805

Note: 95% confidence intervals in brackets, *p<0.1; **p<0.05; ***p<0.01.

The results in Table 8.7 indicate that subsidies have a positive effect on the number of export destinations. For instance, the result of the third column indicates that, keeping all other factors constant, an increase in subsidies of $100 swells the number of export destinations by more than 3. The implication is that subsidies allow for a greater access to export destinations. This finding is echoed in the other two columns, although again the measure of IMF appears the least informative. As to the influence of the control variables, the EBD rank is only significant in the second column, while having a much larger coefficient relative to other columns. Recall that the higher the rank, the worse the business climate, entailing that this result backs up the effect of the subsidy. The general per capita income level appears to have little relevance for this model, but the resource–exports measure indicates that an increase of oil exports per capita of 1 percent decreases the number of export destinations by around 10 countries. The latter effect suggests that the largest resource exporters tend to export with fewer countries.

Table 8.8: Subsidies and export destinations by regions

Export destinations	*Subsidies US$/pc ×100 (Davis)*
All	3.386*** (2.382, 4.390)
Europe	2.342*** (1.189, 3.494)
OECD (*)	2.193*** (0.346, 4.041)
MENA	5.709*** (4.204, 7.213)
Other	3.353*** (2.256, 4.451)

Note: 95% confidence intervals in brackets, *p<0.1; **p<0.05; ***p<0.01.
Each row gives the coefficient a separate regression.

In Table 8.8 the measure of export destinations is disaggregated by region. Similar to the results in Table 8.4, each row presents a separate regression that lists the number of export destinations for one particular region (rescaled to match the interpretation of the world measure) using the subsidy measure of Davis. Does a subsidy affect the access to export destinations by regions? The coefficients obtained suggest that the effect is generally similar, but more than double for MENA destinations compared to Europe and OECD destinations, with the rest of the world hovering in between the latter two. In other words, subsidies positively impact the number of destinations in general, but to a lesser extent toward rich economies.

Summarizing the findings, this chapter finds evidence for a negative effect of the number of export varieties from MENA countries to the rest of the world. The effect is driven by agriculture and some (light) manufacturing, but not by heavy manufacturing and high-technology sectors. There is some evidence that the effect is differentiated between country groups and over export destinations. In particular, subsidies tend to be detrimental for the number of exported varieties toward the EU and OECD. These results, in line with what economic theory postulates, confirm the strong negative relationship between subsidies and trade diversification and corroborate findings from studies that looked specifically at firm performance in relation to energy subsidies in MENA countries.[41] However, these findings are not consistently corroborated by three different subsidy measures. Regarding export destinations, I find that subsidies have a positive effect on the number of export partners, with the strongest effect toward fellow MENA countries, and the smallest (but still positive) effect for European and other OECD countries. Therefore, the findings suggest that those countries that reduce subsidies are able to target their exports specifically to more advanced economies in Europe and the OECD, while limiting the number of export destinations, allowing them to export more varieties.

Conclusion

Energy subsidy reform is a major issue in developing countries in general and the MENA region in particular. Subsidy reform is hard as the short-term political costs are high; and for many in the general population and private sector, so are the expected economic losses. However, over the longer term, subsidy reductions are both fiscally inevitable and a necessary condition to integrate economically with the advanced economies of the world, in particular while dealing with climate change. The overall gains are undeniable.

This study has argued that those MENA countries that have generally lower subsidy levels are better able to export to advanced economies and produce a larger number of varieties. My findings reveal that there is a strong negative relationship between energy subsidies and exported product varieties, but a positive relationship with subsidies and the number of export destinations. Taking a representative estimate, a reduction of energy subsidies of $100 per person would increase the number of exported product varieties, on average by 24 for every 1 million people, i.e. c. 5 percent of additional varieties exported. This effect is almost double for certain sectors, and exports toward European countries and OECD member states are more affected than exports between MENA countries. These are sizeable effects with clear policy implications. They also imply that subsidies have a net negative effect on economic development, and subsidy reductions could be welfare *improving*, especially over the longer term through the channel of economic diversification. These results, therefore, are in line with the Porter hypothesis and imply that subsidy reform would be instrumental in putting MENA countries on a greener economic growth path.

Earlier studies have noted that subsidy reform does not need to be detrimental to economic growth, and from the slight empirical evidence available, subsidy reforms indeed appear to be a boon for MENA economies. The mechanism is that of scarcity driving innovation: countries that reduce their subsidies force firms to innovate in a direction that fits with demand for specific products in the rest of the world, and in advanced economies in particular. Subsidy reforms are one way to harmonize the economic environment of MENA countries with advanced economies, which in turn facilitates access to these markets for the right type of products.

Subsidy reform will have to be combined with other reforms to allow the private sector to innovate successfully and compete in global markets. In particular, some industries or regions might face a fierce adjustment when resource subsidies are abolished. So while a country as a whole may benefit over the long term, those most dependent on subsidized resources are likely to lose in the short term. A failure to compensate firms and consumers for the loss of cheap energy, for instance with more efficient and effective public administration, industrial policy, and anti-trust legislation, could undermine the positive aspects of forcing firms to innovate in the right direction. It is up to governments to strike the right balance, seize the opportunities, and develop a reform agenda and narrative that genuinely prepares their economies for the challenges of the coming decades, internally as well as externally.

9

THE POLITICS OF NATURAL RESOURCES IN THE CASPIAN SEA

A NEW GREAT GAME IN AN ANCIENT WORLD

Abbas Maleki

The Caspian Sea is the largest land-locked body of water on earth. The Caspian occupies a deep depression on the boundary of Europe and Asia with a water level approximately 27 meters below the level of the high seas and a total volume of more than 78,000 cubic kilometers of brackish water. Having been isolated from the earth's oceans at the end of the Pliocene (1.8 million years ago), its ecosystem incorporates remnants of the fauna of the larger regional seas (mainly the Mediterranean and the Arctic biogeographic complexes). A major difference between the Caspian and other large inland water bodies is its meridian orientation and great length (1,200 km), resulting in significant differences in climate over the sea and especially over the catchment area: the northern shores are subject to extreme continental climate, while the southern and southwestern coast is in the sub-tropics.

The isolation of the Caspian basin, its climate, and main biophysical characteristics have created a unique ecological system. The Caspian Sea is home to

Figure 9.1: The Caspian Sea and its basin

810 different species. Today, despite this rich heritage, the Caspian faces a potential catastrophe. Overfishing, discharging wastewater, caviar smuggling, and the exploration and production of gas and oil are degrading many Caspian biotas.[1] The victims of this degradation are many, but the threat is encapsulated by the fate facing the bulk of the world's remaining stock of wild sturgeon, the sea's most famous inhabitant. The Caspian accounted in the past for 80–90 percent of world caviar production, but total catches have declined dramatically, from 27,000 tons in 1990 to less than 1,000 tons in 2010, according to the CaspEco project. Five countries—Azerbaijan, Kazakhstan, Russia, Turkmenistan, Iran—share the Caspian Sea, but the links between science and policy are presently weak, thereby undercutting a much-needed transnational approach to environmental management. The region suffers from the so-called "resource curse" in multiple ways, as this chapter will demonstrate.

The Caspian Sea contains more than 40 percent of the world's inland waters.[2] One of the most important features of the Caspian is its changing water level, a factor that has a significant effect on biodiversity and coastal management in the extensive shallow areas. The level of the Caspian Sea is below that of the world's oceans. The highest water level in recent history, -2.22 meters, was reached 3,800 years ago,[3] but may once have been as low as -64 meters. Up to 1929, the sea level fluctuated around -26.2 meters, later decreasing to -29.0 meters by 1977,[4] the lowest level during the past 400–500 years. In 1978 a rapid rise began, and the sea level reached -26.42 meters by 1995. At present, the Caspian Sea level stands around the -27 meters mark. The causes of sea level change are mainly natural or related to anthropogenic effects on the climate. As an inland sea, the level naturally changes in response to changes in the balance of inputs (mostly river flow) and outputs (primarily evaporation). Geological instabilities play only a small role in water level fluctuations (Figure 9.2).

Both historically and contemporarily, the Caspian basin has enjoyed close relations with the Middle East. Many tribes migrated from the Caspian's littoral regions to various parts of the rest of Asia, Europe, and Africa in ancient history.[5] While it is uncertain where Indo-Europeans originated, many scholars favor the theory that the outmigration from the region began near the western coast of the Caspian and into the Middle East, Europe, and India as early as 4000 BCE.[6] This long tradition of migration has never ceased and has been complemented by the expansion and contraction of empires, trade routes, religious networks, and scholarly communities.

This chapter is mostly concerned with the post-1991 period. After the collapse of the Soviet Union, a "new Middle East" has been emerging. Most of

Figure 9.2: Caspian Sea water levels

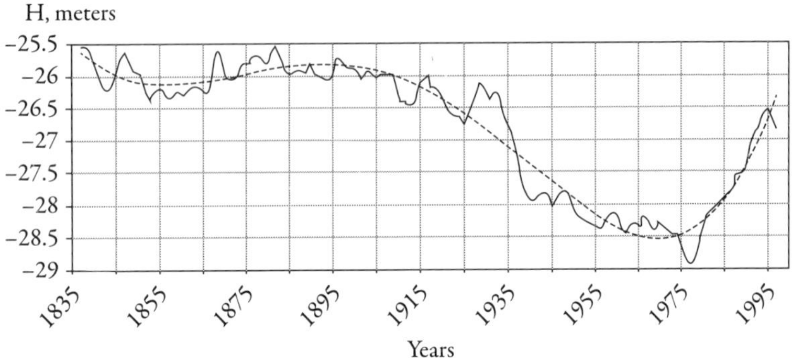

Source: Caspian Environment Programme, *Transboundary Diagnostic Analysis for the Caspian Sea*, vol. 2 (Baku: Caspian Environment Programme, 2002).

the Central Asian and Caucasus states have Muslim majorities; and many look, to a considerable extent, to the actual Middle East and Persian Gulf politically, socially, and culturally. The Russian Federation has sizeable Muslim populations in different republics. The convergence of paths between the Middle East and the Caspian has a feeling of déjà vu about it. While formally the interaction is that between independent nation-states, the legacies of the past influence how geography, ethnicity, religion, and energy presently bring them together.[7]

Both the Caspian and the Middle East are energy-rich regions anticipating significant demographic and economic growth in the coming decades, and striving toward better use of the already existing human resources. Moreover, they are likely to remain the stage for geopolitical competition between traditional powers like the United States, Russia, and China, and emerging players such as the European Union, Turkey, Japan, India, and Iran.

Two-thirds of the world's proven oil reserves exist in just five countries: Saudi Arabia, Iran, Iraq, Kuwait, and the United Arab Emirates (UAE). The picture is much the same for gas. Middle Eastern countries take four of the top six spots in proven gas reserves: Qatar, Iran, Saudi Arabia, and the UAE. Yet the Caspian is attractive, and attracts intense jockeying for influence, precisely because its already considerable oil and gas reserves are not yet fully mapped out. Experts estimate the recoverable hydrocarbon resources there at 20–23 billion barrels of oil and 7,000 billion cubic meters of gas, or 4 percent of the world's proven oil and gas reserves.[8] Even though the Caspian thus cannot currently match the reserves of the Middle East, no new, world-class oil province with the potential of the Caspian has emerged since the discovery of the North Sea oil fields nearly thirty years ago. The competition over access to these lucrative resources is unlikely to remain just a matter of "geo-economics,"[9] but might take on military dimensions.

Iran's strategic position between the Persian Gulf, Caspian Sea, and the Indian subcontinent puts it at the heart of discussions about securing oil and natural gas export outlets for Kazakhstan and Turkmenistan to outside markets. But other players—Russia, Saudi Arabia, and even tiny Qatar—benefit too from their role as gatekeepers of geography. As synergies among these Caspian Sea states develop into closer working relationships, the politically charged issue of where to place regional petroleum export routes will soon be decided by a mix of geopolitical and economic drivers.

This chapter examines the politics of the natural resources of the Caspian Sea as littoral states vie for dominance over its energy resources and its routes to the world markets against a background of climate change, region-wide sustainability challenges, and local pollution. The Caspian is in full transformation and the potential sources of destabilization—which further complicate environmental cooperation and political integration—include radical interpretations of Islam, lack of sustainable development, ethnic violence, corruption, drug trafficking, and external intervention. These destabilizing factors are compounded by the landlocked position of Caspian countries, uncertainty among littoral states as to each other's intentions, and a decaying infrastructure last updated in the Soviet era. This chapter reviews these challenges sequentially, but first turns to the literature on resources and conflict to contextualize the evolving politics of natural resources in the Caspian region.

Conceptual framework

Intuitively, resources loom large in the thinking of many people. Both resource scarcity and abundance have been cited as a primary cause of civil war.[10] Abundance of mineral resources and civil strife appear to be strongly associated. By contrast, there is little evidence that civil strife is related to resource paucity.[11] Auty believes that the risk of civil conflict is highest when a commodity carries high value and production occurs adjacent to porous national borders.[12] Oil has come under particular scrutiny with regard to its destabilizing potential. Norway provides an encouraging example of sound economic and environmental management contributing to decent political governance. However, in the context of the Caspian, many observers doubt whether the Norwegian experience can be replicated. Take Azerbaijan: ordinary Azerbaijanis are rightly concerned over whether their country can handle the potential bonanza from newly discovered oil fields. The heavy reliance on petroleum resources to fund government expenditure places the country at risk of volatility and raises concerns about long-term sustainability and macroeconomic stability. Sluggish growth in recent years underlined the country's vulnerability. The near zero growth in 2011 was the lowest since 1995 and was due to a significant decline in oil production. Given the long time it takes to establish a diversified economy, Baku needs to make greater progress in the non-oil sectors. With a reserve–production ratio of 21.9 as of 2012,[13] oil reserves will essentially be depleted by 2034.[14] For natural gas, Azerbaijan has 0.9 trillion cubic meters and a reserve–production ratio of 57.1.[15] While government officials have promised that oil revenues will go to schools, hospitals, and roads, no formal plans are in the offing. The fact that neighboring Caspian nations are despotically ruled, ethnically divided, and weakened by corruption problems provides a pessimistic background that helps explain the worries of ordinary people.[16] It is undeniable that the development of oil and gas resources provides a unique opportunity for Caspian energy producers to modernize their economies and gain international clout. Yet whether the leaders of Caspian states have the political will and ability to husband their indigenous resources for the long-term benefit and stability of their societies is unclear.[17]

Theoretically, what mechanisms might explain the conditions under which resource abundance becomes a problem rather than part of a solution to development? We know from the literature that export concentration or point source resources—those extracted from a narrow geographic or economic base, such as oil, minerals (such as copper and diamonds)—are strongly associated with weak public institutions, which are, in turn, strongly associated with slower growth.[18] This literature finds that countries rich in natural resources have tended to grow less rapidly and experience higher macroeconomic instability than resource-poor countries. These countries need simultaneously to reduce rent appropriation by the elites and to expand private business opportunities. Political competition leading to more "voice" in decision-making by interest groups not associated with the elites can help to bring about liberalization.[19]

At the center of this argument is the idea that resource wealth reduces the incentives to reform, as reforms would limit the opportunities for direct rent appropriation. Moreover, it allows incumbent elites to remain in power. This was the case in Turkmenistan. Safar Murat Nyazov served as the leader of Turkmenistan from 1985 until his death in 2006. He was first secretary of the

Turkmen Communist Party from 1985 until 1991 and continued to lord over Turkmenistan for fifteen years after independence from the Soviet Union. After his death, there persisted the process of elite formation and the high degree of centralization of the political–economic system, both crucially shaped by Nyazov, because it benefited the ruling circles so much. The new president, Gurbanguly Berdimuhamedov, has maintained the course and has continued to centralize control over hydrocarbon rents to steady intra-elite rivalries, notwithstanding some minor changes due to the new leader's different connection to the traditional structures of Turkmen society.[21]

Historical trajectories clearly matter to how political power and natural resources entwine. Where natural resources were not yet sufficiently developed—as in Azerbaijan and Kazakhstan—and the country depended on outside investment, an initial phase of liberalization during the 1990s was succeeded by a phase of increasing national assertiveness. The latter went hand in hand with a centralization of decision-making and money flows. Therefore, what Kazakhstan, Azerbaijan, and Turkmenistan have in common today are political structures and oligarchies centered on an authoritarian presidential administration and economic structures making entry and entrepreneurship very difficult.[21]

The global background to these systems of resource-based rent-seeking is vital for the Caspian. The complexities of simultaneous interactions at the global, regional, and local levels, with the Caspian Sea at its center, teach us valuable lessons about the complex and still unfulfilled post-Cold War transition, and where we might be heading next. Both soft and hard security threats are emerging from the basin, which are compelling policy responses by littoral and extra-regional actors. This is the subject of the next section.

Geopolitical competition

The collapse of the Soviet Union in 1991 turned the Caspian from a two-states lake into a five-states inland sea. Russia and Iran were joined by Kazakhstan, Azerbaijan, and Turkmenistan on a much more complex map, in terms of both managing political relations and coordinating economic and environmental responses to emerging challenges. Geopolitically, the Caspian Sea is located right at the center of Mackinder's Heartland Theory. In 1904, Halford Mackinder, one of the founders of the London School of Economics and Political Science, gave a paper on "The Geographical Pivot of History" at the Royal Geographical Society, positing political history as a continuous struggle between land and sea empires, with ultimate victory belonging to the continental power. The latter was represented by the world island that consists of Eurasia and Africa.[22] Mackinder called it the Heartland, perceiving it as the greatest natural fortress on earth, surrounded on all sides by geographical barriers. These included the Hindu Kush mountain range and the plateau of Afghanistan and Iran in the southwest, and in the southeast the Caucasus and the plateau of Armenia, sandwiched between the Caspian Sea and the Black Sea.[23]

Stuck in the middle of several regional security complexes, the Caspian Sea has thus long been recognized as a geopolitical battlefield at the heart of the Eurasian landmass. The strategic geographical collocation of the basin—being at the traditional crossroads of empires, trade routes, and cultures—underpins its regional and global significance, in the past as well as contemporarily.

The basin today is littered with conflicts. In addition to widely differing views on the status and content of the legal regime governing the Caspian Sea, flash points include the Nagorno-Karabakh dispute between Azerbaijan and Armenia in the Caucasus, jihadism in the southern regions of Russia (e.g. Dagestan and Chechnya), and uprisings in different parts of Central Asia's Ferghana valley. These conflicts are further complicated by the presence of wide and largely untapped oil and gas reserves.[24] In the post-1991 period, these hydrocarbon sources ensured that the basin rose to the top of the policy agenda of both regional actors and global players, all eagerly eyeing their share of the lucrative pie.

The extraction and transportation of oil and gas from the region have emerged as a major source of geopolitical rivalry. The pipeline routes proposed by companies based outside the region are intended to contain the influence of the region's two powers: Russia and Iran. Big, private multinational companies work hand in hand with governments in Beijing, London, and Washington to draw the Caspian into their sphere of influence. These powers are seeking to increase their leverage by providing alternative energy supply routes to the producing countries—all of them former Soviet republics—so as to reduce their dependence on Moscow.

However, Russia adamantly defends its traditional interests in the Caspian and insists that the bulk of the pipelines pass through its territory. Similarly, Iran too has adopted a strategy that seeks maximum influence by hosting the pipelines within its borders. The major geopolitical contradiction in the Caspian is thus the clash of resource nationalism with the vision of uninterrupted oil and gas flows to Western energy markets (thereby restricting Russian and Iranian control over oil and gas exploration, development, and pipeline routes). The winners in the struggle over pipeline routes will secure major strategic advantages, while the losers risk marginalization.

Since the end of the Cold War, China has gradually recognized the Caspian's increased geostrategic significance. Following 11 September 2001, the United States established a military presence in Central Asia and has sought to preempt China in East and South Asia by strengthening the US–Japan alliance, deploying more strategic submarines, and seeking a closer alliance with India in the context of Barack Obama's "rebalancing" or "pivot" to Asia.[25] The toughening of geopolitical competition over Central Asia has forced the Chinese Communist Party to play a more proactive role. Considering China's 3,000 kilometers of borders with Kazakhstan, Kyrgyzstan, and Tajikistan, Central Asia's importance for China's stability should not be underestimated. Besides, China's thirst for oil and natural gas to support its booming economic growth requires Beijing to develop stable bilateral relations, especially in terms of energy cooperation.[26] One example is the Trans-Asian Pipeline shared between Turkmenistan, Uzbekistan, Kazakhstan, and China. Turkmenistan's eastern natural gas fields, including Galkynysh and the Bagtyyarlyk field group, feed the pipeline, which then enters Uzbekistan and runs to southern Kazakhstan. The pipeline crosses the Kazakhstan–China border at Khorgos and connects to the West–East Gas Pipeline; it is now being expanded to receive natural gas from Kazakhstan's western fields, including Tengiz and Kashagan. More than 125 billion cubic meters of gas (35 percent of China's gas imports) have been transported through the pipeline during 2009–15 through three parallel lines, each running for 1,830 kilometers.[27] Upon completion of all supporting facilities of Line C by the end of 2015, the overall delivery capacity of the Turkmenistan–China gas pipeline hit 55 billion cubic meters per annum. In 2013, China signed inter-governmental agreements with Uzbekistan, Tajikistan, and Kyrgyzstan on the Line D project, as well as to increase gas delivery capacity from Central Asia to 85 billion cubic meters per year. China's grand strategy has two pillars: the security pillar is based on international cooperation along China's borders to prevent sectarian and terrorist activities. The key institution is the Shanghai Cooperation Organization, of which all the Central Asian states plus Russia and Afghanistan are members (Iran, Pakistan, and India are observers). The second pillar is economic integration between China and Eurasian countries.[28] The Silk Road Economic Belt is the development framework proposed by Chinese leader Xi Jinping to boost connectivity between China and the rest of Eurasia.[29]

A smaller but equally active external player is Turkey. Under the leadership of Recep Tayyip Erdoğan, Ankara is trying to find a new role in international relations, focusing on the Middle East and the Turkic-language states. Turkey is facing uncertainty in its relations with the Caspian, driven until now by the contentious interaction between Russian and US policies and interests. During the first decade of the twenty-first century, Turkey has developed closer links with the Caspian states, Russia, and Iran, while maintaining its traditional military alliance with Washington.[30]

The geopolitical competition, for which the Caspian is such a vital theater, extends to the realm of military affairs. The Russo–Persian Treaty of Friendship (1921) and the Soviet–Iranian Agreement of 1940 gave only two coastal states the right of navigation in the Caspian Sea. Any military presence in the Caspian by non-littoral states' ships and flags was not recognized by these accords. After the collapse of the Soviet Union, ship flagging expanded to five littoral states. Iran proposed to demilitarize the Caspian in 2000, but a Russian proposal suggested Caspian Regional Security and Peacekeeping Forces to counter terrorism, smuggling, and the presence of foreign troops in the region. This, in turn, drew opposition from Baku: Azerbaijan is favorably disposed toward hosting foreign forces as it draws substantial income from them. It has rented the Kabala radar base to Russia and has given radar stations in Astara and Khizbon to the United States. Astana participated in maneuvers with American forces as well, though it staged these exercises in eastern Kazakhstan, far from the Caspian.

There is an obvious strategic connection, meaningful to military planners as well as economists, between the Caspian Sea and the Middle East. The Persian Gulf acts as a bridge between both regions. The Gulf has many fishing grounds, extensive coral reefs, and abundant pearl oysters, but its ecology has been damaged by industrialization and oil spills. It is geologically very young, formed around 15,000 years ago. The Persian Gulf and its coastal areas are the world's largest single source of crude oil, and related industries dominate the region. Safaniya oil field, the world's largest offshore oil field, is located in the Gulf. Large gas finds have also been made, with Qatar and Iran sharing a giant field across the territorial median line (North Field in the Qatari sector; South Pars Field in the Iranian sector).

The political economy of hydrocarbons in the Caspian: underpinning authoritarianism

As noted earlier, governments dominated by strong executive powers characterize the Caspian littoral states. Although each state now has a formally elected president, the five countries have reached varying stages of democratization. For Azerbaijan, Kazakhstan, and Turkmenistan, the question of succession dominates current politics. The Islamic Republic of Iran intends to further democratize society, even if conservative factions in Tehran politics, which are less keen on pluralism, often challenge such initiatives.[31] Russia, for its part, has an elected president who has re-centralized authority and who maintains a strong grip on the outlying regions, including the Caspian.[32]

Governmental accountability varies, but is mainly weak. Democratic practices and traditions are more or less absent in a region that has historically been subjected to despotism or colonization of various types. This has led to paternalism on the part of central governments that do not feel a need to consult with or answer to their citizens.[33] Governmental structures are large and economically unsustainable across the region, a phenomenon partly facilitated by governmental control over primary export commodities such as oil and cotton. These oversized structures are cost-inefficient and there is no political will to review their performance via a democratic process. Lack of transparency and abuse of power are rife in the region and are the evident outcome of weak democratic structures and traditions.[34] A related characteristic is the underdeveloped nature of civil society. Non-governmental organizations and community-based organizations are new to the Caspian. Although fast growing in number, these organizations lack the financial and organizational muscle to address, inter alia, environmental issues. Moreover, they also seem to lack the ability to relate to the populace they claim to represent, and to governments that generally view them with suspicion, if not with contempt.[35]

The Caspian region, as a whole, is considered to be among the "High Human Development Countries" when evaluated on the basis of the Human Development Index (HDI) developed by the United Nations Development Programme (UNDP). According to the 2014 HDI list, Russia ranks 50th, Kazakhstan 56th, Iran 69th, Azerbaijan 78th, and Turkmenistan 109th.[36] These apparently high HDI rankings do not adequately reflect the real global economic positions of these countries. High literacy rates in Russia, Kazakhstan, Azerbaijan, and Iran—where considerable investments were made after the 1979 revolution—have helped to raise their HDI. Russia's HDI has fallen from 0.823 in 1990 to 0.798 in 2014; although no comparative figures exist for Azerbaijan, Kazakhstan, and Turkmenistan, it is safe to assume that they too have experienced similar reductions in their HDI, based on overall economic decline during the post-Soviet Union transitional period of the 1990s. Nevertheless, all the littoral countries fall in the lower half of the "high human

Table 9.1: HDI of states of Persian Gulf and Caspian Sea

HDI rank	*Country*	*Value*	*Life expectancy at birth*	*Expected years of schooling*	*Mean years of schooling*	*Gross National Income per capita*	*GNI per capita rank minus HDI rank*
32	Qatar	0.850	78.2	13.8	9.1	123,124	–31
39	Saudi Arabia	0.837	76.3	17.9	9.8	52,821	–27
41	United Arab Emirates	0.835	77.0	13.3	9.5	60,868	–34
45	Bahrain	0.824	75.6	14.4	9.4	38,599	–20
48	Kuwait	0.816	74.4	14.7	7.2	83,961	–46
52	Oman	0.793	76.8	13.6	8.0	34,858	–23
50	Russia	0.798	70.1	14.7	12.0	22,352	–1
56	Kazakhstan	0.788	69.4	15.0	11.4	20,867	–1
69	Iran	0.766	75.4	15.1	8.2	15,440	+4
78	Azerbaijan	0.751	70.8	11.9	11.2	16,428	–11
109	Turkmenistan	0.688	65.6	10.8	9.9	13,066	–28
121	Iraq	0.654	69.4	10.1	6.4	14,003	–44

Source: "Human Development Reports," United Nations Development Programme, 2014, http://hdr.undp.org/en/composite/HDI

development countries," thus reflecting the unsatisfactory human development condition for the region as a whole. The interregional ranking changes significantly when the analysis is based on GDP as an index of economic capacity and performance. Table 9.1 shows the different levels of social and economic development of Caspian and Gulf states.

Caspian economies, just like their Middle Eastern peers, rely disproportionately on the export of primary goods as a major source of government revenue: 57 percent in Russia, 74 percent in Kazakhstan, and 87 percent in Azerbaijan. Furthermore, to various degrees, all littoral Caspian countries are burdened with heavily subsidized and otherwise non-viable industries. During the 1980s and 1990s, in the former Soviet countries, many of these industries shut down for lack of market and finance options, adding tens of thousands to the ranks of unemployed.[37] The agriculture sector in the former Soviet countries provides many job opportunities, yet is technologically and managerially underdeveloped. In Iran, the introduction of relatively new technologies, combined with direct and hidden subsidies, has kept most industries functioning, although quite a few cannot be sustained in the long term. Industrially biased pricing systems and unsettled land tenure hamper agricultural development. The service sector appears to be the major growth pole in most of the littoral countries, although the lines between underground and transparent economic activities in certain countries are murky. The service industry in the former Soviet countries depends heavily on the foreign investment lured by oil and gas exploration.[38]

Energy: the international politics of production

As discussed extensively, energy is crucial for domestic control and rent creation in today's Caspian world. However, the notion of the immense value of oil is not a modern one. As early as 2,600 years ago, ancient peoples were using "fire water" for attack and defense. During Alexander the Great's siege of Persia in 331 BC, the natives of the Caspian shore tried to defend their homelands by setting the invaders' tents on fire with pots of flaming oil. The first documented evidence of oil extraction dates back to the seventh and eighth centuries, when oil was drawn naturally or through primitive extraction methods on the western shores of the Caspian Sea. When Marco Polo traveled through Central Asia, he wrote of oil's medicinal and religious uses by the people of the South Caspian. Large-scale commercialization of oil did not occur until the mid-nineteenth century, when the world's first oil well was drilled near Baku in 1846. Between 1850 and 1891, world oil extraction rose dramatically from 3 million tons to 22.5 million tons. Of this 22.5 million tons, 9.5 came from the US, while the other 11.4 million tons was supplied by Russia, 95 percent of which came from Azerbaijan, a province of Tsarist Russia.[39] The Caspian remained a significant source of oil production for the Soviet Union as well. Only in the second half of the twentieth century did its share of world supply fall, because of stagnating growth and interest in new oil-rich areas such as West Siberia.[40]

Oil reserves in the Caspian outside Azerbaijan remained largely untapped until the collapse of Communism. With several newly independent countries gaining access to valuable hydrocarbon deposits (Kazakhstan and Azerbaijan now have the biggest oil reserves and are the largest export countries, although Turkmenistan's oil and gas exports have been growing rapidly in recent years as well), each state has developed its own approach to developing energy resources. The combination of foreign investment and rising energy prices allowed the coastal countries to shift from diverting oil extraction for local use to supplying both regional and world oil markets. The ability of countries to export greater volumes of Caspian crude oil and natural gas will depend on how quickly domestic energy demand rises, how quickly they can build additional export infrastructure to global markets, and whether expensive projects to develop Caspian resources can attract sufficient investment. At the same time, the lack of regional cooperation has undermined the full exploitation of the Caspian's hydrocarbon riches. Macroeconomic, regulatory, and demographic developments in the region will affect export potential, primarily through the growth in domestic consumption. Shifting legal frameworks create uncertainty for foreign companies. For example, the lack of agreed-upon maritime borders between Turkmenistan, Azerbaijan, and Iran has hampered geologic exploration in the southern Caspian basin and is likely to continue doing so.

It is important to establish some fundamentals in an often polarized discussion on energy in the region. The combined crude oil production in the Caspian region today is recovering from a period of decline in the early 1990s. At peak output, the Caspian is forecast to contribute approximately 17.6 percent of total world crude oil production.[41] Six projects—Kashagan, Tengiz, Karachaganak, Azeri-Chirag-Gunashli, Shah Deniz, and the Severnyi block—contain approximately 17 percent of the littoral states' 298 billion barrels of liquid reserves. The region produced an average of 17.8 million barrel per day of crude oil and lease condensate in 2014, around 20 percent of world crude oil supply. Around 10 percent of that came from offshore fields in the Caspian Sea, with the rest produced in onshore fields in the basin and other parts of the Caspian states.[42]

Future exploration successes could push the eventual decline in production beyond 2020. Azerbaijan, once thought to be the linchpin of future Caspian oil exports, is increasingly seen by energy analysts as a natural gas producer, following a string of disappointments in exploratory drilling. As Azerbaijan developed the Azeri-Chirag-Gunashli (ACG) field group between 2006 and 2008, the country's offshore production began accounting for an increasing part of total Caspian gas production. Following successful exploration efforts in the Kashagan field since 2000, Kazakhstan is now the dominant regional producer and exporter of crude oil and will remain hegemonic over the next two decades. Kazakhstan's onshore oilfields, particularly the Tengiz field, were the biggest contributor to the region's production. Other significant sources of Caspian oil include onshore fields in Turkmenistan near the coast, and production from Russia's North Caucasus region. While most current oil comes from onshore fields, the biggest prospects for future growth will be from offshore fields, which are still relatively undeveloped. Caspian production accounts for virtually all oil production in Azerbaijan and Turkmenistan, yet only a tiny portion for the region's two largest producers, Russia and Iran; production that can reasonably be classified as "Caspian oil" accounts for roughly 17 percent of the total output of the region's countries. Table 9.2 compares Caspian production to total production for the five states. Most of the reserves are offshore or near the Caspian Sea coast, particularly near the northern coast: 41 percent of total Caspian crude oil and lease condensate and 36 percent of natural gas exists in offshore fields. The bulk of offshore oil reserves is in the northern part of the Caspian Sea, while the biggest quantity of offshore natural gas reserves is in the south. An additional 35 percent of oil and 45 percent of gas can be found onshore within 100 miles of the coast, particularly in Russia's North Caucasus region. The remaining oil and natural gas is scattered farther onshore in the large Caspian Sea basins, mostly in Azerbaijan, Kazakhstan, and Turkmenistan.[43]

Caspian gas production peaked in 2014, driven by projects in Kazakhstan's Karachaganak, Tengiz, and Kashagan projects. In the near term, the lion's share of gas export potential will come from Turkmenistan, as it produced 70 billion cubic meters of natural gas in 2014. During the last decade, Turkmenistan exported 16 billion cubic meters annually to Iran via the two pipelines of Dauletabad-Sarakhs and Korbeje-Kurdkuy. A new pipeline is

Table 9.2: Caspian basin proved oil reserves

Country	*Crude oil and condensate (billion barrels)*	*Share of total (%)*	*R/P*	*Production (thousand barrels per day)*	*Share of total (%)*	*Consumption (thousand barrels per day)*	*Share of total (%)*	*Refinery capacity (thousand barrels per day)*	*Share of total (%)*
Russia	103.2	6.1	26.1	10838	12.7	3196	3.5	6338	6.6
Kazakhstan	30.0	1.8	48.3	1701	1.9	276	0.3	–	–
Azerbaijan	7.0	0.4	22.6	848	1.0	101	0.1	–	–
Turkmenistan	0.6	0	6.9	850	0.9	139	0.2	–	–
Iran	157.8	9.3	100.0*	3614	4.0	2024	2.2	1985	2.1
Total Caspian	298.6	17.6	45.6	17851	20.1	5736	6.2	8323	8.6
Total World	1700.0	100.0	52.5	88673	100.0	92086	100.0	96514	100.0

*More than 100 years.

Sources: Data assembled by author from various sources: BP, IEA, EIA, and NIOC.

operational between Turkmenistan and China, carrying 25 billion cubic meters. It is worth noting that only 12 percent of Turkmen gas production actually comes from the Caspian area. The majority of output comes from fields in the south-east, and generally flows to either Iran or China. Russia and Iran are major natural gas producers but have virtually no production in the Caspian area.[44] Table 9.3 shows Caspian basin proven gas reserves.

The post-Soviet heritage: investing in a new geopolitical landscape

As mentioned earlier, the collapse of the Soviet Union at the end of 1991 transformed the Caspian Sea: new states, new borders, new hydrocarbon discoveries, and new points of tension. One of the key actors in this new politics of exploration and investment has been Azerbaijan. The country has been producing oil for over a hundred years, and its recoverable reserves in fields stand at only 7 billion barrels; but it has been utterly crucial in the twenty-five years since the disappearance of the Soviet Union. Azerbaijan involved foreigners in its petroleum industry immediately after achieving independence. International oil companies (IOCs), like Royal Dutch Shell and the Nobel Brothers Petroleum Company, already partook in some of the earliest development of Azerbaijan's petroleum industry. This historic trend was continued after 1991, as Baku signed the largest number of Production Sharing Agreements (PSAs) of any former Soviet states. SOCAR, the country's national oil company, serves as a nominal partner in almost all the country's agreements.

Most of Azerbaijan's oil production comes from the large offshore field complex called ACG after its three principal fields: Azeri (discovered 1986), Chirag (1985), and Gunashli Deep (1977). Azerbaijan International Oil Company (AIOC) operates the field group and estimates 5 billion barrels of technically recoverable oil. AIOC includes SOCAR, as well as foreign companies such as INPEX and Chevron. From 2012, Azerbaijan's oil production struggled to meet production targets because of poor performance from ACG. BP and SOCAR agreed to an output stabilization program from 2013 to prevent future declines from the field.[45]

Historically an oil producer, Azerbaijan is emerging as an important regional natural gas producer as well. About 75 percent comes from offshore fields. Natural gas production comes mostly from the Shah Deniz field, discovered in 1999. Shah Deniz is the largest gas field in the Caspian Sea, located about 40 miles southeast of the ACG complex. According to BP (the project's

Table 9.3: Caspian basin proven gas reserves

Country	*Reserves (trillion cubic meters)*	*Share of total (%)*	*R/P*	*Production (billion cubic meters)*	*Share of total (%)*	*Consumption (billion cubic meters)*	*Share of total (%)*
Russia	32.6	17.4	56.4	578.7	16.7	409.2	12.0
Kazakhstan	0.8	0.4	14.3	19.3	0.6	5.6	0.2
Azerbaijan	1.2	0.6	68.8	16.9	0.5	9.2	0.3
Turkmenistan	17.5	9.3	100*	69.3	0.9	27.7	0.8
Iran	34.0	18.2	100*	172.6	5.0	170.2	5.0
Total Caspian	86.1	46.0	73.8	856.8	24.8	621.9	18.3
Total World	187.1	100	54.1	3460.6	100.0	3393	100.0

*More than 100 years.

Source: Data assembled by author from various sources, including BP, IEA, EIA, and NIGC.

technical operator), it contains an estimated reserve of roughly 840 billion cubic meters of natural gas. Phase one of the development came on-stream in 2006, and began supplying natural gas to Georgia and Turkey a year later through the South Caucasus Gas Pipeline (SCP). Iran's Naftiran International Company owns 10 percent of Shah Deniz shares. Azerbaijan's gas export capacity is tempered somewhat by rising domestic consumption, particularly in the power sector where Azerbaijan is replacing Soviet-era equipment with new combined-cycle gas turbines.

The International Finance Corporation (IFC, part of the World Bank Group), and the European Bank for Reconstruction and Development (EBRD) lent $10 billion to companies developing the Chirag oilfield, a 4 billion-barrel megaproject that is one of the largest private investments in the Caspian. The IFC and EBRD loans to BP Amoco, Exxon, Unocal, LukOil (Russia), and Petrolleri (Turkey) had multiple goals. Not only did they seek to support the refurbishment of existing offshore platforms, but they also intended to set in motion the drilling of new wells and the construction of undersea pipelines in the Caspian, new terminals, and new storage facilities in both Azerbaijan and Georgia. The loans also intended to finance completion of two existing onshore oil pipelines running from Baku across Russia and Georgia for export from the Black Sea ports of Novorossiysk and Supsa. The companies involved view this as a thirty- to forty-year investment.

Recently, doubts have emerged as to whether Azerbaijan can continue to play the prominent role in hydrocarbon investment and geopolitics that is now expected. Baku has been forced to confront a whole series of headaches, economically and politically. In December 2015, Azerbaijan's central bank was forced to abandon its dollar peg and to allow its currency to tumble by almost a third. The central bank said in a statement that as a result of "intensifying external economic shocks" it had switched to a "floating" exchange rate regime. Azerbaijan's move echoed Kazakhstan's move to a free float of its currency in August 2015, triggering a more than 40 percent fall over the subsequent four months. Baku relies on oil and gas for 95 percent of its exports, three-quarters of government revenues, and 40 percent of gross domestic product. The central bank's reserves have fallen sharply, from $13.8 billion at the start of the year to $6.8 billion in October 2015.[46] These economic woes are further compounded by political trouble. In April 2016, thirty soldiers were killed in fighting between Armenian and Azerbaijani forces in the disputed Nagorno-Karabakh region. Nagorno-Karabakh has been under the control of the Armenian military and separatists since the 1994 war between

Armenia and Azerbaijan. Years of negotiations have brought little progress in resolving the dispute, though a fragile truce has been in place. Such instability scares off investors and makes it less likely that much-needed capital will flow to Azerbaijan's oil and gas prospects.

Kazakhstan is another player of global importance that has developed important relations with outside funders. Crude oil production in Kazakhstan is scheduled to grow from 1,701 (thousand barrels per day) in 2014 to 3,100 (thousand barrels per day) in 2040. This may appear impressive, but the numbers veil a track record of considerable ambiguity. Performance has been disappointing at the super-giant offshore Kashagan field, where the project took more than a decade to come online in September 2013, only to have it shut down soon after because of a gas leak. Despite substantial foreign investment, the difficulties of working in Kazakhstan's offshore Caspian terrain have tempered prospects for growth. Outside Kashagan, Kazakhstan has three other major onshore fields—Tengiz, Uzen, and Karachaganak—in the western part of the country. Petroleum production from Tengiz alone doubled between 2004 and 2008, reaching 540 (thousand barrels per day) in September 2008 when its full expansion was completed. The Tengizchevroil consortium (led by Chevron) increased production further, to as much as 1 million barrels per day.

Kazakhstan involved private foreign ownership in the oil sector early on by selling off the majority of shares of Kazakhstan's state oil company. Initially, the government created a state holding company—KazMunaiGas—to oversee oil enterprises inherited from Soviet production in the Caspian basins until multinationals could take over. As Kazakhstan lacked both the technical expertise and funding to develop its offshore Caspian reserves, it sought foreign expertise and cash. The Kashagan reservoir is located more than 5,000 meters below the seabed and is under very high pressure, 770 pounds per square inch. In addition, the reservoir contains high levels of highly toxic and corrosive hydrogen sulfide. Furthermore, conventional drilling and production technologies such as fixed or floating platforms cannot be used because of the shallow water and cold climate. Instead, offshore facilities are installed on artificial islands housing drilling and processing equipment. As a result, costs at Kashagan have ballooned to an estimated $116 billion, rendering it the world's most expensive energy project. The Kazakh government had hoped to ramp up production to 370,000 billion barrels per day by 2015, and within several years to about 1.5 million barrels per day—about 1.6 percent of the world's total, or roughly the amount that Libya produces—until a devastating set of gas leaks disrupted these designs.

At least one investor is still betting that Kashagan will fulfill its potential. In 2013, Chinese President Xi Jinping signed a $45 billion agreement with KazMunaiGas for state-owned China National Petroleum Corporation to purchase an 8.33 percent stake in Kashagan. While little is certain about Kashagan's future, it is clear that when production resumes, it will be with some of the highest production costs in the world, lowering the profit margin for optimistic Western companies that poured into Kazakhstan after Kashagan's discovery fifteen years ago in search of easy money.[47]

Russia is the region's top oil producer. With rich resources and new investments in exploration, it is likely to remain an important liquid fuels producer in the future. At present, much of Russia's oil production comes from fields in the country's West Siberian Basin. Russia is concerned about ensuring its position as one of the world's largest oil producers. In 2013, exploration expenditure by Russian private and state-owned oil companies exceeded $8.4 billion, with another $1 billion contributed by the Russian government. If successful, Moscow expects that about 3 million barrels per day of onshore crude oil production could be added to the country's total output by 2035, with additional production from the Arctic Pechora Sea and offshore resources. In addition, there have been efforts to create incentives to develop Russia's large tight oil resources. Russia's annexation of Crimea in March 2014 and its role in the unrest in eastern Ukraine have dramatically heightened tensions between Russia and the West. So far, Western sanctions targeting specific Russian citizens seem to have had little impact on the Russian energy sector, but a more stringent round of sanctions was announced in July 2014, specifically targeting energy firms. The sanctions, which aim to prevent Russia from obtaining the technology it requires to develop new streams of oil production, could have a profound effect.

Russian production in the Caspian basin traditionally came from onshore fields in the North Caucasus region, particularly from Krasnodar, Stavropol, and Chechnya. The North Caucasus supplies Russia with approximately 65,000 barrels per day. In 2010, Russia's LukOil launched production of the Yuri Korchagin field, the country's first offshore field in the Caspian Sea. Crude output from Korchagin goes to the Makhachkala port in Dagestan to be shipped to the Black Sea port of Novorossiysk via pipeline. Transneft announced plans to expand the Baku-Tikhoretsk pipeline to accommodate increased Russian output from the Caspian to Novorossiysk. LukOil announced its next plan to increase investment into the Filanovsky field, where it expects to be able to produce 120,000 barrels per day. Aside from oil revenues, development of the northern Caspian gives Russian enterprises the opportunity to develop new technologies that could eventually be employed in the Arctic. The Korchagin field was the first field in the world to use an ice-class floating storage offloading vessel to protect against the harsh conditions of the northern Caspian Sea.

Although Russia is one of the world's largest natural gas producers, little of that production currently comes from the Caspian. Gazprom operates a large gas-condensate field and associated processing complex in Astrakhan and produces small amounts of natural gas from a handful of fields in the North Caucasus. LukOil considers the northern Caspian region as a key driver of increased oil and natural gas production in the medium term, particularly from the Filanovsky oil and natural gas field. Industry sources suggest that the field has 28 billion cubic meters of natural gas and 1.1 billion barrels of oil in proven and probable reserves.

Turkmenistan has long been politically an isolated state, but its hydrocarbon reserves have ensured the continued interest and attempts to engage Ashgabat by foreign suitors. The country contains the world's second-largest natural gas field, the South Yolotan-Osman, which was renamed Galkynysh in 2011.[48] Its national gas company, Turkmengaz, controls onshore gas production. Turkmengaz has limited access to international companies, compared to Azeri and Kazakh firms. In 2007, the China National Petroleum Corporation (CNPC) signed a production-sharing agreement with Turkmen authorities to develop natural gas fields in eastern Turkmenistan, as well as potentially exploring the Galkynysh field.

Turkmenistan is unique among resource-rich Soviet successor states in that it retained the ownership structure inherited from the Soviet Union: state control while discouraging foreign involvement. After declaring independence in 1992, President Saparmurat Niyazov asserted that the right to develop petroleum resources belongs to the state and formed fully state-owned oil and natural gas companies. He launched a ten-year development plan in 1993 to become a "second Kuwait," but restricted the ability of foreign companies to invest in the sector, except for joint venture (JV) contracts with some companies. Heavy restrictions resulted in limited development of Turkmenistan's energy resources, particularly in offshore fields. Dragon Oil, an independent company headquartered in the United Arab Emirates, operates the Caspian offshore Cheleken contract area. Other NOCs such as CNPC and Malaysia's Petronas have invested in Turkmenistan energy assets, but do not have significant ownership shares. The Iranian North Drilling Company (NDCO) is working with UAE's Dragon Oil to develop Turkmen offshore fields.[49] Ashgabat has been developing the offshore Cheleken project since the mid-1990s, which it has opened up to some foreign investment. Proven and probable reserves in the contract area are around 3 billion barrels of oil and 80 billion cubic meters of natural gas. Dragon Oil exported 11.4 million barrels in 2011 from Turkmenistan's sector, with most of it going through Azerbaijan to be sold to world markets. Because it is landlocked, Turkmenistan generally focuses on exporting natural gas through pipelines rather than as liquefied natural gas (LNG). The country has a twenty-five-year agreement to reach 100 billion cubic meters per year to Russia from 2010. Russia imposes a monopsony tax on Turkmen gas to Europe.

Last but not least, Iran is the only coastal Caspian country that was not a part of the Soviet Union. The country began to open up the oil and natural gas sector to foreign investment in the mid-1990s, although international sanctions have limited external involvement. The state-owned National Iranian Oil Company (NIOC), under the supervision of the Ministry of Petroleum, is responsible for all upstream oil projects, encompassing both production and export infrastructure. Nominally, NIOC also controls the refining and domestic distribution networks, by way of its subsidiary, the National Iranian Oil Refining and Distribution Company (NIORDC), although functionally there is a separation between the upstream and downstream sectors.

Currently, there is no significant Iranian production in the Caspian. Iran claims 100 million barrels of oil reserves from a field discovered in 2011 named Sardar-e Jangal. The Iranian oil ministry plans to establish a refinery on the Caspian coast and supply it with crude oil derived from the Sardar-e Jangal oilfield, although any development is years away. Industry sources estimate around 1,400 billion cubic meters of gas in Iran's Sardar-e Jangal offshore field, while Iran's Ministry of Petroleum has claimed much higher numbers of offshore natural gas proven reserves in the Caspian.

Two active Iranian companies in the Caspian Sea are Khazar Exploration and Production Company (KEPCO) and North Drilling Company. KEPCO is one of five upstream companies involved in exploration and production under NIOC. KEPCO is tasked with the exploration, development, and production of oil and gas in the Caspian and the three northern provinces of Mazandaran, Gilan, and Golestan. Not only does the North Drilling Company operate as an oil and gas services company in Iran, but it also has foreign activities elsewhere. The company was founded in 1999 and operates as a subsidiary of National Iranian Oil Company, but was privatized in 2009. NDCO owns nine land rigs and three jackup rigs and is managing drilling operations in the Persian Gulf, Caspian Sea, Turkmenistan, and Iran's Khuzestan, Ilam, Khorasan, Bushehr, and Fars provinces.

Pipelines: the politics of transit and exports

The oil and gas trade has grown significantly in the past fifty years. The extraction and transportation of oil and gas from the Caspian have emerged as a major source of contention. Many Caspian states want pipeline grids that will give them options other than exporting through the Russian systems.[50] Relying on Russian pipelines has not been a rewarding experience. Russian officials see Caspian states as potential competitors to their own energy firms, which are critical to state financing.[51] The dilemma for the Russians is that the blunt use of its infrastructural leverage is actually encouraging the construction of alternative pipelines. There has been a succession of problems with gas transit from Russia to Western Europe. When the first Russian gas export line to the region was mooted in the early 1980s, the project faced huge opposition from the US: the Reagan administration saw it as a means for the Soviet Union to exert pressure on European members of NATO. In the event, such fears appeared groundless and East–West gas trading expanded considerably. However, during the 1990s tensions emerged between Russia and Ukraine over the terms of gas transit, relating to (the lack of) payments by Ukraine.[52] Such disputes have encouraged the newly independent Caspian to look for alternatives ever since, to decrease Russia's leverage.

Historically, Caspian oil and natural gas producers have lacked sufficient export infrastructure. The main reason for this is that Moscow saw the Caspian as an internal lake of the Soviet Union, with no need to think of linking the region to international markets. Only after World War II did Moscow design a plan for the exploration and production of Caspian oil, with possible external strategic uses.[53] After 1991, the Caspian basin states developed several approaches for international engagement. Some countries cooperate and jointly develop oil export capacity, while others focus on attracting enough investment to create their own routes. Kazakhstan and Azerbaijan have had the most success in developing oil export capacity through the construction of the CPC and BTC pipelines, which have become the main transit routes for Caspian oil.

European energy interests in the Caspian region are especially distinguished. Firstly, there is the involvement of European energy companies in the region, which have stakes in all spheres of energy but particularly in the upstream sector of the oil and gas industries. Secondly, the European Union has a growing interest in the Caspian as a current and future source of energy for use in Europe itself. The region's oil is already exported to Europe and there are many plans for gas to follow, with pipelines proposed to carry the Caspian region's gas to the heart of the European market. The European Union's Energy Charter, which seeks to address each of the two areas, is just one of a series of initiatives aimed at helping to unlock the entire Caspian region's energy resources.[54]

Geographically and politically, Europe remains the most natural market for the Caspian energy. This is indicated by the obvious export routes lying to the north and west into the EU, which has itself become concerned about the future security of the region's energy supplies. The pipelines heading west to satisfy European markets include:

1. The Caspian Pipeline Consortium (CPC) oil pipeline, commissioned in 2001, running from Kazakhstan's Tengiz oilfield to the Russian port of Novorossiysk on the Black Sea. In 2011, CPC partners began expanding the pipeline capacity to 1.4 million barrels per day. The project is being implemented in three phases, and is expected to provide additional transportation capacity to accommodate increased production from Tengizchevroil.
2. The Baku-Novorossiysk pipeline is 830 miles long and has a capacity of 100,000 barrels per day. The pipeline runs from the Sangachal Terminal to Novorossiysk on the Black Sea. SOCAR operates the Azeri section, and Transneft operates the Russian section. An ongoing dispute between SOCAR and Transneft concerning transportation tariffs occasionally complicates the pipeline's operation. There are proposals to increase the pipeline capacity to between 180,000 and 300,000 barrels per day, a key addition as production grows in the ACG oilfield and throughput from Kazakhstan increases in the future.
3. The Baku-Tbilisi-Ceyhan (BTC) pipeline is a 1-million-barrels-per-day line in Azerbaijan, which came online in 2006. Kazakhstan has a contract with Azerbaijan and the BTC Pipeline Company to ship up to 500,000 barrels per day of oil via BTC. Tankers deliver oil supplies across the Caspian to Baku. The BTC pipeline system runs 1,110 miles from the ACG field in the Caspian Sea via Georgia, to the Mediterranean port of Ceyhan, Turkey. From there, tankers ship oil mainly to European markets.
4. Kazakhstan's other major oil export pipeline, Uzen-Atyrau-Samara, is a northbound link to Russia's Transneft distribution system, which provides

Kazakhstan with a connection to world markets via the Black Sea. The line was upgraded in 2009 by the addition of pumping and heating stations and currently has a capacity of approximately 600,000 barrels per day.

5. Kazakhstan plans on constructing the Kazakhstan-Caspian Transportation System (KCTS). The plan is to export oil produced primarily at Kashagan and Tengiz to international markets via the East–West energy corridor along the route Eskene-Kuryk-BTC. KTCS is expected to supply 300,000 barrels per day through BTC to global markets, gradually increasing to 800,000 barrels per day. Foreign investment will fund part of the estimated $4 billion cost.
6. Caspian natural gas moves to Western Europe through a combination of Soviet-era and newly constructed pipelines. The Central Asia–Center gas pipeline system (CAC), built between 1960 and 1988, carries Caspian Sea natural gas north to Russia where it links up with the wider Soviet-era pipeline network. The two branches of CAC, controlled by Gazprom, meet in the southwestern Kazakh city of Beyneu before crossing into Russia at Alexandrov Gay. The eastern branch of the pipeline, which has a throughput capacity of 62 billion cubic meters, originates in the southeastern gas fields of Turkmenistan. The western branch (3.4 billion cubic meters) originates on Turkmenistan's Caspian coast. Almost all Turkmen and Uzbek gas is delivered via the eastern branch. The western branch is more than thirty-five years old, and sections of it are in disrepair, causing periodic operational problems.
7. The South Caucasus Pipeline (SCP) runs parallel to BTC and supplies natural gas to Georgia and Turkey from Caspian fields. The pipeline began operating in 2007 and has the capacity to transport about 7.8 billion cubic meters of natural gas.

The European market remains the most important one for Caspian states, but the most rapidly growing outlet for hydrocarbons is Asia. As Chinese oil consumption has increased, Beijing has begun investing in Caspian oil and natural gas production to supplement oil from Russia's East Siberia region. Japan is also interested in Caspian oil and natural gas to satisfy growing demand, and the Japan Bank for International Cooperation has expressed interest in financing pipeline projects, such as the Caspian Pipeline Consortium, that could bring more oil to world markets. The main avenue for delivering Caspian oil to the East Asian markets is the Kazakhstan-China oil pipeline, which spans 1,384 miles from Atyrau port in northwestern Kazakhstan to Alashankou in China's northwest Xinjiang Autonomous

Region. It has a crude transportation capacity of 240,000 barrels per day. The pipeline is a joint venture between CNPC and KazMunaiGas, which built the pipeline in segments and began commercial production from phase three in 2009. The pipeline is currently being expanded to increase capacity to 400,000 barrels per day. The burgeoning Asian markets include not only East Asia, but also the Indian subcontinent. India and Pakistan are also witnessing rising energy demands, and for several decades a consortium of countries has planned to construct a pipeline to run from Turkmenistan to India, enabling Ashgabat to diversify its export portfolio. The proposed Turkmenistan-Afghanistan-Pakistan-India (TAPI) pipeline would run for 1,050 miles: 90 miles in Turkmenistan, 460 miles in Afghanistan, and 500 miles in Pakistan, bringing it to the Indian border. The pipeline would have a 28-billion-cubic-meters capacity. India and Pakistan would each get approximately 42 percent of natural gas pumped through TAPI, with the rest going to Afghanistan.

The Caspian and international law: an unresolved legal status

The geopolitics of the region are all the more destabilizing because, for more than twenty-five years now, the legal status of the Caspian Sea has remained unresolved. This failure is the main reason for constant tensions at an inter-state level. As a result of the lack of clear Caspian Sea delineation, several countries dispute ownership over certain offshore resources. For example, Azerbaijan and Turkmenistan both claim the Serdar (Turkmenistan) Kyapaz (Azerbaijan) field, originally discovered in 1959 by Soviet geologists. The five states have promoted conflicting proposals for the sharing or division of Caspian resources and are staking their claims through a mix of diplomatic efforts, international agreements, commercial contracts, and militarization.

The collapse of the Soviet Union complicated an already confusing legal landscape, but cannot be seen as the sole cause. The initial question must be whether there ever existed a shared "Soviet–Iranian regime." The history of Iran–Tsarist Russia and Iran–Soviet relations certainly shows a multitude of treaties and agreements between the two countries, starting with the 1921 Treaty of Friendship between Iran and the Russian Soviet Socialist Republic. The latter confirmed the legal regime of Caspian Sea as a condominium. The 1940 Agreement on Navigation and Trade between Iran and the Soviet Union called the Caspian a "common sea" of both signatories. The dissolution of the Soviet Union increased the number of Caspian littoral states from two to five. Yet, the legal effects of this state succession are subject to heated legal debate.

The position of the five countries in question has evolved since 1992. Iran initially believed that the best way of managing the Caspian would be the principle of common use, or the development of a condominium. But in 1998, Iran posited that, if other states preferred to divide the sea territorially, Iran would require a stake of 20 percent of the Caspian's surface. Overall, Tehran believes that the Iran–Soviet agreements are still valid.[55] Azerbaijan believes that a "sea water division," with reference to how the Caspian was divided during the Soviet era, is the way forward. During the Soviet era, the Caspian was not actually divided between the Soviet Union and Iran, but there are a few maps which show a divided Caspian, by function of oil exploration, among the Soviet Socialist Republics of Azerbaijan, Turkmenistan, Kazakhstan, Dagestan, and Kabardian Balkar.[56] Yet if Azerbaijan wants to base a new legal regime on such maps, Kazakhstan thinks it would be better to divide the Caspian waters afresh between the five littoral states based on the third United Nations Convention on the Law of the Seas.[57] This is a position for which Turkmenistan, which has consistently followed a foreign policy of neutrality, has a lot of sympathy. Russia, for its part, prefers to approach a Caspian legal regime as dual in nature: a division of the seabed, which could be tapped for oil and gas, and a regime for the common use of the sea for purposes of maritime transportation, aviation, fishery, and environmental protection (Figure 9.3).[58]

Despite such wildly differing interpretations of the appropriate legal approach to the Caspian Sea, there have been few summits and ministerial sessions of littoral states' leaders between 1992 and 2016 to sort out these differences. To avert any violence in the settlement of the Caspian dispute and to achieve a resolution by peaceful means, a working group consisting of the deputy ministers of foreign affairs from all five coastal states was established to meet a few times a year to discuss the draft of the future convention on the legal status of the Caspian Sea. However, geopolitical and economic interests of the coastal states explain the lack of progress. Due to clashing interests, each coastal state holds views opposed to those of the others on the principles that are to be applied to the delimitation of the Caspian.

A confrontation between an Iranian military vessel and an Azerbaijani ship conducting geophysical studies in the disputed waters of the Caspian Sea on 23 July 2001 was a stark reminder that the apportioning of the Caspian states' offshore rights has yet to be resolved to the satisfaction of the five Caspian littoral states. The Alov-Araz-Sharg fields, which are claimed by both Azerbaijan and Iran, are not the only disputable area in the Caspian Sea.

Figure 9.3: Caspian straight baselines following UNCLOS, the United Nations Convention on the Law of the Sea: contrivances that have triggered all sorts of injudicious claims against the freedom of the seas.

Source: "The Delimitation of Sea Boundaries," T-FCO, http://www.t-fco.com/englis/unclos/introd.html

Another unresolved border issue is Turkmenistan's ongoing contestation of Azerbaijan's development work on its offshore resources in the Azeri-Chirag-Gunashli oilfields and Sardar-e resources.

Conclusions

The Caspian Sea, the biggest inland lake in the world, is at the center of major internal and external shifts. The dissolution of the Soviet Union signaled industrial decline in the new independent states grouped around the Caspian, but an oil and gas boom has given them a new global role. The well-being of populations and state budgets are intimately tied to fluctuations in hydrocarbon markets.

This chapter has examined the politics of the natural resources of the Caspian Sea as littoral states vie for dominance on energy resources and their routes to world markets against a background of climate change, region-wide sustainability challenges, and local pollution. The Caspian is in full transformation, and solving these problems will require a shift in regional politics toward environmental cooperation and political integration. However, the inherent challenges of such a new approach are compounded by the landlocked position of the Caspian countries, uncertainty among littoral states as to each other's intentions, and a decaying infrastructure, last updated in the Soviet era.

It is undeniable that the development of oil and gas resources provides a unique opportunity for the Caspian energy producers to modernize their economies and gain international clout. Yet, as this chapter demonstrates, whether the respective political leaderships have the will and ability to husband their indigenous resources for the long-term benefit and stability of their societies remains unclear. At the center of this argument is the idea that natural resource wealth reduces the incentives to reform, as reforms would limit the opportunities for direct rent appropriation. Moreover, it allows incumbent elites to remain in power.

International oil companies have been frustrated in their operations in the Caspian so far. On the one hand, rent-seeking by local elites has proven a much greater deterrent to the indigenization of linked economic activity than any inherent reluctance by foreign oil and gas corporations to work with local firms. On the other hand, IOCs have been criticized by civil society at home and abroad for not attaining their stated goals of promoting sustainable development in the Caspian region as part of their corporate social responsibility.

Activists feel that IOCs should focus on neutralizing the potentially negative local impacts of extraction; fostering competitive enterprises to diversify the local economy and generate revenue to sustain the region's stock of produced, human, and social capital; and encouraging resilient social capital.[59]

Oil production is scheduled to increase by 227 percent (excluding Iran), and gas by 64 percent (excluding Iran and Russia) in the Caspian in the 2010–30 period. This heightens the risk of catastrophic oil spills occurring in the future. Ongoing cooperation among the littoral states, using the most up-to-date technology and observing environmental standards, is therefore more essential than ever. Several endemic Caspian species have been listed in the UN-backed Convention on International Trade in Endangered Species of Wild Fauna and Flora. The wild card here remains, of course, oil prices. Fluctuations in world markets could boost production and investment in clean technology, or actually point toward an era of shrinking activity. Most future scenarios suggest that within the next fifteen to twenty years, the center of gravity of the Caspian will move toward the south and east, whereas the north will face negative population growth. Increased urbanization, land filling, and industrial development will result in increased land encroachment and more contamination, and in turn more degradation of landscapes and habitats. Biodiversity and sustainability may be sacrificed in favor of short-term accumulation unless national and regional policies clearly support conservation efforts. A major change in political will is essential, both to contain rising international tensions, and to preserve the Caspian and its abundant resources for future generations. At present, there is unfortunately little reason to be optimistic.

NOTES

INTRODUCTION: THE MIDDLE EAST IN GLOBAL ENVIRONMENTAL POLITICS

1. At the end of the book, the reader can consult a select bibliography comprising the works cited in this introduction.
2. Notable (and increasingly influential) exceptions include Miriam R. Lowi, *Oil Wealth and the Poverty of Politics: Algeria Compared* (Cambridge: Cambridge University Press, 2009); Alan Mikhail, *Nature and Empire in Ottoman Egypt: An Environmental History* (Cambridge: Cambridge University Press, 2011); Alan Mikhail, ed., *Water on Sand: Environmental Histories of the Middle East and North Africa* (New York: Oxford University Press, 2013).
3. Sallie A. Marston, John Paul Jones, Keith Woodward, "Human Geography without Scale," *Transactions of the Institute of British Geographers* 30, no. 4 (2005): 416–32.
4. Michael E. Bonine, Abbas Amanat, and Michael Ezekiel Gasper, eds, *Is there a Middle East? The Evolution of a Geopolitical Concept* (Stanford: Stanford University Press, 2012).
5. World Health Organization, "WHO Global Urban Ambient Air Pollution Database (update 2016)," WHO, 2016, http://www.who.int/phe/health_topics/outdoorair/databases/cities/en/
6. See for instance Mohammad Sharifikia, "Environmental Challenges and Drought Hazard Assessment of Hamoun Desert Lake in Sistan Region, Iran, Based on the Time Series of Satellite Imagery," *Natural Hazards* 65, no. 1 (2013): 201–17.
7. E.g. Jennifer Clapp and Peter Dauvergne, *Paths to a Green World: The Political Economy of the Global Environment* (Cambridge, MA: MIT Press, 2005); John S. Dryzek, *The Politics of the Earth: Environmental Discourses* (Oxford: Oxford University Press, 2013).
8. Clarence J. Glacken, *Traces on the Rhodian Shore. Nature and Culture in Western*

Thought from Ancient Times to the End of the Eighteenth Century (Berkeley, CA: University of California Press, 1967).

9. Benjamin H. Isaac, *The Invention of Racism in Classical Antiquity* (Princeton. NJ: Princeton University Press, 2006), 504.
10. Josef Wiesehöfer, *Ancient Persia* (London: I. B. Tauris, 1996), 79–83.
11. Quoted in J. Donald Hughes, "Early Greek and Roman Environmentalists," in *Historical Ecology: Essays on Environment and Social Change*, ed. Lester J. Bilsky (Port Washington, NY: National University Publications, 1980), 55.
12. Richard P. Turco, *Earth under Siege: From Air Pollution to Global Change* (Oxford: Oxford University Press, 1997), 137.
13. Stephen Frederic Dale, "Ibn Khaldun: The Last Greek and the First Annaliste Historian," *International Journal of Middle East Studies* 38, no. 3 (2006): 431–51.
14. Jean David C. Boulakia, "Ibn Khaldun: A Fourteenth-Century Economist," *Journal of Political Economy* 79, no. 5 (1971): 1114–15.
15. Warren E. Gates, "The Spread of Ibn Khaldun's Ideas on Climate and Culture," *Journal of the History of Ideas* 28, no. 3 (1967): 415–22; Robert Irwin, "Toynbee and Ibn Khaldun," *Middle Eastern Studies* 33, no. 3 (1997): 461–79.
16. Abdelmajid Hannoum, "Translation and the Colonial Imaginary: Ibn Khaldun Orientalist," *History and Theory* 42, no. 2 (2003): 61–81.
17. Diana K. Davis, *Resurrecting the Granary of Rome: Environmental History and French Colonial Expansion in North Africa* (Athens, OH: Ohio University Press, 2007).
18. Cited in Fabien Locher, Jean-Baptiste Fressoz, "Modernity's Frail Climate: A Climate History of Environmental Reflexivity," *Critical Inquiry* 38, no. 3 (2012): 587.
19. E.g. the success of Jared Diamond, *Guns, Germs, and Steel* (New York: W. W. Norton, 1999); and Jared Diamond, *Collapse: How Societies Choose to Fail or Succeed* (London: Penguin, 2005).
20. Carlos J. Castro, "Sustainable Development: Mainstream and Critical Perspectives," *Organization and Environment* 17, no. 2 (2004): 195–225.
21. Al Gore, *Earth in the Balance: Ecology and the Human Spirit* (Boston, MA: Houghton Mifflin, 1992).
22. David Pearce and Jeremy J. Warford, *World without End: Economics, Environment, and Sustainable Development* (New York: Oxford University Press, 1993).
23. William D. Nordhaus, "Resources as a Constraint on Growth," *American Economic Review* 64, no. 2 (1974): 22–6; William D. Nordhaus, *A Question of Balance: Weighing the Options on Global Warming Policies* (New Haven, CT: Yale University Press, 2014).
24. Ronald H. Coase, "The Problem of Social Cost," *Journal of Law and Economics* 3, no. 1 (1960): 1–44.

25. E.g. Holly Lippke Fretwell, *Who is Minding the Federal Estate? Political Management of America's Public Lands* (Lanham, MD: Lexington Books, 2009).
26. J. A. Allan, *The Middle East Water Question: Hydropolitics and the Global Economy* (London: I. B. Tauris, 2001).
27. Julian Simon, *The Ultimate Resource 2* (Princeton, NJ: Princeton University Press, 1998).
28. Marvin G. Weinbaum, *Food, Development, and Politics in the Middle East* (Boulder, CO: Westview Press, 1982); Jane Harrigan, Chengang Wang, and Hamed El-Said, "The Economic and Political Determinants of IMF and World Bank Lending in the Middle East and North Africa," *World Development* 34, no. 2 (2006): 247–70.
29. See, for example, Lynton K. Caldwell, *Science and the National Environmental Policy Act: Redirecting Policy through Administrative Reform* (Tuscaloosa, AL: University of Alabama Press, 1982); Stephanie Pollack, "Reimagining NEPA: Choices for Environmentalists," *Harvard Environmental Law Review* 9, no. 2 (1985): 359–418.
30. Robert Paehlke and Douglas Torgerson, *Managing Leviathan: Environmental Politics and the Administrative State*, 2nd edn (Peterborough, Canada: Broadview, 2005).
31. Bruce A. Williams and Albert R. Matheny, *Democracy, Dialogue and Environmental Disputes: The Contested Languages of Social Regulation* (New Haven, CT: Yale University Press, 1995); Myanna Lahsen, "Technocracy, Democracy, and US Climate Politics: The Need for Demarcations," *Science, Technology and Human Values* 30, no. 1 (2005): 137–69.
32. Will Steffen, Jacques Grinevald, Paul Crutzen, and John McNeill, "The Anthropocene: Conceptual and Historical Perspectives," *Philosophical Transactions of the Royal Society A: Mathematical, Physical and Engineering Sciences* 369, no. 1938 (2011): 842–67.
33. Peter M. Haas, "Introduction: Epistemic Communities and International Policy Coordination," *International Organization* 46, no. 1 (1992): 1–35.
34. Francesca de Châtel, "The Role of Drought and Climate Change in the Syrian Uprising: Untangling the Triggers of the Revolution," *Middle Eastern Studies* 50, no. 4 (2014): 521–35.
35. Peter Schwarzstein, "Inside the Syrian Dust Bowl," *Foreign Policy*, 5 September 2016, http://foreignpolicy.com/2016/09/05/inside-the-syrian-dust-bowl-icarda-assad-food-security-war
36. James N. Rosenau and Ernst-Otto Czempiel, eds, *Governance without Government: Order and Change in World Politics* (Cambridge: Cambridge University Press, 1992); Peter M. Haas, Robert O. Keohane, and Marc A. Levy, *Institutions for the Earth: Sources of Effective International Environmental Protection* (Cambridge, MA: MIT Press, 1993).

37. Ken Conca, *Governing Water: Contentious Transnational Politics and Global Institution Building* (Cambridge, MA: MIT Press, 2006).
38. E.g. Yasemin Atalay, Frank Biermann, and Agni Kalfagianni, "Adoption of Renewable Energy Technologies in Oil-rich Countries: Explaining Policy Variation in the Gulf Cooperation Council States," *Renewable Energy* 85, no. 1 (2016): 206–14; Usama Al-Mulali and Chor Foon Tang, "Investigating the Validity of Pollution Haven Hypothesis in the Gulf Cooperation Council (GCC) Countries," *Energy Policy* 60, no. 9 (2013): 813–19.
39. Morgan Bazilian et al., "Considering the Energy, Water and Food Nexus: Towards an Integrated Modelling Approach," *Energy Policy* 39, no. 12 (2011): 7896–906; Martin Keulertz and Eckart Woertz, "Financial Challenges of the Nexus: Pathways for Investment in Water, Energy and Agriculture in the Arab World," *International Journal of Water Resources Development* 31, no. 3 (2015): 312–25.
40. Daniel L. Nielson and Michael J. Tierney, "Delegation to International Organizations: Agency Theory and World Bank Environmental Reform," *International Organization* 57, no. 2 (2003): 241–76; Jon Birger Skjærseth, Olav Schram Stokke, and Jørgen Wettestad, "Soft Law, Hard Law, and Effective Implementation of International Environmental Norms," *Global Environmental Politics* 6, no. 3 (2006): 104–20; Daniel Bodansky, Jutta Brunnée, and Ellen Hey, *The Oxford Handbook of International Environmental Law* (Oxford: Oxford University Press, 2012).
41. Dogan Altinbelek, "Development and Management of the Euphrates–Tigris Basin," *International Journal of Water Resources Development* 20, no. 1 (2004): 15–33; Aysegul Kibaroglu and Waltina Scheumann, "Evolution of Transboundary Politics in the Euphrates–Tigris River System: New Perspectives and Political Challenges," *Global Governance* 19, no. 2 (2013): 279–305.
42. Salman M. A. Salman, "The Nile Basin Cooperative Framework Agreement: A Peacefully Unfolding African Spring?" *Water International* 38, no. 1 (2013): 17–29; Ana Elisa Cascão and Alan Nicol, "GERD: New Norms of Cooperation in the Nile Basin?" *Water International* 41, no. 4 (2016): 1–24.
43. Elinor Ostrom, Roy Gardner, and James Walker, *Rules, Games, and Common-pool Resources* (Ann Arbor, MI: University of Michigan Press, 1994); Margaret A. McKean, "Success on the Commons: A Comparative Examination of Institutions for Common Property Resource Management," *Journal of Theoretical Politics* 4, no. 3 (1992): 247–81; Arun Agrawal and Clark C. Gibson, "Enchantment and Disenchantment: The Role of Community in Natural Resource Conservation," *World Development* 2, no. 4 (1999): 629–49.
44. E.g. on wastewater management in the MENA region, see Hamed A. Bakir, "Sustainable Wastewater Management for Small Communities in the Middle East and North Africa," *Journal of Environmental Management* 61, no. 4 (2001): 319–28.

45. Lisa Triulzi, "The Bedouin between Development and State: A Syrian Case-Study," *The Arab World Geographer* 5, no. 2 (2002): 85–101.
46. Jeffrey B. Nugent and Nicholas Sanchez, "The Local Variability of Rainfall and Tribal Institutions: The Case of Sudan," *Journal of Economic Behavior and Organization* 3, no. 3 (1999): 263–91.
47. Robert Webking, "Plato's Response to Environmentalism," *Intercollegiate Review* 20, no. 1 (1984): 27–35.
48. Thomas Malthus, *An Essay on the Principle of Population* (London: J. Johnson, 1798), 5.
49. John Avery, *Progress, Poverty and Population: Re-reading Condorcet, Godwin and Malthus* (London: Frank Cass, 1997).
50. Karl Polanyi, *The Great Transformation* (Cambridge, MA: Beacon Press, 1944), 122.
51. Ibid., 122–35.
52. Betsy Hartmann, "Converging on Disaster: Climate Security and the Malthusian Anticipatory Regime for Africa," *Geopolitics* 19, no. 4 (2014): 757–83.
53. John C. Caldwell, "Malthus and the Less Developed World: The Pivotal Role of India," *Population and Development Review* 24, no. 4 (1998): 675–96.
54. Rodney Wilson, *The Economies of the Middle East: The Ghost of Malthus Lingers On* (London: Macmillan Press, 1979): 20–39; Omnia El Shakry, "Barren Land and Fecund Bodies: The Emergence of Population Discourse in Interwar Egypt," *International Journal of Middle East Studies* 37, no. 3 (2005): 351–72; Harry Verhoeven, "The Nexus as Political Commodity: Agricultural Development, Water Policy and Elite Rivalry in Egypt," *International Journal of Water Resources Development* 31, no. 3 (2015): 360–74.
55. Paul Ehrlich, *The Population Bomb* (London: Pan Books, 1971).
56. Donella Meadows, Dennis Meadows, Jørgen Randers, and William W. Behrens III, *The Limits to Growth* (London: Earth Island, 1972).
57. William R. Catton, *Overshoot: The Ecological Basis of Revolutionary Change* (Urbana, IL: University of Illinois Press, 1980); Norman Myers, *Ultimate Security: The Environmental Basis of Political Stability* (London: Norton, 1993).
58. Lester Russell Brown, *Redefining National Security* (Washington, DC: Worldwatch Institute, 1977); Thomas Homer-Dixon, *Environment, Scarcity and Violence* (Princeton, NJ: Princeton University Press, 1999).
59. Joyce R. Starr, "Water Wars," *Foreign Policy* 82, no. 2 (1991): 17–36; Peter H. Gleick, "Water and Conflict: Fresh Water Resources and International Security," *International Security* 18, no. 1 (1993): 79–112; Hussein A. Amery, "Water Wars in the Middle East: A Looming Threat," *Geographical Journal* 168, no. 4 (2002): 313–23.
60. Diane Raines Ward, *Water Wars* (New York: Penguin, 2003).
61. John Bulloch and Adel Darwish, *Water Wars: Coming Conflicts in the Middle East*

(London: Victor Gollancz, 1993); Thomas Naff and Ruth Matson, eds, *Water in the Middle East: Conflict or Cooperation?* (Boulder, CO: Westview Press, 1984).

62. Paul Williams, "Turkey's H_2O Diplomacy in the Middle East," *Security Dialogue* 32, no. 1 (2001): 27–40.
63. Peter H. Gleick, "Water, Drought, Climate Change, and Conflict in Syria," *Weather, Climate, and Society* 6, no. 3 (2014): 331–40; Colin P. Kelley et al., "Climate Change in the Fertile Crescent and Implications of the Recent Syrian Drought," *Proceedings of the National Academy of Sciences* 112, no. 11 (2015): 3241–6.
64. Harald Welzer, *Climate Wars: What People will be Killed for in the 21st Century* (Cambridge: Polity Press, 2012).
65. United Nations Development Programme, *Arab Human Development Report* (New York: UNDP, 2009), 48–9.
66. Gavin Hales, "Under Pressure: Social Violence over Land and Water in Yemen," *Yemen Armed Violence Assessment Issue Brief* 2, Small Arms Survey, October 2010, http://www.smallarmssurvey.org/fileadmin/docs/G-Issue-briefs/SAS-Yemen-AVA-IB2-ENG.pdf; Andreas Gros, Alexander S. Gard-Murray, and Yaneer Bar-Yam, "Conflict in Yemen: From Ethnic Fighting to Food Riots," in *Conflict and Complexity*, ed. Philip Vos Fellman, Yaneer Bar-Yam, and Ali A. Minai (New York: Springer, 2015), 269–80.
67. Mara Hvistendahl, "Young and Restless can be a Volatile Mix," *Science* 333, no. 6042 (2011): 552–4; Sarah Johnstone and Jeffrey Mazo, "Global Warming and the Arab Spring," *Survival* 53, no. 2 (2011): 11–17.
68. Marc F. Bellemare, "Rising Food Prices, Food Price Volatility, and Social Unrest," *American Journal of Agricultural Economics* 97, no. 1 (2015): 1–21.
69. Ban Ki-Moon, "A Climate Culprit in Darfur," *Washington Post*, 16 June 2007, http://www.washingtonpost.com/wp-dyn/content/article/2007/06/15/AR2007061501857.html; United Nations Environmental Programme, *Sudan: Post-Conflict Environmental Assessment* (Khartoum/Nairobi: UNEP, 2007); Jeffrey Sachs, *Common Wealth: Economics for a Crowded Planet* (New York: Penguin, 2008), 48–9.
70. Michael Kevane and Leslie Gray, "Darfur: Rainfall and Conflict," *Environmental Research Letters* 3, no. 3 (2008): 1–10; Harry Verhoeven, "Climate Change, Conflict and Development in Sudan: Neo-Malthusian Global Narratives and Local Power Struggles," *Development and Change* 42, no. 3 (2011): 679–707.
71. Garrett Hardin, "The Tragedy of the Commons," *Science* 162, no. 3859 (1968): 1243–8.
72. William Ophuls, *Ecology and the Politics of Scarcity* (San Francisco, CA: W. H. Freeman, 1977), 12.
73. Karl Wittfogel, *Oriental Despotism* (New Haven, CT: Yale University Press: 1957); see also a special issue on Wittfogelian themes: Christine Bichsel, Peter Mollinga,

Timothy Moss, and Julia Obertreis, eds, "Water, Infrastructure and Political Rule," *Water Alternatives* 9, no. 2 (2016).

74. David Harvey, "The Nature of Environment: Dialectics of Social and Environmental Change," *Socialist Register 1993: Real Problems False Solutions* 29 (1993): 1–51; Rod Neumann, *Making Political Ecology* (Abingdon, Oxon: Routledge, 2014).
75. Richard Peet and Michael Watts, *Liberation Ecologies: Environment, Development, Social Movements* (London: Routledge, 1996); Erik Swyngedouw, *Social Power and the Urbanization of Water: Flows of Power* (Oxford: Oxford University Press, 2004).
76. Arun Agarwal and Sunita Narain, *Global Warming: A Case of Environmental Colonialism* (Delhi: Centre for Science and Environment, 1991); Arturo Escobar, "Whose Knowledge, Whose Nature? Biodiversity Conservation and the Political Ecology of Social Movements," *Journal of Political Ecology* 5, no. 1 (1998): 53–82.
77. Nancy Lee Peluso and Michael Watts, eds, *Violent Environments* (Ithaca, NY: Cornell University Press, 2001).
78. Hussein A. Amery and Aaron T. Wolf, eds, *Water in the Middle East: A Geography of Peace* (Austin, TX: University of Texas Press, 2010).
79. Harry Verhoeven, "Gardens of Eden or Hearts of Darkness? The Genealogy of Discourses on Environmental Insecurity and Climate Wars in Africa," *Geopolitics* 19, no. 4 (2014): 784–805; Eckart Woertz, "Environment, Food Security and Conflict Narratives in the Middle East," *Global Environment* 7, no. 2 (2014): 490–516.
80. Mike Davis, *Ecology of Fear: Los Angeles and the Imagination of Disaster* (New York: Vintage Books, 1998).
81. Timothy Mitchell, *Colonising Egypt* (Berkeley, CA: University of California Press, 1988); Timothy Mitchell, *Rule of Experts: Egypt, Techno-Politics, Modernity* (Berkeley, CA: University of California Press, 2002).
82. Priya Satia, "'A Rebellion of Technology': Development, Policing and the British Arabian Imaginary," in *Environmental Imaginaries of the Middle East and North Africa*, ed. Diana K. Davis and Edmund Burke III (Athens, OH: Ohio University Press, 2011), 23–59.
83. George R. Trumbull IV, "Body of Work: Water and Reimagining the Sahara in the Era of Decolonization," in *Environmental Imaginaries of the Middle East and North Africa*, ed. Diana K. Davis and Edmund Burke III (Athens, OH: Ohio University Press, 2011), 87–112.
84. Daniel R. Headrick, *Power over Peoples. Technology, Environments and Western Imperialism, 1400 to the Present* (Princeton, NJ: Princeton University Press, 2008), 230–31.
85. Harry Verhoeven, *Water, Civilisation and Power in Sudan: The Political Economy of Military-Islamist State Building* (Cambridge: Cambridge University Press, 2015).

86. Jeannie Sowers, "Remapping the Nation, Critiquing the State: Environmental Narratives and Desert Land Reclamation in Egypt," in *Environmental Imaginaries of the Middle East and North Africa*, ed. Diana K. Davis and Edmund Burke III (Athens, OH: Ohio University Press, 2011), 158–91.
87. Jan Selby, *Water, Power and Politics in the Middle East: The Other Israeli–Palestinian Conflict* (London: I. B. Tauris, 2003), 69; Leila M. Harris and Samer Alatout, "Negotiating Hydro-Scales, Forging States: Comparison of the upper Tigris/Euphrates and Jordan River Basins," *Political Geography* 29, no. 3 (2010): 148–56.
88. Edawi Wheida and Ronny Verhoeven, "An Alternative Solution of the Water Shortage Problem in Libya," *Water Resources Management* 21, no. 6 (2007): 961–82.
89. Hazem Beblawi and Giacomo Luciani, eds, *The Rentier State: Nation, State and the Integration of the Arab World* (London: Croom Helm, 1987); Michael L. Ross, "The Political Economy of the Resource Curse," *World Politics* 51, no. 2 (1999): 297–324; Jeffrey D. Sachs and Andrew M. Warner, "The Curse of Natural Resources," *European Economic Review* 45, no. 4 (2001): 827–38.
90. Francesco Caselli and Andrea Tesei, "Resource Windfalls, Political Regimes, and Political Stability," *Review of Economics and Statistics* 98, no. 3 (2016): 573–90. Daron Acemoglu and James A. Robinson, "Economic Backwardness in Political Perspective," *American Political Science Review* 100, no. 1 (2006): 115–31. Thorvaldur Gylfason, "Natural Resources, Education, and Economic Development," *European Economic Review* 45, no. 4 (2001): 847–59. Michael L. Ross, "Does Oil Hinder Democracy?" *World Politics* 53, no. 3 (2001): 325–61.
91. Jill Crystal, *Oil and Politics in the Gulf: Rulers and Merchants in Kuwait and Qatar* (Cambridge: Cambridge University Press, 1990); Clement M. Henry, "Algeria's Agonies: Oil Rent Effects in a Bunker State," *Journal of North African Studies* 9, no. 2 (2004): 68–81. A more positive take can be found in Steffen Hertog, "Defying the Resource Curse: Explaining Successful State-Owned Enterprises in Rentier States," *World Politics* 62, no. 2 (2010): 261–301.
92. Toby Craig Jones, *Desert Kingdom: How Oil and Water Forged Modern Saudi Arabia* (Cambridge, MA: Harvard University Press, 2010); Robert Vitalis, *America's Kingdom: Mythmaking on the Saudi-Oil Frontier* (Stanford, CA: Stanford University Press, 2007); Chad H. Parker, *Making the Desert Modern: Americans, Arabs and Oil on the Saudi Frontier, 1933–1973* (Amherst, MA: University of Massachusetts Press, 2015).
93. E.g. Mehran Kamrava, *Qatar: Small State, Big Politics* (Ithaca, NY: Cornell University Press, 2015).
94. Jeannie Sowers, "Institutional Change in Authoritarian Regimes: Water and the State in Egypt," in *Comparative Environmental Politics: Theory, Practice, and Prospects*, ed. Stacy van Deveer and Paul Steinberg (Cambridge, MA: MIT Press, 2012), 233–7.

95. Begüm Özkaynak, Cem İskender Aydn, Pınar Ertör-Akyazı, and Irmak Ertör, "The Gezi Park Resistance from an Environmental Justice and Social Metabolism Perspective," *Capitalism Nature Socialism* 26, no. 1 (2015): 99–114.
96. David Naguib Pellow, *Resisting Global Toxics: Transnational Movements for Environmental Justice* (Cambridge, MA: MIT Press, 2007).
97. Fikret Adaman, Bengi Akbulut, and Murat Arse, *Neoliberal Turkey and its Discontents: Economic Policy and the Environment under Erdoğan* (London: I. B. Tauris, 2017).
98. See Maarten Hajer, "Discourse Coalitions and the Institutionalisation of Practice: The Case of Acid Rain in Great Britain," in *The Argumentative Turn in Policy Analysis and Planning*, ed. Frank Fischer and John Forester (Durham/London: Duke University Press, 1993), 43–76.
99. David W. Cash and Susanne C. Moser, "Linking Global and Local Scales: Designing Dynamic Assessment and Management Processes," *Global Environmental Change* 10, no. 2 (2000): 109–20.
100. World Bank, *The Sunken Billions Revisited: Progress and Challenges in Global Marine Fisheries* (Washington, DC: World Bank, 2017).
101. Mats R. Berdal and Mónica Serrano, eds, *Transnational Organized Crime and International Security: Business as Usual?* (Boulder, CO: Lynne Rienner, 2002).
102. Michael Klare, *Resource Wars: The New Landscape of Global Conflict* (New York: Metropolitan Books, 2001).
103. Alfred W. Crosby, *Ecological Imperialism: The Biological Expansion of Europe, 900–1900*, new edn (Cambridge: Cambridge University Press, 2004); J. R. McNeill, *Something New Under the Sun: An Environmental History of the Twentieth-Century World* (New York: W. W. Norton, 2000).
104. David Harvey, *Justice, Nature and the Geography of Difference* (Oxford: Blackwell, 1996), 372.

1. ENVIRONMENTAL ACTIVISM IN THE MIDDLE EAST AND NORTH AFRICA

1. My thanks for the insight and helpful feedback on this chapter to the editor, Harry Verhoeven, and Mehran Kamrava, Zahra Babar, and the participants in "Geopolitics of Natural Resources in the Middle East" workshops at the Center for International and Regional Studies, Georgetown University in Qatar; and to Eva Bellin as discussant, and attendees at the panel "New Forms of Authoritarianism and Social Mobilization in the Middle East," Middle East Studies Association Annual Meeting, 20 November 2016.
2. Jeannie Sowers, *Environmental Politics in Egypt: Activists, Experts, and the State* (New York: Routledge, 2013).
3. Jeannie Sowers, "Institutional Change in Authoritarian Regimes: Water and the

State in Egypt," in *Comparative Environmental Politics: Theory, Practice, and Prospects*, ed. Stacy van Deveer and Paul Steinberg (Cambridge, MA: MIT Press, 2012), 231–54.

4. Ramachandra Guha, *Environmentalism: A Global History* (Oxford: Oxford University Press, 2000); Ramachandra Guha, "Environmentalism of the Poor," *Economic and Political Weekly* 37 (2002); Ramachandra Guha and Juan Martínez-Alier, *Varieties of Environmentalism: Essays North and South* (London: Earthscan, 1997); Richard Peet and Michael Watts, eds, *Liberation Ecologies: Environment, Development, Social Movements* (London and New York: Routledge, 2004).
5. Bunyan Bryant and Paul Mohai, *Race and the Incidence of Environmental Hazards: A Time for Discourse* (Boulder, CO: Westview Press, 1992); Bunyan Bryant, ed., *Environmental Justice: Issues, Policies, and Solutions* (Washington, DC: Island Press, 1995); Robert Bullard, *Confronting Environmental Racism: Voices from the Grassroots* (Boston, MA: South End Press, 1999); David Pellow and Robert Brulle, *Power, Justice and the Environment: A Critical Appraisal of the Environmental Justice Movement* (Cambridge, MA: MIT Press, 2005).
6. Hande Paker et al., "Environmental Organisations in Turkey: Engaging the State and Capital," *Environmental Politics* 22, no. 5 (2013): 763.
7. For an Egyptian case study of the Osman Group and the Arab Contractors, see Jeannie Sowers, "Just Green Marketing? State, Business, and Environment in Egypt," in *Growing Pains: Environmental Management in Developing Countries*, ed. Walter Wehrmeyer and Yacob Mulugetta (Sheffield, S. Yorks: Greenleaf Press, 1999), 160–71.
8. For an analysis of the discourse around "hotspots" and efforts to control pollution at state-owned enterprises in Egypt, see Sowers, *Environmental Politics in Egypt*, 38–64.
9. Kaveh Afrasiabi, "The Environmental Movement in Iran: Perspectives from Below and Above," *Middle East Journal* 57, no. 3 (2013): 442.
10. World Bank, "World Development Indicators: Urbanization," 2016, http://wdi.worldbank.org/table/3.12
11. Joel Beinin and Frédéric Vairel, eds, *Social Movements, Mobilization, and Contestation in the Middle East and North Africa*, 2nd edn (Stanford, CA: Stanford University Press, 2013).
12. For Egypt, see Joel Beinin, "The Working Class and the Popular Movement in Egypt," in *The Journey to Tahrir: Revolution, Protest, and Social Change in Egypt*, ed. Jeannie Sowers and Christopher Toensing (London: Verso, 2012).
13. Asef Bayat, "Islamism and Social Movement Theory," *Third World Quarterly* 26, no. 6 (2005): 891–908.
14. Michael Hoffman and Amaney Jamal, "The Youth and the Arab Spring: Cohort Differences and Similarities," *Middle East Law and Governance* 4, no. 1 (2012), 177.

15. Marc Lynch, *Voices of the New Arab Public: Iraq, Al-Jazeera, and Middle East Politics Today* (New York: Columbia University Press, 2007).
16. See Sowers, "Institutional Change in Authoritarian Regimes."
17. Sowers, *Environmental Politics in Egypt*, 20–37.
18. Kerem Okumuş, "Turkey's Environment: A Review and Evaluation of Turkey's Environment and its Stakeholders" (presented at the Regional Environmental Center for Central and Eastern Europe, Szentendre, Hungary, May 2002), 10.
19. Salpie Djoundourian, "Environmental Movement in the Arab World," *Environment, Development, and Sustainability* 13 (2011): 746.
20. Kerem Okumus, "Turkey's Environment" (European Commission: 2002), 15.
21. Graeme Lang and Ying Xu, "Anti-Incinerator Campaigns and the Evolution of Protest Politics in China," *Environmental Politics* 22, no. 5 (2013): 842.
22. Asef Bayat, "Activism and Social Development in the Middle East," *International Journal of Middle East Studies*, 34, no. 1 (2002): 1–28.
23. Asef Bayat, *Life as Politics: How Ordinary People Change the Middle East* (Stanford, CA: Stanford University Press, 2013), 45.
24. Bayat, "Activism and Social Development in the Middle East and North Africa," 3.
25. My thanks to Harry Verhoeven for this observation.
26. Okumuş, "Turkey's Environment," 27.
27. Salpie Djoundourian, "Environmental Movement in Lebanon," *Environment, Development, and Sustainability: A Multidisciplinary Approach to the Theory and Practice of Sustainable Development* 11 (2009): 427–38.
28. Afrasiabi, "The Environmental Movement in Iran," 432–48.
29. Alon Tal et al., "Israel's Environmental Movement: Strategic Challenges," *Environmental Politics* 22, no. 5 (2013): 781.
30. Ibid.
31. Okumuş, "Turkey's Environment," 27–9.
32. Michael Parrish, "Environment Becomes Burning Issue in Kuwait," *Los Angeles Times*, 4 May 1991, http://articles.latimes.com/1991–05–04/news/mn-965_1_kuwait-university
33. Nada Majdalani Azzah, "Mapping of Environmental Actors in the Palestinian Civil Society Sector" (Berlin: Heinrich Böll Stiftung, October 2012), 5, https://ps.boell.org/sites/default/files/downloads/Mapping_Study_FINAL_with_new_cover.pdf
34. Ibid., 17.
35. Ibid., 6.
36. Adaman et al., "Political Economy of Citizens' Participation in Environmental Improvement: The Case of Istanbul," in *Integrating and Articulating Environments: A Challenge for Northern and Southern Europe*, ed. Fatoş Gökşen et al. (Lisse, NL: Swets and Zeitlinger, 2003).
37. Paker et al., "Environmental Organisations in Turkey," 773.

38. Ibid.
39. Sowers, *Environmental Politics in Egypt*, 154–78.
40. Jeannie Sowers, "Nature Reserves and Authoritarian Rule in Egypt: Embedded Autonomy Revisited," *Journal of Environment and Development* 16, no. 4 (2007): 375–97.
41. Djoundourian, "Environmental Movement in Lebanon," 427–38.
42. Tal et al., "Israel's Environmental Movement," 782–3.
43. Gabriel Ignatow, *Transnational Identity Politics and the Environment* (Lanham, MD: Lexington Books, 2007); Hayriye Özen, "Located Locally, Disseminated Nationally: The Bergama Movement," *Environmental Politics* 18, no. 3 (2009).
44. Jeroen Warner, "The Struggle over Turkey's Ilisu Dam: Domestic and International Security Linkages," *International Environmental Agreements* 12, no. 3 (2012): 231–50.
45. Susanne Güsten, "Construction of Disputed Turkish Dam Continues," *New York Times*, 27 February 2013, http://www.nytimes.com/2013/02/28/world/middleeast/construction-of-disputed-turkish-dam-continues.html
46. Ignatow, *Transnational Identity Politics and the Environment*, 86, 92.
47. Kevin O'Brien and Lianjiang Li, *Rightful Resistance in Rural China* (New York: Cambridge University Press, 2006), 62; Lang and Xu, "Anti-Incinerator Campaigns and the Evolution of Protest Politics in China," 841.
48. Fayong Shi and Yongshun Cai, "Collective Resistance in China: Disaggregating the State: Networks and Collective Resistance in Shanghai," *China Quarterly* 186 (2006): 314–32.
49. Ignatow, *Transnational Identity Politics and the Environment*, 53–96.
50. Sharif Elmusa and Jeannie Sowers, "Damietta Mobilizes for its Environment," *Middle East Report Online*, 21 October 2009, http://www.merip.org/mero/mero102109
51. Sowers, *Environmental Politics in Egypt*, 163–6.
52. Ibid., 172–5.
53. Dina Zayed and Jeannie Sowers, "The Campaign against Coal in Egypt," *Middle East Report* 271 (2014): 29–35.
54. Ibid.
55. "Protester Dies During Demonstrations in Beirut," *Al Jazeera*, 24 August 2015, http://www.aljazeera.com/news/2015/08/injuries-protests-lebanon-beirut-intensify-150823183908444.html
56. Abu-Rish Ziad, "Garbage Politics," *Middle East Report* 277 (2015), http://www.merip.org/mer/mer277/garbage-politics
57. Nora Stel and Rola el-Husseini, "Lebanon's Massive Garbage Crisis isn't its First: Here's what that Teaches Us," *Washington Post*, 18 September 2015, http://www.washingtonpost.com/blogs/monkey-cage/wp/2015/09/18/this-isnt-lebanons-first-garbage-crisis-and-what-that-should-teach-us/; Nora Stel and Irna van der

Molen, "Environmental Vulnerability as a Legacy of Violent Conflict: A Case Study of the 2012 Waste Crisis in the Palestinian Gathering of Shabriha, South Lebanon," *Conflict, Security and Development* 14, no. 4 (2015): 387–414.

58. Uwafiokun Idemudia, "Oil Multinational Companies as Money Makers and Peace Makers: Lessons from Nigeria," in *Corporate Social Responsibility and Sustainability: Emerging Trends in Developing Economies*, ed. Gabriel Eweje (Bingley, W. Yorks: Emerald Group Publishing, 2014), 191–213.
59. Tim Boersma, Marie Vandendriessche, and Andrew Leber, "Shale Gas in Algeria: No Quick Fix," Brookings Institute Policy Brief, November 2015, http://www.brookings.edu/~/media/research/files/papers/2015/11/algeria-shale-gas/no_quick_fix_final.pdf
60. For an in-depth and insightful account of Algerian politics during and after the civil war in the 1990s, see Miriam Lowi, *Oil Wealth and the Poverty of Politics: Algeria Compared* (Cambridge: Cambridge University Press, 2009). For the opaque integration of the military command, security forces, and the regime, see Steven Cook, *Ruling but Not Governing: The Military and Political Developments in Egypt, Algeria, and Turkey* (Baltimore, MD: Johns Hopkins University Press, 2007).
61. Ibid., 10.
62. "Algeria: The Curse of Low Oil Prices," *Al Jazeera*, 28 November 2015, http://www.aljazeera.com/programmes/countingthecost/2015/11/algeria-opec-falling-oil-prices-151128182255541.html
63. Linda Pappagallo, "Shale Gas and Fracking Lies Exposed in Tunisia by Local Bloggers," *Green Prophet*, 13 December 2013, https://www.greenprophet.com/2013/12/shale-gas-and-fracking-lies-exposed-in-tunisia-by-local-bloggers/
64. Boersma et al., "Shale Gas in Algeria," 16.
65. US EPA, "Hydraulic Fracturing for Oil and Gas: Impacts from the Hydraulic Fracturing Water Cycle on Drinking Water Resources in the United States," EPA/600/R-16/236F, Washington, DC: US Environmental Protection Agency, 2016.
66. Mohamed Arezki Himeur, "Algerian Heat Wave Claims Lives," BBC News, 26 July 2002, http://news.bbc.co.uk/2/hi/africa/2153886.stm
67. Boersma et al., "Shale Gas in Algeria," 13–15.
68. Djamila Ould Khettab, "We want to Avoid an Ecological Disaster," *Al Jazeera*, 11 March 2015, http://www.aljazeera.com/news/middleeast/2015/03/qa-avoid-ecological-disaster-150311072044323.html
69. Djamila Ould Khettab, "Algeria's Opposition Flares Up amid Fracking Plans," *Al Jazeera*, 7 May 2015. http://www.aljazeera.com/news/middleeast/2015/05/algeria-opposition-flares-fracking-plans-150505114107040.html
70. Wolfram Lacher, "Organized Crime and Conflict in the Sahel-Sahara Region," Carnegie Endowment for International Peace, 13 September 2012, http://carnegieendowment.org/2012/09/13/organized-crime-and-conflict-in-sahel-sahara-region-pub-49360

71. Carlotta Gall, "Shale Gas Project Encounters Determined Foes Deep in the Algerian Sahara," *New York Times*, 25 February 2015, http://www.nytimes.com/2015/02/26/world/shale-gas-project-encounters-determined-foes-deep-in-algerian-sahara.html?_r=0
72. The Bergama resistance movement in Turkey has been very well documented; see for example Murat Arsel, "Risk Society at Europe's Periphery? The Case of the Bergama Resistance in Turkey," in *Integrating and Articulating Environments: A Challenge for Northern and Southern Europe*, ed. Fatoş Gökşen et al. (Lisse, NL: Swets and Zeitlinger, 2003), 29–50; Aykut Coban, "Community-Based Ecological Resistance: The Bergama Movement in Turkey." *Environmental Politics* 13, no. 2 (2004): 438–60.
73. Benjamin Cook et al., "Spatiotemporal Drought Variability in the Mediterranean Over the Last 900 Years," *Journal of Geophysical Research* 121, no. 5 (2016), DOI 10.1002/2015JD023929.
74. "What is CCT?" Cairo Climate Talks, 2017, http://cairoclimatetalks.net/
75. For a summary of highlights and themes at COP22, see United Nations, "COP22—Liveblog," 2016, http://www.un.org/sustainabledevelopment/blog/2016/11/cop22-liveblog/#

2. TUNISIAN PHOSPHATES AND THE POLITICS OF THE PERIPHERY

1. Karen Pfeifer, "How Tunisia, Morocco, Jordan and even Egypt Became IMF 'Success Stories' in the 1990s," *Middle East Report* 210 (1999).
2. Beatrice Hibou, *La Force de l'Obéissance: Economie Politique de la Répression en Tunisie* (Paris: Découverte, 2006).
3. Hamed El-Said and Jane Harrigan, "Economic Reform, Social Welfare, and Instability: Jordan, Egypt, Morocco, and Tunisia, 1983–2004," *Middle East Journal* 68, no. 1 (2014).
4. International Monetary Fund, *Tunisia: Staff Report for the 2012 Article IV Consultation* (2012), https://www.imf.org/external/pubs/ft/scr/2012/cr12255.pdf
5. Former CEO of Compagnie des Phosphates de Gafsa, anonymity requested, interview by Francis Ghilès, Tunis, 1 December 2015.
6. George Joffé, "The Arab Spring in North Africa: Origins and Prospects," *Journal of North African Studies* 16, no. 4 (2011).
7. For examples of other model towns in the world that have been tied to extractive industries, see John Higginson, "Disputing the Machines: Scientific Management and the Transformation of the Work Routine at the Union Minière du Haut-Katanga, 1918–1930," *African Economic History* 17 (1988): 1–21; John Higginson, *A Working Class in the Making: Belgian Colonial Labor Policy, Private Enterprise, and the African Mineworker, 1907–1951* (Madison, WI: University of Wisconsin Press, 1989); Jane Parpart, "The 'Labor Aristocracy' Debate in Africa: The

Copperbelt Case, 1924–1967," *African Economic History* 13 (1984): 171–91; Samuël Coghe, "Reordering Colonial Society: Model Villages and Social Planning in Rural Angola, 1920–45," *Journal of Contemporary History* 52, no. 1 (2016); Greg Grandin, *Fordlandia: The Rise and Fall of Henry Ford's Forgotten Jungle City*, 1st edn (New York: Metropolitan Books, 2009).

8. Françoise and Francis Auvray, "Le gisement des phosphates de Gafsa, Tunisie, Historique de la Découverte et de l'exploitation des phosphates de Gafsa" (Saga Information, no. 325, Mars 2013), http://www.saga-geol.asso.fr/Documents/Saga_325_Phosphates_Gafsa_Tunisie.pdf.; History of Compagnie des Phosphates de Gafsa, http://www.gct.com.tn
9. Robert Vitalis, *America's Kingdom: Mythmaking on the Saudi Oil Frontier* (Stanford, CA: Stanford University Press, 2007).
10. Mohsen Brahmi and Sonia Zouari, "Indicateurs statistiques de performance économique et du positionnement mondial de l'industrie minière en Tunisie (1990–2010): Regard avant la révolution 2011," Association Tunisienne des Économistes, Forum Annuel, 2013, http://www.asectu.org/forum-annuel/forum2013/forum-asectu-2013/164-indicateurs-statistiques-de-performance-%C3%A9conomique-et-du-positionnement-mondial-de-l%E2%80%99industrie-mini%C3%A8re-en-tunisie-1990-2010-regard-avant-la-r%C3%A9volution-2011
11. British Petroleum, "Statistical Review of World Energy 2015," 2015, https://www.bp.com/content/dam/bp/pdf/energy-economics/statistical-review-2015/bp-statistical-review-of-world-energy-2015-full-report.pdf
12. Eqbal Ahmad and Stuart Schaar, "M'hamed Ali and the Tunisian Labour Movement," *Race and Class* 19, no. 3 (1978).
13. Stephen J. King, *Liberalization Against Democracy: The Local Politics of Economic Reform in Tunisia* (Bloomington, IN: Indiana University Press, 2003), 23.
14. Kais Daly, former CEO of CPG and GCT in the 1990s and 2000s, interview by Francis Ghilès, Tunis, 25 November 2015.
15. King, *Liberalization Against Democracy*, 28.
16. Zine el Abidine Ben Ali established Tunisia's military security department, and in 1984 became director general of national security. He was appointed minister of interior in 1986 and prime minister in October 1987, a few weeks ahead of ousting Bourguiba. Throughout the 1980s, Bourguiba's poor health and refusal to appoint a successor allowed Ben Ali to build a strong base of supporters within the system on which he was able to rely at the time of his bloodless *coup d'état*. Gana Nowri, *The Making of the Tunisian Revolution: Contexts, Architects, Prospects* (Oxford: Oxford University Press, 2013).
17. International Monetary Fund, *World Economic Outlook Dataset* (Washington, DC: IMF, 2016), http://www.imf.org/external/pubs/ft/weo/2016/01/weodata/index.aspx

18. Jane Harrigan and Hamed El-Said, *Globalisation, Democratisation and Radicalisation in the Arab World* (Basingstoke: Palgrave Macmillan, 2011).
19. State officials and private businessmen, interview by Francis Ghilès, Tunis, November and December 2015.
20. Kais Daly, former CEO of CPG and GCT, interview by Francis Ghilès Tunis, 25 November 2015.
21. Mohsen Brahmi, Campus Zarruk, Sonia Zaouari, "Indicateurs statistiques de performace économique et du positionnement mondial de l'industrie minière en Tunisie (1990–2010): Regard avant la révolution 2011," working paper, Forum des Economistes, Hammamet, 26–28 May 2016, http://www.asectu.org/forum-annuel/forum2013/forum-asectu-2013/164-indicateurs-statistiques-de-performance-%C3%A9conomique-et-du-positionnement-mondial-de-l%E2%80%99industrie-mini%C3%A8re-en-tunisie-1990-2010-regard-avant-la-r%C3%A9volution-2011; CPG senior engineers interviewed by Francis Ghilès, Tunis, 4 December 2015.
22. Former GCT officials, interview by Francis Ghilès, Tunis, 2 December 2015.
23. Kais Daly, former CEO of CPG and GCT, interview by Francis Ghilès, Tunis, 25 November 2015; and Mohamed Fadhel Khalil, former CEO of CPG in the 1980s, interview by Francis Ghilès, Tunis, 3 December 2015.
24. Sophie Bessis and Souhayr Belhassen, *Bourguiba* (Tunis: Elyzad, 1990). Besides creating a general impression of deterrence, the military help by Morocco, the US, and France included reconnaissance flights and transportation of Tunisian troops. The sangfroid of Tunisian President Bourguiba, who was on holiday in Nefta—100 kilometers west of Gafsa—was exemplified by his decision to go to Gafsa only 48 hours after the coup, where he was triumphantly received.
25. *Khaleeji* is a term used to refer to people of the Arab states of the Persian Gulf. Mahieddine Raoui, "Investissements des pays du Golfe dans le Maghreb," in *Transitions in North Africa in Times of Scarcity: Finance, Employment, Energy, and Food* (Barcelona: CIDOB, 2012), http://www.cidob.org/en/content/download/31710/514747/file/m_MULTIPOLARWORLD_2011.pdf
26. Mohamed Fadhel Khalil, former CEO of CPG, and Ali Boukhris, former CEO of GCT in the early 1980s, interview by Francis Ghilès, Tunis, 21 May 2016.
27. Swati Rathori, "Coromandel phosphoric acid Tunisian joint venture goes on stream," *Times of India*, 13 July 2013, http://timesofindia.indiatimes.com/business/india-business/Coromandel-phosphoric-acid-Tunisian-joint-venture-goes-on-stream/articleshow/21054873.cms
28. Hervé Gaboriau and Abdellah Chik, "Integrated Water Management of Mediterranean Phosphate Mining and Local Agricultural Systems: The El'Maa Project," AFA Eighteenth International Annual Technical Conference and Exhibition, 5–7 July 2005, Casablanca, Morocco, http://elmaa.brgm.fr/Results_publi_en.asp; FAO, "Aquastat," 2016, http://www.fao.org/nr/water/aquastat/data/query/results.html

29. Kais Daly, former CEO of CPG and GCT, interview by Francis Ghilès, Tunis, 15 November 2015.
30. Lakhdar Souid, "Gafsa or the Forgotten Land," *Maghreb Magazine*, July–August 2012.
31. Larbi Chouika and Éric Gobe, "La Tunisie entre la 'révolte du basin minier de Gafsa' et l'échéance électorale de 2009," *L'Année du Maghreb V* (Paris: CNRS Éditions, 2009).
32. Éric Gobe, "The Gafsa Mining Basin," *L'Année du Maghreb V* (Paris: CNRS Éditions, 2009).
33. Éric Gobe, "The Gafsa Mining Basin between Riots and a Social Movement: Meaning and Significance of a Protest Movement in Ben Ali's Tunisia," working paper, January 2010, HAL archives-ouvertes, 6, https://halshs.archives-ouvertes.fr/hals-00557826
34. Walid Belhadj Amor, "Can Southern Tunisia Draw Profit from its Phosphates?" in *Transitions in North Africa in Times of Scarcity: Finance, Employment, Energy and Food*, ed. Francesc Baida i Dalmases, seminar papers by CIDOB and OCP, 11–12 November 2012 (Barcelona: CIDOB, 2013).
35. Pfeifer, "How Tunisia, Morocco, Jordan and even Egypt became IMF 'Success Stories' in the 1990s"; El-Said and Harrigan, "Economic Reform, Social Welfare, and Instability."
36. Gilbert Achcar, *The People Want: A Radical Exploration of the Arab Uprising* (London: Saqi Books, 2013).
37. Bob Rijkers, Caroline Freund, and Antonio Nucifora, "All in the Family, State Capture in Tunisia" (Washington, DC: World Bank, 2014); World Bank, "The Unfinished Revolution: Bringing Opportunity, Good Jobs, and Greater Wealth to All Tunisians" (Washington, DC: World Bank, 2014).
38. Kais Daly, "Quels mécanismes de relance pour le développement regional?" *Forum Atuge* (Association Tunisiennes des Grandes Écoles), Tunis, 18 September 2014. As a former CEO of CPG and GCT, the author is well acquainted with the issues; the statistics are drawn from this conference paper.
39. Ibid.
40. Waleed Hazbun offers an in-depth analysis of how the tourist sector hijacked the economy and was used by Ben Ali to buttress the image of Tunisia as an open country in "Images of Openness, Spaces of Control: The Politics of Tourism Development in Tunisia," *Arab Studies Journal* 15/16, no. 1/2 (2007/2008): 11–35; Abderrazak Lejri, "Les hoteliers et la prédation de l'argent public," *Kapitalis* 26 (2015).
41. Mahmoud Ben Romdhane provides one of the most thorough analyses of the country's economy over half a century in "Tunisie, État, Économie et Société" (Tunis: Sud Éditions, 2011; see p. 190 for an analysis of the banking system); Habib Karaouli, CEO of Banque d'Affaires de Tunisie, "Redimensionner l'apport

des banques et des assurances," *La Presse*, 28 May 2014; and "Réformer nécessite une vision stratégique jusque-là absente," *L'Économiste Maghrébin*, 30 April 2015, http://www.leconomistemaghrebin.com/2015/04/30/reformer-necessite-une-vision-strategique-jusque-la-absente/. A respected banker, he does not shy from criticizing his country's economic failings. Francis Ghilès, "Tunisia's Dangerous Drift," *OpenDemocracy*, 1 July 2015, https://www.opendemocracy.net/francis-ghil%C3%A8s/tunisia's-dangerous-drift

42. Hazbun, "Images of Openness."
43. Indexmundi, Rock Phosphate Monthly Price, http://www.indexmundi.com/commodities/?commodity=rock-phosphate&months=180
44. Gobe, "The Gafsa Mining Basin."
45. On the changing nature of smuggling and security at the frontiers, see International Crisis Group, "La Tunisie des frontières: jihad et contrebande," *Rapport Moyen Orient/Afrique du Nord* 148, 28 November 2013; Francis Ghilès, "Tunisia should escape becoming a bazaar economy," *Notes Internacionals* 82, Barcelona Centre for International Affairs (CIDOB), and "Las Fronteras norteafricanas," *La Vanguardia*, 27 January 2014.
46. Marsha Pripstein Posusney, *Labor and the State in Egypt: Workers, Unions, and Economic Restructuring* (New York: Columbia University Press, 1997); Joel Beinin and Marie Duboc, "A Workers' Social Movement on the Margin of the Global Neoliberal Order, Egypt 2004–2012," in *Social Movements, Mobilization, and Contestation in the Middle East and North Africa*, ed. Joel Beinin and Frédéric Vairel (Stanford, CA: Stanford University Press, 2013), 205–27; Eckart Woertz, "Die Krise der Arbeitsgesellschaft als Krise von Gewerkschaften: Die unabhängige Gewerkschaftsbewegung in Ägypten" (PhD thesis, University of Erlangen-Nuremberg, 1999); Ahmad and Schaar, "M'hamed Ali and the Tunisian Labour Movement"; Joel Beinin, "Workers and Peasants in the Modern Middle East," in *The Contemporary Middle East 2* (Cambridge: Cambridge University Press, 2001); Joel Beinin and Zachary Lockman, *Workers on the Nile: Nationalism, Communism, Islam, and the Egyptian Working Class, 1882–1954* (Princeton, NJ: Princeton University Press, 1987); Joel Beinin, *Workers and Thieves: Labor Movements and Popular Uprisings in Tunisia and Egypt* (Stanford, CA: Stanford University Press, 2015).
47. Ahmad and Schaar, "M'hamed Ali and the Tunisian Labour Movement."
48. In 1964 it was renamed the Socialist Destour Party (PSD), and in 1989 the Constitutional Democratic Rally (RCD).
49. Francis Ghilès, "Something is Rotten in the State of Tunisia," *Notes Internacionals* 139 (Barcelona: CIDOB, January 2016).
50. Stephen J. King, "Structural Adjustment and Rural Poverty in Tunisia," *Middle East Report* 210 (1999); King, *Liberalization Against Democracy*.
51. Roger Owen, *The Rise and Fall of Arab Presidents for Life* (Cambridge, MA: Harvard University Press, 2012).

52. King, *Liberalization Against Democracy*, 32.
53. Salah Hamzaoui, "Champs politique et syndicalisme en Tunisie," *Annuaire de l'Afrique du Nord* 38 (Paris: Éditions du CNRS, 1999): 369–80; Sadri Khiari "Reclassements et recompositions au sein de la bureaucratie syndicale depuis l'indépendance. La place de l'UGTT dans le système politique tunisien" (Paris: Centre d'Études et de Recherches Internationales, Le Kiosque, 2000).
54. King, *Liberalization Against Democracy*, 5, 34; Christopher Alexander, "Labour Code Reform in Tunisia," *Mediterranean Politics* 6, no. 2 (2001).
55. Christopher Alexander, "Authoritarianism and Civil Society in Tunisia."
56. Gobe, "The Gafsa Mining Basin"; Larbi Chouika and Vincent Geisser, "Retour sur la révolte du basin minier. Les cinq leçons politiques d'un conflit social inédit," *L'Année du Maghreb VI* (2010), https://anneemaghreb.revues.org/923; Allal Amin, "Réformes néolibérales, clientélismes et protestations en situation autoritaire. Les mouvements contestataires dans le basin minier de Gafsa en Tunisie (2008)," *Politique Africaine* 117 (2010); Amroussia Ammar, "Le soulèvement des habitants du bassin minier: un premier bilan" (report published by the Parti communiste des ouvriers tunisiens), 12 January 2009, http://www.inprecor.fr/article-Tunisie-Le%20soul%C3%A8vement%20des%20habitants%20du%20bassin%20minier.%20Un%20premier%20bilan?id=633
57. United Nations Development Programme, "Arab Human Development Report 2003: Building a Knowledge Society" (New York: UNDP, 2003) and "Arab Human Development Report 2009: Challenges to Human Security in the Arab Countries" (New York: UNDP, 2009).
58. Mahmoud Ben Romdane and Ali Kadel, "Le basin minier de Gafsa: le désespoir sous les trésors," *Attariq Al Jadid*, 8 June 2008, http://attariq.org/spip.php?article60
59. Gobe, "The Gafsa Mining Basin," 5.
60. Ibid., 7.
61. For an excellent documentary film about the 2008 phosphate riots, see Nomadis Images, *Maudit soit le phosphate*, https://www.youtube.com/watch?v=foZUwchinpY; Karine Gantin and Omayya Seddik, "Révolte du 'people des mines' en Tunisie," *Le Monde Diplomatique*, July 2008, https://www.monde-diplomatique.fr/2008/07/GANTIN/16061
62. Abdelmajid Haouachi, "Gafsa: les raisons de la colère," *Réalités* 1153, 31 January 2008.
63. Kais Daly, former CEO of CPG and GCT, interview by Francis Ghilès, Tunis, 25 November 2015.
64. Gobe, "The Gafsa Mining Basin," 10.
65. Chouika and Gobe, "La Tunisie entre la 'révolte du basin minier de Gafsa.'"
66. Gobe, "The Gafsa Mining Basin," 16.
67. Carole Vann, "Maghreb. La région qui fait du pays le 4e producteur mondial de phosphate est l'une des plus déhéritées du pays," *Le Temps*, 16 October 2008,

quoted in Gobe, "The Gafsa Mining Basin," 16. See also Carole Vann, "En Tunisie, les émeutes du bassin minier de Gafsa se poursuivent malgré la répression," 16 October 2008, http://espace.tunisie.over-blog.com/pages/En_Tunisie_les_emeutes_du_bassin_minier_de_Gafsa_se_poursuivent_malgre_la_repression-791953.html

68. Larbi Chouika and Vincent Geisser, "A Reading of the Revolt in the Gafsa Mining Basin: The Five Policy Lessons of a Unique Social Conflict," *L'Année du Maghreb VI* (2010): 415–26; Ammar Amroussi, "Le Soulèvement des habitants du basin minier."
69. Rijkers, Freund, and Nucifora, "All in the Family"; World Bank, "The Unfinished Revolution." Neither report analyzes the phosphate and fertilizer sector.
70. EIB executive, interviewed by Francis Ghilès, 11 October 2015, Paris.
71. Former senior Tunisian officials and Western diplomats interviewed by Francis Ghilès, Paris and Tunis, October to December 2015.
72. Achcar, "The People Want," 180; Francis Ghilès, "Una prisión al aire libre: el legado de Ben Ali," *El Pais*, 15 January 2011, http://elpais.com/autor/francis_ghiles/a
73. Institut National de la Statistique, Tunis, http://www.ins.tn/fr/themes/industrie#sub-385; Tunisian mining officials, interview by Francis Ghilès, Tunis, 24 May 2016.
74. Francis Ghilès, "Secular Social Movements Confront Radical Temptations," *Notes Internacionals* (Barcelona: CIDOB, 2012).
75. State officials and private businessmen, interview by Francis Ghilès, Tunis, November and December 2015.
76. Oxford Business Group, "Uneven Growth in Tunisia's Industrial Sector Remains a Challenge," 2016, http://www.oxfordbusinessgroup.com/overview/forging-ahead-uneven-growth-industry-subsectors-remains-challenge
77. Tunisian mining official, interview by Francis Ghilès, 24 May 2016.
78. Mongi Marzoug, minister of mines and energy, and his assistant, interview by Francis Ghilès, Tunis, 24 May 2016.
79. Eric Goldstein, "Tunisia's Legacy of Pollution Confronts Democratic Politics," *OpenDemocracy*, 23 May 2014, https://www.opendemocracy.net/arab-awakening/eric-goldstein/tunisia%E2%80%99s-legacy-of-pollution-confronts-democratic-politics
80. Ibid.; and Moez Jemai, "Fishermen en Route for Europe," 27 November 2015, http://www.correspondents.org/node/7136; Sam Kimball, "Phosphate Production Poisoning Tunisian City," *Al Monitor*, 22 January 2015, http://www.al-monitor.com/pulse/originals/2015/01/tunisia-gabes-mineral-production-employment-pollution.html
81. Pascal Croset, *L'ambition au coeur de la transformation. Une leçon de management venue du Sud* (Paris: Dunod, 2012); Patricia Defever-Kapferer and Tristan Gaston-Breton, *OCP: En marche pour l'avenir* (Chesnay and Casablanca: Éditions de marque, 2012).

82. Duncan Pickard, "Challenges to Legitimate Governance in Post-Revolution Tunisia," *Journal of North African Studies* 16, no. 4 (2011); "Researching Arab Mediterranean Youth: Towards a New Social Contract," SAHWA, http://www.sahwa.eu/SAHWA-PROJECT
83. Clement M. Henry, "Algeria's Agonies: Oil Rent Effects in a Bunker State," *Journal of North African Studies* 9, no. 2 (2004).

3. THE SECURITIZATION OF OIL AND ITS RAMIFICATIONS IN THE GULF COOPERATION COUNCIL STATES

1. This is demonstrated vividly in Farah al-Nakib's *Kuwait Transformed: A History of Oil and Urban Life* (Stanford, CA: Stanford University Press, 2016), in which she argues that oil revenues propelled Kuwait's government into policies that transformed a cosmopolitan and closely knit urban Kuwait society—centered on the capital and oriented toward a common good—into a more disconnected and less cosmopolitan society, socially increasingly isolated in suburban villas. The emir's policies not only depopulated the core, but separated Kuwaitis from their natural environment: building parks, closed to the public so they wouldn't get messy, and exiling the opposition to the *diwaniyyas* of the outer villas.
2. On the rentier state literature, Giacomo Luciani, "Allocation vs. Production States: A Theoretical Framework," in *The Arab State*, ed. Giacomo Luciani (Berkeley, CA: University of California Press, 1990), 65–84; and Hazem Beblawi and Giacomo Luciani, eds, *The Rentier States* (New York: Croom Helm, 1987). On the GCC, Jill Crystal, *Oil and Politics in the Gulf: Rulers and Merchants in Kuwait and Qatar* (Cambridge: Cambridge University Press, 1995), an argument updated in Jill Crystal, "Oil and Politics in the Gulf: Kuwait and Qatar," *The New Palgrave Dictionary of Economics Online Edition* (Palgrave Macmillan, 2014).
3. See Heather MacLeod McClain, "Environmental Impact: Oil Fires and Spills Leave Hazardous Legacy," CNN, 2001, http://web.archive.org/web/20061222103323/http://www.cnn.com/SPECIALS/2001/gulf.war/legacy/environment/index.html
4. Alessandria Masi, "Saudi Arabia Thwarts 'Terrorist' Attack in Abqaiq," *International Business Times*, 4 September 2015, http://www.ibtimes.com/saudi-arabia-thwarts-terrorist-attack-abqaiq-worlds-largest-oil-processing-facility-2083386
5. Ali Al-Ahmed, Andrew Bond, and Daniel Morillo, "Security Threats to Saudi Arabia's Oil Infrastructure," Institute for Gulf Affairs, 2013.
6. "Saudi Security Forces Kill 'Terrorist' in Abqaiq: State TV," Reuters, 4 September 2015, http://www.reuters.com/article/us-saudi-security-idUSKCN0R40KK20150904
7. Al-Ahmed et al., "Security Threats to Saudi Arabia's Oil Infrastructure," 46. One of the attackers was a close relative of a leading cleric and head of the religious police.
8. "WikiLeaks Cables Show Worry about Saudi Oil Security," McClatchy Special Reports, 1 June 2011.

9. Ambrose Evans-Pritchard, "Oil Infrastructure at Risk as Mid-East Conflagration Spreads," *Daily Telegraph*, 30 March 2015, http://www.telegraph.co.uk/finance/economics/11505273/Saudi-oil-infrastructure-at-risk-as-Mid-East-conflagration-spreads.html
10. "Terror Threat Puts Kingdom on Top Alert," *Arab News*, 21 April 2015, http://www.arabnews.com/saudi-arabia/news/735551; and Adam Kerlin, "Securing the Kingdom: How the US Military Complex Built Up its Most Important Ally in the Middle East," *Vice*, 17 June 2015, https://www.vice.com/en_us/article/securing-the-kingdom-how-the-us-military-complex-has-built-up-americas-most-important-ally-in-the-middle-east-617
11. "WikiLeaks Cables Show Worry about Saudi Oil Security."
12. Ibid.
13. "Sergeant Slain in Terror Attack," *Arab News*, 5 September 2015, http://www.arabnews.com/saudi-arabia/news/801836.
14. Al-Ahmed et al., "Security Threats to Saudi Arabia's Oil Infrastructure," 14.
15. "WikiLeaks Cables Show Worry about Saudi Oil Security."
16. "NEC to Build Telecommunications and Security Systems for Large-Scale Oil Refinery in Kuwait," NEC Corporation, 17 August 2015, http://www.nec.com/en/press/201508/global_20150817_03.html
17. Justin Lee, "NEC to Provide Biometric Security Solution for Oil Refinery in Kuwait," Biometricupdate.com, 17 August 2015, https://www.biometricupdate.com/201508/
nec-to-provide-biometric-security-solution-for-oil-refinery-in-kuwait
18. "Middle East Enterprises Need New Cybersecurity Incident Response Approach," *Tech News*, 8 September 2013, http://www.ciol.com/middle-east-enterprises-cybersecurity-incident-response-approach
19. Ronke Luke, "Cyber Threat has Oil and Gas Major on Edge," Oilprice.com, 7 July 2015, http://oilprice.com/Energy/Energy-General/Cyber-Threat-Has-Oil-And-Gas-Majors-On-Edge.html
20. Nicole Perlroth, "In Cyberattack on Saudi Firm, U.S. Sees Iran Firing Back," *New York Times*, 23 October 2012; Mike Mount, "U.S. Officials Believe Iran Behind Recent Cyberattacks," CNN, 16 October 2012, http://www.nytimes.com/2012/10/24/business/global/cyberattack-on-saudi-oil-firm-disquiets-us.html
21. Stephen McBride, "No Emails, No Phones, Nothing: How Saudi Aramco—The World's Biggest Oil Company—Survived a Debilitating Cyberattack." Arabianbusiness.com, 10 August 2015, http://www.arabianbusiness.com/-no-emails-no-phones-nothing-how-saudi-aramcoworld-s-biggest-oil-company-survived-debilitating-cyber-attack-602094.html
22. "Kuwait Looks to Boost Cyber Security," Oxford Business Group, 17 June 2014, http://www.oxfordbusinessgroup.com/news/kuwait-looks-boost-cyber-security
23. "Security Framework Keeps Oil Flowing in the Middle East," Booz Allen Hamilton,

http://www.boozallen.com/about/annual-report/annual-report-fy2014/enhancing-analytics-and-network-security/security-framework-keeps-oil-flowing-in-the-middle-east

24. And security more broadly. In April 2016, Qatar National Bank faced a cyberattack affecting data on hundreds of thousands of customers. "QNB: Company Reputation, Not Customers, was Target of Recent Hack," *Doha News*, 1 May 2016, https://dohanews.co/qnb-company-not-customers-target-recent-hack/
25. Jeannie Sowers, "Water, Energy and Human Insecurity in the Middle East," *Middle East Report* 271 (2014).
26. Renee Richer, "Conservation in Qatar: Impacts of Increasing Industrialization," Center for International and Regional Studies, Georgetown University Qatar, Occasional Paper 2, 2008–2009, 6.
27. For a good treatment of Qatar's foreign policy during the Arab Spring, see Kristian Coates Ulrichsen, *Qatar and the Arab Spring* (London: Hurst & Co., 2014).
28. Mari Luomi, *The Gulf Monarchies and Climate Change: Abu Dhabi and Qatar in an Era of Natural Unsustainability* (London: Hurst & Co., 2012), 26.
29. Laurent A. Lambert, "Water, State Power, and Tribal Politics in the GCC: The Case of Kuwait and Abu Dhabi," Center for International and Regional Studies, Georgetown University Qatar, Occasional Paper 14, 2014.
30. Luomi, *The Gulf Monarchies and Climate Change*, 60.
31. World Resources Institute, "Ranking the World's Most Water-Stressed Countries in 2040," 26 August 2015, http://www.wri.org/blog/2015/08/ranking-world%E2%80%99s-most-water-stressed-countries-2040
32. Justin Gengler and Laurent A. Lambert, "Renegotiating the Ruling Bargain: Selling Fiscal Reform in the GCC," *Middle East Journal* 70, no. 2 (2016): 326.
33. "UAE Plans to Build 'Man-made Mountain' to Increase Rainfall," *New Arab*, 2 May 2016. https://www.alaraby.co.uk/english/society/2016/5/2/uae-plans-to-build-man-made-mountain-to-increase-rainfall; "Exclusive: UAE Mulls Man-made Mountain in Bid to Improve Rainfall," *Arabian Business*, 1 May 2016, http://www.arabianbusiness.com/exclusive-uae-mulls-man-made-mountain-in-bid-improve-rainfall-630079.html; "The UAE may Build a Mountain to Make it Rain," *Washington Post*, 2 May 2016, https://www.washingtonpost.com/news/worldviews/wp/2016/05/02/the-uae-may-build-a-mountain-to-make-it-rain/?utm_=.196e515ea784
34. Toby Craig Jones, *Desert Kingdom: How Oil and Water Forged Modern Saudi Arabia* (Cambridge, MA: Harvard University Press, 2010).
35. Luomi, *The Gulf Monarchies and Climate Change*, 73.
36. Brad Plumer, "Saudi Arabia Squandered its Groundwater and Agriculture Collapsed: California Take Note," Vox, 14 September 2015, http://www.vox.com/2015/9/14/9323379/saudi-arabia-squandered-its-groundwater-and-agriculture-collapsed.

37. Fahad al-Attiya, "A Country with No Water," TEDxSummit, April 2012, https://www.ted.com/talks/fahad_al_attiya_a_country_with_no_water
38. Eckart Woertz, "The Governance of Gulf Agro-Investments," *Globalizations* 10, no. 1 (2013): 87–104; Benjamin Shepherd, "GCC States' Land Investments Abroad: The Case of Ethiopia," Center for International and Regional Studies, Georgetown University Qatar, Summary Report 8 (2013), 92.
39. See Mary Ann Tetreault, Deborah L. Wheeler and Benjamin Shepherd, "Win–Win Versus Lose–Lose: Investments in Foreign Agriculture as a Food Security Strategy of the Arab States of the Persian Gulf," in *Food Security in the Middle East*, ed. Zahra Babar and Suzi Mirgani (London: Hurst & Co., 2014), 221–47.
40. See Woertz, "The Governance of Gulf Agro-Investments," 87–104; and Shepherd, "GCC States' Land Investments Abroad: The Case of Ethiopia." Saudi Arabia is also buying farmland in the US, primarily for animal feed. See Jeff Daniels, "Saudi Arabia Buying up Farmland in US," CNBC, 15 January 2016, http://www.cnbc.com/2016/01/15/saudi-arabia-buying-up-farmland-in-us-southwest.html
41. See Eckart Woertz, "The Geo-Economics of Gulf Food Imports," *Jadaliyya*, 13 January 2016, http://www.jadaliyya.com/pages/index/23550/the-geo-economics-of-gulf-food-imports
42. Woertz, "The Governance of Gulf Agro-Investments," 96.
43. Ibid., 88.
44. Eliot Beer, "US Food Exports to GCC hit $3bn," Foodnavigator.com, 7 December 2015, http://www.foodnavigator.com/Regions/Middle-East/US-food-exports-to-GCC-hit-3bn
45. Damian Carrington, "Extreme Heatwaves could Push Gulf Climate Beyond Human Endurance, Study Shows," *Guardian*, 26 October 2015, https://www.theguardian.com/environment/2015/oct/26/extreme-heatwaves-could-push-gulf-climate-beyond-human-endurance-study-shows; Jeremy Pal and Elfatih Eltahir, "Future Temperature in Southwest Asia Projected to Exceed a Threshold for Human Adaptability," *Nature Climate Change*, 26 October 2015, http://www.nature.com/nclimate/journal/v6/n2/full/nclimate2833.html
46. Suzanne Goldenberg, "Saudi Arabia Accused of Trying to Wreck Paris Climate Deal, *Guardian*, 8 December 2015, https://www.theguardian.com/environment/2015/dec/08/saudi-arabia-accused-of-trying-to-wreck-the-paris-climate-deal
47. Lina Eland, "A Brief Guide to Climate Change, COP21 and the Middle East," *Informed Comment*, 7 December 2015, https://www.juancole.com/2015/12/climate-change-middle.html. That said, all the GCC states are working to develop more renewable energy sources. Mohamed Abdel Raouf, "Renewable Energy in GCC," *Arab News*, 23 January 2016, http://www.arabnews.com/economy/news/868856
48. Luomi, *The Gulf Monarchies and Climate Change*, 199.

49. Ibid., 3.
50. For example, in 2013, at least twenty-three oil workers were killed in an attack by a jihadist group on an oil facility in Algeria. Vivienne Walt, "Algeria Attack Poses a Dilemma for Western Oil Companies," *Time*, 19 January 2013, http://world.time.com/2013/01/19/algeria-terror-poses-a-dilemma-for-western-oil-companies/
51. "Kuwait Beefs up Security around Oil Installations after Attack," *Al-Arabiya*, 27 June 2015, http://english.alarabiya.net/en/business/energy/2015/06/27/Kuwait-beefs-up-security-around-oil-installations-after-attack.html
52. Barry Buzan, Ole Waever, and Jaap de Wilde, *Security: A New Framework for Analysis* (Boulder, CO: Lynne Rienner, 1998), 23–4.
53. See F. Gregory Gause III and Sean Yom, "Resilient Royals: How Arab Monarchies Hang On," *Journal of Democracy* 23, no. 4 (2012), who argue that money, cross-cutting coalitions, and foreign patronage largely explain regime survival; and Michael Herb, who focuses more on regime type in "Monarchism Matters," *Foreign Policy*, 26 November 2012, http://foreignpolicy.com/2012/11/26/monarchism-matters/
54. Steven Heydemann, "Mass Politics and the Future of Authoritarian Governance in the Arab World," in *The Arab Thermidor: The Resurgence of the Security States*, Project on Middle East Political Science, 27 February 2015, https://pomeps.org/2014/12/16/mass-politics-and-the-future-of-authoritarian-governance-in-the-arab-world/
55. In 2012 the UAE introduced Cybercrime Law No. 5, which made all forms of electronic abuse and slander illegal. In 2016 Kuwait introduced a new cybercrime law, in addition to those already on the books, which criminalized a range of online behavior including criticizing the government, religious leaders, and foreign leaders. Amnesty International, "Kuwait: Electronic Crimes Law Threatens to Further Stifle Freedom of Expression," 12 January 2016, https://www.amnesty.org/en/latest/news/2016/01/kuwait-electronic-crimes-law-threatens-to-further-stifle-freedom-of-expression/
56. Robert Springborg, "The Resurgence of Arab Militaries," *Washington Post*, 5 December 2014, https://www.washingtonpost.com/news/monkey-cage/wp/2014/12/05/the-resurgence-of-arab-militaries. This was now done in part through recruiting mercenaries, since small militaries were historically part of a coup-proofing strategy. Robert Springborg, "The Role of Militaries in the Arab Thermidor," Project on Middle East Political Science, 12 December 2014, https://pomeps.org/2014/12/12/the-role-of-militaries-in-the-arab-thermidor/
57. This was the case with the basic model for ruling, which Herb calls dynastic monarchism, a model developed in Kuwait and copied by other GCC states after oil was discovered. See Michael Herb, *All in the Family* (Albany, NY: SUNY Press, 1999). It was also the case with the expansion of partially elected consultative assemblies in the 1980s and 1990s.

58. Matthew Gray, *Qatar: Politics and the Challenges of Development* (London: Lynne Rienner, 2013), 235.
59. The government's reaction to the few prominent opposition voices, such as Ali Khalifah al-Kuwari, is detailed in Ulrichsen, *Qatar and the Arab Spring*, 159–65.
60. Ulrichsen, *Qatar and the Arab Spring*, 1.
61. For example, in January 2016 a court jailed a man for three years for insulting the UAE by creating a Facebook page that damaged the country's reputation. Naser Al Rameithi, "Man who Insulted UAE on Social Media gets Three-Year Jail Term," *The National*, 10 January 2016, http://www.thenational.ae/uae/man-who-insulted-uae-on-social-media-gets-three-year-jail-term.
62. Wam, "UAE Anti-Discriminatory Law Bans Hate Speech, Promotion of Violence 'Law Promotes UAE's Coexistence Model,'" *Emirates 24/7 News*, 22 July 2015, http://www.emirates247.com/news/government/uae-anti-discriminatory-law-bans-hate-speech-promotion-of-violence-2015–07–22–1.597389.
63. See "Inside Story—UAE: Arming up with Mercenaries," *Al Jazeera*, https://www.youtube.com/watch?feature=player_detailpage&v=GWjzqR41AM0.
64. Mark Mazzetti and Emily B. Hager, "Secret Desert Force Set Up by Blackwater's Founder," *New York Times*, 14 May 2011. These were not the country's first mercenaries. Most of the soldiers in the 65,000-strong emirati Union Defense Forces are also non-nationals, primarily Arab and Pakistani. Hannah Gurman, "Bigger than Blackwater: Arming the UAE," *Foreign Policy in Focus*, 8 June 2011, http://fpif.org/bigger_than_blackwater_arming_the_uae/.
65. Cited in "li-matha tasta'in al-imirat bi junud al-ajanib 'limurtaziqah' fi al-jaysh wa al-amn al-dakhili," SAS Post, 2 November 2015.
66. "Revealed: The Mercenaries Commanding UAE Forces in Yemen," *Middle East Eye*, 23 December 2015, http://www.middleeasteye.net/news/mercenaries-charge-uae-forces-fighting-yemen-764309832.
67. "Islamists Plot against Gulf: Dubai Police Chief," *Gulf News*, 25 March 2012, http://gulfnews.com/news/gulf/kuwait/islamists-plot-against-gulf-dubai-police-chief-1.999524.
68. Ulrichsen, *Qatar and the Arab Spring*, 155.
69. Ibid.
70. F. Gregory Gause III, "Understanding the Gulf States," *Democracy* 36 (2015): 34.
71. Michael Herb, *The Wages of Oil: Parliaments and Economic Development in Kuwait and the UAE* (Ithaca, NY: Cornell University Press, 2014).
72. At least for the national population; for the expatriate population, it deployed a panopticonic state, which it legitimized through a discourse of Kuwaiti nationalism. See Jill Crystal, "Public Order and Authority: Policing Kuwait," in *Monarchies and Nations: Globalisation and Identity in the Arab States of the Gulf*, ed. Paul Dresch and James Piscatori (London: I. B. Tauris, 2005), 158–81.

73. Amnesty International, "The 'Iron Fist Policy:' Criminalization of Peaceful Dissent in Kuwait," 15 December 2015, https://www.amnesty.org/en/documents/mde17/3080/2015/en/
74. In some cases, however, the terrorism discourse also served the purpose of security theater. Both a spokesman for the oil sector and, separately, for the Kuwait National Petroleum Company, made very public statements following the June 2015 mosque attacks about heightened oil security. "Kuwait Says Security Raised to Highest in Oil Sector," Reuters, 27 June 2015, http://in.reuters.com/article/kuwait-oil-security-idINL5N0ZD08I20150627
75. Khalid al-Shatti, "Beware of Blowback from Forces being Fought," *New York Times*, 15 September 2014, http://www.nytimes.com/roomfordebate/2014/09/15/does-the-us-have-allies-it-needs-to-fight-isis/beware-of-blowback-from-forces-being-fought
76. Suliman Al-Atiqi, "Kuwait is Shielded from Sectarian Strife," Carnegie Endowment for International Peace, Sada Online Journal, 2 July 2015, http://carnegieendowment.org/sada/60801
77. "Kuwait Shiite MPs Boycott Session; Assembly Backs Leadership—E-Media, Anti-Graft Laws Passed, Defense Budget Approved," *Kuwait Times*, 13 January 2016, http://news.kuwaittimes.net/website/shiite-mps-boycott-session-assembly-backs-leadership-e-media-anti-graft-laws-passed-defense-budget-approved/
78. Kristin Smith Diwan, "Kuwait's Balancing Act," *Foreign Policy*, 23 October 2012, http://foreignpolicy.com/2012/10/23/kuwaits-balancing-act/
79. "Kuwait Seeks Death Penalty for 11 of 29 Terror Suspects," *Kuwait Times*, 16 July 2015, http://news.kuwaittimes.net/kuwait-seeks-death-penalty-for-11-of-29-terror-suspects-2-suspects-currently-fighting-with-is-5-to-be-tried-in-absentia/
80. "Kuwait Tightens Security as Emir Attends Joint Prayers," *Daily Star*, 3 July 2015, http://www.dailystar.com.lb/News/Middle-East/2015/Jul-03/304993-kuwait-tightens-security-as-emir-attends-joint-prayers.ashx
81. "Saudis among 26 Held for Kuwait Blast," *Arab News*, 7 July 2015, http://www.arabnews.com/saudi-arabia/news/772966
82. Human Right Watch, "Kuwait: New Counterterror Law Sets Mandatory DNA Testing," 20 July 2015, https://www.hrw.org/news/2015/07/20/kuwait-new-counterterror-law-sets-mandatory-dna-testing
83. Marc Valeri, "Simmering Unrest and Succession Challenges in Oman," Carnegie Endowment for International Peace, 28 January 2015, http://carnegieendowment.org/2015/01/28/simmering-unrest-and-succession-challenges-in-oman-pub-58843
84. In 2015, Saudi Arabia deployed 100,000 troops to secure the hajj, including members of an elite counter-terrorism unit. "Saudi Arabia Says 100,000 Troops to Secure this Year's Hajj," Associated Press, 19 September 2015, https://www.usnews.com/news/world/articles/2015/09/19/saudi-arabia-says-100–000-troops-to-

secure-this-years-hajj; "Saudi Arabia Marks First Day of Hajj—2011," *Al Jazeera*, 5 November 2011, https://www.youtube.com/watch?v=pDazF47rmlk

85. "Saudi Arabia: Mass Execution Largest since 1980," Human Rights Watch, 4 January 2016, https://www.hrw.org/news/2016/01/04/saudi-arabia-mass-execution-largest-1980
86. Majlis al-wuzara al-sa'udi yuqarr nitham jaraim al-irhab wa tamwil, *al-sharq al-awsat*, 14 Safr 1435, http://aawsat.com/home/article/13458
87. Kashmira Gander, "Saudi Arabia Arrests Hundreds of Suspected Isis Jihadists," *Independent*, 19 July 2015, http://www.independent.co.uk/news/world/middle-east/isis-crisis-saudi-arabia-arrests-400-suspected-members-of-extremist-group-10399603.html
88. "Saudi Arabia: Sustained Assault on Free Expression," Human Rights Watch, 11 January 2016, https://www.hrw.org/news/2016/01/11/saudi-arabia-sustained-assault-free-expression
89. An early suggestion that not all may be open to this framing can be found in an op-ed by Nermin Al-Houti in Al-Anbaa, translated by the *Kuwait Times*: "Enough About Subsidy Cuts," *Kuwait Times*, 27 January 2016, http://news.kuwaittimes.net/website/enough-about-subsidy-cuts. It asks, "Before you lift subsidies, why all those who squandered public fund through bogus deals were not punished? Did your proposal look at some names that embezzled and stolen public funds and the law was not applied to them to recover what was taken from state coffers?"
90. "Qatari Emir: Govt can no Longer 'Provide for Everything,'" *Al-Arabiya*, 3 November 2015, https://english.alarabiya.net/en/News/middle-east/2015/11/03/Qatar-Emir-warns-against-dependence-on-state-.html
91. John Chalcraft, "Migration and Popular Protest in the Arabian Peninsula and the Gulf in the 1950s and 1960s," *International Labor and Working-Class History* 79 (2011): 28–47.
92. Sean Yom, "Oil Coalitions and Regime Durability: The Origins and Persistence of Popular Rentierism in Kuwait," *Studies in Comparative International Development* 46 (2011): 217–41.
93. Steffon Hertog, *Princes, Brokers, and Bureaucrats: Oil and the State in Saudi Arabia* (Ithaca, NY: Cornell University Press, 2010), 268; and Mehran Kamrava, "The Political Economy of Rentierism," in *The Political Economy of the Persian Gulf*, ed. Mehran Kamrava (New York: Columbia University Press: 2012).
94. See Steffen Hertog, "The GCC Economic Model in the Age of Austerity," in "The Gulf Monarchies Beyond the Arab Spring: Changes and Challenges," ed. Luigi Narbone and Martin Lestra (Florence: European University Institute, 2015), 5–11.
95. Claudia Carpenter and Sarmand Khan, "U.A.E. Removes Fuel Subsidy as Oil Drop Hurts Arab Economies," *Bloomberg*, 22 July 2015, https://www.bloomberg.com/news/articles/2015–07–22/u-a-e-to-link-gasoline-price-to-global-markets-effect-

aug-1. "Responding to the 'New Normal': Gulf Economic Strategies in an Era of Low-Cost Oil," Gulf State Analytics Monthly Monitor, November 2015, https://gallery.mailchimp.com/02451f1ec2ddbb874bf5daee0/files/Gulf_State_Analytics_November_2015_Report.pdf

96. Gengler and Lambert, "Renegotiating the Ruling Bargain," 321–9, 1.
97. "Gulf States Agree on Key Issues for Implementing VAT, UAE Official Says," Reuters, 7 December 2015, http://gulfnews.com/business/economy/gulf-states-agree-on-key-issues-for-implementing-vat-uae-official-says-1.1633089. Oman, with lower oil revenue, chose to institute a range of measures including raising corporate taxes, deregulating fuel prices at home, increasing visa fees, and halting bonuses for state workers. Giorgio Cafiero, "Can Tourism Save Oman from Cheap Oil?" Atlantic Council, 1 February 2016, http://www.atlanticcouncil.org/blogs/menasource/can-tourism-save-oman-from-cheap-oil
98. "Oman to Cut Benefits for State Employees," *Gulf News*, 4 May 2016, http://gulfnews.com/news/gulf/oman/oman-to-cut-benefits-for-state-employees-report-1.1816265
99. Gengler and Lambert, "Renegotiating the Ruling Bargain," 323.
100. Karen E. Young, "Understanding Vision 2030: Anticipating Economic Change in Saudi Arabia," Arab Gulf States Institute Washington, 28 April 2016, http://www.agsiw.org/understanding-vision-2030-anticipating-economic-change-in-saudi-arabia; Khaled Alaswad, "Towards a New Saudi Economy," *Your Middle East*, 1 May 2016, http://www.yourmiddleeast.com/business/towards-a-new-saudi-economy_40591; Zainab Fattah et al., "What's in Saudi Arabia's Blueprint for Life after Oil?" *Bloomberg*, 26 April 2016, https://www.bloomberg.com/news/articles/2016–04–25/key-elements-of-saudi-arabia-s-blueprint-for-life-post-oil
101. Awad Mustafa, "Half of Saudi Arabia's Military Purchases to be Local," *Defense News*, 25 April 2016, http://www.defensenews.com/story/breaking-news/2016/04/25/united-arab-emirates/83497394/
102. Gengler and Lambert, "Renegotiating the Ruling Bargain," 327.
103. One quiet rumble was a protest in Bahrain's otherwise quiescent parliament by several MPs over a January 2016 cabinet decision to increase gas prices. As MP Mohammad Al Amadi said, "The decision ignored that there's a parliament. We should resign," quoted in Courtney Trenwith, "Why Bahrain's Politicians Must Face the New Reality," *Arabian Business*, 22 January 2016, http://www.arabianbusiness.com/why-bahrain-s-politicians-must-face-new-reality-619412.html
104. "Kuwait Cuts Output in Half as Thousands of Workers Strike," ArabianBusiness.com, 18 April 2016, http://infoweb.newsbank.com/resources/doc/nb/news/15C52C2AAF4FA220?p=AWNB
105. Quoted in Sylvia Westall and Ahmed Hagagy, "Kuwait Freedoms Make Austerity Drive Tricky for Government," Reuters, 2 May 2016, http://www.reuters.com/article/us-kuwait-oil-strikes-idUSKCN0XT0D7

106. Ibid.
107. "12,000 Saudi Citizens Fired by Struggling Binladin Group," *Middle East Eye*, 2 May 2016, http://www.middleeasteye.net/news/over-10000-saudis-fired-struggling-construction-giant-binladin-362509602; Elsa Vulliamy, "Saudi Arabia: Workers Set Fire to Buses, after 50,000 Sacked and Wages Unpaid," *Independent*, 1 May 2016, http://www.independent.co.uk/news/world/middle-east/saudi-arabia-workers-set-fire-to-buses-after-50000-sacked-and-salaries-not-paid-a7008931.html
108. "Saudi Arabia: Foreign Workers Burn Buses after Massive Layoffs," *Telesur*, 2 May 2016, http://www.telesurtv.net/english/news/Saudi-Arabia-Foreign-Workers-Burn-Buses-After-Massive-Layoffs-20160502–0026.html
109. "Bahrain MPs Blast Fuel Price Hike in Heated Session," Reuters, 12 January 2016, http://www.reuters.com/article/us-bahrain-gasoline-parliament-idUSKCN0UQ1JI20160112
110. Gengler and Lambert, "Renegotiating the Ruling Bargain," 328.
111. Among Saudis under thirty (two-thirds of the population), the unemployment rate is estimated at 29 percent. Julia Glum, "Saudi Arabia's Youth Unemployment Problem among King Salman's Many New Challenges after Abdullah's Death," *International Business Times*, 23 January 2015, http://www.ibtimes.com/saudi-arabias-youth-unemployment-problem-among-king-salmans-many-new-challenges-after-1793346
112. Curtis Ryan, "Jordan, Morocco and an Expanded GCC," Middle East Research and Information Project, 15 April 2014, http://www.merip.org/jordan-morocco-expanded-gcc; Richard Lebanon, "The Jordan-Morocco Solution for FCC Defense Masks Bigger Issues", Atlantic Council, 18 April 2014, http://www.atlanticcouncil.org/blogs/menasource/the-jordan-morocco-solution-for-gcc-defense-masks-bigger-issues
113. In May 2016, for example, the Revolutionary Guard's deputy commander said on state television that Iranian forces would close the Strait of Hormuz to the US and its allies should they threaten the country. *Saudi Gazette*, 5 May 2016, cited in *Gulf in the Media*, 5 May 2016. In February 2015, Iran sank a replica of US aircraft carriers near the Strait.
114. Brahim Saidy, "The Gulf Cooperation Council's Unified Military Command," Foreign Policy Research Institute, Philadelphia Papers, October 2014, http://www.fpri.org/article/2014/10/the-gulf-cooperation-councils-unified-military-command/
115. "GCC: Joint Security Agreement Imperils Rights," Human Rights Watch, 26 April 2014, https://www.hrw.org/news/2014/04/26/gcc-joint-security-agreement-imperils-rights
116. Frederic Wehrey and Richard Sokolsky, "Imagining a New Security Order in the Persian Gulf," Carnegie Endowment for International Peace, October 2015,

http://carnegieendowment.org/2015/10/14/imagining-new-security-order-in-persian-gulf-pub-61618

117. US efforts to improve interoperability by developing integrated air and missile defenses had some limited success. Wehrey and Sokolsky, "Imagining a New Security Order in the Persian Gulf."
118. Ghazanfar Ali Khan, "Zayani Backs Creation of a United GCC Police Force," *Arab News*, 10 August 2015, http://www.arabnews.com/featured/news/789076
119. "Kuwait to Send Troops to Saudi Arabia to Fight Yemen Rebels," *Gulf News*, 29 December 2015, http://gulfnews.com/news/gulf/yemen/kuwait-to-send-troops-to-saudi-arabia-to-fight-yemen-rebels-1.1645555. Oman has tried to maintain a degree of distance, agreeing in 2014 to build a natural gas pipeline to Iran and helping broker the nuclear agreement between the US and Iran. Dana El Baltaji, "Oman Fights Saudi Bid for Gulf Hegemony with Iran Pipeline Plan," *Bloomberg*, 22 April 2014, https://www.bloomberg.com/news/articles/2014-04-21/oman-fights-saudi-bid-for-gulf-hegemony-with-iran-pipeline-plan
120. Kristin Smith Diwan, "Soldiers and the Nation," Arab Gulf States Institute in Washington, 18 September 2015, http://www.agsiw.org/soldiers-and-the-nation/
121. See also Harry Verhoeven, "African Dam Building as Extraversion: the case of Sudan's Dam Programme, Nubian Resistance and the Saudi-Iranian Proxy War in Yemen," *African Affairs* 115, no. 461 (2016): 562–73.
122. "Saudi Arabia Willing to Send Ground Troops to Syria," *Al Jazeera*, 6 February 2016, http://www.aljazeera.com/news/2016/02/general-saudi-arabia-set-deploy-troops-syria-160205042542486.html
123. Fahad al-Attiya, "A Country with No Water."
124. Gerald Stang, "Climate Challenges in the Middle East: Rethinking Environmental Cooperation," Middle East Institute Policy Paper 2016–2, http://www.mei.edu/sites/default/files/publications/PP2_Stang_RCS_environment_3.pdf
125. Wehrey and Sokolsky, "Imagining a New Security Order in the Persian Gulf."
126. Gengler and Lambert, "Renegotiating the Ruling Bargain," 325.
127. Regan Doherty, "Top Polluter Qatar Defends Rights to Host Climate Talks," Reuters, 26 November 2012, http://www.reuters.com/article/us-climate-qatar-idUSBRE8AP0V820121126. Cited in Gengler and Lambert, "Renegotiating the Ruling Bargain," 325.
128. "State-Sanctioned Friday Sermon Mandates 'Blessing of Security,'" *Daily News Egypt*, 13 January 2016, http://www.dailynewsegypt.com/2016/01/13/state-sanctioned-friday-sermon-mandates-blessing-of-security/
129. These arguments are developed more fully in "Public Space and Public Protest in Kuwait," *City* 18, 6 (2014): 723–34; and "Towards an Urban Alternative for Kuwait: Protests and Popular Participation," *Built Environment* 40, 1 (2014): 101–17.

4. GREENING GULF LANDSCAPES: ECONOMIC OPPORTUNITIES, SOCIAL TRADE-OFFS, AND SUSTAINABILITY CHALLENGES

1. Harry Verhoeven, *Water, Civilisation and Power in Sudan: The Political Economy of Military-Islamist State Building* (Cambridge: Cambridge University Press, 2015), 13–25.
2. Harry Verhoeven, "The Nexus as Political Commodity: Agricultural Development, Water Policy and Elite Rivalry in Egypt," *International Journal of Water Resources Development* 31, no. 2 (2015): 360–61.
3. Ali El-Keblawy, Arvind Bhatt, and Sanjay Gairola, "Developing Sea Watered Landscapes: A Potential Way to Reduce Stress on Fresh Water Resources," *Current Science* 108, no. 10 (2015): 1773–4.
4. Anna Bramwell, *Ecology in the 20th Century: A History* (New Haven, CT: Yale University Press, 1989).
5. Yogesh Mehta, Srishti Joshi, and Ashwini Mehta, "Composting: A Tool to Save Earth and Go Green," *International Journal of Research in Commerce and Management* 2, no. 5 (2011): 113–15.
6. Keith G. Tidball, "Peace Research and Greening in the Red Zone: Community-Based Ecological Restoration to Enhance Resilience and Transitions Toward Peace," in *Expanding Peace Ecology: Peace, Security, Sustainability, Equity and Gender*, ed. Ursula Oswald Spring, Hans Günter Brauch, and Keith Tidball (Springer International Publishing, 2014), 63–83.
7. Bruce G. Doern, *Green Diplomacy: How Environmental Policy Decisions are Made* (Toronto: CD Howe Institute, 1993).
8. Allison M. Krusky et al., "The Effects of Produce Gardens on Neighborhoods: A Test of the Greening Hypothesis in Post-Industrial City," *Landscape and Urban Planning* 136 (2015): 68–75.
9. *Khaleejis* is a term used to refer to people of the Arab states of the Persian Gulf.
10. Waleed K. Al-Zubari, "Towards the Establishment of a Total Water Cycle Management and Re-use Program in the GCC Countries," *Desalination* 120, no. 1 (1998): 3–14; and Environmental Agency of Abu Dhabi, *Abu Dhabi Water Resources Master Plan* (Abu Dhabi, UAE: Environmental Agency of Abu Dhabi, 2009).
11. Jill Crystal, "Securitization of Natural Resources in the Gulf Cooperation Council" (presentation, Geopolitics of Natural Resources in the Middle East, Georgetown University in Qatar, April 2016).
12. Elie Elhadj, "Dry Aquifers in Arab Countries and the Looming Food Crisis," *Middle East Review of International Affairs* 12, no. 4 (2008): 1–11.
13. Anthony Cordesman, *Bahrain, Oman, Qatar and the UAE: Challenges of Security* (Boulder, CO: Westview Press, 1997); Muhammed F. Al-Rashed and Mohsen M. Sherif, "Water Resources in the GCC Countries: An Overview," *Water Resources Management* 14, no. 1 (2000): 59–75; Adel El-Beltagy, "Strategic

Options for Alleviating Conflicts Over Water in Dry Areas," *ACIAR Monograph Series* 73 (2000): 67–82; Suzan M. Shahin and Mohammed Salem, "Review Future Concerns on Irrigation Requirements of Date Palm Tree in the United Arab Emirates (UAE): Call for Quick Actions" (5th International Date Palm Conference, United Arab Emirates, 2012); Theib Y. Oweis, "Agricultural Water Management Under Scarcity: A Need for a Paradigm Change," *Revista Científica de Produção Animal* 15, no. 1 (2014): 22–30; and Shakhawat Chowdhury and Muhammad Al-Zahrani, "Characterizing Water Resources and Trends of Sector Wise Water Consumptions in Saudi Arabia," *Journal of King Saud University-Engineering Sciences* 27, no. 1 (2015): 68–82.

14. UN-Water, UN-Water Task Force on Indicators, Monitoring and Reporting, *Final Report: Monitoring Progress in the Water Sector: A Selected Set of Indicators* (Perugia, Italy: UNESCO).
15. Safwat Abdel-Dayem et al., *Water Reuse in the Arab World: From Principle to Practice—Voices from the Field*, proceedings of Expert Consultation: Waste Water Management in the Arab World, Dubai, United Arab Emirates (Washington, DC: World Bank, 2012), http://water.worldbank.org/sites/water.worldbank.org/files/publication/Water-Reuse-Arab-World-From-Principle% 20-Practice.pdf
16. Al-Rashed and Sherif, "Water Resources in the GCC Countries," 59–75.
17. Ibid.
18. Environment Agency-Abu Dhabi, *Protecting our Shared Resource: Sustainable Water Use for Organisations* (Abu Dhabi, UAE: Environment Agency-Abu Dhabi, 2016).
19. Ibid.
20. Ibrahim S. Al-Mutaz, "Potential of Nuclear Desalination in the Arabian Gulf Countries," *Desalination* 135, no. 1 (2001): 187–94.
21. Joyce R. Starr, "Water Wars," *Foreign Policy* 82 (1991): 17–36; Mohamed A. Dawoud, "Environmental Impacts of Seawater Desalination: Arabian Gulf Case Study," *International Journal of Environment and Sustainability* 1, no. 3 (2012).
22. Walid A. Abderrahman, "Water Demand Management and Islamic Water Management Principles: A Case Study," *International Journal of Water Resources Development* 16, no. 4 (2000): 465–73; and Ministry of Economy and Planning—The Kingdom of Saudi Arabia, *The Ninth Development Plan (2010–2014)* (Riyadh, Kingdom of Saudi Arabia: Ministry of Economy and Planning, 2010).
23. Chowdhury and Al-Zahrani, "Characterizing Water Resources and Trends of Sector Wise Water," 68–82.
24. Environment Agency-Abu Dhabi, *Water Resources of Abu Dhabi Emirate, United Arab Emirates* (Abu Dhabi, UAE: Environment Agency-Abu Dhabi, 2008).
25. Dawoud, "Environmental Impacts of Seawater Desalination: Arabian Gulf Case Study."

26. Bekele Debele Negewo, ed., *Renewable Energy Desalination: An Emerging Solution to Close the Water Gap in the Middle East and North Africa* (New York: World Bank Publications, 2012).
27. El-Beltagy, "Strategic Options for Alleviating Conflicts," 67–82.
28. Ministry of Agriculture and Water, *Agricultural Statistical Year Book* (Riyadh, Kingdom of Saudi Arabia: Ministry of Agriculture and Water Department of Economic Studies and Statistics, 1992).
29. General Authority for Statistics—Kingdom of Saudi Arabia, "Water Consumption and Number of Subscribers."
30. Cordesman, *Bahrain, Oman, Qatar and the UAE.*
31. Environmental Agency of Abu Dhabi, *Abu Dhabi Water Resources Master Plan.*
32. Ibid.
33. Pernilla Ouis, "'Greening the Emirates': The Modern Construction of Nature in the United Arab Emirates," *Cultural Geographies* 9, no. 3 (2002): 334–47.
34. Second UAE National Report to the UNCCD, 2002.
35. Ouis, "'Greening the Emirates,'" 334–47.
36. Suzan M. Shahin and Mohammed Salem, "Review Future Concerns on Irrigation Requirements of Date Palm Tree in the United Arab Emirates (UAE): Call for Quick Actions" (5th International Date Palm Conference, United Arab Emirates, 2012).
37. Environmental Agency of Abu Dhabi, *Abu Dhabi Water Resources Master Plan.*
38. Ibid.
39. Ahmad, 2000.
40. David R. Dreesen and John T. Harrington, "Propagation of Native Plants for Restoration Projects in the Southwestern US–Preliminary Investigations," in *National Proceedings, Forest and Conservation Nursery Associations*, ed. T. D. Landis and J. R. Thompson, technical coordinators (Portland, OR: USDA Forest Service, Pacific Northwest Research Station, General Technical Report PNW-GTR-419, 1997).
41. General Authority for Statistics—Kingdom of Saudi Arabia, "Water Consumption and Number of Subscribers" in *Saudi Statistical Yearbook* (Kingdom of Saudi Arabia: General Authority for Statistics, 2008).
42. El-Beltagy, "Strategic Options for Alleviating Conflicts," 67–82.
43. Arani Kajenthira Grindle, Afreen Siddiqi, and Laura Diaz Anadon, "Food Security amidst Water Scarcity: Insights on Sustainable Food Production from Saudi Arabia," *Sustainable Production and Consumption* 2 (April 2015): 67–78.
44. Ibid.
45. John Anthony Allan, "'Virtual Water': A Long Term Solution for Water Short Middle Eastern Economies?" (Paper presented at the 1997 Water and Development Session, British Association Festival of Science, University of Leeds).
46. Allan, "'Virtual Water.'"

47. Chowdhury and Al-Zahrani, "Characterizing Water Resources and Trends of Sector Wise Water," 68–82.
48. Abdullah Jaradat and Abdelouahhab Zaid, "Quality Traits of Date Palm Fruits in a Center of Origin and Center of Diversity," *Journal of Food Agriculture and Environment* 2, no. 1 (2004): 208–17.
49. Abu Dhabi Food Control Authority, "Abu Dhabi Food Control Authority Emphasizes the Need to Sustain the Existing Water Storage in the Emirate," news release, March 21, 2012, Abu Dhabi Food Control Authority, http://www.adfca.ae/English/MediaCenter/News/Archived%20News/AuthorityEmphasizes.aspx
50. David Molden et al., "Pathways for Increasing Agricultural Water Productivity," in *Water for Food, Water for Life A Comprehensive Assessment of Water Management in Agriculture*, ed. David Molden (London: Earthscan, 2007).
51. Environmental Agency of Abu Dhabi, *Protecting Our Shared Resource Sustainable Water Use for Organisations* (Abu Dhabi, UAE: Environmental Agency of Abu Dhabi, 2016).
52. Oweis, "Agricultural Water Management under Scarcity," 22–30.
53. Derek E. Tribe, *Feeding and Greening the World: The Role of International Agricultural Research* (CAB International, 1995).
54. El-Beltagy, "Strategic Options for Alleviating Conflicts," 67–82.
55. Al-Zubari, "Towards the Establishment of a Total Water Cycle Management," 3–14.
56. Abdel-Dayem et al., *Water Reuse in the Arab World.*
57. Ibid.
58. Osvaldo Esteban Sala, William J. Parton, L. A. Joyce, and William K. Lauenroth, "Primary Production of the Central Grassland Region of the United States," *Ecology* 69, no. 1 (1988): 40–45.
59. Imanuel Noy-Meir, "Desert Ecosystems: Environment and Producers," *Annual Review of Ecology and Systematics* (1973): 25–51.
60. Jürg Fuhrer, "Agroecosystem Responses to Combinations of Elevated CO_2, Ozone, and Global Climate Change," *Agriculture, Ecosystems and Environment* 97, no. 1 (2003): 1–20.
61. Mohamed Kassas, "Aridity, Drought and Desertification," *Arab Environment: Future Challenges* (2008): 95.
62. United Nations, *United Nations Convention to Combat Desertification in Countries Experiencing Serious Drought and/or Desertification, Particularly in Africa*, U.N. Doc. A/AS.241/27, 33 I.L.M. 1328 (New York: United Nations, 1994).
63. Fernando T. Maestre and Adrián Escudero, "Is the Patch Size Distribution of Vegetation a Suitable Indicator of Desertification Processes?" *Ecology* 90, no. 7 (2009): 1729–35.
64. H. E. Dregne, *Desertification of Arid Lands: Advances in Desert and Arid Land Technology and Development*, vol. 3 (Switzerland: Harwood Academic Publishers, 1983).

65. Johan van de Koppel, Max Rietkerk, and Franz J. Weissing, "Catastrophic Vegetation Shifts and Soil Degradation in Terrestrial Grazing Systems," *Trends in Ecology and Evolution* 12, no. 9 (1997): 352–""56.
66. Ammar A. Amin, "The Extent of Desertification on Saudi Arabia," *Environmental Geology* 46, no. 1 (2004): 22–31.
67. Ali El-Keblawy, Taoufik S. Ksiksi, and Hossameldin E. Alqamy, "Camel Grazing Affects Species Diversity and Community Structure in the Deserts of the UAE," *Journal of Arid Environments* 73, no. 3 (2009): 347–54; Ali El-Keblawy, Mahmoud A. Abdelfattah, and Abdel-Hamid A. Khedr, "Relationships between Landforms, Soil Characteristics and Dominant Xerophytes in the Hyper-Arid Northern United Arab Emirates," *Journal of Arid Environments* 117 (2015): 28–36.
68. Ali El-Keblawy, "Effects of Protection from Grazing on Species Diversity, Abundance and Productivity in Two Regions of Abu Dhabi, United Arab Emirates," in *Desertification in the Third Millennium*, ed. A. S. Alsharhan et al. (Rotterdam: A. A. Balkema/Swets & Zeitlinger, 2003), 217–26.
69. Kamal. H. Shaltout, Esaid F. El-Halawany, and Hassan F. El-Kady, "Consequences of Protection from Grazing on Diversity and Abundance of the Coastal Lowland Vegetation in Eastern Saudi Arabia," *Biodiversity and Conservation* 5, no. 1 (1996): 27–36.
70. El-Keblawy, Ksiksi, and El Alqamy, "Camel Grazing Affects Species Diversity," 347–54.
71. Fridolin Brand, "Critical Natural Capital Revisited: Ecological Resilience and Sustainable Development," *Ecological Economics* 68, no. 3 (2009): 605–12.
72. Deborah M. Finch et al., "Rangeland Drought: Effects, Restoration, and Adaptation," in *Effects of Drought on Forests and Rangelands in the United States: A Comprehensive Science Synthesis*, ed. James M. Vose et al. (Washington, DC: United States Department of Agriculture, Forest Service, 2016).
73. Ali El-Keblawy, "Impact of Fencing and Irrigation on Species Composition and Diversity of Desert Plant Communities in the United Arab Emirates," *Land Degradation and Development* (2016), DOI: 10.1002/ldr.2599.
74. Dawud M. Al-Eisawi and A. M. Hatough, "Ecological Analysis of the Vegetation of Shaumari Reserve in Jordan," *DIRASAT* 14, no. 12 (1987): 81–94.
75. Richard Kinvig and Michael J. Samways, "Conserving Dragonflies (Odonata) Along Streams Running Through Commercial Forestry," *Odonatologica* 29, no. 3 (2000): 195–208.
76. R. C. Pal and Ajay Sharma, "Afforestation for Reclaiming Degraded Village Common Land: A Case Study," *Biomass and Bioenergy* 21, no. 1 (2001): 35–42.
77. Q. Feng, G. D. Cheng, and K. N. Endo, "Water Content Variations and Respective Ecosystems of Sandy Land in China," *Environmental Geology* 40, no. 9 (2001): 1075–83.
78. H. Hamano, Y. Egashira, and T. Kojima, "Numerical Simulation of Infiltration in

Soil of Australian Arid Land," *Kagaku Kogaku Ronbunshu* 26, no. 4 (2000): 581–7.

79. Kerry L. Griffis, Julie A. Crawford, Michael R. Wagner, and W. H. Moir, "Understory Response to Management Treatments in Northern Arizona Ponderosa Pine Forests," *Forest Ecology and Management* 146, no. 1 (2001): 239–45.
80. Ali El-Keblawy and Taoufik Ksiksi, "Artificial Forests as Conservation Sites for the Native Flora of the UAE," *Forest Ecology and Management* 213, no. 1 (2005): 288–96.
81. El-Keblawy and Ksiksi, "Artificial Forests as Conservation Sites for the Native Flora of the UAE."
82. Ibid.
83. El-Keblawy and Ksiksi, "Artificial Forests as Conservation Sites for the Native Flora of the UAE."
84. Ali El-Keblawy and Awatif Al-Rawai, "Impacts of the Invasive Exotic *Prosopis juliflora* (Sw.) DC on the Native Flora and Soils of the UAE," *Plant Ecology* 190, no. 1 (2007): 23–35.
85. Ali El-Keblawy and Mahmoud Ali Abdelfatah, "Impacts of Native and Invasive Exotic *Prosopis* Congeners on Soil Properties and Associated Flora in the Arid United Arab Emirates," *Journal of Arid Environments* 100 (2014): 1–8; Ali El-Keblawy, Arvind Bhatt, and Sanjay Gairola, "Developing Sea Watered Landscapes: A Potential Way to Reduce Stress on Fresh Water Resources," *Current Science* 108, no. 10 (2015): 1773–4.
86. Anamika Dhyani et al., "Analysis of IgE binding Proteins of Mesquite (*Prosopis Juliflora*) Pollen and Cross-Reactivity with Predominant Tree Pollens," *Immunobiology* 211, no. 9 (2006): 733–74.
87. Sue Killian and John McMichael, "The Human Allergens of Mesquite (*Prosopis Juliflora*)," *Clinical and Molecular Allergy* 2, no. 1 (2004): 1.
88. Abdulbari Bener et al., "The Determinants of Breast Cancer Screening Behavior: A Focus Group Study of Women in the United Arab Emirates," *Oncology Nursing Forum* 29, no. 9. (2002).
89. El-Keblawy and Al-Rawai, "Impacts of the Invasive Exotic *Prosopis juliflora*," 23–35.
90. Nikos Alexandratos and Jelle Bruinsma, "World Agriculture towards 2030/2050: The 2012 Revision," *ESA Working paper* 12, no. 3 (2012).
91. David Tilman et al., "Agricultural Sustainability and Intensive Production Practices," *Nature* 418, no. 6898 (2002): 671–7.
92. Tiago F. Jorge et al., "Mass Spectrometry-Based Plant Metabolomics: Metabolite Responses to Abiotic Stress," *Mass Spectrometry Reviews* 35, no. 5 (2015): 620–49.
93. Prateek Tripathi et al., "A Toolbox of Genes, Proteins, Metabolites and Promoters for Improving Drought Tolerance in Soybean Includes the Metabolite Coumestrol and Stomatal Development Genes," *BMC Genomics* 17, no. 1 (2016): 1.

94. Allah Bakhsh and Tahira Hussain, "Engineering Crop Plants Against Abiotic Stress: Current Achievements and Prospects," *Emirates Journal of Food and Agriculture* 27, no. 1 (2015): 24.
95. Michael D. Edgerton, "Increasing Crop Productivity to Meet Global Needs for Feed, Food, and Fuel," *Plant Physiology* 149, no. 1 (2009): 7–13.
96. David W. Lawlor, "Genetic Engineering to Improve Plant Performance Under Drought: Physiological Evaluation of Achievements, Limitations, and Possibilities," *Journal of Experimental Botany* 64, no. 1 (2013): 83–108.
97. Gurdev S. Khush, "What it will Take to Feed 5.0 Billion Rice Consumers in 2030," *Plant Molecular Biology* 59, no. 1 (2005): 1–6.
98. Angelika Hilbeck et al., "No Scientific Consensus on GMO Safety," *Environmental Sciences Europe* 27, no. 1 (2015): 1.
99. Amy Vickers, "New Directions in Lawn and Landscape Water Conservation," *American Water Works Association Journal* 98, no. 2 (2006): 56.
100. Sanjay Gairola, Arvind Bhatt, and Ali El-Keblawy, "A Perspective on Potential Use of Halophytes for Reclamation of Salt-Affected Lands," *Wulfenia Journal* 22, no. 1 (2015): 88–97.
101. Timothy J. Flowers, Hanaa K. Galal, and Lindell Bromham, "Evolution of Halophytes: Multiple Origins of Salt Tolerance in Land Plants," *Functional Plant Biology* 37, no. 7 (2010): 604–12.
102. Edward P. Glenn, J. Jed Brown, and James W. O'Leary, "Irrigating Crops with Seawater," *Scientific American Edition* 279, (1998): 76–81.
103. Edward P. Glenn et al., "*Salicornia Bigelovii* Torr.: An Oilseed Halophyte for Seawater Irrigation," *Science* 251, no. 4997 (1991): 1065–7; Edward P. Glenn, J. Jed Brown, and James W. O'Leary, "Irrigating Crops with Seawater," *Scientific American Edition* 279 (1998): 76–81.
104. Edward P. Glenn et al., "Three Halophytes for Saline-Water Agriculture: An Oilseed, a Forage and a Grain Crop," *Environmental and Experimental Botany* 92 (2013): 110–21.
105. Ibid.; and Ali El-Keblawy, Arvind Bhatt, and Sanjay Gairola, "Developing Sea Watered Landscapes: A Potential Way to Reduce Stress on Fresh Water Resources," *Current Science* 108, no. 10 (2015): 1773–4.
106. Carla Cassaniti and Daniela Romano, "The Use of Halophytes for Mediterranean Landscaping," *European Journal of Plant Science and Biotechnology* 5 (2011): 58–63.
107. M. Ajmal Khan and M. Qaiser, "Halophytes of Pakistan: Characteristics, Distribution and Potential Economic Usages," in *Sabkha Ecosystems* (Springer Netherlands, 2006), 129–53.
108. Ibid.
109. Ibid.
110. Benno Böer and Saif Al-Hajiri, "The Coastal and Sabkha Flora of Qatar: An

Introduction," in *Sabkha Ecosystems vol. 1: The Arabian Peninsula and Adjacent Countries. Tasks for Vegetation Science* 36, no. 8 (2002): 63–70.

111. Benno Böer and Derek Gliddon, "Mapping of Coastal Ecosystems and Halophytes (Case Study of Abu Dhabi, United Arab Emirates)," *Marine and Freshwater Research* 49, no. 4 (1998): 297–301.
112. Mahmoud A. Abdelfattah, Shabbir A. Shahid, and Yasser R. Othman, "Soil Salinity Mapping Model Developed Using RS and GIS—A Case Study from Abu Dhabi, United Arab Emirates," *European Journal of Scientific Research* 26, no. 3 (2009): 342–51.
113. M. M. Yagoub, "Monitoring of Urban Growth of a Desert City through Remote Sensing: Al-Ain, UAE, between 1976 and 2000," *International Journal of Remote Sensing* 25, no. 6 (2004): 1063–76; Nelida Fuccaro, "Visions of the City: Urban Studies on the Gulf," *Middle East Studies Association Bulletin* 35, no. 2 (2001): 175–87.
114. Bill Adams, "Four Aesthetic Reasons to Landscape with Native Plants," *San Diego UrbDeZine*, 12 September 2015, http://sandiego.urbdezine.com/2015/09/12/four-aesthetic-reasons-to-landscape-with-native-plants
115. Dreesen and Harrington, "Propagation of Native Plants for Restoration Projects in the Southwestern US–Preliminary Investigations."
116. Ali El-Keblawy, personal communication with Al-Nakheel Maintenance Department and Ministry of Municipality and Urban Planning.

5. BURNING SOMALIA'S FUTURE: THE ILLEGAL CHARCOAL TRADE BETWEEN THE HORN OF AFRICA AND THE GULF

1. I would like to thank Matt Bryden, Hussein Halane, Salah Omar and Brian O'Sullivan from Sahan Research, and Harry Verhoeven from Georgetown University who assisted with invaluable insight, advice, and support for this chapter.
2. Alex de Waal, *The Real Politics of the Horn of Africa: Money, War and the Business of Power* (Chichester: Polity Press, 2015), 112.
3. In 2015, Transparency International, an anti-corruption NGO, ranked Somalia 167 worst out of 168 countries. Often Somalia is not ranked because it is too dangerous to collect data.
4. Monetary references in this chapter are in United States dollars, unless indicated otherwise. John Norris and Bronwyn Burton, "The Price of Failure," *Foreign Policy*, 5 October 2011.
5. Matt Bryden and Jeremy Brickhill, "Disarming Somalia: Lessons in Stabilization from a Collapsed State," *Conflict, Security and Development* 10, no. 2 (2010): 239–62.
6. Leo C. Zulu and Robert B. Richardson, "Charcoal, Livelihoods, and Poverty Reduction: Evidence from Sub-Saharan Africa," *Energy for Sustainable Development* 17, no. 2 (2013): 127–37.

7. "Illegal Trade in Wildlife and Timber Products Finances Criminal and Militia Groups, Threatening Security and Sustainable Development," United Nations Environment Programme, 24 June 2014, http://www.unep.org/newscentre/default.aspx?DocumentID=2791&ArticleID=10906&l=en
8. *Charcoal TFT Research*, TFT-Earth, February 2015, http://www.tft-earth.org/wp-content/uploads/2015/05/TFT-charcoal-research.pdf
9. "The Charcoal Scourge," Somalia Water and Land Information Management, http://www.faoswalim.org/article/charcoal-scourge
10. Fridah Mugo and Chin Ong, "Lessons from Eastern Africa's Unsustainable Charcoal Trade" (ICRAF Working Paper no. 196, World Agroforestry Centre, 2006).
11. Celeste Hicks, "Chad Charcoal Ban Enflames Public," BBC, 27 January 2009, http://news.bbc.co.uk/2/hi/africa/7853250.stm
12. "Nigeria Bans Exportation of Wood and Charcoal," *Nigerian Eye*, 23 May 2016, http://www.nigerianeye.com/2016/05/nigeria-bans-exportation-of-wood-and.html
13. Sinziana Demian, "Green Charcoal around Virunga Undermines Illegal Trade, Boosts Park Protection," World Wide Fund for Nature, 18 August 2015, http://wwf.panda.org/wwf_news/?251056/Green-Charcoal-around-Virunga-Undermines-Illegal-Trade-Boosts-Park-Protection
14. "The Mafia in the Park, A Charcoal Syndicate is Threatening Virunga" (Washington, DC: Enough Project, 2016), http://enoughproject.org/reports/mafia-park-charcoal-syndicate-threatening-virunga-africa's-oldest-national-park
15. Ibid.
16. Talaat Dafalla et al., "Mesquite in Sudan: A Boon or Bane for Dry Lands? It's Socioeconomic and Management Aspects in Kassala State, Sudan," *Journal of Forest Products and Industries* 3, no. 4 (2014): 182–90.
17. "Somalia Country Overview," World Bank, 9 April 2016, http://www.worldbank.org/en/country/somalia/overview
18. "Reform Strategy and Action Plan 2016–2020," Federal Government of Somalia, Ministry of Finance, Public Finance, June 2016.
19. International Monetary Fund, "IMF Executive Board Concludes 2015 Article IV Consultation with Somalia," 29 July 2015, https://www.imf.org/en/News/Articles/2015/09/14/01/49/pr15360
20. "Somalia Exports 5.3 Million Animals, 6% growth in 2016," FAO, 14 April 2016, http://www.fao.org/emergencies/fao-in-action/stories/stories-detail/en/c/410993/
21. "World Bank Makes Progress to Support Remittance Flows to Somalia," World Bank, 10 June 2016, http://www.worldbank.org/en/news/press-release/2016/06/10/world-bank-makes-progress-to-support-remittance-flows-to-somalia

22. The UAE's assistance to Somalia has become significant enough to be targeted by al Shabaab, which attacked a relief convoy, killing three local staff, in June 2015.
23. "Qatar Offers $18mn Aid for Somalia," *Gulf Times*, 9 May 2013, http://www.gulf-times.com/story/352047/Qatar-offers-18mn-aid-for-Somalia
24. Matt Bryden and Jeremy Brickhill, "Disarming Somalia: Lessons in Stabilization from a Collapsed State," *Conflict, Security and Development* 10, no. 2 (2010): 239–62.
25. Edward Baars, "A Ripe Time for Somalia's Bananas," *New Agriculturalist*, January 2009, http://www.new-ag.info/en/focus/focusItem.php?a=670
26. E. Baars, and A. Riediger, "A Market Analysis of the Somali Banana Sector and its Potential for Export Revival: Experiences of Support to Agricultural Marketing Services and Access to Markets (SAMSAM) Project," (IV International Symposium on Banana: Kenya, 2008), 811–18, DOI: 10.17660/ActaHortic.2010.879.89.
27. Henry Neufeldt et al., "From Transition Fuel to Viable Energy Source: Improving Sustainability in the Sub-Saharan Charcoal Sector" (ICRAF Working Paper no. 196. World Agroforestry Centre, 2015), http://www.worldagroforestry.org/downloads/Publications/PDFS/WP15011.pdf
28. War-torn Societies Project, *Rebuilding Somalia: Issues and Possibilities for Puntland* (London: HAAN Associates, 2001), 101.
29. Federal Government of Somalia, State Minister for Environment, Office of the Prime Minister and Line Ministries and Ministry of Planning, "Somalia's Intended Nationally Determined Contributions," November 2015, http://www4.unfccc.int/ndcregistry/PublishedDocuments/Somalia%20First/Somalia's%20INDCs.pdf
30. F. Rembold et al., "Mapping Charcoal Driven Forest Degradation during the Main Period of Al Shabaab Control in Southern Somalia," *Energy for Sustainable Development* 17, no. 5 (2013).
31. World Bank, "World Development Indicators: Deforestation and Biodiversity," World Bank, 2015, http://wdi.worldbank.org/table/3.4
32. James Fergusson, *The World's Most Dangerous Place: Inside the Outlaw State of Somalia* (London: Bantam, 2013).
33. Inventory of Conflict and Environment, "Somalia's Coal Industry," *ICE Case Studies* 201, May 2007.
34. Federal Government of Somalia, "Somalia's Intended Nationally Determined Contributions."
35. On two research trips to Kismayo in May and June 2016, the author conducted numerous interviews about charcoal with local traders and residents. Figures are also cited in UNDP publications published in 2007.
36. Ibid.
37. *Khaleeji* is a term used to refer to people of the Arab states of the Persian Gulf.
38. Interview with traders and café owners in Doha, Qatar, April 2016.

39. Interviews in Kismayo, Jubaland, May 2016.
40. Report of the Monitoring Group on Somalia and Eritrea (S/2014/726), submitted to the UN Security Council on 10 October 2014 (New York: United Nations Security Council, 2014).
41. United States of America, Sub Committee on African Affairs of the Committee on Foreign Relations, US Senate, 112th congress, first session, 3 August 2011 (transcript).
42. Federal Government of Somalia, "Somalia's Intended Nationally Determined Contributions," November, 2015.
43. UNDP, "UN Resident Coordinator Speech for the Launch Event of Somalia Program for Sustainable Charcoal Production and Alternative Livelihoods (PROSCAL)," 17 April 2013, http://www.so.undp.org/content/somalia/en/home/presscenter/speeches/2013/04/17/un-resident-coordinator-speech-for-the-launch-event-of-somalia-programme-for-sustainable-charcoal-production-and-alternative-livelihoods-proscal-.html
44. In a telephone conversation (5 May 2016) with the UN's environment agency, UNEP, then another with the UN's Development Program, UNDP, officials said that since PROSCAL's launch in April 2013, a lack of UN funding "slowed the project implementation" to starting officially in April 2016. UNDP officials did not reply to further email inquiries.
45. "President Urges every Somali to Plant a Tree," FAO, 18 April 2013, http://www.fao.org/somalia/news/detail-events/fr/c/247644/
46. FAO representatives did not respond to several emails, though on 6 May 2016 one FAO official directed inquiries to their website, which had no new information on the scheme.
47. Nelly Lahoud, *Letters from Abbottabad: Bin Ladin Sidelined?* (West Point, NY: Harmony Program, Combating Terrorism Center, 2012).
48. William McCants, *The ISIS Apocalypse: The History, Strategy, and Doomsday Vision of the Islamic State* (New York: St Martin's Press, 2015).
49. Jihadica: Documenting the Global Jihad, http://www.jihadica.com/wp-content/uploads/2015/03/432-10-CR-019-S-4-RJD-Translation.pdf
50. Martina Fuchs and Tamara Walid, "Bin Laden Criticizes Pakistan Relief, Urges Climate Action," Reuters, 1 October 2010.
51. Harry Verhoeven, "The Self-Fulfilling Prophecy of Failed States: Somalia, State Collapse and the Global War on Terror," *Journal of Eastern African Studies* 3, no. 3 (2009): 405–25.
52. Yool Insight Report, *Al Shabaab Demographics* (February 2016).
53. Matt Bryden, "Peace and Security in Somalia," Center for Strategic and International Studies, 13 July 2016.
54. Tom Keatinge, "The Role of Financing to Defeat al Shabaab," Royal United Services Institute, Whitehall Report, 2–14 December 2014, https://rusi.org/sites/default/files/201412_whr_2-14_keatinge_web_0.pdf

55. *Afghanistan Opium Survey, Cultivation and Production*, UNODC, November 2014, https://www.unodc.org/documents/crop-monitoring/Afghanistan/Afghan-opium-survey-2014.pdf
56. Ahmed Rashid, *Taliban: Islam, Oil and the New Great Game in Central Asia* (London: I. B. Tauris, 2002), 117–20.
57. Azam Ahmed, "Tasked With Combating Opium, Afghan Officials Profit from It," *New York Times*, 15 February 2016, https://www.nytimes.com/2016/02/16/world/asia/afghanistan-opium-heroin-taliban-helmand.html
58. The UN Somalia and Eritrean Monitoring Group reports fluctuating income from charcoal within this range during 2011–15. According to their latest report, tabled before the UN Security Council in October 2016, the monitoring group found "a pattern of a declining volume," in part due to al Shabaab's strategic shift away from the trade and the UAE's "significantly improving its implementation" of a charcoal ban.
59. UN Monitoring Group on Somalia and Eritrea (Report S/2016/919), submitted to the UN Security Council on 31 October 2016 (New York: United Nations Security Council, 2016).
60. "Adopting Resolution 2182 (2014), Security Council Extends Mandate of African Union Mission in Somalia for One Year, Amends Sanctions Regime," United Nations, 24 October 2014, https://www.un.org/press/en/2014/sc11613.doc.htm
61. "Al Shabaab Taxation on Humanitarian Aid in South in Central Somalia," Sahan Research, Nairobi, November 2014.
62. "Mogadishu Area Brief," Sahan Research, Nairobi, December 2016.
63. Ken Menkhaus, "Non-state Security Providers and Political Formation in Somalia," Centre for Security Governance, no. 5, April 2016.
64. David M. Anderson and Jacob McKnight, "Kenya at War: Al-Shabaab and its Enemies in Eastern Africa," *African Affairs* 114, no. 454 (2015): 1–27.
65. "Assistant Secretary Carson's January 30, 2010, Meeting with Kenyan Foreign Minister Wetangula," WikiLeaks, released November 2011, https://wikileaks.org/plusd/cables/10ADDISABABA166_a.html
66. United Nations Mission in Somalia, Integrated Analysis Team, "Regional States: Interests and Engagement in Somalia" Research and Discussion Paper, August 2015.
67. Kenyan Government, "Kenya Troops Re-hat into AMISOM, Nairobi," Embassy of the Republic of Kenya in Ethiopia press release, 6 July 2012, http://www.kenyaembassyaddis.org/2012/07/kenya-troops-re-hat-into-amisom-nairobi/
68. The UN Monitoring Group to Somalia has repeatedly reported that the charcoal trade continued, and in some cases expanded, after Kismayo was liberated from al Shabaab.
69. "Black and White: Kenya's Criminal Racket in Somalia," Journalists for Justice, November 2015, http://www.jfjustice.net/downloads/1457660562.pdf

70. Mike Pflanz, "Kenyan Army Admits that Soldiers Looted Westgate Mall during Siege," *Daily Telegraph*, 29 October 2013, http://www.telegraph.co.uk/news/worldnews/africaandindianocean/kenya/10411403/Kenyan-army-admits-that-soldiers-looted-Westgate-mall-during-siege.html
71. UN Monitoring Group on Somalia and Eritrea (Report S/2016/919), submitted to the UN Security Council on 31 October 2016 (New York: United Nations Security Council, 2016).
72. Interviews conducted with East African sugar industry figures, former UN Dadaab refugee camp workers, and a Human Rights Watch researcher, July 2016.
73. P. D. Williams, "The Battle at El Adde: The Kenya Defence Forces, Al-Shabaab, and Unanswered Questions," *International Peace Institute*, 13 July 2016, https://www.ipinst.org/2016/07/the-battle-at-el-adde-the-kenya-defence-forces-al-shabaab-and-unanswered-questions
74. IPSOS first quarter survey (Social, Political, Economic and Cultural): "Security Issues: Somalia and the al-Shabaab Threat," 21 July 2016.
75. IGAD Security Sector Program, "Al-Shabaab as a Transnational Security Threat," report, August 2016.
76. Independent Policing Oversight Authority, "Monitoring Report on Operation Sanitizing Eastleigh Publically Known as Usalama Watch," July 2014.
77. Omano referred to the allegations as "consistent fabrications" to "create hostility for KDF troops in Somalia and discord within the Somali authorities."
78. The most famous case is probably the Anglo Leasing scheme, which siphoned off hundreds of millions of dollars from the Kenyan treasury while Mwai Kibaki was president (2002–13). See Michela Wrong, *It's Our Turn to Eat: The Story of a Kenyan Whistle-blower* (London: Fourth Estate, 2010).
79. UN Monitoring Group on Somalia and Eritrea (report S/2014/726), submitted to the UN Security Council on 10 October 2014 (New York: United Nations Security Council, 2014).
80. March 2016 interview with Kenyan counter-terror official in Nairobi.
81. Oceans Beyond Piracy, "The State of Marine Piracy 2014," June 2015, http://oceansbeyondpiracy.org/publications/state-maritime-piracy-2014
82. Alex de Waal, *The Real Politics of the Horn of Africa: Money, War and the Business of Power* (Chichester: Polity Press, 2015), 182–92.
83. Paul D. Williams, "Exit Strategies for the AU Mission in Somalia" (Mogadishu: Heritage Institute for Policy Studies, 2016).
84. European Commission, "African Peace Facility Annual Report 2014" (Luxembourg: Publications Office of the European Union, 2015), http://ec.europa.eu/europeaid/african-peace-facility-annual-report-2014–0_en
85. Ben Rawlance, "Why does Al-Shabaab Still Exist?" *New African Magazine*, 9 May 2016, http://newafricanmagazine.com/al-shabaab-still-exist/
86. Ken Menkhaus, "Non-state Security Providers and Political Formation in Somalia," Centre for Security Governance, no. 5, April 2016.

87. The international NGO, Safety Organisation, which monitors security issues in Somalia daily, reported five charcoal-related incidents in the north and south up to May 2016. The clashes saw six people killed, three traders and three al Shabaab. Government police in Puntland and Somaliland arrested numerous charcoal producers, and al Shabaab destroyed property and took prisoners linked to the trade. Al Shabaab attacks are less about enforcing the ban than they are about ensuring that local people pay a price when they do not hand over taxes to the jihadist organization.
88. Interviews in Jubaland, April/May 2016.
89. Ibid.
90. On a research trip conducted at the Kismayo port in May 2016, there was no evidence of charcoal shipments. A cargo ship from Dubai offloaded raw sugar into bags which were then stacked onto beaten-up trucks. A handful of Kenyan soldiers manned the gate and checkpoint to enter the port. About 5 kilometers out of town there were 3-metre-high charcoal stockpiles in green bags on the side of the road. Along the road black soot suggested the movement of charcoal, and a few small donkey-drawn carts carried sacks of charcoal. An interview with the port manager was not possible.
91. Nizar Manek, "DP World May Develop Port in Somali Region, President Says," *Bloomberg*, 22 March 2017, https://www.bloomberg.com/news/articles/2017-03-22/somalia-s-puntland-region-in-talks-with-dp-world-to-develop-port
92. Ioan M. Lewis, *A Modern History of the Somali, Nation and State in Horn of Africa* (Oxford: James Currey, 2002).
93. Ibid.
94. David D. Kirkpatrick, "Leaked Emirati Emails Could Threaten Peace Talks in Libya," *New York Times*, 12 November 2015, https://www.nytimes.com/2015/11/13/world/middleeast/leaked-emirati-emails-could-threaten-peace-talks-in-libya.html
95. Alexander Rondos, "The Horn of Africa, Its Strategic Importance for Europe, the Gulf States, and Beyond," Center for International Relations and Sustainable Development, no. 6 (Winter 2016).
96. Nafeesa Syeed, "A Military Power Rises in the Mideast, Courtesy of One Man," *Bloomberg*, 25 November 2015.
97. Abdirazak Fartaag, "Their Own Worst Enemy: How Successive Governments Plundered Somalia's Public Resources," Fartaag Research and Consulting, 2014, http://www.keydmedia.net/download-files/Their-Own-Worst-Enemy-Fartaag-Report-2014.pdf
98. "Regional States: Interests and Engagement in Somalia," United Nations Mission in Somalia, Integrated Analysis Team, Research and Discussion Paper, August 2015.
99. Fartaag, "Their Own Worst Enemy."

100. UN Monitoring Group on Somalia and Eritrea (Report S/2013/440) submitted to the UN Security Council on 25 July 2013, (New York: United Nations Security Council, 2013).
101. United Nations Mission in Somalia, Integrated Analysis Team, "Regional States: Interests and Engagement in Somalia," Research and Discussion Paper, August 2015.
102. Ibid.
103. The Somali president's office declined several interview requests and said that Gulf state financing was "not such a lovely conversation during an election period (late 2016)." Several Gulf state embassies also declined interview requests. "We want peace," said one Gulf ambassador before hanging up.
104. International Crisis Group, "Kenyan Somali Islamist Radicalisation," Policy Briefing 85, January 2012, https://d2071andvip0wj.cloudfront.net/b085-kenyan-somali-islamist-radicalisation.pdf
105. Fartaag, "Their Own Worst Enemy."
106. See the university's online page, Al Medinah International University website: http://www.mediu.edu.my
107. Interviews in Mogadishu/Kismayo and Nairobi. The effectiveness of the influence obtained by such patronage was limited, as desperate politicians take money from any source with little bearing on its outcome. Funding through Somalia's numerous Islamic sects was seen as the tacit support that individuals received from Saudi and other Gulf states. Interviews conducted May, June, and July 2016.
108. A. Abdirahman, "Somalia Gearing up to Send Domestic Workers to Saudi Arabia," *Horseed Media*, 10 May 2016, https://horseedmedia.net/2016/05/10/somalia-gearing-up-to-send-workers-to-saudi-arabia/
109. Harry Verhoeven, "African Dam Building as Extraversion: The Case of Sudan's Dam Programme, Nubian Resistance and the Saudi-Iranian Proxy War in Yemen," *African Affairs* 115, no. 461 (2016): 562–73.
110. Edmund Blair, "Somalia Received Saudi Aid the Day it Cut Ties with Iran: Document," Reuters, 17 January 2016, http://www.reuters.com/article/us-somalia-saudi-iran-idUSKCN0UV0BH
111. "Saudi Arabia Deposits $1b in Sudan Central Bank," Agence France Presse, 13 August 2015.
112. Salem Solomon, "Saudi Arabia Looks to African Allies during Gulf Crises," Voice of America, 29 March 2016, http://www.voanews.com/a/saudi-arabia-african-allies-gulf-crisis/3260218.html
113. Mohamed H. Gaas, Stig J. Hansen, and Halvard Leira, "Religion, Prestige and Windows of Opportunity (Qatari Peace-making and Foreign Policy Engagement)," ed. Stig Jarle Hansen (Noragric Working Paper no. 48, Department of International Environment and Development Studies, October 2013).
114. "Turkish Permrep Apakan Pays Introductory Call on Ambassador Rice,"

WikiLeaks, 26 October 2009, https://wikileaks.org/plusd/cables/09USUNNEWYORK947_a.html

115. Drazen Jorgic, "Biggest Donor Turkey Stops Direct Budget Support to Somalia," Reuters, 13 February 2014, http://www.reuters.com/article/us-somalia-budget-turkey-idUSBREA1C1S320140213
116. Government of Turkey, Ministry of Foreign Affairs, "Relations between Turkey and Somalia," http://www.mfa.gov.tr/relations-between-turkey-and-somalia.en.mfa
117. Erdoğan has visited Somalia three times, the most of any foreign head of state. His first visit as prime minister in 2011 sparked the beginning of the Turkish Somalia humanitarian program.
118. Mahud Wasuge, "Turkey's Assistance Model in Somalia: Achieving Much with Little," report, Heritage Institute for Policy Studies, 2016, http://www.heritage-institute.org/wp-content/uploads/2016/02/Turkeys-Assistance-Model-in-Somalia-Achieving-Much-With-Little1–1.pdf
119. "Oil Trade off Yemen Coast Grew by 20% to 4.7 Million Barrels Per Day in 2014," US Energy Information Administration, 23 April 2015, https://www.eia.gov/todayinenergy/detail.php?id=20932
120. Alex de Waal, "Africa's 700 Billion Problem Waiting to Happen," *Foreign Policy*, 17 March 2016, http://foreignpolicy.com/2016/03/17/africas-700-billion-problem-waiting-to-happen-ethiopia-horn-of-africa/
121. "Enabling Reforms: A Stakeholder-based Analysis of the Political Economy of Tanzania's Charcoal Sector and the Poverty and Social Impacts of Proposed Reforms," World Bank, 2010, http://documents.worldbank.org/curated/en/998871468246037505/Enabling-reforms-a-stakeholder-based-analysis-of-the-political-economy-of-Tanzanias-charcoal-sector-and-the-poverty-and-social-impacts-of-proposed-reforms
122. Sinziana Demian, "Green Charcoal around Virunga Undermines Illegal Trade, Boosts Park Protection," World Wildlife Fund for Nature, 18 August 2015, http://wwf.panda.org/wwf_news/?251056/Green-Charcoal-around-Virunga-Undermines-Illegal-Trade-Boosts-Park-Protection

6. ILLEGAL FISHING AND PIRACY IN THE HORN OF AFRICA: THE ROLE OF THE MENA REGION

1. Julius Ndumbe Anyu and Samuel B. Moki, "Africa: The Piracy Hot Spot and its Implications for Global Security," *Mediterranean Quarterly* 20, no. 3 (2009): 95–121; James Kraska, "Fresh Thinking for an Old Problem: Report of the Naval War College Workshop on Countering Maritime Piracy," *Naval War College Review* 62, no. 4 (2009): 141–54.
2. Robert Kaplan, "Center Stage for the 21st Century," *Foreign Affairs*, March/April

2009,http://www.foreignaffairs.com/articles/64832/robert-d-kaplan/center-stage-for-the-21st-century

3. Jim Michaels, "Somali Pirate Attacks Plummet," *USA Today*, 20 December 2012, http://www.usatoday.com/story/news/world/2012/12/20/piracy-somalia/1781929/
4. See International Maritime Bureau's annual reports, 2005–12.
5. Fred W. Householder and Donald W. Prakken, "A Ptolemaic Graffito in New York," *Transactions of the American Philosophical Society* 76 (1945): 111–16.
6. Lionel Casson, ed., *The Periplus Maris Erythraei* (Princeton, NJ: Princeton University Press, 1989); Trevor M. Murphy, *Pliny the Elder's Natural History: The Empire in the Encyclopedia* (Courier Corporation, 2004); George Fadlo Hourani and John Carswell, *Arab Seafaring in the Indian Ocean in Ancient and Early Medieval Times* (Princeton, NJ: Princeton University Press, 1995).
7. Muhammad Al-Muqaddasi, *Ahsan al-Taqasim fi Ma'rifat al-Aqalim [The Best Divisions for Knowledge of the Regions]*, trans. George S. A. Ranking and R. F. Azoo (Calcutta, 1897–1910).
8. Duarte Barbosa and Fernão de Magalhães, *A Description of the Coasts of East Africa and Malabar: In the Beginning of the Sixteenth Century*, vol. 35 (London: Hakluyt Society, 1866), 15; Richard F. Burton, *First Footsteps in East Africa: Or, an Exploration of Harar* (Courier Corporation, 2014).
9. William Fitzwilliam Owen, *Narrative of Voyages to Explore the Shores of Africa, Arabia and Madagascar*, vol. 1 (London: Bentley, 1833).
10. Sir Charles Umpherston Aitchison, *A Collection of Treaties, Engagements, and Sanads Relating to India and Neighbouring Countries, Vol. XIII* (Calcutta: Superintendent Government Printing, 1909).
11. Sir Charles Umpherston Aitchison, *A Collection of Treaties, Engagements, and Sunnuds Relating to India and Neighbouring Countries, Vol. VII* (1865).
12. Aitchison, *A Collection of Treaties, Engagements, and Sanads Relating to India and Neighbouring Countries*, 197.
13. Robert Lambert Playfair, "Massacre of Two Boats Crew of H. M. S. *Penguin*," personal report contained in Playfair personal collection, pages 131–40. "Playfair was an active diplomat in the area, which is illustrated throughout PLFR6/3 (msdep 14/6/3), in which there are copies of his dispatches and reports of his negotiation of a peace treaty between the settlements of Miat and Hais in a bloody dispute over guano in 1859, the rescue of sixty-three slaves from traders in 1860, the rescue of shipwrecked British sailors in 1861, and investigation into the murder of the crew of HMS *Penguin* in 1862, together with his personal reports of a massacre of Europeans at Mecca and insurgency against Turkish domination of the Yemen in 1856 and 1859. Further details of these and other of his diplomatic activities are to be found in PLFR6/6 (msdep 14/6/6)." https://standrewsrarebooks.wordpress.com/2012/06/11/robert-lambert-playfair-and-his-account-of-aden-a-new-acquisition-adds-to-substantial-archive.

14. Jade Lindley, *Somali Piracy: A Criminological Perspective* (Farnham: Ashgate, 2016).
15. Charles J. Cruttenden, "Report on the Mijjertheyn Tribe of Somalis Inhabiting the District Forming the North East Point of Africa," *Transactions of the Bombay Royal Geographical Society* 7 (1846): 111–26. Italy initially signed a protection treaty with Sultan of Obbia on 9 February 1889 and with Majeerteen Sultan on 7 April 1889. In 1889, Italy obtained a 25-year lease agreement from the Sultan of Zanzibar for the Benadir coast, including Mogadishu, Merca, Brava, and Ursciech (Warsheik), and then purchased it from him on 13 January 1905. Italy then started expanding its rule over Somali lands and declared in 1908 that the country was its colony. Britain established its Somaliland protectorate under different treaties signed with Somali sultans and elders in 1886, and proclaimed it British Somaliland Protectorate in July 1887.
16. Afyare A. Elmi et al., "Piracy in the Horn of Africa Waters: Definitions, History, and Modern Causes," *African Security* 8, no. 3 (2015): 147–65.
17. The report, "BMP4: Best Management Practices for Protection against Somalia Based Piracy," defines the High Risk Area as an area bound by Suez and the Strait of Hormuz to the north, 10°S and 78°E (Witherby Publishing, August 2011), http://eunavfor.eu/wp-content/uploads/2013/01/bmp4-low-res_sept_5_20111.pdf
18. Elmi, "Piracy in the Horn of Africa Waters," 147–65.
19. Jack Lang, "Report of the Special Adviser to the Secretary-General on Legal Issues Related to Piracy off the Coast of Somalia," United Nations Security Council report, 24 January 2011, Paragraph 89.
20. Sarah M. Glaser et al., "Securing Somali Fisheries," One Earth Future Foundation (2015). DOI: 10.18289/OEF.2015.001.
21. Food and Agriculture Organization of the United Nations, "International Plan of Action to Prevent, Deter, and Eliminate Illegal, Unreported and Unregulated Fishing," 2001, http://www.fao.org/docrep/003/y1224e/y1224e00.htm; Malcolm Barrett, "Illegal Fishing in Zones Subject to National Jurisdiction," *James Cook University Law Review* 5 (1998).
22. Food and Agriculture Organization, "International Plan of Action."
23. Ibid.
24. Joshua Reichert, "As the UN Tightens the Net around Illegal Fishing, Now is the Time to Act," *Guardian*, 20 May 2016, https://www.theguardian.com/sustainable-business/2016/may/20/illegal-fishing-fight-thieves-seafood-international-treaty
25. Sean A. Hagan, "Too Big to Tackle: The Persistent Problem of Pirate Fishing and the New Focus on Port State Measures," *Suffolk Transnational Law Review* 37 (2014): 113.
26. Steve Trent, Juliette Williams, and Louis Buckley, "Pirates and Profiteers: How Pirate Fishing Fleets are Robbing People and Oceans," Environmental Justice Foundation (2005), http://ejfoundation.org/sites/default/files/public/Pirates%20%20Profiteers.pdf

27. Trent et al., "Pirates and Profiteers."
28. Ibid.
29. Food and Agriculture Organization, "Profile: The Somali Republic," January 2005, http://www.fao.org/fi/oldsite/FCP/en/SOM/profile.htm
30. United Nations Security Council, "Report of the Monitoring Group on Somalia and Eritrea Pursuant to Security Council Resolution 2060 (2012): S/2013/413."
31. Scott Coffen-Smout, "Pirates, Warlords and Rogue Fishing Vessels in Somalia's Unruly Seas," Chebucto Community Net, 1998, http://www.chebucto.ns.ca/~ar120/somalia.html
32. Glaser, "Securing Somali Fisheries."
33. Ibid.
34. Mohamed Abshir Waldo, "The Two Piracies in Somalia: Why the World Ignores the Other," International Monitoring, Control and Surveillance (MCS) Network for Fisheries-related Activities, 2009, http://imcsnet.org/imcs/docs/somalias_twin_sea_piracies_the_global_aramada.pdf
35. "Pirate Fishing," Greenpeace International, http://www.greenpeace.org/international/en/campaigns/oceans/which-fish-can-I-eat/pirate-fishing
36. Hagan, "Too Big to Tackle," 109.
37. Abdi Ismail Samatar, Mark Lindberg, and Basil Mahayni, "The Dialectics of Piracy in Somalia: The Rich Versus the Poor," *Third World Quarterly* 31, no. 8 (2010): 1377–94.
38. "Proclamation by the President of the Federal Republic of Somalia," United Nations, 30 June 2014, http://www.un.org/Depts/los/LEGISLATIONANDTREATIES/PDFFILES/SOM_2014. Proclamation.pdf.
39. Andrew Palmer, *The New Pirates: Modern Global Piracy from Somalia to the South China Sea* (London: I. B. Tauris, 2014).
40. United Nations Security Council, "Somalia report of the Monitoring Group on Somalia and Eritrea submitted in accordance with resolution 2060 (2012)," S/2013/413, 12 July 2013, http://www.un.org/ga/search/view_doc.asp?symbol=S/2013/413
41. Elmi, "Piracy in the Horn of Africa," 147–65.
42. Awet T. Weldemichael, "When Elephants Fight, the Grass Suffers: A Report on the Local Consequences of Piracy in Puntland" (Halifax: Marine Affairs Program, Dalhousie University, 2014).
43. Glaser, "Securing Somali Fisheries."
44. Awet T. Weldemichael, "Maritime Corporate Terrorism and its Consequences in the Western Indian Ocean: Illegal Fishing, Waste Dumping and Piracy in Twenty-first-century Somalia," *Journal of the Indian Ocean Region* 8, no. 2 (2012): 110–26; and Waldo, "The Two Piracies in Somalia."
45. There is anecdotal evidence suggesting that toxic waste was dumped in Somali waters in the early 1990s. However, for the last decade things have changed, accord-

ing to the United Nations. The European companies responsible are no longer engaged in dumping.

46. Lang, "Report of the Special Adviser to the Secretary-General."
47. Ghassan Schbley and William Rosenau, "Piracy, Illegal Fishing, and Maritime Insecurity in Somalia, Kenya, and Tanzania" (Alexandria, VA: Center for Naval Analyses, 2013).
48. Ibid., 3.
49. Sarah Percy and Anja Shortland, "The Business of Piracy in Somalia," *Journal of Strategic Studies* 36, no. 4 (2013): 541–78.
50. Elmi, "Piracy in the Horn of Africa," 147–65.
51. Ibid.
52. Jay Bahadur, *The Pirates of Somalia: Inside Their Hidden World* (New York: Vintage, 2011).
53. Stig Jarle Hansen, "Debunking the Piracy Myth: How Illegal Fishing Really Interacts with Piracy in East Africa," *RUSI Journal* 156, no. 6 (2011): 26–31.
54. Elmi, "Piracy in the Horn of Africa," 147–65.
55. See International Maritime Bureau annual reports, www.icc-ccs.org/piracy-reporting-centre
56. Lindley, *Somali Piracy*; see also "Piracy: No Stopping Them," *Economist*, 3 February 2011, www.economist.com/node/18061574
57. Christian Bueger, "Drops in the Bucket? A Review of Onshore Responses to Somali Piracy," *WMU Journal of Maritime Affairs* 11, no. 1 (2012): 15–31.
58. Glaser, "Securing Somali Fisheries," 32.
59. United Nations Security Council, "Report of the Monitoring Group on Somalia," 2013.
60. Personal communication with a cabinet minister of the Somali government, January 2016, Doha, Qatar.
61. Glaser, "Securing Somali Fisheries."
62. Ahmed H. O. Gulaid, "Feasibility Report on the Fisheries Sector in Somaliland: Current Status, Opportunities and Constraints," United Nations Development Programme (2004), p. 35, www.somalilandlaw.com/sl_fisheries_feasibility_report.pdf
63. Glaser, "Securing Somali Fisheries."
64. A. J. Kulmiye, "Assessment of the Status of the Artisanal Fisheries in Puntland through Value Chain Analysis," draft report for VSF Suisse and UNDP Somalia (2010), http://shuraako.org/sites/default/files/documents/Assessment%20of%20the%20Status%20of%20the%20Artisanal%20Fisheries%20in%20Puntland%20Through%20Value%20Chain%20Analysis.pdf
65. Glaser, "Securing Somali Fisheries."
66. "International Energy Outlook 2013," US Energy Information Administration, 2013.

67. See International Maritime Bureau annual reports, www.icc-ccs.org/piracy-reporting-centre
68. When piracy peaked in 2009–12, a number of solutions were advanced. The insurance industry wanted to keep paying ransoms and increasing premiums. For them, the statistical analyses justified their conclusion. This was seen as a self-serving proposal. The shipping industry, seafarers, and countries have paid a heavy price.
69. Interviews with private security companies in London, 2013; see also "BMP4 HRA Revision—Pragmatic Decision or Dangerous Gamble?" Dryad Maritime, 8 October 2015, www.dryadmaritime.com/bmp4-hra-revision-pragmatic-decision-or-dangerous-gamble
70. "Vigilance Still Crucial as Piracy High Risk Area in the Indian Ocean Reduced," BIMCO, 8 October 2015, www.bimco.org/News/2015/10/08_HRA_reduced_press.aspx
71. "The Pirates of Somalia: Ending the Threat, Rebuilding a Nation," World Bank, 2013, http://documents.worldbank.org/curated/en/182671468307148284/pdf/76713-REPLACEMENT-pirates-of-somalia-pub-11-2-15.pdf
72. Ibid.
73. Anna Bowden and Shikha Basnet, "The Economic Cost of Maritime Piracy," One Earth Future Foundation, 2010, http://oceansbeyondpiracy.org/sites/default/files/economic_cost_of_piracy_2011.pdf
74. "The Pirates of Somalia," World Bank.
75. "Yemen Losses Reach US$150 mln Due to Piracy in 2009," Yemen News Agency (Saba), 27 October 2010. www.sabanews.net/en/news227455.htm
76. Kennedy K. Mbekeani and Mthulie Ncube, "Economic Impact of Maritime Piracy," *Africa Economic Brief* 2, no. 10 (2011), www.afdb.org/fileadmin/uploads/afdb/Documents/Publications/Maritime%20Piracy_Maritime%20Piracy.pdf
77. Faiza Saleh Ambah, "After Oil Tanker Hijacking, Saudi Arabia to Join Anti-piracy Efforts," *Washington Post*, 19 November 2008, www.washingtonpost.com/wp-dyn/content/article/2008/11/18/AR2008111801167.html
78. "Pirates Capture Saudi Oil Tanker," BBC, 18 November 2008, http://news.bbc.co.uk/2/hi/africa/7733482.stm
79. Bowden and Basnet, "The Economic Costs of Maritime Piracy."
80. "The Pirates of Somalia," World Bank.
81. Ibid.
82. United Nations Security Council, "Report of the Monitoring Group on Somalia and Eritrea Pursuant to Security Council Resolution 2182 (2014): Somalia," S/2015/801 (19 October 2015), 33.
83. United Nations Security Council, "Report of the Monitoring Group on Somalia and Eritrea Pursuant to Security Council Resolution 2002 (2011)," S/2012/544 (13 July 2012), 8.
84. Elmi, "Piracy in the Horn of Africa."

85. Haneen Dajani, "Pirates who Hijacked UAE Ship Sentenced to Life in Prison," *The National UAE*, 23 May 2012, www.thenational.ae/news/uae-news/courts/pirates-who-hijacked-uae-ship-sentenced-to-life-in-prison
86. Quy-Toan Do, Lin Ma, and Claudia Ruiz, "Pirates of Somalia: Crime and Deterrence on the High Seas," Policy Research Working Paper 7757 (Washington, DC: World Bank, 2016), http://pubdocs.worldbank.org/en/689501484733836996/pirates-of-Somalia-on-the-high-seas.pdf
87. Ladan Affi et al., "Countering Piracy through Private Security in the Horn of Africa: Prospects and Pitfalls," *Third World Quarterly* 37, no. 5 (2016): 934–50.
88. Sheikh Abdullah bin Zayed Al Nahyan, "Preface," for the conference Global Challenges, Regional Responses: Forging a Common Approach to Maritime Piracy, Dubai, 18–19 April 2011.
89. "UAE Concludes Fourth Counter Piracy Conference," Emirates News Agency, 30 October 2014, www.wam.ae/en/news/emirates/1395271693861.html
90. David J. Agnew, John Pearce, Ganapathiraju Pramod, Tom Peatman, Reg Watson, John R. Beddington, and Tony J. Pitcher, "Estimating the worldwide extent of illegal fishing," *PLOS One* 4, no. 2 (2009): e4570, 1.
91. Emily Andrews-Chouicha and Kathleen Gray. *Why fish piracy persists: the economics of illegal, unreported, and unregulated fishing*, OECD, 2005, 37.
92. "Addressing the Overcapacity Issue in Small-Scale Fisheries," February 2014, Coastal Resources Center, Graduate School of Oceanography, University of Rhode Island, 5.
93. Lo Persson, Alasdair Lindop, Sarah Harper, Kyrstn Zylich, and Dirk Zeller, "Failed state: reconstruction of domestic fisheries catches in Somalia 1950–2010," *Fisheries catch reconstructions in the Western Indian Ocean* 2010 (1950), 111.
94. Glaser, "Securing Somali Fisheries," 9.
95. Persson, "Failed State," 2.
96. Jack Lang, "Report of the Special Adviser to the Secretary-General on Legal Issues related to Piracy off the Coast of Somalia," United Nations, New York, January, 2011, Paragraph 89.
97. See the signatory parties to the Port State Measures Agreement, www.fao.org/fishery/psm/agreement/parties/en
98. Indian Ocean Tuna Commission, "Report on presumed IUU fishing activities in the EEZ of Somalia," 2015, www.iotc.org/documents/report-presumed-iuu-fishing-activities-eez-somalia
99. Tim Cashion, Sarah M. Glaser, Lo Persson, Paige M. Roberts, and Dirk Zeller, "Fisheries in Somali waters: Reconstruction of domestic and foreign catches for 1950–2015," *Marine Policy* 87 (2018): 276; Todd Jennings, "Controlling Access in the Absence of a Central Government: The Somali Dilemma1," *Ocean Yearbook Online* 15, no. 1 (2001): 412.
100. Puntland coastguards attacked and arrested four Iranian vessels illegally fishing

from the Lasqoray coast. During the operation, one of the Somali guards hired by the Iranian boats was killed. For Somali media coverage, see www.garoweonline.com/so/news/puntland/qof-ku-dhintay-weerar-ka-dhacay-laasqoray-dhagayso. The research team also communicated with a member of the coastal community in January 2016, confirming these findings.

101. Pramod Ganapathiraju et al., "Estimates of Illegal and Unreported Fish in Seafood Imports to the USA," *Marine Policy* 48 (2014): 102–13.
102. Hagan, "Too Big to Tackle," 109.

7. LEARNING GEOPOLITICAL PLURALISM: TOWARD A NEW INTERNATIONAL OIL REGIME?

1. The author wishes to thank Harry Verhoeven and David Prindle for their encouraging feedback to early drafts of this chapter. It was written before the US presidential elections of 2016, but may prove more relevant in light of their outcome.
2. Roger Stern, "Oil Scarcity Ideology in US Foreign Policy, 1908–1997," *Security Studies* 25 (2016): 214–57.
3. Zbigniew Brzezinski. *The Grand Chessboard: American Primacy and its Geopolitical Imperatives* (New York: Basic Books, 1997), 10.
4. Ibid., 225. Brzezinski's representation of its hydrocarbon reserves is technically correct: they indeed "dwarf those of Kuwait, the Gulf of Mexico, or the North Sea," but certainly not those of the Middle East more generally, or Saudi Arabia's in particular.
5. David C. Hendrickson, "The Grand Chessboard, American Primacy and its Geostrategic Imperatives," *Foreign Affairs* 76, no. 6 (1997): 159–60. In his review, Hendrickson prophetically observed that Brzezinski's "grand design is problematic for two reasons: one is that the excessive widening of Western institutions may well introduce centrifugal forces into them; a second is that Brzezinski's test of what constitutes legitimate Russian interests is so stringent that even a democratic Russia is likely to fail it. Russia, in effect, is to be accorded the geopolitical equivalent of basketball's full court press."
6. Ibid., 225 and 192.
7. Halford J. Mackinder, "The Geographical Pivot of History," *Geographical Journal* 170, no. 4 (1904): 298–321; Halford J. Mackinder, *Democratic Ideals and Reality* (London: Philip & Son, 1919), 150; Brzezinski, *The Grand Chessboard*, 121.
8. Brzezinski, *The Grand Chessboard*, 198.
9. Richard N. Haass, "The New Middle East," *Foreign Affairs*, November–December, 2006.
10. Brzezinski, *The Grand Chessboard*, 123–4.
11. Zbigniew Brzezinski, *Strategic Vision: America and the Crisis of Global Power* (New York: Basic Books, 2012), 116.

12. Zbigniew Brzezinski, *The Loss of Order: Project Syndicate's 2014 Year Review* (Project Syndicate, 2015), Kindle edition, loc. 117. Brzezinski further noted concerning the Middle East, "In these volatile circumstances, greater attention must be given to the national interests of countries such as Turkey, Iran, Saudi Arabia, Egypt, and Israel. By the same token, the interest of any one of them must not be allowed to become the total interest of the US."
13. At Harvard in the early 1960s, Kissinger (born 1923) and Brzezinski (born 1928) were already rivals, protégés respectively of Professors William Yandell Elliott and Carl Joachim Friedrich, the two heavyweights in the Department of Government.
14. Henry Kissinger, *World Order: Reflections on the Character of Nations and the Course of History* (London: Allen Lane, 2014); Samuel P. Huntington, *Clash of Civilizations and the Remaking of World Order* (New York: Simon & Schuster, 1996).
15. "Hillary Clinton Reviews Kissinger's World Order," *Washington Post*, 4 September 2014, https://www.washingtonpost.com/opinions/hillary-clinton-reviews-henry-kissingers-world-order/2014/09/04/b280c654–31ea-11e4–8f02–03c644b2d7d0_story.html?utm_term=.08758a7ee221
16. Joseph S. Nye, Jr, *Soft Power: The Means to Success in World Politics* (New York: Public Affairs, 2004).
17. Henry R. Luce, "The American Century," *Life Magazine*, 17 February 1941, http://www.informationclearinghouse.info/article6139.htm
18. Joseph S. Nye, Jr, *Is the American Century Over?* (Cambridge: Polity Press, 2015).
19. Clyde Prestowitz, *Rouge Nation: American Unilateralism and the Failure of Good Intentions* (New York: Basic Books, 2004), 1.
20. John J. Mearsheimer and Stephen M. Walt, *The Israel Lobby and U.S. Foreign Policy* (New York: Farrar, Straus and Giroux, 2006).
21. Maxime Rodinson popularized this characterization of Israel after the 1967 war in his *Israel: A Colonial-Settler State?* (New York: Pathfinder Press, 1973). For Israel in a more general context of colonial settler states, see Lorenzo Veracini, *Settler Colonialism: A Theoretical Overview* (Basingstoke: Palgrave Macmillan, 2010).
22. George W. Ball, *Error and Betrayal in Lebanon: An Analysis of Israel's Invasion of Lebanon and Their Implications for US–Israeli Relations* (New York: Foundation for Middle East Peace, 1984).
23. Seymour Hersh, "Target Qaddafi," *New York Times Magazine*, 22 February 1987.
24. George Bush and Brent Scowcroft, *A World Transformed* (New York: Alfred A. Knopf, 1998).
25. Samantha Power, "US Diplomacy: Realism and Reality," *New York Review of Books*, 18 August 2016, http://www.nybooks.com/articles/2016/08/18/us-diplomacy-realism-and-reality/
26. Jason Brownlee, *Democracy Prevention: The Politics of the U.S.–Egyptian Alliance* (Cambridge and New York: Cambridge University Press, 2012).

27. Kirk J. Beattie, *Congress and the Shaping of the Middle East* (New York: Seven Stories Press, 2015).
28. William R. Polk, *Violent Politics: A History of Insurgency, Terrorism, and Guerrilla War, from the American Revolution to Iraq* (New York: HarperCollins, 2007); William R. Polk, "Falling into the ISIS Trap," *Consortium News*,17 November 2015, https://consortiumnews.com/2015/11/17/falling-into-the-isis-trap
29. Stockholm International Peace Research Institute (SIPRI), "Importer/Exporter TIV Tables," http://armstrade.sipri.org/armstrade/page/values.php. From 2011 to 2015 the United States and Russia respectively exported totals of $46.9 and $36.2 billion worth of military equipment in constant 1990 US dollars, as expressed in SIPRI's Trend Indicator Values. China came in third place with $8.5 billion, just ahead of France, Germany, and the UK in descending order. Note: $1 (1990) = $1.85 (2016).
30. Robert O. Keohane, *After Hegemony: Cooperation and Discord in the World Political Economy* (Princeton, NJ: Princeton University Press, 1984), 59.
31. International Energy Agency, "Energy Supply Security 2014: Emergency Response of IEA Countries," IEA/OECD, Paris, 2014, https://www.iea.org/publications/freepublications/publication/ENERGYSUPPLYSECURITY2014.pdf
32. Theorizing about regimes taking on lives of their own, Robert O. Keohane understood US hegemony to have ended in the 1960s, in his *After Hegemony*, 15 and 138–9.
33. Enrico Mattei, who wanted access for his Italian oil company, coined the expression Seven Sisters. They were Exxon, Royal Dutch Shell, British Petroleum, Mobil, Gulf, Texaco, and Chevron, joined by an eighth bit player, la Compagnie Française des Pétroles.
34. Theodore H. Moran, "Managing an oligopoly of would-be sovereigns: the dynamics of joint control and self-control in the international oil industry past, present, and future," *International Organization* 41, no. 4 (1987): 575–607.
35. Ibid.
36. Ibid., 585.
37. Moran, "Managing an oligopoly of would-be sovereigns."
38. In fact its writ was worldwide. The international companies priced their oil at the Galveston, Texas, f.o.b. (free on board) freight price plus the ("phantom") freight rate from Galveston to wherever the oil was being shipped. Although TRC allocations generally favored the small independent Texas producers at the expense of the big ones like Humble Oil (Exxon), the management of a steady price baseline amply reimbursed the cartel. Costs of production were much higher in Texas than in the Middle East, and the TRC fixed prices were high enough to keep expensive stripper wells in operation. David F. Prindle, *Petroleum Politics and the Texas Railroad Commission* (Austin, TX: University of Texas Press, 1981), 40–55.
39. Daniel Yergin, *The Prize: The Epic Quest for Oil, Money, and Power* (New York: Simon & Schuster, 1991).

40. Moran, "Managing an Oligopoly of Would-be Sovereigns," 603.
41. John Kay, *Other People's Money: The Real Business of Finance* (New York: Public Affairs, 2015); Mahmoud El-Gamal and Amy Jaffe, *Oil, Dollars, Debt, and Crises: The Global Curse of Black Gold* (New York: Cambridge University Press, 2010).
42. BP Statistics indicate that Saudi Arabia annually produced a daily average of 5.2 million barrels in 1986, 4.6 million in 1987, and 5.7 million in 1988.
43. Kate Gillespie and Clement M. Henry, eds, *Oil in the New World Order* (Gainesville, FL: University Press of Florida, 1995), 11.
44. From 1998 to 1999, Saudi production diminished from an average of 9.4 million barrels per day to 8.8 million, while Iran cut its production of 3.9 million barrels by an average of about 250,000 barrels per day.
45. Mehran Kamrava, *Qatar: Small State, Big Politics* (Ithaca, NY: Cornell University Press, 2015).
46. Alfred B. Prados, "Saudi Arabia: Current Issues and US Relations," Congressional Research Service, 2005.
47. Price-Smith (2015) notes the waning of Saudi spare capacity after 2003, especially in 2006–8: Andrew T. Price-Smith, *Oil, Illiberalism, and War. An Analysis of Energy and US Foreign Policy* (Cambridge, MA: MIT Press, 2015), 34, 59.
48. Robert Keohane, *After Hegemony*, 223.
49. IEA (Ingency), *Energy Policies and Programmes of IEA Countries, 1979 Review* (Paris: OECD/IEA, 1980), 12, cited by Keohane in *After Hegemony*, 228.
50. During the week of 26 August 2016, the US imported 8.9 million barrels, some of which were destined for the SPR. US Energy Information Administration, "Weekly U.S. Imports of Crude Oil," 2017, https://www.eia.gov/dnav/pet/hist/LeafHandler.ashx?n=PET&s=WCRIMUS2&f=W
51. British Petroleum, *BP Statistical Review of World Energy June 2016*, https://www.bp.com/content/dam/bp/pdf/energy-economics/statistical-review-2016/bp-statistical-review-of-world-energy-2016-full-report.pdf; Adam Sieminski, "International Energy Outlook 2016," Center for Strategic and International Studies, U.S. Energy Information Administration, Washington, DC, 2016, http://www.eia.gov/pressroom/presentations/sieminski_05112016.pdf
52. Francis P. Sempa, *Geopolitics: From the Cold War to the 21st Century* (New Brunswick, NJ: Transaction Publishers, 2009).
53. Barry R. Posen, *Restraint: A New Foundation for U.S. Grand Strategy* (Ithaca, NY: Cornell University Press, 2014).
54. The Chinese vision of "One Belt, One Road" for restoring the Silk Route refers respectively to the land and sea routes between China and the Middle East and Europe.
55. Johannes Feige, "Why China's Djibouti Presence Matters," *The Diplomat*, 13 April 2016, http://thediplomat.com/2016/04/why-chinas-djibouti-presence-matters/; Geoffrey Kemp, *The East Moves West: India, China, and Asia's Growing Presence in the Middle East* (Washington, DC: Brookings Institution Press, 2012).

56. Harry Verhoeven, "Is Beijing's Non-Interference Policy History? How Africa is Changing China," *Washington Quarterly* 37, no. 2 (2014): 55–70. DOI: 10.1080/0163660X.2014.926209.
57. Robert D. Kaplan, *Asia's Cauldron: The South China Sea and the End of a Stable Pacific* (New York: Random House, 2014).
58. British Petroleum, *BP Statistical Review of World Energy June 2016.*
59. See also Jill Crystal's Chapter 3 in this volume.
60. Angelina Rascouet, "Saudi Arabia's Break-Even Oil Price Plunges as Spending Drops," *Bloomberg News*, 25 April 2016, http://www.bloomberg.com/news/articles/2016–04–25/
saudi-arabia-tightens-belt-most-as-break-even-oil-price-declines
61. Figures 7.2 and 7.3 are based on OPEC data, whereas BP 2016, the source of Figure 7.1, presents higher yearly production data for Saudi Arabia.
62. British Petroleum, *BP Statistical Review of World Energy June 2016.*
63. David Prindle in an email communication with the author, 17 November 2016.
64. Robert Vitalis, "The Twentieth-Century Origins of a Twenty-First Century Pseudoscience," *Montreal Review*, June 2013, http://www.themontrealreview.com/2009/America-s-Kingdom.php
65. Robert Axelrod, *The Evolution of Cooperation* (New York: Basic Books, 1984).

8. SCARCITY DRIVES ECONOMIC DEVELOPMENT: THE EFFECT OF ENERGY SUBSIDIES ON EXPORT DIVERSIFICATION IN THE MIDDLE EAST

1. I am grateful to the two referees and to Harry Verhoeven for their helpful comments on this chapter. United Nations Development Programme, "Arab Human Development Report 2016—Youth and the Prospects for Human Development in a Changing Reality," 2016, http://www.arabstates.undp.org/content/dam/rbas/report/AHDR%20Reports/AHDR%202016/AHDR%20Final%202016/AHDR2016En.pdf; and "Arab Human Development Report 2002—Creating Opportunities for Future Generations," UNDP, 2002, http://www.arab-hdr.org
2. Julia C. Devlin, "Challenges of Economic Development in the Middle East and North Africa Region," in *World Scientific Studies in International Economics*, ed. Robert M. Stern (Singapore: World Scientific, 2010); Melani Cammett et al., *A Political Economy of the Middle East*, 4th edn (Boulder, CO: Westview Press, 2015); Mélise Jaud and Caroline Freund, *Champions Wanted: Promoting Exports in the Middle East and North Africa, Directions in Development* (Washington, DC: World Bank, 2015); Pedro de Lima et al., "What's Holding Back the Private Sector in MENA? Lessons from the Enterprise Survey" (Washington, DC: World Bank Group, 2016).
3. Cammett et al., *A Political Economy of the Middle East.*
4. Shanta Devarajan, "How the Middle East and North Africa can Benefit from Low

Oil Prices," Brookings Institute, 6 April 2016, https://www.brookings.edu/blog/future-development/2016/04/06/how-the-middle-east-and-north-africa-can-benefit-from-low-oil-prices/

5. For a review of studies, see Jennifer Ellis, "The Effect of Fossil-Fuel Subsidy Reform: A Review of Modelling and Empirical Studies" (Winnipeg: International Institute for Sustainable Development, Global Subsidies Initiative, 2010).
6. Jean-Marc Burniaux, Jean Chateau, and Jehan Sauvage, "The Trade Effects of Phasing Out Fossil-Fuel Consumption Subsidies," OECD Trade and Environment Working Papers (Paris: OECD, 2011); Jean-Marc Burniaux, Jean Chateau, and Jehan Sauvage, "Mitigation Potential of Removing Fossil Fuel Subsidies: A General Equilibrium Assessment," OECD Economics Department Working Papers, no. 853 (Paris: OECD, 2011).
7. David Coady et al., "How Large are Global Energy Subsidies?" IMF Working Paper (Washington, DC: International Monetary Fund, 2015); Masami Kojima, "Fossil Fuel Subsidy and Pricing Polices: Recent Developing Country Experience," policy research working paper, no. 7531 (Washington, DC: World Bank, 2016); Devarajan et al. "Middle East and North Africa Economic Monitor October 2014: Corrosive Subsidies," *MENA Economic Monitor* (Washington, DC: World Bank, 2014).
8. For an overview of studies, see Kojima, "Fossil Fuel Subsidy and Pricing Polices."
9. Ellis, "The Effect of Fossil-Fuel Subsidy Reform."
10. Aziz Atamanov, Jon Jellema, and Umar Serajuddin, "Energy Subsidies Reform in Jordan: Welfare Implications of Different Scenarios," policy research working paper, no. 7313 (Washington, DC: World Bank, 2015); and José Cuesta, AbdelRahmen El-Lahga, and Gabriel Lara Ibarra, "The Socioeconomic Impacts of Energy Reform in Tunisia," policy research working paper, no. 7312 (Washington, DC: World Bank, 2015).
11. Frederick Van der Ploeg, "Natural Resources: Curse or Blessing?" *Journal of Economic Literature* 49, no. 2 (2011): 366–420; Anthony J. Venables, "Using Natural Resources for Development: Why has it Proven so Difficult?" *Journal of Economic Perspectives* 30, no. 1 (2016): 161–84.
12. All monetary references in the paper are in US dollars, unless indicated otherwise. William Wallis, "Nigeria Audit: State Oil Company Siphoning Oil Revenues," *Financial Times*, 28 April 2015.
13. Javier Arze del Granado, David Coady, and Robert Gillingham, "The Unequal Benefits of Fuel Subsidies: A Review of Evidence for Developing Countries," *World Development* 40, no. 11 (2012): 2234–48. See also Coady et al., "How Large are Global Energy Subsidies?"; and Kojima, "Fossil Fuel Subsidy and Pricing Polices."
14. Ellis, "The Effect of Fossil-Fuel Subsidy Reform," 10.
15. Maria Vagliasindi, *Implementing Energy Subsidy Reforms: Evidence from developing countries* (Washington, DC: World Bank, 2013); and Simeon Kerr, "Saudis Face Fuel Price Jump under New Austerity Plan," *Financial Times*, 2 January 2016.

16. Daron Acemoglu et al., "The Environment and Directed Technical Change," *American Economic Review* 102, no. 1 (2012): 131–66; Philippe Aghion et al., "Carbon Taxes, Path Dependency and Directed Technical Change: Evidence from the Auto Industry," *Journal of Political Economy* 124, no. 1 (2016): 1–51; and Joshua S. Gans, "Innovation and Climate Change Policy," *American Economic Journal: Economic Policy* 4, no. 4 (2012): 125–45.
17. Acemoglu et al., "The Environment and Directed Technical Change."
18. Michael E. Porter, "America's Green Strategy," *Scientific American* 264, no. 4 (1991): 168; Michael E. Porter and Claas van der Linde, "Toward a New Conception of the Environment-Competitiveness Relationship," *Journal of Economic Perspectives* 9, no. 4 (1995): 97–118; Karen Palmer, Wallace E. Coates, and Paul R Portney, "Tightening Environmental Standards: The Benefit-cost or the No-cost Paradigm?" *Journal of Economic Perspectives* 9, no. 4 (1995): 119–32.
19. The first tendency can be readily observed in the increasing standards required for the mileage of automobiles or the measurement of energy use of electrical equipment in OECD countries. The second assertion is debatable and relates to the "carbon leakage" discussion. While energy-intensive industries are shifting from countries where fossil fuels are taxed to where fossil energy is cheaper, the products that are exported back are currently not taxed based on their carbon footprint.
20. Even though this chapter focuses on energy subsidies, note that reform will have welfare and income implications for various societal groups. Therefore, reforms should include both compensation for the lowest income groups and potential regulatory reforms to allow firms to compete successfully with international peers. Overhauling the business climate would become even more urgent once subsidies are abolished.
21. Jaud and Freund, *Champions Wanted*; and de Lima et al., "What's Holding Back the Private Sector in MENA?"
22. E.g. Julien Gourdon, "FDI Flows and Exports Diversification: Looking at Extensive and Intensive Margins," in *Trade Competitiveness of the Middle East and North Africa: Policies for Export Diversification*, ed. José R López-Cálix, Peter Walkenhorst, and Ndiamé Diop (Washington, DC: World Bank, 2010), 13–46; and Stephen R. Bond and Adeel Malik, "Natural Resources, Export Structure, and Investment," *Oxford Economic Papers* 61 (2009): 675–702.
23. Gourdon, "FDI Flows and Exports Diversification."
24. Aggregate imports and exports can be de-aggregated over product categories. Roughly speaking, the 1-digit level corresponds to sectors such as agriculture, commodities, chemicals, manufacturing, high-tech etc. Increasing the number of digits therefore allows analysis of trade data at close to individual product categories. Whereas most countries will export and import products at the 1-digit level, it

becomes increasingly probable that certain product categories are not exported at a higher level of disaggregation. I am using the information on the number of product varieties for individual countries to deduce a measure of export diversification. Although the database has a 6-digit product categorization, this does not mean that there are 999,999 product categories. At the 6-digit level for the sample of countries and years used, there are 6,274 different product categories recorded.

25. Elhanan Helpman, Marc Melitz, and Yona Rubinstein, "Estimating Trade Flows: Trading Partners and Trading Volumes," *Quarterly Journal of Economics* 123, no. 2 (2008): 441–87.
26. International Monetary Fund, "Energy Subsidy Reform: Lessons and Implications" (Washington, DC: International Monetary Fund, January 2013); International Energy Agency, "World Energy Outlook 2011" (Paris: OECD, 2011); International Energy Agency, "World Energy Outlook 2012" (Paris: OECD, 2012); Vagliasindi, *Implementing Energy Subsidy Reforms*; Lucas W. Davis, "The Economic Cost of Global Fuel Subsidies," *American Economic Review*, papers and proceedings 104, no. 5 (2014): 581–5. Davis distinguishes between gasoline and diesel subsidies per capita. For the empirical analysis, I take the sum of the two.
27. E.g. Jane O. Ebinger, "Measuring Financial Performance in Infrastructure: An Application to Europe and Central Asia," policy research working paper, no. 3992 (Washington, DC: World Bank, 2006).
28. Lulu Shui and Peter Walkenhorst, "Regional Integration: Status, Developments and Challenges," in *Trade Competitiveness of the Middle East and North Africa*, ed. José R. López-Cálix, Peter Walkenhorst, and Ndiamé Diop (Washington, DC: World Bank, 2010), 267–97; and Cammett et al., *A Political Economy of the Middle East*.
29. Identified by the first two digits of 6-digit product variety: 27.
30. The qualitative results in the rest of the paper are not affected by its inclusion.
31. Demographics can be an endogenous outcome of public policy too, except that they work over generations rather than over the shorter time-span that concerns me here. The simple correlation between population and varieties for the entire sample period of 1991–2015 is 0.37 (with both figures in log it is 0.25). A panel regression with country and year fixed effects, and controlling for GDP per capita, gives a coefficient of 0.42 with a standard error of 0.12.
32. Vagliasindi, *Implementing Energy Subsidy Reforms*; Atamanov et al., "Energy Subsidies Reform in Jordan."
33. Vagliasindi, *Implementing Energy Subsidy Reforms*. The chapter on Turkey in Vagliasindi's study (ch. 11) referred only to Turkey's subsidies in the electricity sector, rather than general subsidies, and is therefore not included in the graph. This level was, however, relatively small, at 0.2 percent of GDP in terms of hidden subsidies for natural gas on average between 2000 and 2003, and 2 percent

of GDP for electricity, decreasing to 0.5 percent in 2003. These numbers cited by Vagliasindi are based on Ebinger, "Measuring Financial Performance in Infrastructure."

34. Bond and Malik, "Natural Resources, Export Structure, and Investment."
35. Kevin M. Morrison, "Oil, Nontax Revenue, and the Redistributional Foundations of Regime Stability," *International Organization* 63, no. 1 (2009): 107–38.
36. The inclusion of country fixed effects rather than group fixed effects is impossible due to the lack of time variation in the different subsidy measures.
37. Based on Vagliasindi's data, it is possible to create an indicator variable to designate for each country the period of subsidy reforms, thereby exploiting the time dimension of reforms. However, the results of regressions with this indicator were sensitive to the particular measure of varieties and inclusion of control variables. The regressions that are presented here are not sensitive to the specific measure of varieties (e.g. total number of varieties, or the log of varieties). For the measure of varieties per capita, results are sensitive to the inclusion of the fixed effects, but not for the alternative measures. Since the subsidy measures do not vary over time, one could question the use of any time dimension in the regressions. Results not presented here show that while using the time average for each of the measures over the period 2011–14, a regression of the group indicators and control variables on the subsidy measures gives qualitatively the same results.
38. See UN Comtrade, "Commodities List": agriculture, 01–24; commodities, 25, 26; oil and gas, 27; raw chemicals, 28, 29, 31; processed chemicals, 30, 32–36, 38–40; light manufacturing, 41–71; heavy manufacturing, 72–83; machines and electric, 37, 85–91; miscellaneous, 92–99; http://comtrade.un.org/db/mr/rfCommoditiesList.aspx
39. The results using the IEA measure indicate that all sectors are affected, while using the IMF measure gives mostly statistically insignificant results.
40. In this respect, the coefficient and standard errors for the coefficient of the OECD are actually quite interesting. The coefficient is very close to zero, but the confidence interval is very tight, and much smaller compared to the intervals of the other regions. This combination of a small coefficient and small standard error indicates that the estimate is quite precisely estimated and the result should not be dismissed immediately for lack of statistical significance.
41. De Lima et al., "What's Holding Back the Private Sector in MENA?" 99.

9. THE POLITICS OF NATURAL RESOURCES IN THE CASPIAN SEA: A NEW GREAT GAME IN AN ANCIENT WORLD

1. UNDP, *The Caspian Sea: Restoring Depleted Fisheries and Consolidation of a Permanent Regional Environmental Governance Framework* (CaspEco, 2009).
2. Felix Stolberg and Olena Borysova, "The Caspian Sea Regional Report," Global International Waters Assessment, 2006, http://www.unep.org/dewa/giwa/areas/area23.asp

3. David G. Aubery, *Sea Levels, Land Levels, and Tide Gauges* (New York: Science, 1991).
4. Aleksey N. Kosarev and Anna Yablonskaya, *The Caspian Sea* (London: SPB Academic Publishing, The Hague, 1994).
5. Arthur Koestler, *The Thirteenth Tribe* (London: Random House, 1976).
6. Rayna Baily, *Global Issues: Immigration and Migration* (New York: Infobase Publishing, 2008), 10.
7. David Menasheri, *Central Asia Meets the Middle East* (London: Frank Cass, 2002), 3–4.
8. Frits van der Leeden, Fred L. Troise, and David Keith Todd, eds, *The Water Encyclopedia*, 2nd edn (Chelsea, MI: Lewis Publishers, 1990), 196; Gal Luft and Anne Korin, eds, *Energy Security: Challenges for 21st Century* (Oxford: ABC Clio, 2009); Thomas W. Wälde, ed., *The Energy Charter Treaty: An East–West Gateway for Investment and Trade*, International Energy and Resources Law and Policy Series, vol. 10 (London: Kluwer Law International, July 1996).
9. Edward N. Luttwak, "From Geopolitics to Geo-economics: Logic of Conflict, Grammar of Commerce," *National Interest* 20 (1990): 17–23.
10. Jonathan Isham, Michael Woolcock, Lant Pritchett, and Gwen Busby, "The Varieties of Resource Experience: Natural Resource Export Structure and the Political Economy of Economic Growth," *World Bank Economic Review* 19, no. 2 (2005): 141–74.
11. Indra de Soysa, "The Resource Curse: Are Civil Wars Driven by Rapacity or Paucity?" in *Greed and Grievance: Economic Agendas in Civil Wars*, ed. Mats Berdal and David M. Malone (Boulder, CO: Lynne Rienner, 2000), 113.
12. Richard M. Auty, "Natural Resources and Civil Strife: A Two-Stage Process," in *Geopolitics of Resource Wars: Resource Dependence, Governance and Violence*, ed. Philippe Le Billon (London: Frank Cass, 2004), 30.
13. Reserve–production ratio (R/P) is the remaining amount of a non-renewable resource expressed in time. The reserve portion of the ratio is the amount of a resource known to exist in an area and to be economically recoverable (proved reserves). The production portion of the ratio is the amount of resource produced in one year at the current rate.
14. Asian Development Bank, "Country Partnership Strategy: Azerbaijan, 2014–2018," 2014, https://www.adb.org/sites/default/files/linked-documents/cps-aze-2014-2018-ea.pdf
15. "BP Statistical Review," British Petroleum, 2014.
16. Isham et al., "The Varieties of Resource Experience," 143.
17. Sergej Mahnovski, "Natural Resources and Potential Conflict in the Caspian Sea Region," in *Faultlines of Conflict in Central Asia and the South Caucasus: Implications for the US Army*, ed. Olga Oliker and Thomas Szayna (Santa Monica, CA: Rand Arroyo Center, 2003), 109–44.

18. Dani Rodrik, Arvind Subramanian, and Francesco Trebbi; "Institutions Rule: The Primacy of Institutions over Integration and Geography in Economic Development," *Journal of Economic Growth* 9, no. 2 (2004): 131–65.
19. Akram Esanov, Martin Raiser, and Willem Buiter, "Nature's Blessing or Nature's Curse: The Political Economy of Transition in Resource-based Economies" (working paper, EBRD no. 65, 2001).
20. Slavomir Horak, "The Elite in Post-Soviet and Post-Niyazow Turkmenistan: Does Political Culture form a Leader?" *Demokratizatsiya* 20 (2012): 371–85.
21. Humera Iqbal, "Democracy and Central Asian States," *Regional Studies* 25, no. 4 (2007): 66–99; Tanya Charlick-Paley, Phil Williams, and Olga Oliker, "The Political Evolution of Central Asia and South Caucasus: Implications for Regional Security," in *Fault lines of Conflict in Central Asia and the South Caucasus*, ed. Olga Oliker and Thomas Szayna (New York: RAND Publications, 2003), 7–34; E. Wayne Merry, "Governance in Central Asia: National in Form, Soviet in Content," *Cambridge Review of International Affairs* 17, no. 2 (2004): 286–91; Stephen Blank, "Rethinking Central Asian Security," *China and Eurasia Forum Quarterly* 6, no. 2 (2008): 23–39.
22. Halford John Mackinder, "The Geographical Pivot of History," *Geographical Journal* 23 (1904): 421–37.
23. Pascal Venier, "The Geographical Pivot of History and Early 20th Century Geopolitical Culture," *Geographical Journal* 170, no. 4 (2004): 330–36.
24. Andre Gunder Frank, "The Centrality of Central Asia," *Studies in History* 8, no. 1 (1992): 43–97.
25. For US policy on the Caspian during Bush, Amy Myers Jaffe and Ronald Soligo, "Re-evaluating US Strategic Priorities in the Caspian Region: Balancing Energy Resource Initiatives with Terrorism Containment," *Cambridge Review of International Affairs* 17, no. 2 (July 2004): 251–89. For policy under Obama, Sam Raphael and Doug Stokes, "US Oil Strategy in the Caspian Basin: Hegemony through Interdependence," *International Relations* 28, no. 2 (June 2014); and Kurt Campbell and Brian Andrews, *Explaining the US Pivot to Asia* (London: Chatham House, 2013).
26. Gue Xuetang, "The Energy Security in Central Eurasia: The Geopolitical Implications to China's Energy Strategy," *China and Eurasia Quarterly* 4, no. 4 (2006): 117–37.
27. Huseyn Hasanov, "Turkmenistan Becomes China's Biggest Strategic Partner in Gas Provision," *Trend News Agency*, 28 September 2015, http://en.trend.az/business/energy/2437384.html
28. Alyson Bailes et al., *The Shanghai Cooperation Organization*, Stockholm International Peace Institute policy paper (2007).
29. Michael D. Swaine, "Chinese Views and Commentary on the One Belt, One Road Initiative," *China Leadership Monitor* no. 47 (2015).

30. Laurent Rusekas, "Turkey and Eurasia: Opportunities and Risks in the Caspian Pipeline Derby," *Journal of International affairs* 54, no. 1 (2000): 217–36.
31. Abbas Maleki, "Decision Making in Iran's Foreign Policy: A Heuristic Approach," *Journal of Social Affairs* 19, no. 73 (2002): 31–56.
32. Daniel S. Treisman, *After the Deluge: Regional Crises and Political Consolidation in Russia* (Ann Arbor, MI: Michigan University Press, 2001).
33. Alexander Warkotsch, "Normative Suasion and Political Change in Central Asia," *Caucasian Review of International Affairs* 2, no. 4 (2008): 240–49.
34. Mariya Y. Omelicheva, "Democracy and Dictatorship in Central Asia," in *Oxford Bibliographies in Political Science* (New York: Oxford University Press, 2012).
35. Caspian Environment Programme, *Transboundary Diagnostic Analysis for the Caspian Sea.*
36. "Human Development Reports," United Nations Development Programme, 2014, http://hdr.undp.org/en/composite/HDI.
37. Simon Commander and Fabrizio Coricelli, *Unemployment, restructuring, and the labor market in Eastern Europe and Russia* (Washington, DC: World Bank, Economic Development Institute, 1995), 147–92.
38. Caspian Environment Programme, *Transboundary Diagnostic Analysis for the Caspian Sea.*
39. Alice J. Barnes and Nicholas S. Briggs, "The Caspian Oil Reserves: The Political, Economic and Environmental Implications of 'Black Gold' in the World Market," *EDGE* (2003), http://web.stanford.edu/class/e297a/Caspian%20Oil%20 Reserves.pdf
40. Gue Xuetang, "The Energy Security in Central Eurasia: the Geopolitical Implications to China's Energy Strategy," *China and Eurasia Quarterly* 4, no. 4 (2006): 117–37.
41. Wood Mackenzie, "Drop in exploration ahead for Caspian region. Production to rise," *Offshore Energy Today*, 30 January 2015, http://www.offshoreenergytoday.com/wood-mackenzie-drop-in-exploration-ahead-for-caspian-region-production-to-rise/.
42. British Petroleum, "BP Statistical Review."
43. Total proven oil reserves globally reached 1,700 billion barrels at the end of 2014, sufficient to meet 52.5 years of production. Over the past decade, proven reserves have increased by 24 percent, or more than 330 billion barrels. The US Geological Survey (USGS) assessed the Caspian basin using published geological information on commercial oil and natural gas field data to estimate undiscovered resources. The USGS estimates a mean of about 20 billion barrels of crude oil and 6.8 trillion cubic meters of natural gas in technically recoverable, conventional undiscovered resources. USGS estimates around 65 percent of the undiscovered oil and 81 percent of the natural gas in the South Caspian basin, reflecting the more limited exploration of the south-eastern part of the Caspian Sea near Iran and

Turkmenistan because of territorial disputes. The Arctic-like north of the Caspian Sea is also relatively unexplored, and USGS estimates significant amounts of undiscovered resources there as well. For further discussion: Gregory F. Ulmishek, *Petroleum Geology and Resources of the Middle Caspian Basin, Former Soviet Union*, USGS Bulletin no. 2201-A (2001), https://pubs.usgs.gov/bul/2201/A/

44. EIA, "Overview of oil and natural gas in the Caspian Sea region," EIA, 2013.
45. Sources: BP, IEA, EIA, and NIGC.
46. Jack Farchy, "Azerbaijani Manat collapses after government abandons dollar peg," *Financial Times*, 21 December 2015, https://www.ft.com/content/b5f46eac-a7c4-11e5-9700-2b669a5aeb83
47. John C. K. Daly, "Kashagan Oil Field Comes Back to Life," *Silk Road Reporters*, 10 July 2015, http://www.silkroadreporters.com/2015/07/10/kashagan-oil-field-comes-back-to-life
48. "Rising China, Sinking Russia," *Economist*, 14 September 2013, http://www.economist.com/news/asia/21586304-vast-region-chinas-economic-clout-more-match-russias-rising-china-sinking
49. http://www.ndco.ir/Default.aspx?tabid=166
50. Shah Alam, "Pipeline Politics in the Caspian Sea Basin," *Strategic Analysis* 26, no. 1 (2002): 5–26.
51. Richard E. Ericson, "Eurasian Natural Gas Pipelines: the Political Economy of Network Interdependence," *Eurasian Geography and Economics* 50, no. 1 (2009): 28–57.
52. Paul Stevens, *Transit Troubles: Pipelines as a Source of Conflict* (London: Chatham House, 2009).
53. Guive Mirfendereski, *A Diplomatic History of the Caspian Sea: Treaties, Diaries, and other Stories* (New York: Palgrave, 2001).
54. For further information, refer to "International Energy Charter," http://www.energycharter.org
55. Abbas Maleki and Kaveh Afrasiabi, "Iran's Foreign Policy after 11 September," *Brown Journal of World Affairs* 9, no. 2 (Spring 2003): 254–89.
56. Rustam Mamedov, "International Legal Status of the Caspian Sea: Issues of Theory and Practice," *Turkish Yearbook* (2001): 217–59.
57. Natalie Klein, *Dispute Settlement in the UN Convention of Law of the Seas* (New York: Cambridge University Press, 2004).
58. Stanislav Cherniavskii, "Problems of the Caspian," *Russian Politics and Law* 40, no. 2 (April 2002): 85–94.
59. Jedrzej George Frynas, *Beyond Corporate Social Responsibility: Oil Multinational and Social Challenges* (New York: Cambridge University Press, 2009).

BIBLIOGRAPHY FOR INTRODUCTION ONLY

Acemoglu, Daron, and James A. Robinson. "Economic Backwardness in Political Perspective." *American Political Science Review* 100, no. 1 (2006): 115–31.

Adaman, Fikret, Bengi Akbulut, and Murat Arse. *Neoliberal Turkey and its Discontents: Economic Policy and the Environment under Erdoğan*. London: I. B.Tauris, 2017.

Agarwal, Arun, and Sunita Narain. *Global Warming: A Case of Environmental Colonialism*. Delhi: Centre for Science and Environment, 1991.

Agrawal, Arun, and Clark C. Gibson. "Enchantment and Disenchantment: the Role of Community in Natural Resource Conservation." *World Development* 2, no. 4 (1999): 629–49.

Allan, J. Anthony. *The Middle East Water Question: Hydropolitics and the Global Economy*. London: I. B. Tauris, 2001.

Al-Mulali, Usama, and Chor Foon Tang. "Investigating the Validity of Pollution Haven Hypothesis in the Gulf Cooperation Council (GCC) Countries." *Energy Policy* 60, no. 9 (2013): 813–19.

Altinbelek, Dogan. "Development and Management of the Euphrates–Tigris Basin." *International Journal of Water Resources Development* 20, no. 1 (2004): 15–33.

Amery, Hussein A. "Water Wars in the Middle East: A Looming Threat." *Geographical Journal* 168, no. 4 (2002): 313–23.

Amery, Hussein A., and Aaron T. Wolf, eds. *Water in the Middle East: A Geography of Peace*. Austin, TX: University of Texas Press, 2000.

Atalay, Yasemin, Frank Biermann, and Agni Kalfagianni. "Adoption of Renewable Energy Technologies in Oil-Rich Countries: Explaining Policy Variation in the Gulf Cooperation Council States." *Renewable Energy* 85, no. 1 (2016): 206–14.

Avery, John. *Progress, Poverty and Population: Re-reading Condorcet, Godwin and Malthus*. London: Frank Cass, 1997.

Bakir, Hamed A. "Sustainable Wastewater Management for Small Communities in the Middle East and North Africa." *Journal of Environmental Management* 61, no. 4 (2001): 319–28.

Bazilian, Morgan, et al. "Considering the Energy, Water and Food Nexus: Towards an Integrated Modelling Approach." *Energy Policy* 39, no. 12 (2011): 7896–906.

Beblawi, Hazem, and Giacomo Luciani, eds. *The Rentier State: Nation, State and the Integration of the Arab World*. London: Croom Helm, 1987.

Bellemare, Marc F. "Rising Food Prices, Food Price Volatility, and Social Unrest." *American Journal of Agricultural Economics* 97, no. 1 (2015): 1–21.

Berdal, Mats R., and Mónica Serrano, eds. *Transnational Organized Crime and International Security: Business as Usual?* Boulder, CO: Lynne Rienner, 2002.

Bichsel, Christine, Peter Mollinga, Timothy Moss, and Julia Obertreis, eds. "Water, Infrastructure and Political Rule." *Water Alternatives* 9, no. 2 (2016).

Bodansky, Daniel, Jutta Brunnée, and Ellen Hey. *The Oxford Handbook of International Environmental Law*. Oxford: Oxford University Press, 2012.

Bonine, Michael E., Abbas Amanat, and Michael Ezekiel Gasper, eds. *Is there a Middle East? The Evolution of a Geopolitical Concept*. Stanford, CA: Stanford University Press, 2012.

Boulakia, Jean David C. "Ibn Khaldun: A Fourteenth-Century Economist." *Journal of Political Economy* 79, no. 5 (1971): 1105–18.

Brown, Lester Russell. *Redefining National Security*. Washington, DC: Worldwatch Institute, 1977.

Bulloch, John, and Adel Darwish. *Water Wars: Coming Conflicts in the Middle East*. London: Victor Gollancz, 1993.

Caldwell, John C. "Malthus and the Less Developed World: The Pivotal Role of India." *Population and Development Review* 24, no. 4 (1998): 675–96.

Caldwell, Lynton K. *Science and the National Environmental Policy Act: Redirecting Policy through Administrative Reform*. Tuscaloosa, AL: University of Alabama Press, 1982.

Caselli, Francesco, and Andrea Tesei. "Resource Windfalls, Political Regimes, and Political Stability." *Review of Economics and Statistics* 98, no. 3 (2016): 573–90.

Cascão, Ana Elisa, and Alan Nicol. "GERD: New Norms of Cooperation in the Nile Basin?" *Water International* 41, no. 4 (2016): 1–24.

Cash, David W., and Susanne C. Moser. "Linking Global and Local Scales: Designing Dynamic Assessment and Management Processes." *Global Environmental Change* 10, no. 2 (2000): 109–20.

Castro, Carlos J. "Sustainable Development: Mainstream and Critical Perspectives." *Organization and Environment* 17, no. 2 (2004): 195–225.

Catton, William R. *Overshoot: The Ecological Basis of Revolutionary Change* (Urbana, IL: University of Illinois Press, 1980).

Clapp, Jennifer, and Peter Dauvergne. *Paths to a Green World. The Political Economy of the Global Environment*. Cambridge, MA: MIT Press, 2005.

Coase, Ronald H. "The Problem of Social Cost." *Journal of Law and Economics* 3, no. 1 (1960): 1–44.

Conca, Ken. *Governing Water: Contentious Transnational Politics and Global Institution Building*. Cambridge, MA: MIT Press, 2006.

Crosby, Alfred W. *Ecological Imperialism: The Biological Expansion of Europe, 900–1900*, new edn. Cambridge: Cambridge University Press, 2004.

Crystal, Jill. *Oil and Politics in the Gulf: Rulers and Merchants in Kuwait and Qatar*. Cambridge: Cambridge University Press, 1990.

Dale, Stephen Frederic. "Ibn Khaldun: The Last Greek and the First Annaliste Historian." *International Journal of Middle East Studies* 38, no. 3 (2006): 431–51.

Davis, Diana K. *Resurrecting the Granary of Rome: Environmental History and French Colonial Expansion in North Africa*. Athens, OH: Ohio University Press, 2007.

Davis, Mike. *Ecology of Fear: Los Angeles and the Imagination of Disaster*. New York: Vintage Books, 1998.

de Châtel, Francesca. "The Role of Drought and Climate Change in the Syrian Uprising: Untangling the Triggers of the Revolution." *Middle Eastern Studies* 50, no. 4 (2014): 521–35.

Diamond, Jared. *Guns, Germs, and Steel*. New York: W. W. Norton, 1999.

——— *Collapse: How Societies Choose to Fail or Succeed*. London: Penguin, 2005.

Dryzek, John S. *The Politics of the Earth: Environmental Discourses*. Oxford: Oxford University Press, 2013.

Ehrlich, Paul. *The Population Bomb*. London: Pan Books, 1971.

El Shakry, Omnia. "Barren Land and Fecund Bodies: The Emergence of Population Discourse in Interwar Egypt." *International Journal of Middle East Studies* 37, no. 3 (2005): 351–72.

Escobar, Arturo. "Whose Knowledge, Whose Nature? Biodiversity Conservation and the Political Ecology of Social Movements." *Journal of Political Ecology* 5, no. 1 (1998): 53–82.

Fretwell, Holly Lippke. *Who is Minding the Federal Estate? Political Management of America's Public Lands*. Lanham. MD: Lexington Books, 2009.

Gates, Warren E. "The Spread of Ibn Khaldun's Ideas on Climate and Culture." *Journal of the History of Ideas* 28, no. 3 (1967): 415–22.

Glacken, Clarence J. *Traces on the Rhodian Shore: Nature and Culture in Western Thought from Ancient Times to the End of the Eighteenth Century*. Berkeley, CA: University of California Press, 1967.

Gleick, Peter H. "Water and Conflict: Fresh Water Resources and International Security." *International Security* 18, no. 1 (1993): 79–112.

——— "Water, Drought, Climate Change, and Conflict in Syria." *Weather, Climate, and Society* 6, no. 3 (2014): 331–40.

Gore, Al. *Earth in the Balance: Ecology and the Human Spirit*. Boston, MA: Houghton Mifflin, 1992.

Gros, Andreas, Alexander S. Gard-Murray, and Yaneer Bar-Yam. "Conflict in Yemen: From Ethnic Fighting to Food Riots." In *Conflict and Complexity*, ed. Philip Vos Fellman, Yaneer Bar-Yam, and Ali A. Minai, 269–80. New York: Springer, 2015.

Gylfason, Thorvaldur. "Natural Resources, Education, and Economic Development." *European Economic Review* 45, no. 4, (2001): 847–59.

Haas, Peter M. "Introduction: Epistemic Communities and International Policy Coordination." *International Organization* 46, no. 1 (1992): 1–35.

Haas, Peter M., Robert O. Keohane, and Marc A. Levy. *Institutions for the Earth: Sources of Effective International Environmental Protection*. Cambridge, MA: MIT Press, 1993.

Hajer, Maarten. "Discourse Coalitions and the Institutionalisation of Practice: The Case of Acid Rain in Great Britain." In *The Argumentative Turn in Policy Analysis and Planning*, ed. Frank Fischer and John Forester, 43–76. Durham/London: Duke University Press, 1993.

Hales, Gavin. "Under Pressure: Social Violence over Land and Water in Yemen," *Yemen Armed Violence Assessment Issue Brief* 2, Small Arms Survey. October 2010. http://www.smallarmssurvey.org/fileadmin/docs/G-Issue-briefs/SAS-Yemen-AVA-IB2-ENG.pdf.

Hannoum, Abdelmajid. "Translation and the Colonial Imaginary: Ibn Khaldun Orientalist." *History and Theory* 42, no. 2 (2003): 61–81.

Hardin, Garrett. "The Tragedy of the Commons." *Science* 162, no. 3859 (1968): 1243–8.

Harrigan, Jane, Chengang Wang, and Hamed El-Said. "The Economic and Political Determinants of IMF and World Bank Lending in the Middle East and North Africa." *World Development* 34, no. 2 (2006): 247–70.

Harris, Leila M., and Samer Alatout. "Negotiating Hydro-Scales, Forging States: Comparison of the Upper Tigris/Euphrates and Jordan River Basins." *Political Geography* 29, no. 3 (2010): 148–56.

Hartmann, Betsy. "Converging on Disaster: Climate Security and the Malthusian Anticipatory Regime for Africa." *Geopolitics* 19, no. 4 (2014): 757–83.

Harvey, David. "The Nature of Environment: Dialectics of Social and Environmental Change." *Socialist Register 1993: Real Problems False Solutions* 29 (1993): 1–51.

——— *Justice, Nature and the Geography of Difference*. Oxford: Blackwell, 1996.

Headrick, Daniel R. *Power over Peoples: Technology, Environments and Western Imperialism, 1400 to the Present*. Princeton, NJ: Princeton University Press, 2008.

Henry, Clement M. "Algeria's Agonies: Oil Rent Effects in a Bunker State." *Journal of North African Studies* 9, no. 2 (2004): 68–81.

Hertog, Steffen. "Defying the Resource Curse: Explaining Successful State-Owned Enterprises in Rentier States." *World Politics* 62, no. 2 (2010): 261–301.

Homer-Dixon, Thomas. *Environment, Scarcity and Violence*. Princeton, NJ: Princeton University Press, 1999.

Hughes, J. Donald. "Early Greek and Roman Environmentalists." In *Historical Ecology: Essays on Environment and Social Change*, ed. Lester J. Bilsky, 45–59. Port Washington, NY: National University Publications, 1980.

Hvistendahl, Mara. "Young and Restless can be a Volatile Mix." *Science* 333, no. 6042 (2011): 552–4.

Irwin, Robert. "Toynbee and Ibn Khaldun." *Middle Eastern Studies* 33, no. 3 (1997): 461–79.

Isaac, Benjamin H. *The Invention of Racism in Classical Antiquity*. Princeton, NJ: Princeton University Press, 2006.

Johnstone, Sarah, and Jeffrey Mazo. "Global Warming and the Arab Spring." *Survival* 53, no. 2 (2011): 11–17.

Jones, Toby Craig. *Desert Kingdom. How Oil and Water Forged Modern Saudi Arabia*. Cambridge, MA: Harvard University Press, 2010.

Kamrava, Mehran, *Qatar: Small State, Big Politics*. Ithaca, NY: Cornell University Press, 2015.

Kelley, Colin P., Shahrzad Mohtadi, Mark A. Cane, Richard Seager, and Yochanan Kushnir. "Climate Change in the Fertile Crescent and Implications of the Recent Syrian Drought." *Proceedings of the National Academy of Sciences* 112, no. 11 (2015): 3241–6.

Keulertz, Martin, and Eckart Woertz. "Financial Challenges of the Nexus: Pathways for Investment in Water, Energy and Agriculture in the Arab World." *International Journal of Water Resources Development* 31, no. 3 (2015): 312–25.

Kevane, Michael, and Leslie Gray. "Darfur: Rainfall and Conflict." *Environmental Research Letters* 3, no. 3 (2008): 1–10.

Kibaroglu, Aysegul, and Waltina Scheumann. "Evolution of Transboundary Politics in the Euphrates–Tigris River System: New Perspectives and Political Challenges." *Global Governance* 19, no. 2 (2013): 279–305.

Ki-Moon, Ban. "A Climate Culprit in Darfur." *Washington Post*, 16 June 2007. http://www.washingtonpost.com/wp-dyn/content/article/2007/06/15/AR2007061501857.html

Klare, Michael. *Resource Wars: The New Landscape of Global Conflict*. New York: Metropolitan Books, 2001.

Lahsen, Myanna. "Technocracy, Democracy, and US Climate Politics: The Need for Demarcations." *Science, Technology and Human Values* 30, no. 1 (2005): 137–69.

Locher, Fabien, and Jean-Baptiste Fressoz. "Modernity's Frail Climate: A Climate History of Environmental Reflexivity." *Critical Inquiry* 38, no. 3 (2012): 579–98.

Lowi, Miriam R. *Oil Wealth and the Poverty of Politics: Algeria Compared*. Cambridge: Cambridge University Press, 2009.

Malthus, Thomas. *An Essay on the Principle of Population*. London: J. Johnson, 1798.

Marston, Sallie A., John Paul Jones, and Keith Woodward. "Human Geography without Scale." *Transactions of the Institute of British Geographers* 30, no. 4 (2005): 416–32.

McKean, Margaret A. "Success on the Commons: A Comparative Examination of Institutions for Common Property Resource Management." *Journal of Theoretical Politics* 4, no. 3 (1992): 247–81.

McNeill, J. R. *Something New Under the Sun: An Environmental History of the Twentieth-Century World*. New York: W. W. Norton, 2000.

Meadows, Donella, Dennis Meadows, Jørgen Randers, and William W. Behrens III. *The Limits to Growth*. London: Earth Island, 1972.

Mikhail, Alan. *Nature and Empire in Ottoman Egypt: An Environmental History*. Cambridge: Cambridge University Press, 2011.

Mikhail, Alan, ed. *Water on Sand: Environmental Histories of the Middle East and North Africa*. New York: Oxford University Press, 2013.

Mitchell, Timothy. *Colonising Egypt*. Berkeley, CA: University of California Press, 1988.

——— *Rule of Experts. Egypt, Techno-Politics, Modernity*. Berkeley, CA: University of California Press, 2002.

Myers, Norman. *Ultimate Security: The Environmental Basis of Political Stability*. London: Norton, 1993.

Naff, Thomas, and Ruth Matson, eds. *Water in the Middle East: Conflict or Cooperation?* Boulder, CO: Westview Press, 1984.

Neumann, Rod. *Making Political Ecology*. Abingdon, Oxon: Routledge, 2014.

Nielson, Daniel L., and Michael J. Tierney. "Delegation to International Organizations: Agency Theory and World Bank Environmental Reform." *International Organization* 57, no. 2, (2003): 241–76.

Nordhaus, William D. "Resources as a Constraint on Growth." *American Economic Review* 64, no. 2 (1974): 22–6.

——— *A Question of Balance: Weighing the Options on Global Warming Policies*. New Haven, CT: Yale University Press, 2014.

Nugent, Jeffrey B., and Nicholas Sanchez. "The Local Variability of Rainfall and Tribal Institutions: The Case of Sudan." *Journal of Economic Behavior and Organization* 3, no. 3 (1999): 263–91.

Ophuls, William. *Ecology and the Politics of Scarcity*. San Francisco, CA: W. H. Freeman, 1977.

Ostrom, Elinor, Roy Gardner, and James Walker. *Rules, Games, and Common-Pool Resources*. Ann Arbor, MI: University of Michigan Press, 1994.

Özkaynak, Begüm, Cem İskender Aydın, Pınar Ertör-Akyazı, and Irmak Ertör. "The Gezi Park Resistance from an Environmental Justice and Social Metabolism Perspective." *Capitalism Nature Socialism* 26, no. 1 (2015): 99–114.

Paehlke, Robert, and Douglas Torgerson. *Managing Leviathan: Environmental Politics and the Administrative State*, 2nd edn. Peterborough, Canada: Broadview, 2005.

Parker, Chad H. *Making the Desert Modern: Americans, Arabs and Oil on the Saudi Frontier, 1933–1973*. Amherst, MA: University of Massachusetts Press, 2015.

Pearce, David, and J. J. Warford. *World without End: Economics, Environment, and Sustainable Development*. New York: Oxford University Press, 1993.

Peet, Richard, and Michael Watts. *Liberation Ecologies: Environment, Development, Social Movements*. London: Routledge, 1996.

Pellow, David Naguib. *Resisting Global Toxics: Transnational Movements for Environmental Justice*. Cambridge, MA: MIT Press, 2007.

Peluso, Nancy Lee, and Michael Watts, eds. *Violent Environments*. Ithaca, NY: Cornell University Press, 2001.

Polanyi, Karl. *The Great Transformation*. Cambridge, MA: Beacon Press, 1944.

Pollack, Stephanie. "Reimagining NEPA: Choices for Environmentalists." *Harvard Environmental Law Review* 9, no. 2 (1985): 359–418.

Rosenau, James N., and Ernst-Otto Cziempel, eds. *Governance without Government: Order and Change in World Politics*. Cambridge: Cambridge University Press, 1992.

——— "The Political Economy of the Resource Curse." *World Politics* 51, no. 2 (1999): 297–324.

Ross, Michael L. "Does Oil Hinder Democracy?" *World Politics* 53, no. 3 (2001): 325–61.

Sachs, Jeffrey D., and Andrew M. Warner. "The Curse of Natural Resources." *European Economic Review* 45, no. 4 (2001): 827–38.

Sachs, Jeffrey D. *Common Wealth: Economics for a Crowded Planet*. New York: Penguin, 2008.

Salman, Salman M. A. "The Nile Basin Cooperative Framework Agreement: A Peacefully Unfolding African Spring?" *Water International* 38, no. 1 (2013): 17–29.

Satia, Priya. "'A Rebellion of Technology': Development, Policing and the British Arabian Imaginary." In *Environmental Imaginaries of the Middle East and North Africa*, ed. Diana K. Davis and Edmund Burke III, 23–59. Athens, OH: Ohio University Press, 2011.

Schwarzstein, Peter. "Inside the Syrian Dust Bowl." *Foreign Policy*, 5 September 2016. http://foreignpolicy.com/2016/09/05/inside-the-syrian-dust-bowl-icarda-assad-food-security-war.

Selby, Jan. *Water, Power and Politics in the Middle East: The Other Israeli–Palestinian Conflict*. London: I. B. Tauris, 2003.

Sharifikia, Mohammad. "Environmental Challenges and Drought Hazard Assessment of Hamoun Desert Lake in Sistan Region, Iran, Based on the Time Series of Satellite Imagery." *Natural Hazards* 65, no. 1 (2013): 201–17.

Simon, Julian. *The Ultimate Resource 2*. Princeton, NJ: Princeton University Press, 1998.

Skjærseth, Jon Birger, Olav Schram Stokke, and Jørgen Wettestad. "Soft Law, Hard Law, and Effective Implementation of International Environmental Norms." *Global Environmental Politics* 6, no. 3 (2006): 104–20.

Sowers, Jeannie. "Remapping the Nation, Critiquing the State: Environmental Narratives and Desert Land Reclamation in Egypt." In *Environmental Imaginaries of the Middle East and North Africa*, ed. Diana K. Davis and Edmund Burke III, 158–91. Athens, OH: Ohio University Press, 2011.

——— "Institutional Change in Authoritarian Regimes: Water and the State in Egypt." In *Comparative Environmental Politics: Theory, Practice, and Prospects*, ed. Stacy van Deveer and Paul Steinberg, 231–54. Cambridge, MA: MIT Press, 2012.

Starr, Joyce R. "Water Wars." *Foreign Policy* 82, no. 2 (1991): 17–36.

Steffen, Will, Jacques Grinevald, Paul Crutzen, and John McNeill. "The Anthropocene: Conceptual and Historical Perspectives." *Philosophical Transactions of the Royal Society A: Mathematical, Physical and Engineering Sciences* 369, no. 1938 (2011): 842–67.

Swyngedouw, Erik. *Social Power and the Urbanization of Water: Flows of Power*. Oxford: Oxford University Press, 2004.

Triulzi, Lisa. "The Bedouin between Development and State: A Syrian Case-Study." *Arab World Geographer* 5, no. 2 (2002): 85–101.

Trumbull, George R. IV. "Body of Work: Water and Reimagining the Sahara in the Era of Decolonization." In *Environmental Imaginaries of the Middle East and North Africa*, ed. Diana K. Davis and Edmund Burke III, 87–112. Athens, OH: Ohio University Press, 2011.

Turco, Richard P. *Earth Under Siege: From Air Pollution to Global Change*. Oxford: Oxford University Press, 1997.

United Nations Development Programme. *Sudan: Post-Conflict Environmental Assessment*. Khartoum/Nairobi: UNEP, 2007.

——— *Arab Human Development Report*. New York: UNDP, 2009.

Verhoeven, Harry. "Climate Change, Conflict and Development in Sudan: Neo-Malthusian Global Narratives and Local Power Struggles." *Development and Change* 42, no. 3 (2011): 679–707.

——— "Gardens of Eden or Hearts of Darkness? The Genealogy of Discourses on Environmental Insecurity and Climate Wars in Africa." *Geopolitics* 19, no. 4 (2014): 784–805.

——— "The Nexus as Political Commodity: Agricultural Development, Water Policy and Elite Rivalry in Egypt." *International Journal of Water Resources Development* 31, no. 3 (2015): 360–74.

——— *Water, Civilisation and Power in Sudan: The Political Economy of Military-Islamist State Building*. Cambridge: Cambridge University Press, 2015.

Vitalis, Robert. *America's Kingdom: Mythmaking on the Saudi-Oil Frontier*. Stanford, CA: Stanford University Press, 2007.

Ward, Diane Raines. *Water Wars*. New York: Penguin, 2003.

Webking, Robert. "Plato's Response to Environmentalism." *Intercollegiate Review* 20, no. 1 (1984): 27–35.

Weinbaum, Marvin G. *Food, Development, and Politics in the Middle East*. Boulder, CO: Westview Press, 1982.

Welzer, Harald. *Climate Wars: What People will be Killed for in the 21st Century*. Cambridge: Polity Press, 2012.

Wheida, Edawi, and Ronny Verhoeven. "An Alternative Solution of the Water Shortage Problem in Libya." *Water Resources Management* 21, no. 6 (2007): 961–82.

Wiesehöfer, Josef. *Ancient Persia*. London: I. B. Tauris, 1996.

Williams, Bruce A., and Albert R. Matheny. *Democracy, Dialogue and Environmental Disputes. The Contested Languages of Social Regulation*. New Haven, CT: Yale University Press, 1995.

Williams, Paul. "Turkey's H_2O Diplomacy in the Middle East." *Security Dialogue* 32, no. 1 (2001): 27–40.

Wilson, Rodney. *The Economies of the Middle East: The Ghost of Malthus Lingers on*. London: Macmillan Press, 1979.

Wittfogel, Karl. *Oriental Despotism*. New Haven, CT, Yale University Press: 1957.

Woertz, Eckart. "Environment, Food Security and Conflict Narratives in the Middle East." *Global Environment* 7, no. 2 (2014): 490–516.

World Bank. *The Sunken Billions Revisited: Progress and Challenges in Global Marine Fisheries*. Washington, DC: World Bank, 2017.

World Health Organization. "WHO Global Urban Ambient Air Pollution Database (update 2016)." WHO, 2016. http://www.who.int/phe/health_topics/outdoorair/databases/cities/en.

INDEX